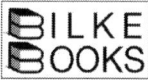

BILKE
BOOKS

Published by **Bilke Books,** an imprint of:

Peter Weisz Publishing, LLC
7143 Winding Bay Lane
West Palm Beach, FL 33412 USA
info@peterweiszpublishing.com

FULL CIRCLE; My circular search for the real me

Fixler, Elliot • All rights reserved
            Memoir — Biography —Business — Personal Improvement

ISBN: 9 781435 780163
Printed in the United States of America by Blurb.com
1 2 3 4 5 6 7 8 9 10

Full Circle

My circular search for the real me.

Elliot Fixler

with

Peter Weisz

BILKE BOOKS

Elliot Fixler

Dedication

To my mother, Rose,
My son, Mathew
and
My wife, Lorraine

Elliot Fixler

All my life's a circle;
But I can't tell you why;
Season's spinning round again;
The years keep rollin' by.

—*Harry Chapin*

Elliot Fixler

Contents

(continued)

Introduction

To say that Elliot Fixler is a *mensch* is like saying Tom Brady plays football. It just doesn't tell the half of it. Elliot takes "*mench*-ness" to an entirely new level. He is also, to put it mildly, a study in contrasts; caring and biting, loving and acerbic, generous and opinionated, methodical and manic. At this point, I have probably known Elliot Fixler longer than any other living person. I've learned that he believes that in order to be a true friend, it's occasionally necessary for him to kick you in the ass. I discovered this the very first time we met.

The year was 1953 and, because of my popularity, I was regarded as the third grade's "Leader of the Pack" among the schoolyard tough guys at Public School 66, located on Buffalo's Tacoma Avenue. In fact, we were known as the Polisner Gang and we ruled the playground during recess. On one fateful day, we spotted a new kid who had recently transferred to our school. He looked funny. He talked funny. And he wore a baseball cap at all times. So, naturally, we wasted no time tormenting him.

After a game of "keep away" using the kid's cap, we began to taunt and tease him mercilessly. The kid stood his ground and looked us up and down and determined that I was the "head honcho." He put his head down and ran straight at me. He then proceeded to beat the living crap out of me.

1

That pugnacious kid was Elliot, and as I lay panting on the playground tarmac, I remembered my father's advice, "If someone can beat you up, it's better to be his friend than his enemy." Elliot and I have been best friends ever since. And friends like Elliot don't grow on trees, although, as you will read, some of Elliot's clients swing from them.

I am proud to say that I have been at Elliot's side through thick and thin, and I'm not just talking about the hair on his head. We've shared moments of magnificent splendor atop Masada in Israel, as well as periods of the deepest despair imaginable. In this amazing memoir, Elliot recounts many of the cherished memories of our Buffalo boyhood. For example: Scraping the snow from our driveway so we could spend the afternoon shooting baskets in front of our garage, after which my mother introduced Elliot to non-kosher food for the first time in his life (pepperoni pizza). Elliot also unabashedly shares tales of other sorts of "forbidden fruit" that he and I indulged in.

I believe it was Elliot who popularized my nickname that has stuck with me all my life. "Polisner" somehow got slurred into "Parsner" which sounds like parsnip. And Parsnip eventually got whittled down to simply "Snip."

Some of my most enduring memories from our misspent youth include listening to Elliot's mother, Rose, *kvetch* at me for having a *shiksa* (non-Jewish) girlfriend. I also clearly recall the day Elliot and I were playing tackle football with our high school buddies; full contact with no equipment. One of our teammates suffered a serious compound fracture of his forearm, the splintered bone protruding

2

through the skin. I think that was the day Elliot decided to stick to basketball.

As he matured, Elliot's athletic prowess kept up with his skills as a courtroom litigator. But sometimes he would push the envelope a bit too far. I recall going on a ski vacation to Vail with Elliot when he was in training for an upcoming marathon competition. Despite the wintery weather and unmindful of the unfamiliar Rocky Mountain elevation, he felt compelled to carry out his daily morning jog. Big mistake. He returned blue and barely alive. I was required to assist him into the closest jacuzzi where I served him a Jim Beam breakfast to revive him. I'm pretty sure that was Elliot's last marathon race.

Reading the pre-release version of this book was, naturally, a sentimental journey for me. I learned a great deal about a friend I thought I knew inside and out. What I found in these pages touched my heart and often caused me to really LOL (laugh out loud). I am convinced that, even though you may not know Elliot as well as I do, you will feel the same way as you make your way through his remarkable life saga.

One caveat: in this book, as in real life, Elliot often portrays himself as a curmudgeon and a grouch. Don't be fooled. It's a persona that he developed as part of his courtroom image. In reality, Elliot is one of the most generous, intelligent, well-read and compassionate people I have ever known. The following tale illustrates my point.

Many members of the schoolyard gang from PS 66 have, incredibly, managed to stay in touch over what has now been seven decades. Recently, one of our group had fallen on hard times. He swallowed his pride and shared with me the fact that, at age 78, he was unable to make ends meet on Social Security alone. Could I help him out?

I put out the word to several of the others in our grade school group—some of whom are today very well off financially. I was stunned as my plea was rejected by men who willingly direct their philanthropic dollars toward worthy causes benefiting complete strangers, but who now refused to help a friend in need. The one shining exception was Elliot, whose immediate response was simply "Sure. How much does he need?"

Finally, I feel that the title of this book, *Full Circle,* is highly appropriate describing Elliot's diverse and distinguished circle of friends. It is a circle that is "full" of exceptional people, many of whom you will meet in the pages of this memoir. I am proud to count myself among those within this "full circle" of friendship.

I am aware that this book is part of Elliot's quest to resolve many unanswered questions surrounding his family background. I applaud this effort and am deeply moved that he allowed me to offer my words as the Introduction to this extraordinary volume. I am particularly gratified that by invoking the memories of that Buffalo boyhood schoolyard where we first met, I believe I am helping him to, once again, come full circle.

Richard (Snip) Polisner, DPM, MJ
Ponte Vedra, Florida
March, 2022

Author's Foreword

I think it was author Norman Mailer who said that writing a book is about as close to childbirth as a man will ever get. I cannot attest to that, but I can swear that writing this book, like giving birth, involved a lot of labor and for the most part, it was a labor of love. To carry the metaphor a bit further, both undertakings initially require the planting of a seed. In my case, oddly enough, it was my daughter, Sarah, who got me "knocked up" in a literary sense.

Sarah understood, perhaps better than most, that my life had been plagued by unanswered questions about my origins and family background. She was also aware that I had, over the past few years, actively attempted to fill some of the gaps in my life story. Why was my mother living in Budapest when she gave birth to me in 1944? Where and when did my parents get married? How did my mother and I manage to survive the Nazi onslaught that succeeded in murdering so many members of our family? The most aggravating question I faced was, "Why had I failed to question my family members about these things when I had the chance? Why had I waited until they were gone before I began my search?"

Sarah understood my frustration and more than once had commented: "Wouldn't it be nice if my grandmother had writ-

5

ten a book about her life? You could just read the book and your questions would be answered."

I agreed that it would be nice, but, as we both knew, neither she, nor my father, had written any such book.

"Well, then," she replied. "Don't make that same mistake."

"Hunh?"

"You should do what they failed to do," she advised. "I don't want to be in the same boat after you've gone. It's important to record your story in a book, a book that I and my brothers and our kids can read to learn about you and our family history."

"Wow," I thought to myself. *"How did I manage to raise such a smart kid?"*

Her point struck me immediately. She was entirely correct. I should not leave my children in the dark about their past, a darkness that I had lived with and dreaded for years. I should write down whatever I have been able to put together about my own history and those who came before me, no matter how spotty or incomplete the information may be. Plus, I should record the high points—and low points—of my own life, not only for the sake of my heirs, but for anyone who might find such an account to be of interest or benefit. *"But were there really such people out there?"* I wondered.

I got my answer at a dinner party during the summer of 2021, when COVID vaccinations had started giving people the courage to socialize once again. I had monopolized the majority of the evening's conversation by regaling my friends with a few stories from my wicked wayward past.

My old buddy, restauranteur and businessman, Paul Iacuone, turned to me during dessert and said, "Ell, have you ever thought about writing a book? You've got some amazing stories there that people would really enjoy reading."

Paul's wife, Terry, agreed, as did the other guests: Dave Festa, Raymond Kolkman and their wives.

"That's funny," I replied, "because my daughter, Sarah, has been bugging me to do just that. I just wasn't sure if anyone outside my family would be all that interested."

The encouragement of my friends appeared to be sincere and I put a lot of stock in their judgement. So, I made up mind.

"O.K.," I announced. "I'll do it."

Now what? I've written legal briefs and articles for law journals, but I had no idea about how to go about writing a memoir. Interestingly, it would be in my capacity as a Holocaust survivor that I would find the help I needed. Not long after, I was invited to testify at a public Palm Beach County School Board meeting. It seemed that a certain high school principal had stirred up a controversy when he had replied to a parent who had inquired as to why the school did not offer a Holocaust education program as specified under Florida law. The principal responded in writing that since some parents held differing opinions about the existence of the Holocaust, and since their beliefs had to be respected, he could not inject one particular point of view into the school curriculum.

Once his words were made public, the principal was labeled a Holocaust-denier, and calls for his termination echoed throughout the county. The school board invited members of the public to address them about whether they should fire the principal. As I waited to offer my remarks in the five minutes allotted to each witness, I was seated amidst dozens of other witnesses; other Holocaust survivors as well as representatives of area synagogues and Jewish communal organizations. As I chatted with a slightly younger man seated next to me, I learned that his parents, like mine, had been Hungarian Holocaust survivors. He revealed he was a writer who assisted clients in authoring and publishing their memoirs. He handed me his card and suggested I contact him if I ever decided to write my life story. I thanked him, stuck the card into my wallet, and then moved to the podium to offer my testimony—through the mandatory face mask. Within a few weeks, the errant principal had been fired and I had connected and agreed to work with the memoir writer to produce and publish this book.

Thus began a process that was at times gratifying and other times terrifying. I was required to organize my many disparate memories into some sort of cohesive narrative. Most challenging was confronting some of the long-buried ghosts of my past, whom I had not thought about for decades. The range of emotions this process brought to the surface was both compelling and cathartic. Eventually, the process of viewing my life from an objective vantage point allowed me to discern certain distinct patterns taking shape.

For example, my life's journey began in Budapest, Hungary. Years later, I would return to Budapest where I would pick up the tattered threads of my story and weave them into the tapestry of my life. It was, in a sense, a feeling of having come full circle. This same feeling arose when I thought back to my early Jewish education, conducted by an Orthodox rabbi who was part of the Lubavitch sect known for their "Chabad" movement. I had remained distant from my heritage for most of my life, only to again come full circle, back to Chabad in later years, right here in Palm Beach Gardens.

There is one more instance of having come full circle that illustrates this pattern that accounts for the title of this book.

As I prepare to bring this accounting to an end and thereby bring about a sense of closure regarding the mysteries of my life, I, at the same time, recognize that this book represents a new beginning for my kids and grandkids. The beginning of their understanding about who I am and the values I have attempted to impart. I am most grateful that I was able to complete this book before I "closed the circle," as Apple Watch owners like to say.

I invite you to travel vicariously with me through these pages, pages that chronicle the major memories—both good and bad—of my life's journey. I know you will find the trip provocative, amusing, tragic and, at times, uplifting and inspiring. Once you have come full circle and reached the final chapter, perhaps you will find yourself motivated to write your own life story

If this book inspires just one person— be it family member, friend or stranger—to write his or her own memoirs, then I will rank this literary labor as a glorious success. When I, at some future point, find myself holding a book in my hands; a book created by someone who was prompted to write it because of *this* book, then I will consider myself as truly having come full circle.

Elliot Fixler
March, 2022

Chapter One

Someday You'll Understand

"Secrecy involves a tension which, at the moment of revelation, finds its release."

—Georg Simmel

R evelation arrived in my parents' bedroom closet on a sultry summer afternoon in 1958. Past Bar Mitzvah age, at 14, I was deemed sufficiently mature to be left at home unattended. I had recently graduated from Public School 66 in North Buffalo and was spending my summer working alongside my dad as a painter's assistant. By the 1950s, North Buffalo had solidified its place as the historic center of the local Jewish community. Our little family recently moved from a house behind a flower shop, one of the many "two-flats" along Hertel Avenue, to a more spacious place located at 196 North Park Avenue. Most of Buffalo's non-Orthodox Jewish families have since that time relocated to the more upscale suburban neighborhoods of Amherst and Williamsville. But North Buffalo still retains its ethnic flavor. It is today home to a "Little Italy" community, complete with fine Italian trattorias that dot Hertel Avenue where kosher delis once stood.

Back in those days, my Jewish friends came from conservative and reform families that had assimilated into American mainstream culture. Because we were a post-war immigrant family, our religious observance was, by contrast, strictly Orthodox and that was the reason I sported a baseball cap that was nearly permanently affixed to my head. It also meant I would walk to *shul* with my father every week on *Shabbos*. Most importantly, my Orthodox orientation was about to cast me into a future that would drastically diverge from that of my *"Amerikanische"* friends. This fact weighed heavily on my mind on that fateful summer's day.

When I arrived home, I quickly realized I was alone. My father, Sam, was at work painting houses and my mother, Rose, had left by bus to the market. As an only child, I was accustomed to spending time alone and would only occasionally experience a pang of loneliness or a twinge of isolation. I delighted in the hours spent lying on the carpet with our huge "international-style" radio tuned in to sports broadcasts. Buffalo Baseball Hall of Fame announcer, Bill Mazer, whose coverage of the Buffalo Bisons minor league baseball team, along with his "ticker-tape" reporting of major league games, was a particular favorite of mine. Mazer would read each play from the ticker and then rely upon his imagination alone to inject color and context into his narrative. This was how I was able to follow the legendary New York Yankees and the exploits of my baseball hero, slugger Mickey Mantle. I since learned that Mazer's real first name was Morris, that he was Jewish and born in Ukraine.

My time home alone was also devoted to books about my other childhood hero, famed attorney Clarence Darrow. Darrow worked on some of the most celebrated legal cases during the first half of the twentieth century, including the Scopes "Monkey Trial" and the Leopold and Loeb murder case. My deep admiration for this "sophisticated" country lawyer with brilliant defense strategies would eventually guide me toward a career in the legal profession.

But on this day, I was not thinking about Clarence Darrow or the Yankees winning the pennant. I was consumed with concern about my own future. The night before, I overheard my parents talking after I went to bed. My father was showing my mother papers he had received from the Hebrew parochial high school, Yeshiva Torah Vodaath, located on South Third Street in the Williamsburg section of Brooklyn, New York. While I had assumed I would be attending Buffalo's Bennett High School in the fall along with my classmates, my parents evidently had other plans.

All I knew about Torah Vodaath, a Jewish boarding school connected to the Mesifta Talmudical Seminary, was that it required strict adherence to Jewish dietary laws and that half of every school day would be devoted to the study of the Torah and other Judaic texts. I had to learn more about this place. I needed to see those brochures and application forms that my father had shown my mom.

I quickly set to work scouring the premises in an effort to locate those Torah Vodaath materials. My search led me to the large closet in my parents' bedroom. This was territory into which I had not yet ventured since our recent move to the North Park Avenue address. Scanning the shelves and floor of the closet, I spotted something.

It was a weathered and well-worn grainy leather valise that some might call a portfolio. It protruded from among the shoe and hat boxes on the top shelf. I gingerly pulled it out. Opening the metal clasp, I surmised that this was something my parents had carried with them from Europe and then to Israel. It had obviously been though a lot.

13

And although the valise could easily contain the documents I was seeking, what I found was far from what I was expecting.

Instead of Torah Vodaath paperwork, I discovered a collection of old black and white photographs, along with what appeared to be various old transit documents written in either Czech or Hungarian. Leafing through the photos, it was clear they had been taken long ago, before or during the war. Some were candid photos of family life with surroundings indicating a quaint European village. There were also two photos of a group of well-dressed older men, each of whom wore a square-topped elegant black hat. A Jewish star was stitched onto the breast area of each man's overcoat. There was something haunting and somewhat disturbing about the way each man peered solemnly into the camera.

Eventually, I came across a large collection of professionally produced wedding photos. The only face I recognized belonged to a younger version of my mother, Rose. I wondered why my parents kept these old photos stuffed away in the closet and never showed them to me. After all, there were plenty of family photo albums, sitting on the dining room bookshelf, chronicling my childhood years in fading Kodachrome. Why were these photos secreted away in the closet?

As I pored over the images, I eventually came across a full-size photographer's portrait of the wedding couple. It featured my mother in a flowing white satin wedding gown. But there was something horribly wrong with this picture. The man next to her, decked out in a double-breasted dark suit, was *not* my father! This was clearly a formal wedding photo; not a candid shot with the bride posing with a wedding guest. No, this was the happy couple on their wedding day. But why did I recognize the bride and not the groom?

The weight of a thousand questions landed heavily on my shoulders as I sat on the floor with the open valise across my lap. "Was this older couple my grandparents who were murdered in the Holocaust?" I wondered as I flipped feverishly through the photos. "Did my mother have another husband at some point and, if so, where is this man now?"

I sat there for what seemed like hours, deep in troubled thought as I forgot all about the Yeshiva and my future education. After several long moments puzzling over these matters, I put everything back just as I had found it in the valise and placed it back on the shelf. I decided that I would confront my mother about these photos as soon as possible—but not in the presence of my father.

My dad, Sam Fixler, and I, did not enjoy a typical father-son relationship, at least as far as I could determine by observing how friends and relatives interacted with their fathers. Sam, whom I called Tatte, never engaged with me outside of my role as his assistant on house painting jobs; no ball games, no fishing trips, not even a round of catch in the backyard. There was certainly no love lost or gained between us. Instead, there existed a sort of chilling distance. I grew inured to his lack of fatherly affection to the point that it didn't really bother me that much. I had come to resign myself to my relationship with a dad that was, well…different.

The next morning, after Sam had left for work, I sat down at the kitchen table where my mother was drinking her morning coffee and asked her, in a very offhanded and casual manner:

"Mom, you know those pictures in your closet...?" The blood immediately drained from her face as she jerked her head swiftly my way—both eyes boring into me.

"What!?" she exclaimed. "What were you doing in there?" I explained that I was searching for the stuff about Yeshiva High School and had come across the old leather valise. We sat in silence for a long and ponderous moment.

"Did you see the wedding photos?" she ventured shakily.

I nodded.

"So, you want to know 'Who is the man? Who was the *chasan*?'" using the Yiddish word for bridegroom. I nodded again, a bit warily. My mother reached out and placed her hand atop mine.

"I knew this day would come, Ellie," she said softly. "I just thought you'd be a little older when it did."

I thought back to the many times I questioned my mother about why my father was not like the other dads. "Someday you'll understand," she would invariably and cryptically reply. "Someday you'll understand."

Finally, choosing her words carefully, my mother began to recite her story—actually, our story.

"That man, the groom in the pictures, was called Marton Adlersheim," she explained patiently. "Mortzy was the finest most wonderful man who ever I knew," she continued, in a husky voice tinged with emotion.

"He..he was your husband?" I asked shakily, trying to make it easier for her. "Before you married Dad?"

My mother nodded with a wistful smile.

"Yes, *shaffeleh* (little bushel)," she got out. "He was my first husband and...," Here she paused and looked into my eyes squarely. "...and he was your father."

I sat in stunned silence as my stomach churned and the scales fell from my eyes. A flood of questions began bubbling up immediately as the meaning of what I had just heard sunk in.

"Why had I never met my real father?"

"Where is this man, Marton 'whatever'? What happened to him?"

"Why was Sam posing as my father?"

"Is my mother really my mother?"

Once I had recovered somewhat from the shock, things started making sense to me. If this man, Sam, was an imposter and not my true father, that would resolve many of the questions that I had been struggling with. It would, in part, explain that emotional wall that existed between us. It would also explain certain mysteries that had confounded me regarding our religious observance.

I had for years accompanied Sam on foot every *Shabbos* to our nearby Lubavitch *shul* (synagogue). It was there that I would, since becoming a Bar Mitzvah, be called up to the *bimah* (altar) to read from the Torah. As per tradition, I would be called by my Hebrew name, "Eliahu Tzvi ben Mordechai." The final two parts of the name mean "son of Mordechai." But my father's name was not Mordechai. It was Shmuel. This puzzled me, but not wishing to make waves, I had never questioned it. Now, I understood. Mordechai was Mortzy, my real father.

17

Another thing about the Torah ritual bothered me. According to Orthodox tradition, the honor of reading the first segment of the weekly Torah portion (the first *aliyah*) is given to a descendant of the tribe of Aaron the *Kohane,* while the second *aliyah* goes to a member of the tribe of Levi. Whenever I was called to the Torah, it was to read the second *aliyah.* Also, when the sexton called my name, it would be amended with the word "HaLevi," indicating that I was a hereditary member of the Levites. Yet when my father's name was called, no such distinction was announced. Since tribal affiliations were a matter of patrilineal descent, how could this be? How could I be a Levite when my father was not? I now had the answer.

I also had the beginnings of an answer as to why there was this tangible disaffection between Sam and me. Sam's brother, Jacob, was the father of two daughters who would visit from time to time. I would always notice Sam's interactions with his two nieces. His demeanor towards them was in stark contrast to the way he behaved toward me. I saw that he could be a warm, loving and strongly affectionate man—just not with me.

As these initial insights flooded my mind, I found that I still needed many more answers. I greatly wanted to interrogate my mother about all the details. How did my father die? How did she meet Sam? Did I have any unknown brothers or sisters?

But I did not ask. I held back.

It sounds strange, perhaps, but I somehow felt that probing too deeply into this alternate universe of my past might be seen as an act of disloyalty to the man who had raised me as his son. I held my tongue. Nevertheless, sensing my desire to know more, my mother sweetly and patiently related her story to me in broad strokes as she sipped her morning coffee.

My mother, Rose, was originally from the Ruthenian village of Bilke, in what is now the Ukraine, while my father's birthplace was a nearby village, some three kilometers away. I believe Rose and Mortzy were married in Budapest. After years of trying, at age 38, she managed to get pregnant with me in the summer of 1943. Hungarian Jews, at the time, were living in an insulated bubble, blissfully oblivious to the impending onslaught of the Nazi "final solution," that would soon engulf their lives and signal their doom. I was born in Budapest on March 30, 1944, eleven days after German forces occupied Hungary on March 19. Shortly before my birth, Mortzy, my biological father, had been among the first Jews rounded up by the Nazis and their fascist henchmen, the Arrow Cross. My father was sent to the Mauthaussen concentration camp, from which he never returned. As far as I have been able to determine, he never saw me, his only child.

My mother, with her newborn baby, found refuge in what was labeled the International Ghetto on the Pest side of the Danube. She miraculously survived the mass deportations to Auschwitz that led to the murder of more than 400,000 Hungarian Jews.

Shortly after the war's end, Rose made her way back to Budapest and connected with her brother-in-law, Sam Fixler. Sam had been married to my mother's sister, Raisele, and, like Rose, had lost his spouse in the inferno of the Holocaust. In a sort of reverse Levirate marriage, the couple wed. After a short stay in Israel, our little family immigrated to the US, settling in Buffalo. Although he never legally adopted me, Sam Fixler gave me his name and raised me, so to speak, as his son. Wisely or not, my parents decided to put off telling me about my true provenance until I grew older.

My parents' story is more fully recounted in the following chapters, but I begin this book with this seminal moment of personal revelation, because it stands as a critical inflection point that would influence my life's journey moving forward. The impact of that discovery has taken shape in many ways, but perhaps the most salient lesson I learned was this: The truth must be sought out. Things are not always as they first appear. One must dig deeper — snooping around in a dusty old closet, perhaps — to arrive at the truth.

During the course of my legal career, I have often been required to look deeper. I was required to delve into every detail of a witness' testimony to determine if some detail was being hidden. I was frequently required to probe into the personalities of jurors to uncover any biases that might go against the interests of my client.

Just as my parents were reluctant to come forward with the truth about my origin for fear of embarrassment or other such reasons, parties involved in a lawsuit often attempt to conceal what is at the heart of their battle. But just as the pieces of my life fell into place upon my discovery, the facts surrounding a legal proceeding are often brought into clear focus under the bright illumination of the truth.

I have been fortunate, over the years, to have been involved in many fascinating cases, some of which you are invited to read about in the subsequent chapters. Whenever I was called upon to sum up a case before a jury in a courtroom trial, I frequently invoked the memory of my mother. I would point out that she was extremely wise, despite the fact that she was not an educated woman.

"Don't think you so smart just because you go to school," she would admonish me in her charming European accent. "I got a *Life School*." I always urged juries to reflect upon the value of common sense and to trust their "street smarts" as they began their deliberations.

I invite you to join me on this literary look at my life's circular path. A path that led me from my birthplace in Budapest, to the courtrooms and basketball courts of New York, to the sunny fairways of south Florida, and eventually, in a search for my origins, coming full circle back to Budapest. I promise it will be a fascinating journey of revelation and redemption.

Welcome to my world.

Elliot Fixler

Chapter Two

From Bilke to Buffalo

"Dare to ask questions and seek answers to the puzzles of life."
—Lailah Gifty Akita, *Ghanaian author*

Although I have always believed that one should fear regret more than failure, I begin this account of our family history and my early years with an admission of regret. As you will soon read, my familiarity with the course of our family's journey may be described as spotty at best. Major gaps and unanswered questions as to who did what, when, and where loom large and have fueled my ongoing remorse. I missed opportunities to obtain answers from those who knew the facts first-hand but who have, by now, passed from the scene. Nevertheless, I have tried my best, in recent years, to reconstruct what I could about our family's tattered saga through research, coupled with delving and digging into family artifacts. This book is a part of that belated process. Hence, what you are about to read must be regarded as equal parts fact, speculative deduction. and pure imagination.

My mother Rose's, or Roisa's, people came from the village of Bilke, a picturesque town, tucked into the elbow of the Borzhava River Valley, in what was once known as Ruthenia. Bilke is today located in eastern Ukraine and lies about 50 kilometers to the east of the provincial capital of Munkacs (Mukachevo). According to legend, the original village was named after the daughter of a medieval nobleman whose daughter had drowned while bathing in the big river. The town was once part of the eastern Austro-Hungarian Empire that encompassed the scenic Carpathian Mountain region. Bilke found itself within the borders of the newly created nation-state of Czechoslovakia after World War I. The community's colorful history and natural beauty was of little value, however, to the ten thousand people (of which two thousand were Jews) who struggled there in the crushing poverty that prevailed when my mother, Rose, the eldest of three children, was born to Meier Berger and his wife, Faige, in the year 1906. From what little I have been able to learn about my grandfather Meier, he was a respected town elder to whom the Jews of Bilke would often turn for advice and assistance. He was known as a lover of music who enjoyed performing the popular Yiddish klezmer tunes of the day.

The citizenry of Bilke was far from homogeneous. In addition to Jews, Bilke was home to a variety of diverse Christian ethnicities that included Ukrainians, Ruthenian peasants, Hungarians, Czechs and Slovaks. Hence, my mother was required to learn a number of languages in addition to her native Yiddish that was spoken in her home and at the *cheyder* (school). Jews did not live in a segregated *shtetl*, or ghetto, in Bilke. My mother's home may have had Hungarian neighbors. While the family maintained the Jewish dietary laws, along with a mezuzah on the doorpost, they still integrated themselves into the mainstream culture of the community.

My biological father, Marton (Mortzy) Adlersheim, was born in 1898 into an even smaller community, roughly nine kilometers to the west of Bilke. Little is known about the village of Il'nytsya, apart from its identity as the home of the famed Protection of the Theotokos Eastern Orthodox wooden church, which was erected in 1925 and later renovated in 2000.

I have been unable to discover where and when my parents met. Since I was not even aware of the existence of Marton Adlersheim until I was fourteen years old, I naturally gathered nothing about his life as I grew up. Based on snippets and hunches, I have put together this possible, even probable, scenario regarding the experiences of my parents during the years leading up to my birth.

I suspect that my father, Marton, met his future wife while living in rural Il'nyitsya. There were many occasions for young Jewish men from the countryside to travel to a nearby town to attend *shul* (synagogue) during Jewish holidays. It was only a short hop to the Great Synagogue in Bilke where they likely met.

I feel that Marton, wishing to escape the confines of his rural hamlet, decided to leave home in the mid-1930s to seek opportunity and employment. He was likely motivated by the collectivization process put into place by the Soviet regime in what was then the U.S.S.R. Many Jewish men during this period flocked to urban areas after being forced to forfeit their farmland to the state. Conscription into the Red Army was also a driving factor. So, he said goodbye to his paramour, Rose, and set out for the big city of Budapest.

The Jews of Bilke were aware of the rise of Hitler and knew that his ascent to power was not going to be *"Gut fer der Yiden."* (good for the Jews). Thanks to the appeasement in Munich, the year 1938 saw the Germans take possession of the nearby Sudetenland, put Bohemia and Moravia under their so-called "protection," and turn Slovakia into a puppet regime. Despite these sinister signals, most Jews of Bilke felt immune from danger and confident that the wild anti-semitic ravings of a mustachioed madman in Berlin would never reach their idyllic town.

I would like to think that my father anticipated the events that were about to unfold and recognized the threat more clearly than most. Instead of waiting for events to overtake him, he chose to act. I suspect that Marton decided to leave home and make his way alone to the Hungarian capital of Budapest. At the time, the region was allied with Germany under the Horthy regime and not yet occupied or under Nazi political control. My father considered himself an ethnic Magyar and spoke Hungarian fluently. While he may have wished for Rose to join him on his sojourn to Budapest, she was obligated to remain in Bilke, serving as a caregiver to an invalid older relative.

It was also at about this time that my mother's older brother, Maurice, bid farewell to his home in Bilke and sought his fortune in the United States. In so doing, he removed himself from the approaching conflagration.

If my assumptions as to his motives are correct, Marton's fears were well founded and his decision to leave home was a sound one. In early 1939, Bilke and the entire Carpathian region was ceded by the Germans to Hungary under the terms of the Treaty of Trianon. This greatly displeased Ukrainian nationalists who quickly began seditionist activity. Bilke became the hotbed of a rising resistance movement. On March 13, 1939, the Ukrainians declared an independent Ruthenian Republic in Bilke. It was quickly put down by the Hungarians, who subdued the short-lived, but bloody, uprising. Conditions were deteriorating rapidly, especially for Bilke's Jews.

My guess is that around this time—but at a point prior to Germany's invasion of Poland on September 1, 1939, an act of naked aggression that triggered World War II—Marton managed to bring Rose from Bilke to Budapest. They would wed not long thereafter, at a time when more than one and a half million Jews had already been exterminated in the Nazi Holocaust that was raging across Europe.

It no doubt seemed to them that the Jews of Hungary were safe from the genocidal Nazi onslaught thanks to the protection of Admiral Miklos Horthy, the regent of the Kingdom of Hungary. Unfortunately, this sense of security turned out to be a pitiful pipe dream that would soon go up in smoke.

For their livelihood, Marton and Rose operated a small grocery store housed on the first level of a four-story building located on the Buda side of the city. They lived in an apartment on one of the floors above the store (Our return to this building will be described in a later chapter). The couple initially remained childless until finally, at age 38, Rose became pregnant in the summer of 1943. I was the child about to emerge from her womb into a world swathed in danger and teetering on the precipice of disaster.

In early 1944, with a likely German defeat, Hitler received word that Regent Horthy had approved secret plans for his nation to abandon the Axis and forge a separate peace with the conquering Allies. Aiming to prevent the Hungarians from turning against Germany, the

27

Nazi high command responded by launching Operation Margarethe, a.k.a. the German invasion of Hungary.

On the Ides of March 1944, Regent Horthy arrived in Berlin at the invitation of Hitler. Once there, he was escorted to the Schloss Klessheim near Salzburg, Austria, where Horthy was told that the Fuhrer wished to meet with him privately on March 18. This charade was a ruse to get the Hungarian head of state out of the country while German troops marched in on March 19. The tactic worked. The Hungarian Army, deprived of their leader who was being held in isolation in an Austrian castle, passively permitted the invaders to quickly and bloodlessly capture control of the country. When Horthy returned to Budapest the following day, he was greeted by German troops who escorted him from the station and kept him under close watch until his resignation and subsequent arrest in October.

Fast on the heels of the German invasion came SS leader Adolf Eichmann, one of the major architects of the "Final Solution," tasked with the mission of destroying the largest Jewish community still free in Europe. While he and the Nazi industrial death apparatus eventually succeeded in transporting 440,000 Hungarian Jews to Auschwitz, where most were gassed upon arrival, those early days of occupation were filled with confusion and trepidation for Budapest's Jews.

The round-up of Jews from the provinces began in April and the mass deportations that saw Jews cruelly packed into boxcars for days without food, water, or facilities, would be fully underway in May. But the detention and deportation of certain high-profile Jews began immediately. My father had likely attained such a leadership position in Budapest since he was arrested in late March and sent to the Mauthausen concentration camp in northern Austria. He never returned.

Marton was interned at Mauthausen, along with his wife's brother-in-law, Samuel Fixler, who survived the ordeal. I only learned this in 2016 during a trip to the Czech Republic. Until then, I wondered how my mother could have known about the details surrounding her husband's demise. It seems that she was informed by her brother-in-law and soon-to-be husband, Sam Fixler, who was also interned at Mauthausen at the time of my father's murder.

In early 1945, my father was included in a group of prisoners ordered to march from the camp to a nearby work detail. Sam Fixler was either a member of that group or heard what happened from other prisoners who were.

At a certain point, the commandant ordered the crew to stop, then announced, "Anyone who is having trouble walking today, take two steps forward." My father, who was suffering severe leg pains, did as ordered and was immediately shot in the head by the commandant. Sam Fixler, who also lost his spouse (my aunt) during the Holocaust, would survive Mauthausen and go on to marry my widowed mother after the war, thereby becoming my stepfather.

As a result of my actual father's immediate arrest during the first days of the Nazi occupation of Budapest, he was not present on March 30 when his wife, Rose, gave birth to her first and only child. She named her son, Illés Adlersheim. That boy was me.

My mother, and her infant fatherless son, managed to somehow survive Nazi-occupied Budapest. And as is the case with every survivor's story, our salvation was the result of random happenstance mixed with profound good fortune. But what about the family left behind in Bilke? Theirs was an all too typical tale of sorrow and devastation.

On the day following the last day of Passover 1944, the Hungarian gendarmerie were ordered to round up the Jews of Bilke and assemble them in the courtyard of the Great Synagogue. From there some 1,500 souls—including women, children, the elderly and the infirm—were force-marched to the train station where they were loaded tightly onto the awaiting rolling stock.

Among the Jews of Bilke rounded up that day were my maternal grandparents, Meier Berger and his wife, Faige, as well as Faige's brother, Samuel Heisler and his wife, Sarah. Also taken that day were the Heislers' two youngest sons still living at home, Eddie and Jack. My great-aunt and uncle, Samuel and Sarah, were the parents of 10 children. Bernard, who had immigrated to the US in the 1930s, was the oldest and Faige, my grandmother, was their youngest. Bernard, whom I would later call Uncle Bernie, had emigrated from Bilke and settled in Buffalo, New York. He would go on to serve in the U.S. Army under General Dwight Eisenhower in North Africa.

Also deported were Meier's brother and next-door neighbor, Jacob. Both men lived across the street from the Great Synagogue, which was obliterated by fire. During the 1930s, Meier's brother-in-law, Samuel Heisler, was a builder who had provided substantial tracts of timber to the town's home construction trade. Along with my grandfather, Samuel Heisler also owned several fruit orchards that dotted the fertile river valley. Workers from the countryside would travel to Bilke on weekends to pick fruit. Among their ranks was a young Jewish man named Samuel Fixler. During these visits, Fixler would often be put up at Meier Berger's home. My two cousins who lived nearby, Jack and Eddie Heisler, remember Sam Fixler as uncouth and a bit "wacky." It was undoubtedly here that Sam Fixler met Meier Berger's two daughters, Raisele and Rose. While he was prone to tease Rose, he was smitten by her younger sister, Raisele. He would eventually marry not one, but both of the Berger sisters, and go on to become my stepfather.

The train carrying my family and all the Jews of Bilke stopped and unloaded its human cargo in the outskirts of Berehove, some 50 kilometers to the southwest. The Jews were then herded into an open-air brick factory where they joined hundreds of other Jews collected from the surrounding provinces to await the mass deportation. With Jews arriving by the hour, the population inside the fenced-in and heavily guarded brickyard swelled to more than 15,000. Thanks to Eichmann's extreme efficiency, the established pattern of genocide was executed with lightning dispatch. In other European Jewish communities, the process of identification, isolation, "ghettoization," deportation, and extermination could take months and even years. Eichmann's system had been streamlined in the Carpathian communities so that Jews from Bilke were relegated to the ashes of Auschwitz within weeks of Nazi occupation.

By the end of May, every last Bilker Jew, including the family I would never know, had been deported via train transports, populated by about 2,500 persons each, that were destined for the slaughterhouse in Poland, known as Auschwitz-Birkenau. The beloved Jewish community that had persevered in Bilke for more than three hundred years reached its inexorable end.

Although rumors were rampant, it is doubtful that my mother, struggling to survive in Budapest, was aware of the fate of her family and home community. Even if she had been informed of the truth by a credible source—such as Rudolph Vrba, a Hungarian Jew who escaped Auschwitz with meticulous notes detailing the atrocities—she most likely would not have believed such outlandish stories. Transporting entire Jewish villages hundreds of miles by train only to murder them upon arrival? It made no sense.

I can only imagine my mother's anguish during those chaotic days in late 1944 as the Red Army made its way toward Budapest. Alone with only her infant son and her frustrating uncertainty about the fate of her husband, my mother also had to contend with the vicious Arrow Cross fascists who had taken control of the city.

On October 16, Regent Horthy was officially deposed by force and replaced with the Nazi puppet regime headed by fascist Ferenc Szalasi. This gave Szalsi's followers, Hungary's nationalist version of Nazi brownshirt thugs (the Arrow Cross), unrestricted reign in the capital. While most Jews from the provinces had already been sent to Auschwitz, close to 200,000, including my mother and me, remained in Budapest, facing a highly uncertain future. And now, the Arrow Cross had declared open season on us.

Determined to prevent even a single Jew from remaining alive by the time the Russians reached Budapest, the fascist gangs took to their bloody and evil work with relish. Atrocities abounded as the reign of terror accelerated across the capital. Fascist gangs targeted

Jewish orphanages and joyously bludgeoned the children to death with their rifle butts, in order not to waste precious bullets on mere youngsters. There were endless accounts of Jewish families forced to march to the banks of the icy Danube River. Once there, they were ordered to remove their shoes, as these were the only remaining items of value in their possession. They were then lashed together tightly with rope in groups of ten or twelve. An Arrow Cross officer would then calmly shoot every other Jew in the head with his pistol before dumping the entire group into the rushing river. This method conserved precious ammunition, as the weight of the dead dragged the living down to the river's lethal depths.

Thanks to the efforts of "righteous gentiles" such as Swedish diplomat, Raoul Wallenberg, a significant number of Jews found refuge from the marauding bands in safe houses and the embassies of neutral nations, such as Switzerland. Hundreds found sanctuary in the storied Glass House, which served as an adjunct to the Swiss embassy and became home to Jews lucky enough to have obtained forged foreign protection documents called *Shutzpasses*.

In November, the Nazis, deprived of boxcars that were needed at the Eastern front to evacuate retreating German troops, ordered 70,000 of the city's Jews to march on foot from the Obuda suburb to camps in Austria, some 500 kilometers away. Thousands were shot during this notorious Death March and even more died from the cold, deprivation, and exposure.

In late November, with the Red Army drawing ever closer, the Arrow Cross ordered the city's Jews who were not holding *Shutzpasses* into a designated ghetto on the Pest side of the Danube. My mother and I were included in this group. Although approximately 20,000 Jews from this ghetto were taken out and shot by the Arrow Cross in December, my mother somehow managed to avoid this fate. She also succeeded in keeping me alive during those harrowing days at no small risk to herself. I recall my mother recounting the following story:

> It was winter and we were all packed into the ghetto in Pest and I needed to feed you. Due to the cold and the lack of food, I had stopped lactating. I needed to find some milk and there was none to be had inside the ghetto. So, I ventured across the Chain Bridge to the Buda side looking for some milk for you. A *Nyilas* (Arrow Cross) soldier spotted me with my big yellow star on my coat and ordered me to go with him to the train yard. I could see they were loading Jews onto the boxcars headed to God-knows-where. I pleaded with the soldier.
>
> "Please let me return to the ghetto," I begged. "My baby is there and he needs milk." At this,. the bastard took his rifle butt and slammed me hard in the belly. I fell to my knees in pain and began wailing. But I did not spill the milk.
>
> "Get moving," he growled at me.
>
> By some miracle, a Hungarian officer heard the commotion and came over to investigate. After assessing the situation, the officer, who outranked the Arrow Cross soldier, ordered him to release me. The kind officer permitted me to keep the milk I had fetched and return to the ghetto so I could give it to you.

Her eyes glistened with tears while recounting this episode, suggesting that this was the closest brush with death that my mother experienced during these treacherous years. She was, at that point, unaware of the mortal danger she and her child faced as a ghettoed Jew during the days of waning Nazi occupation.

The ghetto that we, along with 70,000 other trapped Jews, were forced to inhabit was known as the General Ghetto to distinguish it from the International Ghetto, where roughly 30,000 Jews with *Schutzpasses* and other protective documents were housed.

On December 23, 1944, Eichmann and his henchmen fled the city ahead of the Red Army that had reached the outskirts of Budapest. Wishing to destroy all evidence and witnesses to his crimes, Eichmann issued a final order to General Gerhard Schidhuber, the SS Commandant of both ghettos. The order called for the transfer of Jews from the International Ghetto to the General Ghetto, prior to its complete destruction. Jews from the International Ghetto were quickly relocated amid the planting of dynamite throughout the General Ghetto. Next, the ghetto was surrounded by SS machine gun batteries. The plan was to set the ghetto ablaze, set off the explosives and then gun down any Jew attempting to flee the conflagration.

Somehow, Swedish diplomat and Holocaust hero, Raoul Wallenberg, got wind of the diabolical plan and decided to act. On January 3, 1945, he contacted the Arrow Cross leader, Ference Szalasi, who was in charge of Jewish affairs following Eichmann's departure. Wallenberg informed Szalasi that if he did not intervene to prevent this mass massacre—which he labeled as bestial and insane—Wallenberg would see to it that Szalasi was held responsible in any subsequent war crimes trials.

Fearing the gallows, Szalasi responded by calling off the plan. As a result, my mother and I, along with 100,000 other innocent Jews were spared a fiery horrific fate.

Red Army forces entered the city a few days later and by February 13, 1945, Hungary was liberated from Nazi occupation. It would be 16 years before Adolf Eichmann would be captured in Argentina by Mossad operatives. He was placed on trial in Jerusalem and is the only person to have been officially executed by the State of Israel. Despite his efforts to cooperate with Wallenberg and later with the Soviets, Ference Szalasi was placed on trial by the Hungarian courts and held responsible for the murder of 15,000 Jews in Budapest. He was executed for Crimes Against Humanity on March 28, 1945. Sadly, our savior, Raoul Wallenberg, was arrested by the Russians shortly after they took control of the city. He was secretly imprisoned in Moscow where he is presumed to have died some thirty years later.

Shortly after liberation, my mother learned that her parents, Meier and Faige Berger, along with her younger sister, Raisela, had been put to death in the gas chambers of Auschwitz. As mentioned, her older brother, Maurice had emigrated to America and settled safely in Buffalo in 1937. It appears that at the end of the Nazi occupation of Budapest, my mother returned with me to the house above the grocery while she attempted to rebuild her life and try to discover the fate of her other loved ones.

Eventually, she learned that my great-uncle, Samuel Heisler, had also perished in Auschwitz. Miraculously his two sons, Eddie and Jack, survived that nightmare. Throughout their ordeal, the brothers kept their sister Leona's American street address, on Buffalo's Hickory Street, frontmost in their thoughts. It was this enduring hope of joining the family in America someday that had gotten them through the unspeakable horrors of Auschwitz.

Upon liberation, the two brothers made their way back to Bilke. Due to the devastation, only remnants of their home remained in place. The house had been stripped bare and all the furnishings were gone. With the exception of a single room, even the windows had been removed. The brothers fixed up that one room as best they could and used it for sleeping quarters as they took stock of their situation. When they ventured into what was once the family's orchard to pick some fruit to eat, the neighbors drove them away. These neighbors, they discovered, had taken possession of the furniture they procured from the Heisler home after the deportations. They had likewise taken possession of all of the family's property.

Like all survivors, the brothers were anxious to learn which family and former community members had survived. They learned that among the few who remained alive was their cousin, Rose Adlersheim, my mother, living in Budapest with a small child. So, they made their way to the capital where they reunited with their cousin Rose, who put them up in her apartment above the grocery store.

A detailed retelling of the brothers' post-liberation journey, written by Eddie Heisler, appeared in the June 2007 issue of *Together Magazine*. The following account is drawn from that article.

Not long after arriving to Budapest, my cousins Eddie and Jack, to whom I referred as my uncles since they were significantly older than I was, saw a man on the street that caused them to question their own eyesight. Dressed in the uniform of a US Army G.I., the man walked down the main boulevard of Budapest, stopping people on the street and questioning them. As they drew closer, they could make out the soldier's features only to discover that he was their older brother, Bernie, who had emigrated to the United States in 1937.

Uncle Bernie, as previously mentioned, had spent the war in the U.S. Army serving under Eisenhower in North Africa. He found himself in Marseilles, France after VE day and immediately requested a furlough—but not to go home to see his newborn son, Aaron—but to travel to Hungary and search for his surviving relatives.

Incredibly, the three brothers literally bumped into each other on a street in a city with a population of two million souls. A tearful sidewalk reunion ensued as Jack and Eddie informed their brother about the fate of their father and other lost family members. The furlough, which was supposed to last three days, was extended to several weeks as Bernie started the process of bringing his brothers to America. Thanks to this fortuitous reunion, Uncles Jack and Eddie did not have to wait as long as we did to enter the United States. Uncle Bernie assisted them in emigrating first to France and then, after a bit of palm greasing, to the United States. Jack and Eddie landed in Buffalo in 1947. It would take another four years for my mother and me to join our relatives in New York. We did not arrive alone. We were accompanied by a man, Sam Fixler, whom I called Tatte. A man whom I mistakenly believed was my father for the first fourteen years of my life.

I have been unable to reconstruct the exact sequence of events that enabled my widowed mother to connect with her widower brother-in-law, Sam Fixler, but I suspect a scenario similar to this probably is what took place:

Rose found herself in post-war Budapest, alone with a one-year-old child and a future that looked quite bleak. Her past had been burned away in the crucible of the Holocaust, leaving her only with her determination—a determination to build a better future for her infant son. She decided that she had to find the boy a father.

Sam Fixler, the young man who used to stay with mother's family when he traveled to Bilke to pick fruit from the family's orchards, had married my aunt Raisele, who perished in Auschwitz. Sam, who had been interned at Mauthausen along with my father, Marton, had miraculously managed to survive. He arrived in Budapest every bit as alone as my mother. Connecting with his late wife's sister seemed like the natural thing to do. The couple soon grew close.

For reasons that remain unclear, Rose and Sam left Budapest to set up a home in the Czech river port town of Usti Nad Labem, which means "Mouth of the Elba River." The area was part of the Sudetenland that had been ceded to Germany under the terms of the Munich Pact in 1938. The scant 200 Jews who previously lived among the town's 80,000 residents had been a sufficiently large contingent to inflame the antisemitic predispositions of the Christian community. On January 1, 1939, local Nazis burned down the town's only synagogue and replaced it with a pork processing factory. Rose and Sam undoubtedly were, at this point after the war, the town's only Jews, since the entire Jewish population had been wiped out during the Holocaust.

It is unlikely that the couple wed in Usti since the town had no synagogue or rabbi to officiate. It can therefore be assumed that they married before departing from Budapest. Their *ketubah*, or Jewish wedding contract, is dated 1947, but does not list the location of matrimony. It is a near certainty that before marrying my mother, Sam was required to obtain a *ghet* (a bill of divorcement) from a Jewish religious court known as a *bet din*. Such documents were vital in the case of many Jewish widows who did not know the ultimate fate of their missing husbands. The *bet din* tribunal typically asked for evidence that the original husband had died before granting the *ghet* to the widow. In this case, Sam was no doubt able to provide such evidence, since he was with my father at Mathausen and could credibly testify as to his fate.

Although he never officially adopted me, Sam Fixler became my stepfather and I became Illés Fixler when he married my mother. My parents, wisely or not, decided to conceal the fact that the man I called Tatte was actually my stepfather. I grew up believing that Sam Fixler was my biological father. As recounted in Chapter One, I did not learn the truth until that fateful day in 1958 when, at age 14, I decided to rummage through my parents' closet.

My memories of Usti are understandably dim and distant. I do recall living in an attractive high-rise apartment building across the street from a lovely park. But like the old photographs that I still own from that period, my memories have also faded.

Nevertheless, I managed to hang on to a few salient recollections from that time and place. Most of them are painful and indicative that I was highly accident prone as a child. I seemed to attract disaster. At age three, I fell from a wooden fence while playing in the yard and broke my right arm. On another occasion, I fell hard on pavement and cracked the back of my head, requiring surgery and stitches.

When my stepfather, who worked as a house painter, repainted our apartment and needed to remove a massive, framed mirror that hung on a wall in order to paint the area behind it, something slipped. The mirror crashed to the floor sending shards of sharp glass everywhere. While I was unhurt, Sam was cut and bloody and had to be taken to the hospital for stitches.

In another painful memory, I was seated on the hospital steps after my tonsils had been removed. I had overheard the doctors telling my mother that things had not gone well and that they had almost lost me during the operation. I recall being frightened and begging my mother to take me to the sweet shop for the ice cream that had been promised me. Thankfully, she agreed.

Eventually my mother and stepfather, whom I will refer to as my parents going forward, came to the conclusion that residing in Usti as the town's only Jews was not in my best interests and set their sights on emigrating to America. They wished to join our family that had put down roots in Buffalo. Unlike Uncles Eddie and Jack, my parents did not have a member of the US military to assist them in this effort. They decided to take a different route. A route that took us through the Holy Land.

The newborn Jewish state of Israel was declared in May 1948, and immediately found itself in a death grip battle for survival against its Arab neighbors. The new nation was anxious to welcome Jews from all over the world to implement the "ingathering of the exiles." Israel viewed itself as the successor to the biblical Jewish Davidic Kingdom of Judea. Jews who immigrated there were considered to be making "*aliyah*" and were accepted under the state's Law of Return. Absorption centers and temporary housing, consisting of tents and shacks, were set up across the nation. The new State of Israel was faced with the massive absorption and assimilation of both the ravaged remnants of European Jewry and the hundreds of thousands of Sephardic Jews, known as the Mizrachi, who had been expelled from the Arab lands upon the creation of the State of Israel; expelled from lands in which their ancestors had dwelt for dozens of generations.

It was into this quagmire of conflict and redemption that my family found itself as we arrived in Petach Tikvah, outside of Tel Aviv, in the summer of 1948. We were assigned to temporary housing in a long rectangular barracks-style building that measured roughly 20 feet wide and 300 feet long. Each family occupied a small, partitioned area and had access to a common outdoor latrine, which was a circular wooden structure near the end of the barracks. At about seven feet tall and ten feet in diameter, this makeshift facility was divided by partitions into individual wedges to afford a modicum of privacy. In the space where one might expect to find a toilet, there was but a hole dug in the dirt.

Our dormitory structure was constructed at an elevation higher than street level and separated by a deep swale or culvert from the road in front of it. How clearly I can remember the huge python snake that we found one day curled up in that hollowed area by the road. The *olim*, or new immigrants, were alerted and brought their shovels and brooms to quickly dispense with the threat.

The car rides from our home in Petach Tikva to the beach in Tel Aviv are also remarkably clear in my memory. These excursions are especially notable because they were typically made on the sabbath. Driving a car on *Shabbat* is strictly prohibited by Jews who consider themselves observant, or *Shomer Shabbos.* Once in America, I do not recall my stepfather ever driving a car on *Shabbat*. Thinking back, I now consider our regular car trips during our time in Israel surprising. Evidently, my stepfather was not as pious during those early days after the Holocaust. It's certainly not astonishing that the religious convictions of many survivors were shaken to the core by the profound question of "How can I worship a God who let such horrible things happen?"

Perhaps my most cherished memory is of my stepfather taking us to Jerusalem and our visit to *Kever David Ha-Melekh,* or King David's Tomb on Mount Zion. While historians and archeologists have cast doubt as to whether King David is actually buried there, the site has powerful symbolic significance for Jews of the diaspora. With the partition of Palestine in 1948 through the liberation of Jerusalem by Israeli forces during the Six Day War in 1967, the Old City was under the sovereignty of Jordan. During this period, Jews were denied the right to worship at their holiest site, the Western Wall of the Second Temple known as the Kotel. Hence, the Tomb of David was, during those years, promoted as a suitable substitute place of worship for observant Jews and pilgrims. The roof of the building, above the Christian holy site known as the Upper Room or

Cenacle, was famous for its dramatic view of the Temple Mount and, as a result, became a symbolic place of yearning. I was spellbound as my stepfather pointed to the Temple Mount, occupied by the Al Aqsa Mosque and the Dome of the Rock. Someday, he told me, Jews will once again *"daven"* (pray) at this holy spot off in the distance. He turned out to be correct.

Like my mother, my deceased biological father, Marton, also had a brother living in the United States. But unlike Uncle Maurice, who would soon help our family legally enter the country, Marton's brother, Frank, refused to provide us with any assistance, whatsoever.

Despite this, our little family soon experienced great good fortune in the form of invaluable assistance from a relative named Jacob Feurstein, a Buffalo real estate broker and part-time bootlegger. Because Fuerstein agreed to sponsor us and warrant that we would not become wards of the state, we received our entry visas after spending a year and a half in Israel. In addition, Max Yellen, an attorney who owned the Century Movie Theater in downtown Buffalo, also signed an identical affidavit attesting that he would likewise guarantee the financial solvency of our family. I will be forever indebted to these two men who facilitated our family's entry into the *"Goldeneh Medinah."*

We made that journey from Haifa Harbor to the Port of New York in the summer of 1951. It was a rocky crossing that nearly resulted in me being swept overboard as I played along the top deck railing during a powerful squall. That terrifying moment has been deeply etched into my memory for all these years.

We finally sailed under the watchful eye of the Statue of Liberty and disembarked on Ellis Island. Our family was among the last of the 12 million immigrants that passed through this historic and hallowed intake facility during the 62 years it was operational. While many immigrants look back with fondness at the experience of entering America's "golden door," my memory of Ellis Island is a bit more painful. I had brought with me—stuffed into my little rucksack—a big golden Jaffa orange. A true memento from the land of Israel. But when an immigration officer discovered it, my citrus souvenir was swiftly confiscated. "No fruits or vegetables allowed," read the big sign that the officer pointed out. Since English was not yet a language I had mastered, that didn't mean too much to me.

Although this first taste of America was a tart one, I soon fell in love with my new homeland and began my transformation into an "All American Boy."

Elliot Fixler

Chapter Three

A Buffalo Boyhood

"No language has ever had a word for a virgin man."
—Will Durant

We were met in New York Harbor by my Uncle Maurice and his big 1950 blue-grey Custom Dodge. We were also met by something I had never seen in sunny Petach Tikva: fluffy white flakes falling from the morning sky and covering the ground with an icy frosting. It was snow, glorious snow. I recall opening my mouth skyward just to be able to taste the stuff on my tongue. To my seven-year-old eyes, snow was a magical powder, but to Uncle Maurice, the accumulation and drifting posed a hazard for the long drive back to Buffalo. The Dodge performed admirably and after spending more than eight hours in the back seat peering out the windows at this ocean of land, covered in white, we finally arrived at my uncle's humble home where our little family took up residence on the second floor.

My uncle, Maurice Berger, a soft-spoken, genial and warm-hearted fellow, was married to a vivacious woman who bore the same first name as my mother, Rose. This made things a bit confusing with two ladies named Rose living under the same roof, but I distinguished them. One was Mommy and the other was Aunt Rose. Maurice and Aunt Rose were first cousins. Maurice's mother, Faige Berger (née

Heisler), was the sister of Aunt Rose's father, Samuel Heisler. Consanguine marriage was an accepted practice among the Jews of Eastern Europe and is still considered as such today among orthodox Hassidic sects. Uncle Maurice and Aunt Rose had immigrated to the United States in the mid-1930s and thereby averted the fiery fate of the family members they had left behind. They settled in Buffalo, which was home to Aunt Rose's older brother, Bernard, who had preceded her to America in 1935. By the time our little family arrived in 1951, Buffalo was brimming with Heislers.

After getting settled at the home of Uncle Maurice, Aunt Rose and their baby daughter, Carol, I was soon enrolled at nearby Public School 81 on Tacoma Avenue. I shall never forget my first day of school in America. I was a bit older than the other first graders and, of course, could not speak a word of English. This fact, along with my odd Hungarian first name, Illes, prompted them to bully me in the schoolyard as soon as classes let out. I turned tail and ran, but a gang of them pursued me all the way back home, shouting and mocking me. I made two important decisions that day. I would learn English as quickly as possible and I would change my name. It was by listening to the radio (and later watching a lot of TV) that I quickly mastered the language. And it was Aunt Rose who dubbed me with my new American name.

"From today on, you will be known as Elliot Fixler," she proclaimed to the family with a dramatic flourish.

She then tutored me on the correct spelling. "Two L's and one T," she had me repeat after her, a phrase that has become an oft-repeated mantra over the course of my life. Only seven years old and I had already had three names. This one, however, stuck.

We lived with my aunt and uncle in North Park for a little less than two years before finding our own home on Hertel Avenue. Today, a gentrified boulevard in the heart of the city's Italian district, in the 1950s Hertel Avenue was the main drag of Buffalo's vibrant Jewish community. In addition to Mastman's and Blitzer's delis, the latter owned by the family of well-known CNN news-blabberer, Wolf Blitzer, and numerous synagogues, Hertel was also home to a plethora of small family-owned shops, including North Park Florists. It was into a $26 per month first-floor flat situated directly behind that flower shop that our life in America began to bloom as our family took root in Buffalo.

I was, at this point, at an age of self-discovery and sexual curiosity. Unfortunately, my pre-pubescent sex life was cut short unduly because, of all things, the Communist Party. Let me explain.

Entry into our building could only be gained by first traversing a narrow passageway that led from Hertel Avenue to the back alley. This tunnel was about three feet wide and ran for forty feet alongside the florist shop. Next door to the florist was both the home and place of business of an optometrist by the name of Dr. Robert Tobin. Tobin and his wife, Sylvia, had two daughters. The younger, Nancy, was my age and my classmate at school. Did I mention that she was very cute?

It was with the mischievous and marvelous Nancy Tobin that I experienced my first proto-sexual experience in her bedroom as her father was administering eye tests to patients one floor below. Nancy not only expanded my knowledge of female anatomy, she also enlarged my vocabulary by teaching me the meaning of words like "gynecologist." It was not long after that first game of playing doctor with Nancy that I found myself in her father's darkened exam room as he shined his penlight into my dilated pupils during an eye exam. It felt a bit awkward knowing that just a few days before I had been one flight up probing his daughter with what appeared to be the same penlight.

After checking me out on the phoropter, Tobin diagnosed my condition as amblyopia, also known as lazy eye. It's a disorder found among children wherein the nerve pathways from one eye to the brain are not properly stimulated and the brain starts to favor one eye over the other. Sadly, I was past the age of eligibility for therapy. As a result, I have been plagued by impaired vision in my right eye since childhood.

Despite my lazy eye, I was able to keep it focused on Nancy for quite a while. This came to an abrupt halt, however, when her mother, Sylvia, was called to testify before the House UnAmerican Activities Committee. As part of the prevailing witch hunt known as the McCarthy Era, the Committee had come to Buffalo and was holding hearings to ferret out members of the Communist conspiracy. A witness, known only as Mr. Regan, testified that Sylvia Tobin had been a member of the Communist Party in New York in the 1930s, a charge she vigorously denied. Nevertheless, the times were so charged that the scandal resulting from the mere allegation of Communist affiliation resulted in Dr. Tobin closing his office and the family moving to parts unknown. And thus, came to an ignominious end my earliest sexual adventures.

Moving to the house on Hertel Avenue placed me into a different school district from where I had attended PS 81. It also was a different district from the one frequented by my many Heisler cousins. Although it was only a few miles away, it may as well have been light years. I wound up having much less contact with my American cousins than expected.

Our immediate family had settled in Buffalo in order to be near our relatives. But, as things turned out, we only saw the Heislers and my Uncle Maurice's family during Jewish holidays, on family outings and life cycle events like Bar Mitzvahs, weddings, and funerals. With the exception of Yom Kippur, the one common thread that ran through all such family get-togethers, was food. Lots of food. I guess you could call us a gastronomical clan, although I felt it takes more than mere creamed cheese and schmaltz herring to hold a family together. Such feelings cast me in the role of an outsider and left me feeling uncomfortable and a bit unwelcome at such gatherings.

It's hard to say if this sense of estrangement from my Buffalo relations was their fault or my own, but it was clearly something real and palpable that persisted as I grew older. The only two Buffalo cousins with whom I enjoyed close friendships over the years was my Uncle Bernie's son, Aaron Heisler, who died in 2009 and my second cousin, Andrew Hahn. Andy is the son of Bernie's sister-in-law, Lillian and her husband Fred.

Another factor adding to my alienation from the family was the fact that my father and I attended a small Orthodox synagogue about

a half mile's walk from our home, while the rest of the family belonged to Brith Sholem, better known as the Pine Street Shul, an
even smaller establishment, located in a different part of town. This
synagogue was actually located at 1052 Hertel Avenue, but it retained the name of the street where it resided during the first half of
the 20th century. The Pine Street Shul was also Orthodox, although
only two members of my extended family, my cousins Leona and
Ethel, were considered to be *Shomer Shabbos* or strictly observant.
The Pine Street Shul was also home to brothers Max and Jack Yellen.
Max was the attorney who had signed the affidavit that enabled our
family's entry to the United States (more about his brother, Jack, a
bit later in this chapter).

Our *shul* was operated by the Lubavitchers, a chassidic sect that
created the Chabad movement, an outreach program designed to
bring more Jews back to traditional Judaism. I attended Hebrew
School at the Lubavitcher *shul* three times a week after regular
school. This fact naturally cut down on my ability to interact with my
friends after school. At this point, my religious training did not result
in any real resentment on my part, although it certainly would do so
after I entered high school.

My most salient memory from Hebrew school (aka *cheyder*) was
a confrontation I had with our instructor, Rabbi Begun. It was before
the Jewish New Year in September 1957 that the venerated Talmudic
scholar announced to our class that we Jews were about to celebrate
the arrival of the year 5719. He attached great numerological significance to the fact that the Hebrew year was the reverse of the secular

year. Precocious kid that I was, I raised my hand and asked what the numbers meant.

"The Hebrew year counts how long it has been since God created the universe as we studied in *Bereshit* (the Book of Genesis)," he explained.

"But what about evolution and cavemen and dinosaurs?" I challenged. "That was *more* than 6000 years ago."

"All those things were created by God 5719 years ago," the Rabbi assured me. The answer left me scratching my head and highly skeptical of what I was being taught. I didn't buy it then and I don't buy it now.

The family outings I mentioned earlier were most often held in Grand Island, a town northwest of Buffalo, near Niagara Falls. It was at such Sunday picnics that I had a chance to observe how my cousins' fathers interacted with them. Vastly different from the way my stepfather, Sam, related to me. I had to say I felt somewhat envious as I watched how my cousins would hug and embrace their fathers in unabashed displays of public affection. I recall sometimes asking my mother about Sam's clear absence of outward endearment towards me.

"Are you sure that Tatte is really my father?" I would ask her, only half-joking. It would not be until I discovered that Sam Fixler was not actually my biological father (see Chapter One) that I began to understand the true nature of our relationship and the not-very-attractive nature of the man.

My buddies at my new North Park school, PS 66, were mostly middle and upper-class Jewish guys whose families attended Conservative or Reform synagogues. Unlike mine. I was the only kid in the entire school who was Orthodox. And, at that time and place, being Orthodox was associated with being somehow lower class, socially. It also meant that since I came from a kosher home, I was required to bring my brownbag lunch with me each day. But the most isolating feature of my childhood existence was my cap. I was required to keep a baseball cap planted on my head at all times. This was during a period when wearing such team logo caps was not in fashion and viewed as somehow "weird" by my classmates. The baseball cap made me a target for all of the schoolyard punks and bullies. Their favorite method of taunting me was grabbing my cap and playing "keep away" with it, tossing it to each other as I chased back and forth trying desperately to retrieve it, much to their amusement.

Another reason behind my schoolmates labeling me a "weirdo,"… were the chickens. Often, when my friends were at our home, they would venture into the bathroom to discover that the bathtub was filled with freshly plucked dead chickens, covered in a layer of kosher salt. According to Jewish dietary laws, meat must be "*kashered*" within 72 hours of slaughter to remove the blood before it has a chance to congeal. Soaking the meat in a salty brine is the most common way of accomplishing this, although the practice looked very strange to my less observant friends.

I also recall a snotty Catholic kid named Bobby who loved taunting me every Saturday morning as I passed by his house, located across from the massive St. Mark's Cathedral and parochial school. My stepfather and I were forced to walk past Bobby's house on our way to *shul*. Bobby loved to razz me about my formal wardrobe. My stepfather and I both dressed in suits and ties and wore our black fedoras whenever we attended Shabbat services at the Lubavitcher *shul*. While I grudgingly tolerated his taunts back then, years later I encountered an opportunity to pay Bobby back for his antisemitic abuse. The details of that avenging altercation are recounted in Chapter Four.

The experience of being the lone *"frum"* (observant) kid in grade school and enduring the scorn and persistent teasing of my peers resulted in toughening me up to the point that I was no longer afraid to get into a fight if the situation called for it. I recall one fracas with an Italian boy who claimed *he* was the toughest kid in our class. I soon disabused him of that errant notion. A few swift punches and... *Presto*! I retained my title.

One fight that stands out in my memory took place in the third grade against a kid named Richard Polisner, better known by one and all as Snip. I don't recall what triggered the skirmish, but I do remember clearly that I was the victor. Snip decided, as he nursed his bloody nose, that he would be better off being my friend than my enemy. We have been lifelong pals ever since. Today, Dr. Richard Polisner is a Florida Certified Supreme Court civil and family mediator and a board-certified podiatrist. He still mentions that fight every time he introduces me to someone.

When it came to our family's social standing, what they said about us was true. We *were* lower class. After all, Sam Fixler, my stepfather, was a moonlighting house painter. I could not afford the preppy attire—button-down oxford cloth shirts, khaki slacks, Bass Weejun penny loafer shoes—favored by my wealthier classmates. My wardrobe was strictly J.C. Penny's.

At age twelve, I underwent a naturalization process and emerged a full-fledged citizen of the United States of America. My pride at this passage point was minimal, particularly since this was the time I began work as a painter's assistant for my stepfather every summer.

Sam Fixler was not a union painter and so when he took on a job where this was an issue, he would only be able to work at night, unobservable by the union shop stewards who might report him were he to conduct his painting during daylight hours.

Sam was a darned good painter and I'm proud to say I did an acceptable job as his assistant. It was exhausting, filthy labor that saw me working both days and nights mixing paint, removing wallpaper, hauling ladders and scaffolds and anything else that needed to be done.

One nocturnal off-the-books job I recall most vividly was a big one at the Sample Shop on Hertel Avenue. Our benefactor, Max Yellen's brother, Jack, worked for the owner, Anne Bunis, and Max had recommended my stepfather to Jack when the need arose to paint the interior of the large dress boutique. We worked every night till the wee hours of the morning for weeks.

In addition to working at the Sample Shop, Jack was an accomplished musician and successful songwriter. Both brothers belonged to the Pine Street Shul, mentioned earlier, and it was the son of Pine Street's cantor, young Hyman Arluck, who, at age seven became the prodigy star of the congregation's choir. In the mid-1920s, Hyman, who by then had a budding career in show business, changed his name to Harold Arlen and began writing songs for New York City's Cotton Club. His collaborator on many of these tunes was Jack Yellen. Arlen would go on, with another partner, Yip Harburg, to compose the music for *The Wizard of Oz* and such timeless hits as *Over the Rainbow, Ain't She Sweet, Stormy Weather,* and FDR's campaign song, *Happy Days Are Here Again.*

Our family owes a great debt to the compassionate and talented Yellen brothers in more ways than one.

Unlike my mother, who was accurately regarded as a kind-hearted woman with a gentle demeanor, my stepfather was not liked by *anyone* as far as I could tell. He had no friends, or so I thought at the time. He was considered to be pretty much of a nobody by the rest of the family. The only place where this did not hold true was at the synagogue. Tatte was blessed with a beautiful singing voice and often served as the volunteer *chazan* (cantor) during services. This fact came into play when I delivered his body for burial on the Mount of Olives in Jerusalem. According to biblical prophesy, it is at this spot where the *Mashiach* (messiah) is to appear in order to raise the dead. So being buried on this holy site has been the devout desire of Orthodox Jews for centuries. Sam, along with his brother, Jacob Fixler, both had purchased burial plots there. I will discuss this further in a future chapter.

I was quite fond of our ethnic Hertel Avenue neighborhood. On our block alone there was an appliance store, a local bank, and a Chinese restaurant. A music store and the huge Catholic church and parochial school—the one that Bobby the bully belonged to—were situated on the next block over. That block also was home to the aforementioned Blitzer's, a Jewish delicatessen owned by the father of CNN news anchor, Wolf Blitzer. Mr. Blitzer the Elder was an outgoing man who eventually sold out to his partner, a Mr. Friedman, and then went on to become a successful homebuilder. Friedman, unfortunately, lost a couple fingers while operating an electric meat slicer, but he never lost his sense of humor. "Let me know if you find a fingernail in that pastrami," he would often joke.

Next to Blitzer's was the North Park Movie House. This spot remains notorious in my memory and not only for being the place where I snuck into the theater in the dark to see my first movie (*David and Bathsheba* starring Gregory Peck and Susan Hayward, as I recall). It was also the site of my first real sexual experience since my dalliance with the eye doctor's daughter. The dirty deed took place when I was in the sixth grade and in the same alleyway behind the theater where I would someday exact my revenge on Bobby the bully.

While the experience was exciting, it was also terrifying. My paramour was a girl whose big brother was a really BIG brother and a well-known menacing tough guy who lived on my block. The fear that he would find out that I was diddling his little sister and come after me succeeded in giving me nightmares. Fortunately, he never did find out (unless he's reading this now).

For the most part, my grades at school were exemplary. I earned A's and my test scores were always 95 or higher. I shined in every subject except for one, "Deportment." In those days, teachers would evaluate students not only academically, but also on their general behavior and good manners. Being the class tough guy naturally meant

I did not possess much in the way of "respectable" manners. My grade in this area was usually around 75 or lower. One of the incidents that I recall contributing to my low Deportment scores was the time I squirted my seventh-grade teacher in the face with my squirt gun. My dear mother was so upset when she learned about this that she threatened to tell my stepfather—a man who had responded to my previous misbehaviors by applying his belt to my naked backside. My mother, bless her soul, never went through with her threat.

Not surprisingly, when my stepfather would review my report card each term, he never once mentioned my outstanding grades in academic subjects. His desultory and negative comment would invariably refer to my poor showing in Deportment. This pattern of always seeking out the worst persisted in high school and beyond.

My reputation as a kid with poor Deportment also contributed to a rather traumatic experience in the eighth grade. Our teacher, Mrs. Finkelstein, was conducting tryouts for the annual citywide public speaking competition. She would select the winner from among the students in our class by means of tryouts. The winner would go on to compete against all the other public schools in Buffalo as the representative of PS 66. I had worked diligently, polishing my solemn delivery of Lincoln's Gettysburg Address and performed it to perfection before the class. Yet, I was not the winner. When Mrs. Finkelstein selected another student, Gerald Nover—whose speech was far inferior to mine—I was outraged, absolutely livid. Why was I denied the award? I'll never know for sure, but I am convinced that "poor deportment" had a lot to do with it.

The lingering effects of that childhood disappointment stayed with me later in life as I advanced in my legal profession. I would work diligently on honing my public speaking skills in an unconscious effort to prove that Mrs. Finkelstein had selected the wrong winner back in the eighth grade. As a result, I grew into an effective trial attorney, thanks to the public speaking skills I had developed partly because of this juvenile desire for redemption and proper recognition.

As an only child, my free time—what there was of it—was devoted to two things: sports and reading. Looking back, my budding interest in sports was surprising, given the fact my immigrant parents knew nothing whatsoever about American athletics. I played basketball and softball (3rd base and shortstop) on the PS 66 school team. In addition, I played basketball in the youth leagues organized by the Jewish Community Center. I also enjoyed sports as a spectator and a devoted fan. As described in Chapter One, I would lie on the carpet listening to radio broadcasts of Yankee baseball games, made exciting by the skills of Bill Mazer, the "Voice of the Buffalo Bisons," our local minor league team.

On those days (holidays and the Sabbath) when listening to the radio was "*verboten*," I would spend the hours curled up with a book that most often recounted the exploits of my boyhood hero, attorney Clarence Darrow. As stated, it was my admiration for him that would later propel me on the path toward the legal profession.

It was also forbidden to watch TV (or use any form of electricity) on the Sabbath, but I managed to get around this obstacle in order to watch my beloved NBA Saturday basketball games. Directly across the street from our home on Hertel Avenue stood the Pierson Layer Appliance Store. The front of the store was filled with the latest model TV sets and a row of chairs had been positioned in front of them for potential customers to sit and view the TVs in action as they made up their minds about which one to buy. It was many an unforgettable NBA Saturday basketball game featuring such legends as Bob Cousy, Bill Russell, Bob Pettit, and Paul Arizin that I watched at Pierson's, eyes glued to the screen and seated in a comfy chair for hours at a stretch.

There was another solitary pursuit that I, as an isolated child, would engage in. Whenever I had the time, I would make my way around the corner to where I had painted a rectangle on the side of a multistory brick building. The box represented a baseball batter's strike zone and I would spend hours pitching a tennis ball at that wall trying to nail it inside the box. Actually, since I only had one tennis ball, most of my time was spent retrieving it. But, after some practice, I got to be pretty consistent and was able to toss off a fastball or a screwball with a passable degree of accuracy. My aim in improving my pitching skills was to shine at our favorite playground game. A similar strike zone box existed in our schoolyard and one kid would stand in front of it with a baseball bat. Our task, as pitchers, was to strike out the batter by getting the tennis ball past him and have it hit the wall inside the strike zone box. All that solitary practice helped and, after a while, I began to earn a reputation for my pitching prowess.

I didn't recognize it at the time—I was just a kid—but that brick wall in the alley was a metaphor for my life. Rough and unpolished, but also upright and unyielding. It was one of many walls in my life at that time, not the least of which was the wall that emotionally separated me from the man who was supposed to be my father. I would soon begin to break through that wall and move beyond it.

My mother, on the other hand, was always supportive and never critical…with one exception. Although I had loved to sing from an early age, I could not carry a tune for the life of me. Whenever I would break into song within earshot of my mom, she would declare, in Yiddish: *"Oy Elly. Es shurli gegangen tsu regn"* which translates to: "My goodness, Elly. It surely is about to rain."

Now, while you might find this non sequitur confusing (what does a weather forecast have to do with a person singing badly?), I always understood it as her way of gently urging me to mercifully cease my vocalizations for fear it would bring on a thunderstorm, and I would always comply.

I did keep on singing, despite my limited abilities, when I was out of my mother's earshot. I would belt out pop tunes as I traversed the tunnel leading from Hertel Avenue to our home behind the flower shop. The enclosed space provided an echo chamber-like environment. I would, of course, sing in the shower and the bath. I loved all kinds of music, particularly that put out by the early Rock 'n Roll heroes like Elvis Presley, Buddy Holly and Jerry Lee Lewis. I even formed a singing duo in the seventh grade with a talented buddy and we would vocalize tunes like *"Peggy Sue"* and *"Heartbreak Hotel,"* but never before an audience. Just for our own amusement.

I was absolutely delighted when I learned, only a few years ago from a book about the history of the Jews of Bilke, that my grandfather, my mother's father, Meier Berger, who had perished in Auschwitz, had been a lover of music. This fact represents the sum total of all I know about my grandfather. It was not only his physical body, but his entire history that was reduced to ashes in the Nazi ovens.

Although none of them, like me, are able to carry a tune, I'm pleased to report that all my children share my deep love of music, a love I always, as a parent, encouraged. I recall pleading with my own parents to buy me some sort of musical instrument and pay for lessons, but that, like most such "rich kid" luxuries, was out of the question. After much strenuous begging, I did succeed in getting them to purchase a brand-new maroon and white Shelby bicycle. I rode it proudly to school and all over the neighborhood until one day I decided to visit the Buffalo Zoo in Delaware Park. I left the bike standing in a rack outside the gates of the zoo and when I returned I discovered that it had been stolen. My parents did not have enough money to buy me a bike lock and so that was the end of my two-wheeled galivanting—for a while.

As my elementary school years drew to a close, my parents purchased a house on North Park Avenue, a few blocks away, and we said good-bye to the rental flat behind the flower shop on Hertel Avenue. By the time I reached eighth grade, I was once again the owner of a bicycle that I rode to school and back each day. Of course, being somewhat of a showoff, I liked to ride while perched on the bike's handlebars. Not too surprisingly, I fell off, hit the pavement and wound up breaking my arm. I spent the rest of my grade school career sporting a plaster cast.

I finished eighth grade in 1958 with an impressive academic record and was primed to join my friends at the public secondary school, Bennett High, in the fall after once again spending the summer working for my stepfather as a painter's assistant. It turned out to be an exciting summer in more ways than one.

In June, I had my first experience, at age 14, of driving a car by myself. One of my stepfather's helpers gave me his keys and said, "Take her for a spin, son," obviously trying to ingratiate himself with the boss's kid.

Although my feet reached the pedals and I knew how to brake, shift and steer, I had never been behind the wheel of a real automobile before in my life. It was a frightening experience navigating the narrow streets of the neighborhood all alone. I managed to get both myself and the car back to the job site in one piece and without any mishaps.

As that last summer of innocence wound down, I was successful in sweet-talking a girl from my graduating class to meet me by the train tracks at midnight for some randy railroad romance. She complied and it was at this point that I saw my sex life truly get back on track.

My train yard trysts were a wonderful way to end that summer before entering high school, but what I ran into next was anything but. I had overheard my stepfather telling my mother that he intended to send me not to Bennet High in Buffalo, but to a yeshiva in Brooklyn, New York. A place that trained young men to become rabbis. I was shocked. I was dumbstruck. And I was very upset. Not only by the fact that I would not be going to high school along with my friends, but even more galling was the fact that I was not being consulted about this matter. It looked like I was not slated to become the "All-American Boy" after all. It seemed I was fated to become something entirely different.... an Orthodox rabbi. Oy!

I knew that Sam had shown my mother the brochure and application form from the yeshiva and I was determined to find them to learn exactly what he had in store for me. As described in Chapter One, it was during a room-to-room search the following day that I came across the old valise holding the wedding photos of my mother and her first husband, my true father, Marton Adlersheim, who, up until that moment, I never knew had existed.

At that point, everything changed for me and I knew that my life would never be as it had been before.

Elliot Fixler

Chapter Four

The Yeshiva Years & Beyond

*"When I look back on all the crap I learned in high
school, it's a wonder I can think at all."*
—Paul Simon (Opening lyric from "Kodachrome")

Despite my protestations and apprehensions about being packed off to a religious seminary some 400 miles away, in September of 1958 I found myself in the heart of the heavily Orthodox Jewish community of Brooklyn, New York, known as Williamsburg. I had been enrolled by my parents at Yeshiva Torah Vadaath, a school that still bills itself as "The Mother of the Yeshiva movement in America." It was a mother, alright. Opened in 1926, the *Mesivta* (high school) was headed by Rabbi Nesanel Quinn, who served as its principal. Reb Quinn started out as a student and remained affiliated with the school for nearly 80 years until his death, at age 96, in 2006.

But I did not yet know about the "Mighty Quinn," or much else about my new home, as I trudged up the four flights to my dormitory room in the building adjacent to the school. I soon met my roommate, a likable fellow who will remain nameless for the simple reason that not long after the start of the school year he tried to have sex with me.

I was more puzzled than outraged by his advances. "Aren't you an observant Torah-true Jew?" I asked him. "Have you read in *Vayikra,* where God instructs us that for a man to lie with another man is an abomination? *(Leviticus 18:22)*" He seemed to shrug off my appeal to his presumed religious convictions, so I was forced to resort to more basic methods to make my point.

"If you ever touch me like that again, I'll break your fucking neck with my bare hands." He got the message and I was not bothered by the sins of Sodom ever again.

The school day was divided into morning and afternoon sessions. We would start the day with Torah and Talmudic studies under the tutelage of a dreary Lubavitch rabbi named Mordechai Avrohom Yeshaya Groner. Rabbi Groner sported a long black beard and I dubbed him "Blackbeard, the Pirate" in the imaginary universe where I would often retreat to find solace from the soul-draining world to which I had been relegated. Blackbeard had a disgusting habit of regularly placing his chin hairs into his mouth and then using his fingers to pull them out from his face. Even more revolting was the stomach-wrenching behavior of a tall, pimply classmate who loved to dig deeply into his nostrils with his forefinger and then munch happily on whatever he was able to extract.

Looking back, there are only two things that I remember from all my classes at Torah Vadaath. One was flunking Algebra and the other was sneaking into the kitchen late at night for a midnight snack of cold kosher roast beef. I have retained nothing else, intellectual or otherwise, from my first year of high school. Torah, Talmud and three thousand years of Jewish history just washed over me and was swept away into the void.

In order to maintain its accreditation with the State Board of Regents, the school had to offer a minimal contingent of secular courses which we would sit through as we struggled to stay awake through the shank of each afternoon. The content of these "English" courses, as they were called, adhered to my brain more thoroughly than did the Hebrew, but not by much.

As an only child, I didn't have a great need to make new friends. About the only true friendship that I recall was with an older student named David. David and I played one-on-one basketball in the schoolyard constantly. When, toward the end of the school year, I was expelled from both the school and the dormitory (as explained later), it was David who put me up at his Brooklyn home until the school year came to a close.

I did not find very much about my situation enjoyable. In fact, my classes and classmates were barely tolerable. There was one bright light in the firmament, as I recall. Her name was Harriet and she was *frum* which means orthodox or observant. As such, she was prohibited from riding any form of transportation during *Shabbos,* which began each week on Friday night at sunset and ended with sunset on the following day. I would spot Harriet walking down Bedford Avenue at such times and occasionally I would ask to join her. As we walked, we talked as about everything from theology to psychology and I found her to be highly intelligent and quite charming. Of course, we were unable to discuss anything relating to popular culture since she was forbidden to watch television or go to the movies. Eventually, she was regarded as my girlfriend by our classmates, but it was not a particularly serious relationship and we lost touch after I got into trouble and was forced to leave school. Let me explain.

Toward the end of the school year, I felt as though I could lighten up on my dreary studies a bit and try to have a little fun. For me, that meant taking a glass bottle and dropping it from my fourth-floor dormitory window onto the pavement below just to see what would happen. What happened was that someone spotted me and reported my act of vandalism to the *Rosh* (Head of the School). It was decided that I would be expelled from the Hebrew Division although I would be permitted to continue my secular studies. I would also be allowed to remain in the dormitory, although I was moved away from any windows.

I had developed my penchant for practical jokes back in middle school when some buddies and I decided to sabotage a soft drink vending machine located at the Jewish Community Center. In those days, the machines would hold large tanks of syrup and soda water. When a customer put in his ten cents, a paper cup would slide down behind a clear plastic door and the ingredients would then be poured into the cup where they would blend. I was elected to stick my arm up inside the machine and withdraw a stack of empty paper cups. We neatly removed the bottom floor of each cup and then shoved them all back up into the machine. We would then hide nearby, but in sight of the machine, and watch with glee as people would put in their coins and view haplessly as, behind the door, the contents of their soft drink would flow through the bottom of the cup and down the drain.

After my partial expulsion, I continued to live in the dorm and attended classes only in the afternoon. Although I no longer had to contend with Hebrew and the Torah fixation that prevailed during the morning sessions, I still found the English afternoon classes to be insurmountably boring. Finally, in order to inject some excitement into our studies, I brought along a string of firecrackers and set them off during class. Not surprisingly, this bit of theatrics did not sit well with the teacher who immediately remanded me to the principal's office. This was the last straw, I was told. I was summarily drummed out of the school entirely. As a result, I had to forfeit my lodgings in the dormitory. This meant I would need to head home before the school year ended, making it clear to my parents that I had been expelled. I felt a bit lost and at sea—like Holden Caulfield in *The Catcher in the Rye*—as I pondered my future. Fortunately, my friend David said I could board at his apartment for the balance of the school year. I was also allowed to take the New York State Regents' Exams to obtain credit for the courses I had been booted out of.

I'm not sure exactly how, but my parents did learn about my expulsion and, not surprisingly, were very upset. Instead of concluding that perhaps I was not a good fit for an orthodox yeshiva, my stepfather came up with the ultimate punishment for my bad behavior. He would send me to a different orthodox yeshiva. The Yeshiva University High School for boys located in Washington Heights (today known as the Manhattan Talmudical Academy, or MTA).

I knew little of the school's impressive history. Founded in the early 20th century and originally known as the T.A. or Talmudic Academy, the school was located on New York's Lower East Side. It moved to Brooklyn in the 1920s and back to Manhattan in the 1940s. It is recognized as the first Jewish high school in America. It was also the first Jewish high school in the world to offer a dual curriculum consisting of both Hebrew and English studies.

Although I looked to my mother for a reprieve from this dismal sentence, she chose not to intervene. I suspect she felt putting some distance between me and Sam was a good idea. She also knew that if I stayed at home, she would be forced to listen to Sam complain about my antics. Something she understandably wished to avoid.

Once there, I was pleased to discover that this school was far more "Modern Orthodox" in its orientation than was my previous one. Modern Orthodox is an American movement within Orthodox Judaism that seeks to integrate Jewish values and rituals with the secular, modern world. Nevertheless, it had the same class schedule format as my previous school. With Torah studies in the morning, and afternoons devoted to the "English" program, as they called it.

Amazingly, I cannot recall the name of a single one of my teachers in either the Hebrew or English divisions. The only staff member I can recollect with any clarity is Mr. Abrams, a diminutive bespectacled, bald fellow who served as the school's much feared administrator. The reason he sticks in my memory—and in my craw—is because he loved to confront me at the end of the school year about...what else?...my deportment.

My roommate at YU High was Larry Lerner, who hailed from Michigan and is the younger brother of Ted Lerner. Ted Lerner would one day become the billionaire real estate developer and owner of the Washington Nationals baseball team. I remember Larry as a rather introverted fellow—slight with horn-rimmed glasses—who, unlike me, tended to walk the straight and narrow. They say opposites attract, and Larry and I became fast friends and enjoyed our regular Friday lunches of corned beef on rye at a nearby corner deli.

My taste for larceny also needed to be satisfied on the day I found myself at a formal school luncheon reception. The buffet table was decorated with a few whole watermelons. I decided that one of those would look very nice back in my dorm, so I ambled out the door with a hefty melon tucked tightly under my arm. No one observed and I made my way home through the back alleys. I didn't care to be seen walking down the boulevard carrying a watermelon.

My backstreet route was impeded by a chain-link fence that I decided to climb over. As I descended on the other side I heard a rip as the seat of my fancy houndstooth trousers caught on the fence and produced a long rip in the fabric. Such are the wages of sin, but all I could think at the time was, *"Thank God I didn't drop the watermelon."*

I cherished those houndstooth trousers and the pain of losing them has stayed with me over the decades. So, imagine my utter joy at finding a similar pair at Macy's not long ago. I wear them with pride these days and make a point of staying away from chain-link fences.

At the beginning of the following fall semester, I found myself attending the obligatory High Holiday services at the school's synagogue. Even though there was a *mechitsa* (barrier wall) separating the men from the women, I still managed to catch a glimpse of a certain young lady each time the congregation was required to rise. She was what I would term as "super-cute" and I found myself attracted

73

to her. I soon learned that her name was Fredda Lerner (no relation to my roommate, Larry) and that she lived around the corner from the school on nearby 187th Street. Our relationship soon became serious and intimate as we spent the after-school hours in her bedroom doing what comes naturally to two horny teenagers when no parents are at home.

Fredda's father was a soft-spoken, low voltage electrician and her grandfather was a friendly neighborhood butcher. I loved both of them dearly. With their warm-hearted and generous affection toward Fredda, they were such a stark contrast to my own bloodless stepfather. I did not get on so well with Fredda's domineering mother, however. I suspect she was aware of, and resented, the time I spent with her daughter behind closed doors. Or perhaps she thought her daughter was too good to go out with a house painter's son.

YU High had a decent basketball program, but as a sophomore, I was relegated to the Junior Varsity team. Our team managed to make it to the league finals where, unfortunately, we lost the championship game. I was double teamed during most of the game and, as a result, turned in the worst performance of my short basketball career.

As my sophomore school year drew to a close, I was summoned to the office of that mini-martinet, Mr. Abrams. He looked me in the eye as I stood stiffly in front of his desk and he came right to the point:

"Feexler. You masturbate?" he inquired in his heavy Yiddish accent.

"Of course not," I replied quickly.

"Vell, I dunt believe you vun bit," he retorted. "But it dunt matter cause you are not gonna be coming back here next year."

"What?!?" I couldn't believe it. I was being expelled for whacking off? The sad part was that I was actually telling the truth. I had no need to masturbate and neither was I the "master of my domain." I had something better than porno and wet dream fantasies to relieve my hormonal urges. I had Fredda. Maybe someone had ratted on me about my liaison with the electrician's daughter. I suspected Fredda's mother to be the squealer. She viewed me as an uncouth marauder who had deflowered and corrupted her innocent young daughter. She probably wanted me gone from her daughter's life and thought that complaining about me to the school would do the trick. If so, she was right—for a while.

To be honest, I was not at all choked up about, once again, being unceremoniously booted out of another Jewish educational institution. About the only thing I would miss would be my romps between the sheets with Fredda. Once I was back in Buffalo, I did stay in touch with her as best I could. Hertel Avenue was dotted with public phone booths in those pre-cell phone days and I selected one near our home that I would regularly use to call Fredda. I'd show up with a bag of nickels, dimes and quarters and start feeding them into the phone's coin slot. It was impossible for me to call her from our home since the long-distance charges would have infuriated my stepfather.

After a while, I learned a slick trick that saved me lots of coinage. Someone showed me how to unbend a wire coat hanger and insert it up into the coin return slot. If I jiggled it just right, I would be able to coax the phone into returning the money I had just deposited even though my call had been put through. First soda pop machines and now pay phones, I was moving up and turning into a real con artist mechanic.

I did not have to fear the wrath of my stepfather after this second expulsion in as many years. By this time, I stood a foot taller than he did and he had not raised a hand to me since he declined my invitation to arm wrestle back in the seventh grade. I do believe, however, that he had finally abandoned his dream of my becoming a rabbi. Ain't gonna happen. And he knew it. I was thrilled that I would be back in a "normal" public school system and back with my old friends from grade school.

My Junior and Senior years were spent at Bennett High School in Buffalo's University Heights section. As I reconnected with my few old friends, they urged me to pledge a high school fraternity even though I'd be doing so a year later than usual, as a Junior instead of a Sophomore. Since I was friends with the upperclassmen, I found that pledging was relatively painless, with one exception that remains painfully evident in my memory. As part of the fraternity's initiation ritual, it was required that my scrotum be swathed with Bengay mentholated rub. OUCH!

It was after my junior year in high school, during the summer of 1961, that I once again crossed paths with Bobby, the anti-Semitic bully you may remember from Chapter Three. As I entered the lobby of the plush North Park Theater I observed a group of teenage punks in one corner of the huge lobby harassing a short kid, a friend of mine by the name of Moshe. As I drew closer, I could tell that the ringleader was that same Catholic kid who used to mock me and my stepfather as we walked past his house to *shul* every *Shabbos*. It was none other than Bobby, the bully. He had not changed that much, but I had. I was now 6 feet tall (thanks to my Heisler genes) and in great shape. This gave me the confidence I needed to approach him even though he was surrounded by an entourage of eight or ten fellow would-be tough guys.

"Hey," I shouted at Bobby as I swung him around toward me by his shoulder. "Remember me? Why don't you pick on someone your own size?" I could tell that he recognized me and I sensed that he feared my righteous retribution. Like all bullies, Bobby became a complete coward when challenged.

"C'mon," I ordered. "Let's take it outside."

He followed me and Moshe to the alley behind the theater and his cheering section followed along in step. As soon as I turned towards him, Bobby hit me with a swift kick to the crotch. A crotch that was still recovering from that Bengay treatment. Whereas I was merely annoyed by his behavior before, this cowardly low blow got me steaming mad. I decided I would persuade this bigot, once and for all, that picking on Jewish kids was a bad idea. If I couldn't make him see the light, I would make him see the darkness.

I lunged at him and we fell to the ground in a double bear grip as I pummeled him hard. He was clearly getting the worst of it, but interestingly, all of his cohorts merely stood around and did not lift a finger to intervene or come to his aid. By the time I was finished, I had beaten the living crap out of him. Bobby was nothing but a bloody heap, unable to get up. He had to be carried off by his buddies. Afterwards, Moshe thanked me and I, for that moment, felt like I was the Jewish Superman. Bobby, the bully, had learned the hard way that Jew-baiting was not a great idea and, as far as I know, he never did so again.

Entering Bennett High at the Junior level, as I did, resulted in some definite challenges. It was too late for me to join any of the after-school clubs and getting on a school sports team was a fruitless endeavor. I went out for the basketball team but saw immediately that the freshmen and sophomore players already had set positions. My religious commitments also complicated matters when it came to playing sports. Games on Friday night and Saturday practice were out since such activity is prohibited on the Sabbath.

I did manage to get on a basketball team at our local Jewish Community Center, however. We played against other JCC teams from surrounding cities. The annual state JCC tournament was held in Rochester and, instead of a hotel, team members were put up in private Jewish homes. I really enjoyed traveling with the team and meeting new kids from different communities. We emerged victorious in Rochester, but an even bigger thrill was scoring with a cute young lady in whose house I was assigned to spend the night.

We then moved up to the national JCC basketball tournament held in Harrisburg, Pennsylvania. Although our team did not win the championship, I was fortunate to have been named to the tournament's All-Star Team. I still cherish the trophy I was awarded in recognition of this honor.

I did not go in very much for extra-curricular activities in high school. I recall being cast in a minor role in a school production of ARSENIC AND OLD LACE. My mini career as a thespian reached its zenith when I was assigned to play the part of a woman in full drag. I was six feet tall at this point and I was required to perform a dance number with a rather pint-sized student named Gary. Our Mutt 'n Jeff appearance elicited howls of laughter from the audience as we went through our routine. And, when I picked up little Gary and carted him bodily off the stage, we brought down the house.

Not long after my return to Buffalo, I was riding a bus to the JCC in order to attend a community event. Seated alone by the window was a very attractive girl a few years my junior. I asked if I could sit down next to her. She agreed and flashed me a million-dollar smile. By the time I learned her name was Judy, I had already fallen in love with her. Judy became my girlfriend from that point through the duration of my high school years. She was a freshman at Bennett and we soon became an item as we embarked on a fun-filled teenage romance.

Judy's mother, I felt, looked down her nose at me because my father was a house painter. I found this ironic since Judy's father owned a paint store. Even though Judy's mother did not appear to care for me, her dad was a pretty good guy. He even gave me a part-time job in his paint store. This position allowed me to become familiar with the father's work schedule, enabling me to strategically time my visits to their home to frolic with Judy. My most cherished memories of that period involve making wild passionate love to Judy whenever her parents were not at home while listening to Ravel's *Bolero* on the record player. Pure Heaven on Earth. Bear in mind, this was 25 years before the Bo Derek movie, "10", in which that piece played a significant role.

Speaking of sexual escapades, the summer following my junior year was an unforgettable one that has left its lusty imprint on me to this day. I was invited by one of my Junior year teachers to stop by her house one afternoon on some pretense. It was only one block away from our place and so I agreed. Once inside her darkened living room, she came on to me. It wasn't exactly a Mrs. Robinson situation, but not far off. One thing led to another and pretty soon I found myself in her bedroom and between her legs. Afterwards, we were both pretty casual about it. We, of course, kept things secret. I never publicized or boasted about what happened to anyone. I actually felt some pride in the fact that she found me, a rising high school Senior, to be sexually attractive.

It was during that sultry summer that the families of many of my friends had purchased or rented bungalows in a resort-style community known as Crystal Beach. Situated on the eastern shore of Canadaigua Lake in Ontario County, New York, the property straddled the US-Canadian border and was the site of an outstanding amusement park that would close in 1989 after a century of service.

Judy's family owned one of the bungalows where I found myself spending a good number of my summer days—often spending the summer nights as well. The bungalows were located across the Peace Bridge on the Canadian side of the park. As we drove back over the bridge upon our return to the U.S., a border guard would ask everyone in our party the same question, "Where were you born?" I would look him squarely in the eye each time I answered.

"In the United States of America," I lied.

That seemed a pretty easy entrance requirement at the time, but I guess today, under the current administration in 2022, people crossing our southern border don't even get asked that much before being granted entry.

The amusement park was home to a classic wooden roller coaster and a Victorian Ferris wheel with hand-carved horses imported from Italy. My favorite spot, however, was the beach and the adjacent outdoor basketball court where I loved to hang out, practicing foul shots and layups until late into the night.

Judy and I would enjoy strolling along the boardwalk and stopping at the various eateries and hot dog stands. There was an establishment that was patterned after Nathan's on Coney Island that sold the world's greatest French fries. Being a voracious French fry fiend, I would typically buy a huge order that I would douse with tomato catsup. Judy used to annoy me by always pilfering my French fries.

"I'll buy you your own," I protested.

"No, no. I don't want any. I just want a bite of yours," she replied. I found this behavior highly annoying and it often led to spats and hard feelings. Come to think of it, the only thing we ever argued about was French fries.

To illustrate the depths of my depraved obsession with French fries, let me share the following account. On Sunday evenings, my mom would typically prepare hot dogs and French fries for our supper. The fries were made from peeled and hand-cut Idaho potatoes. They were served in a large bowl that contained a sufficient amount of fries to feed six people. I would eat half the bowl immediately at supper. The other half would be put away in the cupboard and I would consume them cold a few hours later. I have, since those days, joined a 12-step program called Potato Heads Anonymous and I'm proud to say that I now have my deep-fried demons under control… sort of.

Judy and I would drive up to Crystal Beach in my tiny two-seat roadster and often used it as a "motel on wheels" for some horny hanky-panky. I was a six-footer and Judy was also quite long of limb. You can just picture the contortions we put ourselves through, twisting our bodies around steering wheels and gearshift knobs, all for the sake of making love.

One day, as I was practicing my lay-ups in the Crystal Beach basketball court, I was approached by a guy who towered over me. At 6 foot 5 inches, he could have been a college or NBA athlete. The fellow challenged me to a one-on-one match and I arrogantly accepted. I was known to play a strong defense and could lay them up to the basket with either hand. And one-on-one was my strong suit. I had never lost…till now. This giant pushed his butt directly into my stomach and backed me down the court making short easy shots. I lost big time and was forced to swallow my hubris.

Before acquiring my roadster, I relied on my best friend in high school, Richard Polisner, better known as Snip, for my transportation needs. Snip had access to a car and he did a lot of the driving as we engaged in the time-honored Jewish teenage tradition of Cruisin' and Schmoozin.' Unfortunately, Snip was an aggressive driver. Moreover, I learned how to drive from Snip and thereby inherited all of his bad habits. Like Snip, I had little regard for the posted speed limit signs, generating a rap sheet of traffic citations that wound up nearly costing me my first legal job.

Snip's father owned a pharmaceutical chemical distribution business for which he employed a long station wagon to make his delivery rounds. The car did not have an automatic transmission, but rather it was a stick shift with the shift handle mounted on the right side of the steering column. Snip enjoyed access to the station wagon during off-duty hours and I used to marvel how adeptly he managed to shift gears with his left hand while keeping his girlfriend, Lois, in a tight front seat embrace with his right. That took true talent.

Snip and Lois would often go on double dates with Judy and me on Friday nights. Snip would pick up Judy at her home first and then pick me up at a street corner where I stood waiting. I was forced to sneak out of the house because, had my stepfather seen me riding in a car on the Sabbath, he would have read me the riot act. It was another type of intolerance that would eventually force Lois to stop seeing Snip. Once her father found out that his daughter's boyfriend was Jewish, he chased him out of the house and then went straight to Snip's father at his pharmaceutical business to warn him that his son had better stay away from his Christian daughter.

Judy was an easy-going and endearing young lady who was vastly different from the other girl in my life, Fredda Lerner. Judy and I split up over some silly reason. Perhaps I had had enough of her French fry thievery or she was tired of being a contortionist in order to make love in my tiny roadster. Whatever the reason for our break-up, I soon regretted it and begged her to agree to get back together. But Judy wouldn't hear of it. She was done with me. I eventually re-established my relationship with Fredda just as I was going off to college. A relationship we maintained on a long-distance basis during my college years.

While most of my high school buddies were accepted by out-of-town colleges and universities, the only college to which I applied was the University of Buffalo (later known as the State University of New York at Buffalo). This was an economic imperative. Neither my parents nor I had the funds to send me to a school where I would need to pay for room and board. I could go to college, but I would have to live at home.

I was accepted by the University of Buffalo with my tuition paid for by a State Regents scholarship I had applied for and received. My only out-of-pocket expense was for books. As the next chapter reveals, I was on my way...or so I thought.

Chapter Five

Shuffling Off to Buffalo

"College is the reward for surviving high school."
—*Judd Apatow*

While I may have hoped that graduating from high school and moving on to college would mean an end to my days of painting walls and cleaning brushes, things did not turn out that way. The money I was awarded through a New York State Regents' scholarship paid my tuition, but not my other expenses, such as textbooks. That meant I needed to find employment while enrolled at the University of Buffalo. I found a part-time job at the Niagara Falls Hotel where I was put to work repainting guest rooms and hallways.

By the early 1960s the hotels and motels along Niagara Falls Boulevard and Pine Avenue had already started to go into decline as tourists bypassed the "Gateway to the Falls" in favor of the new interstate highway that got them there much quicker. Plus, the closing down of the railroad's "Honeymoon Express" in 1961 no longer encouraged visitors to travel the Boulevard.

The University of Buffalo was home to three Jewish fraternities. Buffalo locals, like me, tended to gravitate towards Beta Sigma Rho. Founded at Cornell in 1910 as Beta Samach (that's one Greek letter followed by a Hebrew letter), it was notable because it did not require members to pay initiation fees or dues. By the 1920s, when the Delta chapter was established at Buffalo, the name had been changed to Beta Sigma Rho. The frat would grow to 15 chapters, including two in Canada, before being absorbed by a larger Jewish fraternity, Pi Lambda Phi.

I decided to pledge Beta Sig and found that it wasn't too difficult. In fact, it was a lot of fun. I was confident that the upperclassmen, most of whom I knew as friends, wanted me in the house, so I wasn't concerned about being blackballed. Frat parties included the requisite beer guzzling and general "Animal House"-like behavior.

I recall one riotous episode that would have made an ideal scene in that movie. A group of pledges, including me, were delivered to a raunchy blue-collar dive on the "wrong side of the tracks." We entered en masse and ordered beers all around. Suddenly, two of the upperclassmen who had brought us to the place jumped up and began to fake a loud rehearsed argument.

They faced each other and placed their hands on their belt buckles, as if to unclasp them, and began shouting at each other, back and forth:

"Mine's longer than yours!"

"Oh yeah? Well, I'll show you, buddy. Mine is definitely longer than yours!"

All heads turned toward the pair. The patrons of the bar naturally assumed that the two were talking about their penises.

The joke was that when one exclaimed, "Oh yeah? Then whip it out and let's see," they would pull out their belts from their trouser loops, hold them up vertically next to each other as if to compare their lengths, and one would announce, "Hmm. I guess you're right. Your belt *is* longer than mine."

It was supposed to generate a big laugh. But they never got a chance to deliver the punchline.

At the point where one of them shouted, "Whip it out!" the place went nuts. The local denizens of the establishment became enraged at the antics of these ill-mannered college kids and a full-scale riot ensued. I was soon dodging an attack by an enraged bar patron who came at me brandishing a wooden chair over his head. Fortunately, I was standing in a doorway when he came down with it and the chair splintered against the door jamb instead of me. We ran for our lives, barely escaping the wrath of the intoxicated and infuriated mob.

I did go out for the basketball team as a walk-on, but once I came into contact with the coach and team members, I realized I would not be very welcome since I had not been recruited. The mentality was, "If he was any good, why wasn't he recruited?"

I also realized that I would face the same sort of Sabbath violation issues that I endured in high school. So that was that.

At some point, during my Sophomore year, I had become disenchanted with fraternity life and less and less active in-house activities. This corresponded to the time I smoked my first marijuana joint. For us local Buffalo guys, pot was not really a part of our repertoire, as it was with the boys from the Bronx and Long Island. After that first experimentation, I never tried it again until I was much older and in the company of my adult children.

Most of my time was spent studying, working at the hotel, socializing with my buddies, and playing basketball for fun. My grades were good and most of my courses were not particularly memorable. The exception was Psychology 101.

I found Psyche class interesting and I actually learned a few things that turned out to be valuable in my later legal career. For example, we studied something called Intermediary Responses developed by pioneering psychologist, B.F. Skinner. In a later chapter, I will explain how my understanding of this concept, one that Skinner demonstrated using monkeys and bananas, was to benefit me in such areas as jury selection. I was also fond of my History professors and for a brief instant I considered becoming one myself. But that delusion passed quickly.

I particularly recall a public speaking class instructor who assigned us to prepare and deliver an advocacy speech on a topic we did not necessarily support. I took things to the extreme and delivered an address in which I laid out far-right Nazi principles. Despite the fact that I found such thinking abhorrent, I delivered my remarks in the context of a serious and enthusiastic campaign speech designed to win converts to the cause of Naziism. The class was spellbound and hung on my every word. The result—much like the denouement in Mel Brooks' *The Producers*— both the teacher and the other students reacted as if they were watching a performance of *Springtime for Hitler*—they laughed uproariously. I got an A and the teacher explained that the only reason I did not receive an A+ was because a few times I permitted a smile or a giggle to escape my lips, destroying the desired effect. I took that as a lesson for the future and strived to develop a stoic poker face at all times, even though it gets me in trouble occasionally when people have a hard time telling if I am joking or not.

I was not involved romantically with anyone during this period and after a while, I began to think about Fredda, my old flame. I just couldn't seem to get her out of my system. I called her and, when she expressed similar feelings toward me, we rekindled the romance and embarked on a long-distance relationship that would endure for many long years.

My resurrected romance with Fredda necessitated numerous trips from Buffalo to New York City—a journey that today takes a little over six hours by car, but before the completion of Interstate 80, took me close to eight hours each way under normal driving conditions. One particularly harrowing experience along the byways of upstate New York remains etched in my memory. I was winding my way back to Buffalo on the New York State Thruway. It was a frosty winter morning and I was driving my beloved green MG Midget 2-seat roadster while singing along with the radio to a country-western version of Nat King Cole's immortal *"Mona Lisa."*

Mona Lisa, Mona Lisa, men've gone and named ya.

You're jes' like that lady with that ol' mystic smile.

Is it 'cause you're lonely they've gone and blamed ya, darlin'?

For that ol' Mona Lisa strangeness in your smile?

As the winds picked up and the snowfall became denser, I realized I was driving into blizzard conditions. I suddenly lost control of the vehicle and hit the brakes, skidding into a roadside barrier. I got out and surveyed the situation to discover I was now stuck in a two-foot snowbank. I reckoned my location as near a small town called

Westmoreland, about two hundred miles from home. I couldn't budge the car so, in those pre-cell phone days, there was nothing left to do but wait for someone to rescue me.

After about an hour of waiting, I began to shiver and actually started worrying about my very survival. I tried to remember the statistic I had read about how many motorists freeze to death by the side of the road each year. To my overjoyed relief a state trooper spotted me and pulled up behind my immobilized car. My joy was short-lived however, since the first thing he did was hand me a speeding ticket for driving too fast given the weather conditions. Evidently, I was not the first motorist who had gone off the road at this juncture and the trooper was intent on making sure that the hamlet of Westmoreland lived up to its reputation as a speed trap.

Before long, my car was hauled into town and I was hauled before the local Justice of the Peace for arraignment. He set bail and a court date and asked me if I had money for a train ticket (I did). The trooper then delivered me to the depot where I dejectedly shuffled off to Buffalo, leaving my heavily damaged roadster behind. I was told that the trooper was the J.P.'s brother-in-law and convicting speeders was the town's main source of revenue. I don't know if all of that was true, but I can attest to the fact that they were two of the biggest assholes I have ever dealt with—and I've dealt with plenty.

On the train ride back home, I pondered my situation. I would need to return to Westmoreland to retrieve my car once it was repaired. Could that happen at the same time I was required to appear in court or would I need to make two trips? I recognized that the charge against me would never hold up at trial. The trooper could not possibly know how fast as I was driving at the time I swerved off the road. I had no idea how fast I was going (my attention was diverted, singing along with Conway Twitty), so how could the cop? He also could not attest to the weather conditions at the time of accident since it happened an hour before he arrived on the scene. The prosecution would have zero chance of proving my guilt beyond a reasonable doubt, which is what the law called for.

We'll never know the outcome of my trial because there wasn't one. I was busy with classes and exams on the appointed trial date and failed to return to Westmoreland to make an appearance. I presumed that the judge would just put it over again and I would be notified about a later trial date, but that's not what happened. My failure to appear was deemed to indicate my acknowledgement of guilt and I was issued a conviction for speeding. This was problematic because it was my third moving violation within the previous 90 days (as mentioned earlier, neither Snip nor I paid much attention to speed limits). I was notified that my driver's license was suspended for six months. This made retrieving my car problematic and made my visits with Fredda much less frequent. Nevertheless, our relationship endured despite such challenges.

By the first semester of my Senior year at Buffalo, Fredda and I jointly had come to the conclusion that we wished to spend the rest of our lives with each other. She accepted my proposal of marriage and we set the date to correspond with my graduation at the end of May 1966. Fredda insisted that the engagement was not official unless I bought her an engagement ring. I must have been totally bedazzled because, in response, I withdrew every last dollar of my life's savings, about $3,000, and used it to purchase a one carat emerald-cut diamond ring. I never understood the logic of her desire to have a fancy ring and a penniless husband. This was the first time, but probably not the last, that I ever did anything so fiscally foolish. The true value of the situation was not in the piece of extravagant jewelry, it was in my learning about what has true and lasting value in life.

Based to some degree on my admiration for famous lawyers like Clarence Darrow (and possibly Perry Mason), I decided to pursue the law as my career path. Hence, I sat for the Law School Aptitude Test (LSATs) and submitted applications to several Buffalo and New York City law schools. LSAT scores are supposed to predict how well a student is likely to perform in law school. Hence, the scores are used by a law school's admissions office as a qualification criterion for entry. My scores were not good enough to earn me admission into any of the nation's elite law schools (i.e., Harvard, Stanford, Yale, etc.), not that I could have afforded them even if I had qualified. I was accepted at both the New York Law School, located in Manhattan's Tribeca neighborhood, and the University of Buffalo School of Law. Fredda made it plain that she did not wish to move from New York and insisted that I enroll at NYLS, which had recently received its accreditation from the American Bar Association. So, that's what I did.

It was not long after being accepted at NYLS that I received some devastating news. Fredda had undergone a change of heart and wished to break off our engagement. She evidently had met someone else who had captured her affections. I had, at this point, one more semester to complete in order to receive my bachelor's degree. I was all set to get married and attend law school in New York after that and now found out that my fiancé had been unfaithful to me. Now what?

I fought through the despair, gathered my courage and did what I had to do. I begged. I pleaded with Fredda to stay with me. She replied that she could not endure the long absences while I was in Buffalo. She had needs and required someone nearby to fulfill them. The only way she would put the engagement ring back on was if I agreed to carry out my final undergraduate semester in New York City. Like an obedient puppy, I agreed.

I transferred out of the University of Buffalo and into NYU. Fortunately, my scholarship covered the cost of tuition. And, for the third time in my life, I was back in the Big Apple to attend school. During that final semester, I found lodging directly across the street from Fredda at her grandparents' apartment. Arriving in town with empty pockets, I was forced to quickly find some sort of gainful employment. I found a part-time position at Caligor's Physicians and Hospital Supply at 83rd and Lexington, a job that I held till it was time to begin classes at NYLS.

At some point, the subways stopped running temporarily and I was required to use a small kiddie bicycle to get to work. Pedaling down Lexington Avenue from 187th Street all the way to 83rd Street every day was an experience I'll never forget. It was a true adventure navigating the backstreets and alleyways of Harlem, especially on the ride back uptown at the end of each day.

Ironically, I received my bachelors' degree (from the University of Buffalo) on the same day I ceased being a bachelor. I was unable to attend the commencement exercises in Buffalo on May 28th, 1966—a date that would "live in infamy" for the rest of my life—due to a prior commitment; our wedding. I consider that date to be so onerous that when I recently received an invitation to the wedding of a close friend's son to be held on May 28, 2022, I informed him that I would only attend if they changed the date.

My mother had pleaded with me not to marry Fredda. She simply didn't like her. But I would not listen. I was focused on going to law school and becoming an attorney. I did not want anything to upset the game plan that Fredda and I had put together. Looking back, I should have listened to Mom. I may have been headed to Law School, but my mother had received a broader education at a place she called Life School.

Our nuptial ceremony turned into the biggest disaster to hit the Bronx since the 1936 Schmeling-Louis fight. It was held on an early summer Saturday night which meant my observant parents could not leave their lodgings in Brooklyn until sunset at around 7:30 pm. As a result, the ceremony did not take place until 9:30 pm. The drizzly weather added further to the stress experienced by Fredda, me and the wedding guests who were unhappy about having to wait for my parents to arrive. Not a great way to start a marriage, or, if you're superstitious, definitely a bad omen.

I began my law school classes in the fall of 1966 and expected to complete my studies in the spring of 1969. Fredda and I moved into an efficiency apartment in Rego Park, Queens, and I would commute daily into Lower Manhattan to the NYLS building at 57 Worth Street. I enjoyed my studies and did reasonably well during my first year. As a result, I was asked to join the New York Law Review, the school's journal of legal scholarship. My poorest grade was in Torts, which was odd because I loved the subject and considered it my favorite. Two factors contributed to my poor showing. My disdain for the incompetent instructor and my less than legible handwriting. This last point was evidenced by the fact that there were two young women in our class, both with excellent penmanship, who earned top grades despite not being particularly astute.

I suffered an even worse instructor in my Contracts class. A sitting judge from the Bronx, he was a totally inept educator. For example, we were assigned to study textbook cases, each one of which represented an important precedent or principle of the law. The judge never expounded on these cases. Instead, he would lazily call on a student to rise and describe a case and state its significance. Whatever the student said, be it right or wrong, was accepted and not questioned by the judge. He would simply shout, "Next case," and move on to the following student without comment. Years later, I would at times represent clients in a Bronx courtroom before this judge. I discovered, to no one's surprise, that he was no better a jurist than an educator.

Fredda had been trained at New York's Fashion Institute of Technology (FIT), located at 27th Street and Seventh Avenue in the heart of the garment district. This enabled her to find work as a clothing buyer in Manhattan's booming "*shmatteh*" industry. Fredda became friendly with a co-worker named Gary Hodes and we would often socialize with him and his wife. My days were devoted to study at home whenever I was not attending classes or working at the medical supply store. During these times, Fredda was off at work and I was typically at home when the postman arrived. One day, as I was bringing in the mail, I noticed a letter addressed to Fredda that had come from Gary. This struck me as odd, so I proceeded to open it. What I read floored me. It was nothing less than an impassioned love letter. I naturally became distraught and confronted Fredda with it as soon as she arrived home. To her credit, she did not deny the relationship and began to apologize and ask my forgiveness immediately. She begged me not to end our marriage and after some deep soul searching, I agreed. Our marriage did not end that day, but something else did: my love for my childhood sweetheart, my love for my wife.

I was determined not to permit my wife's infidelity to derail my career plans nor distract me from my studies. The realization that she had taken up with a man so stupid as to write love letters and send them by mail to the home she shared with me, only added insult to injury. I had made up my mind on that first day of law school—when the Dean announced to the incoming class that only one third of us would complete the program and that both the student seated to my right and the one seated to my left would likely not be receiving a law degree—that I would not be among the casualties.

To add to the complexity of my situation, it was not long after that I learned that Fredda was pregnant. The specter of my own dysfunctional upbringing rose to immediately haunt me. Would I raise it as Sam Fixler had raised me—at a distance? I swore that no matter what the case, I would never treat this child the way my stepfather had treated me. In fact, I may have overcompensated a bit when bringing up Mitchell.

So here I was, married to an adulterous wife, fighting my way through law school with a baby on the way when I am forced to come face to face with another of life's cruel realities. We needed money. We simply could not get by on Fredda's paltry *shmatteh* salary and my meager part-time earnings. Not with a kid on the way. There was no way around it. I would have to find full-time employment. Now.

I immediately transferred my law school studies to the evening division that would free up my daytime hours but would add another year of study before I would be granted my law degree. I contacted Dean Daniel Gutman in order to apply for a scholarship. In addition to serving as Dean at NYLS, Gutman had been a legal counsel to New York Governor Averell Harriman and had founded a night small claims court. He was well-liked by both students and faculty and had introduced an English course into the law school's curriculum intended to improve students' ability to better express themselves in writing and in speech. I was pleased to learn that, based on my exemplary performance to date, Dean Gutman approved my request and my tuition fees disappeared. I had a chance to thank him years later when he and I became neighbors.

Thanks to this change, I was able to accept a full-time position at Caligor's at double my previous salary. I held that job for my remaining three years of law school. I suppose it would have made sense for me to find employment at a law firm instead of a hospital supply company, given my ambition to practice law, but the only such jobs available to me were internships and they paid far less than I was making at Caligor's.

During the summer months, I would ride my bike to work from Rego Park, over the 59th Street Bridge (feeling groovy), and uptown to Caligor's. I had moved up from the kiddie bike and was now pedaling a spiffy green 3-speed 26-inch Raleigh. Riding my bike was less of a hassle than switching subway lines to get into Manhattan from Queens, plus I liked the exercise. I would arrive to work pretty sweated up from pedaling ten miles in the summer heat. I'd need to stop in the storage room at Caligor's before clocking in to get cleaned up and wipe off the perspiration. I'm happy to report that, unlike back in Buffalo, I now owned a good bike lock and managed to keep my wheels from being stolen.

Before the year was out, Fredda gave birth to our first son, after a long and arduous delivery. I recall spending close to 18 hours in the hospital maternity ward working on a law review article as we awaited the stork's arrival. I met our new son just as I finished the final paragraph of the article. Two years later, our second son, Jason, joined our family.

The ensuing years of law school went by swiftly and I was fortunate to be blessed with a few outstanding instructors. One standout was Professor Leon Silverman who taught me Property Law. He was always available to dispense valued, albeit cryptic, advice.

When he learned my stepfather was a house painter, he counseled me, "You don't drink paint. So, don't drink whiskey. They both contain alcohol." I have heeded his advice and have avoided drinking paint ever since.

I recall how one of my classmates, during my final year in law school, likewise gave me some excellent advice. He said that I should get involved in politics because it was a good way to attract clients and plenty of legal work. Towards that end, he managed to get me invited to a cocktail reception at a penthouse condo owned by Andrew Stein, who would go on to become the last president of the New York City Council. Stein was the son of Jerry Finkelstein, the multi-millionaire publisher of the essential New York Law Journal. Stein shortened his name when he entered politics.

Two things stand out about that evening. One was a "Mount Everest" made up entirely of jumbo shrimp. It was the tastiest shrimp this formerly Kosher kid had ever tasted. Even more memorable was my conversation with Andrew Stein. I was purportedly there to meet Stein and then go on to work on his campaign for the presidency of the City Council. After chatting with him, I quickly concluded that he was an overly privileged idiot and I could not work to get someone so stupid elected to political office. And so ended my nascent political career...until years later when the person I tried to get elected was me.

to the position of a part-time judge. But that's a story for later.

In addition to the fellow who introduced me to Andrew Stein, I had made a few other friends at law school and we all wound up studying for the New York bar exam together. I had taken off work in order to study full-time. I recall going from Queens to the NYLS building in downtown Manhattan on my newly acquired motorcycle. The inexpensive but sporty Czechoslovakian-made Jawa 250 was my first motorcycle, but it would not be my last. After a few hours of study in the school library, I would hop back on my Czech chopper and barrel down Sixth Avenue to a midtown hotel where I was enrolled in a bar review study course.

On one particular rainy afternoon, as I was making my dash down Sixth Avenue, I gave it the gas in order to speed up and try to make every stoplight just before each one turned red. As I zoomed through an intersection, a young man suddenly stepped from the curb and began to cross the street, bringing him directly into my path. There was no time for me to stop on the rain-slicked cobblestone road surface. I could not avoid striking him. He was thrown in one direction while I was thrown in another. The bike slid sideways till it came to a stop next to a parked car. To this day, I remember my blue helmeted head bouncing along the cobblestone pavers of Sixth Avenue.

I managed to survive the crash more or less unscathed, but the young tourist from Cleveland was not so fortunate. He wound up in the hospital where I soon appeared to visit him. He was very understanding and appreciated my concern. I suspect that is why he decided not to sue me although I knew enough about the law at this point to determine that had he opted to do so, he would have had an excellent case against me.

All that biking and booking paid off when it came time to take my exam. My most salient memory of the experience was a bonus essay question involving the statute of perpetuities. I was totally clueless and forced to leave my answer completely blank. I was not at all interested in that subject and never truly understood it. And I have never needed it during the course of my legal career. I felt sure that not answering would doom my chances of passage. But, happily, it did not. I was relieved and proud to learn that I had indeed passed the bar on my first attempt. With flying colors, no less.

When, many years later, I again sat for an exam in order to gain admission to the Florida Bar, I found things had changed dramatically. For one thing, back in the 1960s, we all dressed like lawyers going to court in our suits and ties. We felt that it was important to look the part. Today, law students dress far more casually. Another difference is the growth in the percentage of female law students. There were only two women in our law school graduating class in 1970. Today, fifty percent of all law degrees are awarded to women. This is undoubtedly a positive trend, although it does come with some consequences.

I found that preparing for the Florida Bar Exam was a truly onerous experience. Not only that, when I took the exam I was seated next to a buxom candidate who was fighting a losing battle to keep her ample breasts from being exposed. For some reason, I found this to be distracting. Despite such unfair hindrances, I managed to prevail and was admitted to the Florida Bar. That was a great feeling, but it did not compare to the joy and exuberance I felt back in 1970 when I found myself to be a freshly minted New York lawyer ready to take on the world.

Elliot Fixler

Chapter Six

My Bronx Apprenticeship

"The only real lawyers are trial lawyers. And trial lawyers
try cases to juries."
—Clarence Darrow

Upon my graduation from law school, Fredda and I sought out and secured an apartment in the newly constructed Co-Op City high-rise complex, located in the northeast section of the Bronx. Built on reclaimed marshland that had been home, for several years, to the Freedomland U.S.A. Amusement Park, Co-Op City eventually grew into the largest housing cooperative in the world. It was divided into five sections. Ours, Section 1, had its streets all named after famous people whose last names started with the letter A. Hence, our building was on Asch Loop, named after author Sholem Asch.

Fredda and I set to decorating our 14th floor flat that afforded a panoramic view of the Sawmill River in the distance. It also allowed us to glimpse a less scenic view: several of the city's nearby junkyards. Not too attractive, but a good place to look for a cheap used car. The search led us to one of the sprawling salvage yards owned by a character who could have stepped out of a Damon Runyon story, Joe McGiver, alias Joey Do-All. He was known as a go-to guy for whatever you needed to get done. This despite his pronounced strabismus (crossed eye). I needed an affordable car that would take me to work and back every day. Joey came through and sold me a charming yellow Volkswagen bug. Joey and I would cross paths twice more. Once when I was in the prosecutor's office and again when I was in private practice. I'll tell you more about this colorful character then.

I was fortunate to be accepted as an Assistant District Attorney (ADA) in the Bronx County Prosecutor's Office. It was a great place to learn the ins and outs of the criminal justice system and I soon became familiar with how the office was structured and how it functioned. The Prosecutor's Office was divided into six bureaus, arranged in a sort of hierarchy. At the lowest level was the Criminal Court Bureau. This was where new ADAs began their apprenticeships. It was located in what was called the Criminal Court Building on 161st Street, about one mile from the County Courthouse on the Grand Concourse, the Bronx's "main drag". Looking out from the back of the building, I was afforded a great view of Yankee Stadium, otherwise known as the "House That Ruth Built". Although his career ended before my time, I had been a staunch admirer of El Bambino since boyhood. So, I would at times imagine, as I stared down at the diamond, the dugout and the bleachers, that I could hear the echoes of Ruth's Louisville Slugger cracking one over the fence.

The D.A.'s offices were located on the seventh and eighth floors where our Criminal Bureau shared space with (in ascending order of importance) the Homicide Bureau, the Fraud Bureau, the Appeals Bureau, the Grand Jury Bureau and the Supreme Court Bureau. Each of the bureaus were headed by one ADA and all assistants worked their way up, getting promoted, getting re-assigned, or getting canned.

Like most other "fresh-out-of-law-school" ADAs, I started life in the Criminal Court Bureau. We were responsible for handling all cases right from the moment of arrest and—if the case was a misdemeanor—all the way through to its resolution. Oftentimes, a felony arrest might be reduced to a misdemeanor as part of a plea bargain. It was our job to make sure those bargains were good ones and the people got something of value in return for the charge reduction. Felony arrests were held for preliminary hearings but if there was no probable cause, the case would usually be dismissed. In some cases, however, it might be held over for the Grand Jury Bureau to investigate.

It was pretty much an assembly line operation that had been in place for decades inside that dilapidated old Criminal Court building that was our home. Every arrest, no matter how trivial or serious, was processed in our bureau. The process began with the arresting officer presenting the defendant before a magistrate in order to enter a plea. Guilty pleas were dispensed with quickly, but if a defendant entered a "not guilty" plea, he or she would be entitled to a preliminary hearing to determine if probable cause existed. Felony cases were sent to the Grand Jury in an attempt to secure an indictment. Because of the enormous caseload, many felony defendants were offered a reduced charge to a misdemeanor if they would agree to plead guilty and thereby eliminate the need for a preliminary hearing, probable cause, or a need for the Grand Jury. We prosecutors could offer a suggested reduced sentence in such cases in order to reach a plea bargain deal with the defendant's attorney, but a judge would

105

have to approve every such deal via a ruling that would actually determine the sentence.

We ADAs had a good deal of discretion in structuring those plea bargain deals. We each had to deal with 50 to 60 cases each day and the only way we could possibly do so was by disposing of most of them by means of a plea bargain. These negotiated deals were all carried out in the morning, leaving our afternoons filled with preliminary hearings and trials.

The only saving grace of the run-down edifice in which we conducted the county's business was that it was located across the street from another property that included a first-rate basketball court. Many was the lunch hour that saw me and another young ADA named Al Tomaselli engaged in a pick-up game of one-on-one. On such days, I would travel directly from the basketball court to the criminal court—hoping to score big in both places.

It was grunt work, but looking back, I must admit that the Criminal Court Bureau was a terrific training ground that provided a solid, hands-on foundation for any aspiring trial lawyer. From learning how to interview crime victims, witnesses and cops, to figuring out how to correctly evaluate the evidence in a case to determine the likelihood of prosecutorial success. We were cutting our teeth by being constantly immersed in the inner workings of the criminal justice system. Through often bitter experience and with the guidance of judges and senior assistant D.A.'s, we learned in which cases we should offer the defendants a deal and which cases we should take to trial.

We also gained experience in the skills that we would later use as private trial lawyers, defending the same sort of people we were now intent on prosecuting. We learned how to question witnesses and how to conduct effective cross examinations, and how to prepare and deliver compelling opening statements and summations. Most importantly, I was developing my communication skills that would empower me to effectively deal with judges, opposing counsel, and court personnel. Hardly a day would go by when such skills weren't put to the test, especially when the defendant's lawyer wanted to get cute with my last name.

I have never particularly liked my last name, especially when I discovered I had been unwittingly yoked to it by the man who married my mother. If it had not been for Hitler, my last name would have been a decidedly more impressive one, I often mused. "Chief Justice Elliot Adlersheim" had a great ring of gravitas, I thought. If I had been Adlersheim instead of Fixler, I might have had a shot at having a street named after me in Section 1 of Co-op City in the Bronx (since Adlersheim started with an A). But, as things stood, my last name was an open invitation for every wise-cracking knuckle-headed defense attorney who fancied himself a wit to prattle off such pathetic rejoinders as: "Say, Mr. Fixer, can I talk you into putting in the fix on this case?"

The only time I did not cringe at this witless wordplay was when my daughter Sarah was recruited by her high school basketball team. A local sportswriter penned a highly laudatory full-page newspaper article about her at the time she won the Athlete of the Month title awarded by the North County News, a paper that covered Westchester, Putnam, and Dutchess Counties in New York. The boldface headline at the top of the page reads: "THE FIX IS IN AT MA-HOPAC HIGH!"

Undoubtedly, the most enduring and valuable skill I honed during my two-year stint in the Bronx D.A.'s office was the fine art of negotiation. As mentioned, the only way to plow through the crowded docket of cases we were faced with each day was to come to terms with the cadre of defense attorneys who regularly inhabited our world. After a while, I got to know them well and was able to gauge how far I could push each one. Before sitting down to haggle, I was required to honestly assess not only the strengths and weaknesses of the prosecution's case, but likewise those of my opponent. Only then was I able to negotiate an equitable deal from a position of strength.

These skills would serve me well in the future and not only in criminal cases. The same type of analysis had to take place whether negotiating a contract on behalf of a corporate client, arriving at an amenable divorce settlement, or arm-wrestling with an insurance company in a personal injury case. The area of the law in which I found my negotiating skills most needed was when it came to mediation and arbitration work. This may sound odd, coming from a lawyer, but the key principle in all such scenarios is *honesty*. I'm not talking about being 100% honest in your dealings with your opposite number. No, I mean being scrupulously honest with yourself when assessing your client's plusses and minuses. Self-delusion and denial are the anathema of any effective negotiating strategy. This fact was drilled into me during those years inside that crumbling old building that housed the heart of the Bronx criminal justice system.

I also found that the negotiating skills I had developed back then to be quite valuable in many other areas of life outside of my profession. Buying a car or a house, for example, both involve a give and take that requires an honest appraisal of the situation. If I don't accept the seller's price for a new home, how likely is it, really, that someone else will swoop in and scoop it up? Just as with legal issues, success in all areas involving negotiation depends upon your ability to accurately recognize all the prevailing factors. And to do that requires conducting the research and spadework that will enable you to make informed decisions. Successful negotiation, as any winning poker player will tell you, also requires one more thing, balls.

The desired outcome of a negotiation, be it in a D.A.'s office or in a car dealer's showroom, is not unconditional victory. It is reaching a compromised settlement that both parties regard as fair and equitable. Nevertheless, success in negotiating, like victory, is not for the faint-hearted nor the weak-kneed. Many was the time that a settlement was finally reached thanks to my proposing a daring, and at times risky, solution.

In the immortal words of the Kenny Rogers ballad, *The Gambler*, composed by Don Schlitz:

> You've got to know when to hold 'em.
> Know when to fold 'em.
> Know when to walk away
> And know when to run
> © Sony/ATV Music Publishing LLC

Unlike many lawyers I have known, I was never attracted to standard gambling or games of chance. When I was a teenager, I didn't have the spare change to join in any of the penny ante poker games that were popular with my peers. Once I became a practicing lawyer, I found myself handling cases that involved hundreds of thousands and sometimes millions of dollars. Making decisions and advising my clients with stakes that high was all the gambling I needed in life. I never craved the extra pressure or kicks represented by casinos or even sports betting.

I handled such an abundance of cases during my tenure in the D.A.'s office that most of them blend into one big blur. But a lawyer never forgets his or her first case. I was friends with a law school classmate named Zoltán Hanovszky who was, at that time, employed by the Legal Aid Society, a charitable entity that provides free legal counsel to defendants unable to afford the services of a lawyer. Zoltán, like many Hungarians, immigrated to the U.S. as a child in the wake of the anti-Soviet Hungarian Revolt of 1956. Zoli was representing a client who had been arrested after he had threatened a passenger on a Bronx subway train with a crossbow. He had been charged with the Class B misdemeanor of menacing, as well as a Class A misdemeanor of being in possession of a dangerous weapon. The second charge entitled the defendant to a jury trial and, since no plea agreement could be reached, a trial was docketed and took place.

It was my first jury trial and I was petrified as I paced back and forth during the jury selection process. I knew it was important to make a good impression on the jurors and appearances mattered. But I was so nervous that my shirt was soaked with flop sweat and I was sure that would turn off the jurors.

Sadly, I lost the case—but not because of my sweaty shirt—when the jury decided to acquit the defendant on the weapons charge. Although I was devastated at this disheartening beginning to my courtroom career, I was consoled by the fact that the loss wasn't really my fault. This was not a rationalization on my part. The defendant was freed due to a loophole in the New York criminal statute that specified which weapons were to be regarded as "dangerous." The legislators in Albany who had drafted the law saw fit to include a list of such weapons. The list included certain types of knives, pistols, rifles, etc. but it did not include crossbows. Evidently, the lawmakers were not well-versed in medieval history.

As I licked my wounds and tried to recover from the pain of this initial setback, I received a call a few days after the trial from the forelady of the jury. She told me that she was so impressed with my abilities in the courtroom that she wished to retain me to represent her regarding some estate issues she was facing. I considered this a sincere compliment and it served to buoy my sodden spirits.

Naturally, I inquired about the jury deliberations and she verified that the jury members felt they had no choice but to acquit since the statute failed to identify a crossbow as a dangerous weapon. They all had felt I had done an excellent job in establishing the guilt of the defendant, but she also confided something about my courtroom manner that I found to be very helpful. She had found my incessant pacing back and forth whenever I addressed the jury to be terribly distracting. I took that advice to heart and have never forgotten it across forty plus years of trying cases. I realized that although I had lost the case, I had gained something of true value, a means of im-

111

proving the quality and effectiveness of my future interaction with juries.

There was another more well-known individual who helped to shape my courtroom skills, although I did not particularly appreciate his guidance at the time. I am referring to the legendary Bronx D.A. and later Supreme Court Justice, Burton B. Roberts. Roberts had started his career much like I had, as an Assistant D.A. under New York County prosecutor, Frank Hogan. It was there that he began using his stentorian voice (once described as "a few decibels below the roar of a jet engine") as a weapon of "mass detention" as he bellowed against petty criminals and corrupt politicians alike. He became known for his trademark fiery red hair which matched his incendiary temper.

Roberts moved to the Bronx in 1966 and was elected to serve as the Bronx County District Attorney in 1968. He immediately began expanding the office in a move that resulted in tripling the number of prosecutors. I was brought in as part of that expansion.

Burt Roberts' no-nonsense courtroom manner served as the model for the larger-than-life character Myron Kovitsky in Tom Wolfe's 1987 bestseller, *The Bonfire of the Vanities.* Wolfe dedicated the book to Roberts, whom he admired greatly. Alan Arkin was slated to portray the Burt Roberts' character in the Brian DePalma 1990 film version but was ultimately replaced by Morgan Freeman.

In 1973, Roberts was elected to a 14-year term as a Supreme Court Justice where he ruled the courtroom with an iron fist, using his booming voice and expansive personality to chide prosecutors, keep defense attorneys focused, and even upbraid witnesses when necessary. I considered myself very fortunate to land a job working under him. During my two years in the prosecutor's office, our paths crossed three times, two of them during my service in the Criminal Court Bureau.

The first encounter was during the early days of my tenure. I was summoned to the D.A.'s office and it triggered painful memories of being ordered to the principal's office back in high school. I immediately thought, *"Uh-oh. How did I manage to fuck up so soon?"*

As I entered Roberts' sizable office, I found him seated in a huge, upholstered leather chair behind his battleship-sized desk. At his elbow was his constant sidekick, Chief Assistant D.A., Sy Rotker. Roberts waved me to sit down at the nearby conference table. I did so and watched as he finished leafing through a folder in front of him. Finally, he looked up at me and thundered, "What is this shit?"

A dozen thoughts raced through my head. I had recently been hired and had taken the bar exam but had not yet received the results. If I failed to pass, I would not be allowed to keep the job. Is that what this was about? I had also completed a detailed application form that the office used as the basis to conduct a vetting investigation into my background. Had they discovered some dirt? I began to sweat .45 caliber bullets.

"What do you mean, sir?" I said forthrightly.

"I see you lost your driver's license because of a bunch of speeding convictions. What the hell is that all about?"

I couldn't think of anything to say in my defense, so I opted for the truth. I shrugged and came out with: "I'm always in a hurry."

He stared at me pensively as he considered this. I guess he decided that a young ADA in a hurry would be a worthy addition to the team. After a beat he closed the file and waved me out the door with, "OK. Get outta here....and slow down."

I got out of there quickly. And I have never slowed down.

I knew that Burt Roberts was fond of positive publicity focused on the prosecutor's office. And so, to demonstrate my efficiency, I jumped on a high-profile case that had been lingering on my calendar for a while. The defendants were two upstanding liquor store owners who had gotten themselves into a bit of difficulty. The store had been plagued by nocturnal burglaries and so they decided to hire someone to stand guard each night inside the premises. Instead of shelling out for an actual security guard, the frugal partners offered the job to a homeless guy from the street. Not surprisingly, the fellow turned out to be an alcoholic. One night he went on a bender and started drinking up the inventory. They found him dead on the floor the next morning clutching an empty Chivas Regal bottle. It was like hiring Colonel Sanders to guard a chicken coop.

Instead of calling the police, the publicity-shy partners decided that since the fellow had no family, no one would really miss him. So, after wrapping him in some jumbo trash bags, they furtively drove the body down to the local landfill and unceremoniously dumped it. Sadly, for them, their crime was witnessed by some dumpsite staff who reported it to the authorities.

The story of the "Liquor Store Stiff" caught the attention of the local press and hence the case wound up on Burt Roberts' radar screen. He again called me into his office, this time to discuss the case.

"This is a true victimless crime, Fixler," he boomed, "and the newspapers are all over it. The perps have no priors and are well-loved citizens of the community. Let's see if we can't get the misdemeanor reduced to something like disorderly conduct or an ACD (adjournment in contemplation of dismissal). I want us to come out looking like heroes."

Of course, I complied and the body-dumping businessmen got off with a mere slap on the wrist.

After ten months of toiling in the trenches of the Criminal Court Bureau, I was promoted to the Grand Jury Bureau and moved to their offices located in the courthouse on the Grand Concourse. Compared to the constant *sturm und drang* of the Criminal Court Bureau, it was an utter bore. Our job was to interview the victims and the witnesses and then put together a case for the prosecution that we would present to the twenty-three members of the Grand Jury. They would then decide to indict or not. There was no cross examination and no presiding judge. Just a prosecutor, a stenographer, a witness and the members of the Grand Jury. Defendants would almost never make an appearance. It was more or less a rubber stamp ritual.

A wag once said, "A Grand Jury would indict a ham sandwich if the ADA asked them to." Very true.

Perhaps the most noteworthy event that took place while I was in the Grand Jury Bureau was meeting an arresting police officer who would frequently enter testimony about the circumstances of a case. Years later, when I was in private practice, this officer was himself arrested in Westchester County for beating up a black man in front of fifteen witnesses. He hired me to defend him. More about that case in a later chapter.

I also recall, during my Grand Jury Bureau days, again running into Joey McGiver, aka Joey Do-All from the junkyard. He had been charged with running a chop shop for stolen cars on his premises. Since we were friends, I was glad I had not been assigned to prosecute his case. I found out that he had beat the rap. He told me about it some years later, after I had just gone into private practice in Putnam County and Joey had become my very first client.

You might recall from my description of Joey at the beginning of this chapter, that he had one crossed eye. The lyrics of one of my favorite Country & Western tunes at that time would remind me of Joey every time I heard it. And I listened to it constantly. It was a ballad by Tom Russell about a Mexican cock fighter and his rooster called Gallo del Cielo. The lyrics went like this:

El Gallo Del Cielo was a rooster born in heaven,
So, the legends say.
His wings they had been broken,
He had one eye
Rollin' crazy in his head
©BMG Rights Management

More about Joey Do-All in a forthcoming chapter.

I was still assigned to the Grand Jury Bureau when we all received our Bar Exam results a few days before they were published in the legal newspaper. I was happy to see that I had passed and since we all worked for the D.A.'s office, we received preferential treatment that enabled us to be sworn in ahead of the others being admitted into the Bar. We rejoiced at the news since it translated into a raise that bumped our salaries up to $15,000 per year.

After a few months of dealing with the Grand Jury Bureau's monotonous grind, I was delighted to learn that I had been promoted to the Appeals Bureau. I should not have been so delighted. It turned out to be even more mind-numbing than the Grand Jury. I missed....no, I craved, the rough and tumble action of courtroom trials.

Our office handled a good number of Corum Nobis cases. Also known as Writ of Corum Nobis and Corum Vobis, they are relatively rare today and only used in a handful of states. It is a plea made by the counsel of a convicted defendant to set the conviction aside "in the interests of justice" because of a fundamental error that had been made in the original trial. Becoming familiar with this stratagem served me well early in my private practice career when I represented two police officers who had pled guilty to a misdemeanor and now wished to have the convictions expunged to avoid injuring their careers. I successfully used a Corum Nobis to have their convictions set aside.

After a very brief stint, I complained to my supervisor that I really did not belong in the Appeals Bureau and he asked me why. I brazenly told him that once I got into private practice I did not plan on losing many cases, so the learning experience offered in the Appeals Bureau was being wasted in my case. He agreed and wasted no time in transferring me out of the bureau.

My next assignment was in the Supreme Court Bureau where I was tasked to handle more serious trials. Hearing both civil and criminal cases, the New York Supreme Court is the state's highest level trial court. Supreme Court judges are often referred to as Justices.

Just as in the Criminal Courts, most Supreme Court Justices prefer to have cases resolved via plea bargaining. All cases needed to be worked up as if they were going to be adjudicated at trial, but in reality, very few went the full distance. Once again, my cases all tend to blur together in my memory, but once again, my first Supreme Court case stands out prominently.

Unlike in the Criminal Court Bureau, where a prosecutor appears before a variety of different judges in various courtrooms, in the Superior Court Bureau an ADA is assigned to a particular courtroom (known as a Part) and goes before the same Justice every day. The Justice who presided over my courtroom was Judge George Starke, and I initially thought highly of him. Late in his career, he was censured by the Appellate Division for his prejudicial behavior that resulted in a defendant being denied a fair trial. I saw evidence of this early on, in the first case I tried in the Supreme Court before him.

At this time, I sported a thick mustache and Judge Starke harassed me about it on a steady basis. He frequently would publicly urge me to shave it off and it started to get on my nerves. Behind his back, I began referring to him as "Judge Starke Raving Mad."

Jury selection in criminal trials is conducted in front of the judge in a procedure dubbed Voir Dire. It is the judge's job to control this process of counsel interviewing prospective jurors. This case involved a man accused of coming home from work one day to discover his wife in bed with another woman. He allegedly had become enraged and beat the wife severely.

As Judge Starke looked on, I began to question an older female prospective juror. It soon became obvious that she was hard of hearing. For this reason, and others, I determined that having her on the jury would not be in the best interests of our case. But I did not wish to offend or embarrass the lady by excusing her, since doing so might be viewed as harsh by the other jurors whose good will we relied upon.

I naively decided to confer privately with Judge Starke and request his help. I asked if he would excuse the juror so I would not appear to be the "bad guy." I also did not wish to use up one of my preemptory challenges which would permit me to reject a prospective juror without having to provide cause. He agreed and I expected him to discretely excuse the juror on behalf of the court and thank her for fulfilling her jury duty obligation. Instead, he did the following:

Justice Starke: Hey lady. You got a hearing problem?

Juror: No, your honor. It's just that the D.A.'s words get muffled in his mustache.

Justice Starke: Ma'am, I understand completely. I've been telling him to shave that nasty thing off since he showed up in my courtroom.

"Thanks a bunch for your help, your honor," I thought to myself. Not only did he embarrass the juror, he made me out to be some sort of disrespectful hippie in the eyes of the other jurors. I was reluctantly forced to use one of my challenges to have the lady excused from the jury.

Eventually the jury was selected and the case was tried. The defendant was found guilty of a lesser charge of misdemeanor assault rather than the more serious charge of felony assault that we had asked for. I considered the outcome to be a loss, but interestingly, I later learned that the defense also viewed it as a loss. The defendant had been capably represented by a legal aid lawyer named Stanley Green who would go on years later to serve as a Supreme Court Justice in Manhattan. My son, Jason, who is today an attorney with the New York law firm of Fixler & LaGattuta, often appears before Judge Green. Whenever he does, the Judge never fails to remind Jason how I was defeated years ago in that lesbian wife-beater case. I racked it up as a loss because we failed to get the felony conviction. The opposing side also regarded it as a loss because they failed to obtain an acquittal. Definitely a Lose-Lose situation.

I became friends with another ADA in the prosecutor's office, Howard Finger. Howard introduced me to his brother, William, who enjoyed a successful criminal defense practice. In order to supplement my meager income, I asked Howard if his brother might hire me to work part-time on weekends. William agreed and I began my duties at his office reviewing files and making sure they were all in order for trial. Among his clients was a major drug dealer who rewarded William lavishly for keeping him one step ahead of the law.

As I witnessed the enormous sums (by my standards) being earned by William in private practice, I began to get the itch to start making more money myself. The itch was made more intense thanks to Howard who, in addition to introducing me to his brother, had also introduced me to the music of an artist named Elton John. This was long before Elton had become a household name. Howard got me thinking that it might be time for me to say *Goodbye Yellow Brick Road* and to move on from the Bronx District Attorney's office toward greener (as in "money") pastures.

My motives were not only fueled by fiscal factors. I had gotten to know some outstanding lawyers, with sharp legal minds, stagnating in place as they spent their prime earning years working for Bronx County. Irv Goldsmith was the chief of the Homicide Bureau. He was about sixty and was definitely a lifer. Also at the Homicide Bureau was Bruce Goldstone who had produced a consecutive string of successful murder convictions. He certainly wasn't going anywhere. I realized two things. One, in order to achieve long-term success in this realm, you had to be adept at office politics. Burt Roberts, Irv Goldsmith, Bruce Goldstone all knew how to play the game well, but I did not care for it. Two, although these men were all highly skilled and top-of-the-line lawyers, they all lacked the fire-in-the-belly ambition to cast out on their own and take the risks that were necessary if one hoped to make it big time as a lawyer. I recognized that unlike them, I had that burning ambition and I was determined to act upon it.

It was about this time that Fredda and I decided we would like to move from the Bronx to more upscale Westchester County to the north. We located a charming house in the Millbrook community and tendered an offer that was rejected. The owners, who had already moved out of the country, were being represented by a local attorney. Despite the fact that they did not come back with any counter offers, I submitted more bids, each higher than the previous one. I finally agreed to the original asking price which should have closed the deal. But it was also rejected. Evidently, in the interim, the house had begun generating more buyer interest, so the lawyer squelched the listed asking price and put the house up for bid. I was outraged. If a buyer accepts a seller's asking price in writing and puts up the requisite earnest money, it is considered to be a binding contract. I pointed this out to the attorney who told me he didn't care and continued with the auction. The bids came through and we lost the house to the highest bidder. I vowed to myself to never be placed into that position again. I kept that vow for forty years, until I didn't...as described in a forthcoming chapter.

We were eventually successful in landing a house in Somers, a lovely bedroom community in northern Westchester County, New York. My parents agreed to loan us $10,000 toward the cost of the down payment and we closed on our family dream house. The sellers even threw in a dog, a friendly German shepherd, to complete the package. I named her *Shtarkeh*, which means "strong" in Yiddish. I felt like I was living the American dream inside a portrait of the All-American family. A wife, two kids, a house, a dog and a mortgage. What more could a little Hungarian immigrant kid ever hope to dream for.

But there were serious cracks in that portrait. While Fredda and I managed to make it appear that things were okay between us, she still insisted on being Fredda—a not-very-nice person. My first consideration in those days was becoming a great lawyer and achieving real financial success. Improving our marriage was not a major priority. And ending it would, at best, have been a major distraction. But we both understood that my love affair with Fredda was long over and, to tell the truth, there wasn't much there to like, either.

The real estate broker we had used to purchase the house in Somers, Richard Lawson, turned out to be a great guy who became a good friend. I had shared with him some of my hopes of leaving the D.A.'s office and going into private practice. He advised me that opening a practice in Somers or, even better, in Putnam County, just north of Somers, would be a great idea. The entire area was developing rapidly and there was likewise a growing need for lawyers to serve both businesses and families. Richard said that if I was interested, he could introduce me to another young lawyer who had opened a practice in Putnam County a few years before. Perhaps he might have some overflow work available. I told him I would think about it and let him know.

We soon got settled in and I began commuting to the Bronx each day. At a certain point, not long after, I reached the decision that it was time for me to cut loose. I asked Richard to introduce me to the young lawyer he had mentioned and a meeting was soon arranged. The lawyer's name was Howard Stockfield and he operated out of a one-room office in a private home next to the Putnam County courthouse. It was situated in the scenic county seat known as Carmel Hamlet just over the county line with Westchester County to the south.

When I got to Howard's office, he greeted me warmly at the door. For my part, I tried not to let my face disclose the major surprise I had just encountered. Richard had described Howard as a bright young lawyer, so, after speaking with him on the phone, I had a certain mental image of what he looked like. This was definitely *not* it. I was looking at a man about my height, but at least 40 lbs. overweight and with a balding, white-haired pate. Young lawyer? I would have guessed him to be at least sixty.

Well, I guess I should not consider working at a carnival guessing people's age and weight. It turns out that Howard was thirty, just two years older than me at the time. He informed me that he had been doing a lot of real estate work, both commercial and residential. I thought to myself that sort of work must make a man age prematurely. He shared that he had been representing clients on both sides of real estate transactions, something you can get away with in small suburban communities, I surmised. He indicated that if I were to join him in his practice, he could give me the other end of these deals so both buyer and seller would be represented by independent counsel. This would provide some basic income and a steady cash flow. I looked around and surveyed the cramped quarters he was currently occupying. Howard responded by explaining that his wife owned a vacant private house across the street from a major shopping plaza. We could obtain it at no cost, fix it up, and turn it into a respectable law office for the both of us. He said if I agreed, he wouldn't charge me anything for the overhead or staff labor until I started earning some serious money.

To my ears, this sounded like an offer I could not possibly refuse. I didn't have to think too long to realize that here was an opportunity to launch a practice with zero capital outlay in a burgeoning community, located only a short hop from my home.

"Does this sound like what you're looking for, Elliot?" he asked me.

"You bet," I said with a smile as we shook hands. I told him I would need some time to give notice and to wrap up my pending cases.

"Not a problem," said Howard. "Let me know when you're ready to start things rolling."

We said our good-byes and on the way home I anguished over exactly how I was going to inform Mr. Burt Roberts, with his fiery red hair and temperament, that I was planning to leave the D.A.'s office.

I braced myself for my third visit in two years to D.A. Roberts' office. Once again, Roberts was seated behind his massive desk with his lapdog lackey, Rotker, at his side. Rotker was clutching my resignation letter and it was he who addressed me this time.

"What is this shit?" he exhorted while waving the letter in the air. I had heard that same line the first time I had entered this office.

"Do I need to remind you that you gave us a commitment when we hired you? You promised to stay three years. You've only been here two years. So, what's going on?"

By this time, Rotker had insinuated his weaselly face directly into mine. Roberts looked on with a bemused expression on his broad face. I had my answer prepared.

"What you say is true, Mr. Rotker," I began. "I did make a commitment at the time of hire, but so did you."

At this point, I dramatically turned my gaze to Roberts. I pointed out the fact that Roberts had accepted a seat on the New York Supreme Court and would be leaving the prosecutor's office as well.

"In fact, and in my heart, the commitment I made two years ago was made to Mr. Burton Roberts, a man I admire greatly," I went on as if I were conducting a trial summation before a jury.

"Commitment is a two-way street. A street called equity," I argued. "Mr. Roberts had likewise made a commitment to me and he, not me, was the first to breach that commitment. Once he did so, my commitment evaporated and I am no longer under any obligation to honor it."

Rotker was dumbfounded. Roberts, still smiling, rose to shake my hand and wish me good luck. I thanked him sincerely for all he had allowed me to learn about the law over the past two years.

And that was that. I said a final fond farewell to this chapter of my life and headed north to meet my new destiny in Putnam County.

Chapter Seven

Off and Running

"Young lawyers must learn by doing. Once young lawyers acknowledge that they have a lot to learn and see learning as part of the process, things gets easier."

—Cyndee Todgham Cherniak

O nce out the door at the Bronx District Attorney's Office, the reality of my situation began to sink in. The last time I had been self-employed was when I was hired to paint rooms and hallways at the Niagara Falls Hotel. But back then it was just me. At this point, I had a wife, two kids, and a dog to support, not to mention a hefty home mortgage. Yikes!

One of the main reasons I took the plunge was the assurance I received from Howard Stockfield to steer business my way. I hoped to take on real estate clients he could not ethically represent as well as litigation work he preferred not to handle. In other words, I would start life as a private practice lawyer feeding off of Howard's leftovers.

U.S. Route 6 was, at that time, a two-lane highway that cut an east-west swath across the southern protrusion of New York State, running from the Pennsylvania state line at Port Jervis to the Connecticut border, just east of Brewster. After skirting the northern edge of the New York City metro area, it veers north at Baldwin Place and enters Putnam County, where it follows the south shore of Lake Mahopac and reaches a village with the same name. It next curves past the south end of the West Branch Reservoir where it connects with State Road 52 just outside of the county seat of Carmel. It was a two-story frame house along Route 6 in Carmel in which Howard and I set up shop.

In addition to our own office space on the first floor, we fixed up the basement and leased it out to a State Farm Insurance agency. I insisted that Howard should occupy,m nbvcx nbvc the larger office. It was the least I could do to express my gratitude for his generosity. The main floor also contained two secretarial stations and a break room. We planned to put a conference room and more offices upstairs at some point. We were definitely planning for growth.

The Putnam County Courthouse was situated a few miles away on Gleneida Avenue. Built in 1814, it stands as the second-oldest extant county courthouse in New York. Howard showed me around the building, then introduced me to some of the town's real estate brokers who had been referring clients to him. I continued this process by traveling up and down Route 6, popping into real estate brokerages, dropping off business cards and introducing myself as a new attorney in town who would appreciate any referrals they could send my way. I assured them that I would take excellent care of any clients they directed to me and I would handle the paperwork expeditiously. Little by little, this sort of self-promotion began to pay off.

Howard graciously informed me once again that he would not expect me to chip in to cover the overhead until I got established and started bringing in some business. He understood that it would take some time and I have always appreciated this classy gesture.

It was not long after we opened our doors in Carmel that I got a phone call from Joey Do-All, my old junkyard car dealer buddy from the Bronx. As recounted in the previous chapter, Joey had been hauled before the Grand Jury for operating a chop shop that trafficked in stolen cars. This time, Joey had gotten himself busted for the same offense up in Mahopac, the next town along Route 6. Somehow he had learned that I had opened an office in nearby Carmel and he asked me to represent him.

"Sure, Joey," I told him.

"One thing, Mr. Fixler," he said softly. "I'm broke. I can't pay you." I said nothing.

"But I can give you a swell new car as payment." The car turned out to be a baby blue 1965 Jaguar XKE roadster. I checked the book value. It was worth $4,600, so I agreed. Given Joey's background, I was a bit leery about the provenance of the vehicle. But Joey assured me that he had bought it legitimately from an insurance company and when he took delivery the title and registration were all in order. Interestingly, Howard also drove a Jaguar XKE coupe. The parking area outside our office resembled a mini-Jaguar road rally. I had my first client, but I still had no cash to kick into the kitty.

I took care of Joey's case by convincing him to enter a guilty plea and got him off with only probation and no jail time. Joey found this to be a great outcome and happily turned the car over to me. It drove like a dream, until the dream turned into a nightmare.

The Jag had been parked in our lot for several days in the dead of winter. As I pulled in on that frosty morning in my yellow VW bug, I thought it a good idea to start up the Jag and run the engine for a while. I swept off the snow, turned on the ignition, and let it idle while I went inside to make some calls. About ten minutes later, Howard came in the door and commented that much of our staff probably would not be showing up today.

Then he added, as he passed by my desk, "Oh, by the way, Elliot, your car's on fire." I dropped the phone and ran out the door to witness with horror the all-consuming flames and plumes of black acrid smoke from my car's fiery funeral pyre. And that was the end of that. No regrets, except when I realized that car would sell for between $250,000 and $300,000 today. I lost track of Joey Do-All, but knowing that he was a junkie, I suspect he came to a bad end.

As hoped, the spadework I had done among the town's real estate professionals began bearing fruit. In this small-town environment, it was often the case that I became friendly with both the agents and the clients they would direct my way. Some of these friendships have endured to this day, I'm pleased to say. One such Route 6 realtor and friend was Roland Merlino. It was Roland who sent me my first real estate client. *"Great,"* I thought. *"I'll be collecting a cash fee on this deal and can start contributing to the office overhead."*

Roland sent me a gentleman who wished to purchase a house in Carmel, owned by a Mr. Richard Gannon. Gannon was being represented by my partner, Howard. The parties reached an agreement and the house was taken off the market while we prepared the documents for the closing. I was supposed to receive my fee at that time, but I never did…because there was no closing.

A few days before the appointed date, Roland called me to say that Gannon wanted to back out of the deal because his son had been diagnosed with leukemia and he was going through a traumatic time. Reluctantly, I was able to convince my client, the buyer, to agree to a cancelation of the deal and start searching for another house. Sadly, my cash flow still remained less than a trickle.

Even though I did not collect a fee, I did receive something of lasting value from that deal. A long-term friendship with Dick Gannon. I'll tell you more about him later.

It was through another early real estate deal that I met one of the most colorful characters I've ever known. I was representing the buyer and the deal went down without a hitch. After the closing, I got a call from the seller. A gentleman by the name of Jay Maxwell.

"I like the way you handled yourself, Fixler," he said, "and I want you to represent me in some deals I've got cooking." I agreed to meet with him and that led to one of the most enduring, and amazing, friendships of my life. More about Jay Maxwell later.

Within one month of hanging out my shingle, I had already embarked on friendships that would last a lifetime. Both Jay and Dick were extraordinary figures and had become fixtures in my practice and my life. I will share more about them later in this chapter.

I really enjoyed working with Howard—even when we were each representing clients on opposite sides of a deal. He was sharp, outgoing and had a truly generous spirit. Within a few months, I was generating enough revenue to start contributing toward the rent and expenses, a great relief. After a year of working as officemates we thought it would make sense for us to form a professional partnership. It was a handshake deal that never saw us draw up any actual partnership documents. The only hiccup was that Howard wanted a majority position. I balked at this since I felt it should be an equal partnership. I made my case ("We both need to agree to do something or we don't do it.") and Howard relented. And thus began a twenty-year period that arguably marked the best years of my life.

After two decades of being hitched in harness, Howard decided he'd had enough of practicing law and concluded that he could never get rich charging by the hour. I was sorry to see the partnership dissolve, but I did not wish to stand in the way of his happiness. After we disbanded, Howard connected with a client who was in the construction business and wound up doing very well.

During the early years of my practice, our family's home was in a little hamlet called Shenorock, located in nearby Somers, New York. Fredda was also working and we were busy raising Mitchell, age five and Jason, age three. We were able to hire a live-in au pair who helped with the childcare.

Our next-door neighbors were the Bishops who had two boys the same age as Mitch and Jay. Roy Bishop, their father, was a mounted officer with the NYPD. At six foot four, Roy cut an imposing figure on horseback. Not surprisingly, he was also a talented basketball player, with whom I enjoyed many rounds of one-on-one on my driveway half-court. It was through Roy that I signed up to play in a basketball league in nearby Kent, north of Carmel. Dick Gannon had likewise hooked me up with a local softball team. So, I was staying in shape and having a great time as a suburban double threat athlete. Two teammates—one from each sport—got me involved in one of the most unusual cases of my early career.

Andy Kinash played on my basketball team while Bill Balzano was one of my softball teammates. Both men were police officers on the Town of Kent Police Force. The two of them, along with a few friends, had gone deer hunting in a rural area of neighboring Dutchess County, just north of town. One of the two had mistakenly shot a doe. At that time, hunters were only permitted to shoot bucks with antlers. This changed over time and today doe and antler-less deer may be hunted in season when they are not likely to be pregnant. But back then shooting a doe was unlawful and considered a misdemeanor under state law.

Andy and Bill were arrested and held in the county lock-up under a $5,000 bond for the both of them. They were told that they would remain in jail until bail was posted. If they pled guilty, however, they would be immediately released and the $5,000 would be considered to be their fine. They accepted the deal without having retained a lawyer. The pair were not told that they would be pleading guilty to a misdemeanor and were led to believe that if they agreed, the whole matter would be kept hush-hush and there would be no repercussions back in Kent where they were police officers in good standing. They were wrong.

Six months after their arrest, the case broke in the local newspapers. "Two Kent Police Officers Convicted of Misdemeanor in Union Vale," blared the headline. Andy and Bill learned that, as a result of the publicity, their jobs were now in jeopardy. They came to me for help. Proving that all knowledge has value, I told them I thought there was a way I could help them out. As described in the previous chapter, the only thing of value I learned during my stint in the Appeals Bureau of the Bronx prosecutor's office, was how to file a Writ of Coram Nobis. This was a procedure for the purpose of setting a conviction aside due to some manner of flaw in the original trial. I thought that such a maneuver might work in this case.

I entered a Coram Nobis, pleading with the court, alleging that Andy and Bill's convictions were obtained in violation of their constitutional rights. I was soon granted a hearing by the Appellate Court and the trial was held in the Dutchess County night court. I subpoenaed the Justice of the Peace from Union Vale who had taken the original guilty plea and instructed him to bring along the Docket Book that held the details about cases that came before him.

I first called Andy, and then Bill, to the stand to testify as to what had happened that day. The Union Vale J.P. took the stand next, clutching the huge Docket Book tightly to his chest. I began a line of questioning and found the witness uncooperative. He soon made it clear that he believed he was not obliged to answer my direct questions. After all, he was a presiding officer in a courtroom of his own jurisdiction and not used to being grilled in the dock. I appealed to the presiding judge to permit me to question the J.P. as a hostile witness—even though he was *my* witness. This meant I would be permitted to ask him leading questions, whereas such questions are not permitted in the case of non-hostile witnesses. The judge ruled in my favor and I continued with my line of intense questioning, intended to wear down the witness.

"What was the amount of the bail you set?" I asked him. This sent him flipping through the pages of the giant Docket Book to find the answer.

"Why was it set so high for such a minor infraction? Did you honestly think that two police officers from a neighboring community represented a flight risk?" He said nothing.

"This wasn't really bail at all, was it? It was really ransom. Am I correct?" I accused. "You were holding these two police officers hostage until you got your five grand. Isn't that right, Mr. Justice of the Peace?" He shook his head weakly.

"As an officer of the court you surely must be familiar with the laws pertaining to illegal confinement," I went on. "Isn't it a fact that by denying these officers their constitutional rights to counsel and a fair hearing, you were guilty of illegal confinement?" I was only getting warmed up by this point and the J.P. was already visibly perspiring.

After about an hour of this, I finally confronted the man with the key question, "Are you willing to admit, under oath, that requiring these men to plead guilty and pay you $5000 in order to gain their freedom was an act of utter highway robbery?"

And then something really bizarre happened.

The J.P. slammed shut his Docket Book, stood up and proclaimed: "I don't have to answer any more of your questions."

He then quickly stepped down from the witness stand and strutted briskly out of the courtroom before anyone could do anything to stop him. I have never, before or since, seen anyone do that in a court of law. The look on the District Attorney's face was priceless. And the judge was frozen in shock.

When the judge recovered, he looked to the prosecutor and asked "Well, what are you going to do now?" The D.A. just shrugged, but I was smiling at what I considered to be a thing of real beauty. The J.P.'s unprecedented action clearly established the strength of my case. His walkout was regarded as an admission that he had, in fact, violated the civil rights of my clients and thus established grounds for a dismissal of all charges.

The charges were dropped, the two officers retained their jobs, and Bill Balzano went on to become Chief of Police of the Town of Kent. I have never been one to charge a fee to my friends who retain me to represent their interests, so I did not send them a bill. Even though I received no cash compensation for my brilliant and career-saving courtroom tactics, I did obtain something of true lasting value. In appreciation of my pro bono service, the Kent Police Benevolent Association presented me with an official police shield. I found a special type of wallet that allowed me to display two badges and I placed the PBA shield next to the one I was given as a Bronx Assistant District Attorney. I kept the wallet in my car and would flip it open whenever I was stopped for exceeding the speed limit, something that happened quite often. As I had told DA Burt Roberts back in the Bronx, I was still a man in a hurry.

As you will learn a bit later, my second wife is named Lorraine. She and the kids would travel with me from Putnam County to Buffalo when my mother became ill and needed to be hospitalized. On one such 360-mile dash, I was stopped for speeding by a New York State Trooper. I was duly contrite and respectful as I pulled out the driver's license from my weighty wallet and made sure the trooper got a good look at my two badges. I explained that I was rushing because my mother had just been taken to the hospital. He handed back my license and released me with a stern, "Be careful."

Fast forward two months and I am again barreling down Interstate 86 toward Buffalo with Lorraine and the kids when I was once again pulled over. I opened the window and began to present my shiny credentials, when the trooper greeted me with, "Mr. Fixler. I see you're in a hurry again. How's your mother doing?"

The trooper again admonished me to be careful and declined to issue a speeding ticket. My kids, impressed by the protective power of my badges, still talk about that incident to this day.

After several years of plying my profession in Putnam County, Fredda and I were finally in a financial position to afford a family vacation. After some deliberation, we decided to travel to Smugglers' Notch for some skiing.

Smugglers' Notch is located in a mountain pass along the scenic Vermont-Canadian border. It derives its name from the time that President Thomas Jefferson, acting to prevent U.S. involvement in the Napoleonic Wars, signed the 1807 Embargo Act making trade with Canada illegal. Intrepid Vermont farmers and traders ignored the embargo and persisted in smuggling goods through the Notch into Montreal. It was also used before the Civil War by escaped slaves heading northward and during Prohibition by bootleggers smuggling whiskey southward.

We arrived toward the end of the ski season and rented "ski in - ski out" rooms on one of the slopes. We were all set for a great winter vacation, except for one thing. At age 28, I still didn't know how to ski. To remedy this, I scheduled a private lesson the following

morning at 9 am. Despite the fact I was suffering from costochondri-
tis due to a recent basketball rib injury, I was raring to go. In fact, I
couldn't wait till 9 am. Decked out in my spiffy new jeans and
leather bombardier jacket and toting my rented short skis, I walked to
the ski lift at 8:15 and got on.

In short order, I spotted a nice flat area ahead. I assumed this
would be a good place to get off. It wasn't. People immediately started shouting at me to get out of their way. I soon learned that the correct spots to disembark from a chairlift were all elevated to allow you
to slide safely away. The flat area I had mistakenly used was for
skiers who wished to go up to a higher elevation. Oops!

I moved into position and was poised for my first ever run down
the mountain. Surveying the landscape and the steepness of the ski
trail, I decided that going straight down was a bad idea. Basing myself on principles of physics that had somehow penetrated my brain
even though I had slept through most of my high school physics
classes, I determined that the best way for me to proceed was to go
from one side of the trail to the other in small increments until I safely reached the bottom. Of course, executing this maneuver required
that I know how to turn and, most importantly, how to stop. These
are the first things a novice skier is taught during an initial lesson.
Unfortunately, I had not yet had that lesson and therefore knew nothing. One thing that I did know how to do, however, was fall down. I
did that quite well and rather often. But getting up was a challenge
and, because of my injury, horribly excruciating. So, that was how I
made my way down the slope. Ski from the right side of the trail to
the left. Fall down. Get up. Ski from the left to the right. Repeat. Oy!

By the time I reached the base after a half an hour of stress and struggle, I was totally soaked with sweat on the inside of my leather jacket and dripping wet from the snow on the outside. I was a sorry mess by the time I showed up for my lesson. Nevertheless, my hearty instructor directed me to the bunny hill and patiently showed me the basics of "Downhill Skiing 101."

By the end of the week, I was doing a respectable job of not falling down and could almost pass for an actual skier. The run that had taken me 30 minutes that first dreadful day, I could now traverse in about fifteen seconds. The boys took to the sport and eventually both Mitchell and Jason became highly skilled skiers. And before long, I, too fell in love with the whole ski slope experience.

My love for skiing was so great that, by the following November, I marked the beginning of the ski season by purchasing a pair of orange Olin skis and boots as well as a matching Beconta ski jacket and pants. Trying on the ensemble, I looked something like a Formula One driver as I admired myself in a full-length mirror. I had gone to Mahopac in order to make the purchase. There I contacted David Kellogg who was one of the owners of Tom Kat Sporting Goods. His father had opened the store in 1948 and it had been a go-to fixture in Mahopac for many years, offering a full array of ski equipment as well as ski fashions and accessories. Although the store has since closed its doors, David's daughter, Alison, continues to operate a virtual Tom Kat Sporting Goods enterprise online. I eventually bought the building that housed the store, but that's another story.

Now I was really ready to hit the slopes, or so I thought. I had the stylish outfit. I was injury-free. I was an experienced downhill skier.

All I needed was some decent powder and I'd be tearing down those trails in no time. On Thanksgiving weekend, I was looking at the snowfall reports and saw there was some decent precipitation coming down at Hunter Mountain, about an hour and a half north of our home. I called up one of the "Route 6 realtors" I had met when I was trying to establish my practice. Terry Simone and I had become friends and I knew he was an experienced ski instructor. I prevailed upon Terry to join me on a jaunt to Hunter Mountain and he gladly agreed.

The day turned out to be a disaster. The snow was hard and trails were covered with ice. I learned the meaning of a "head plant" as I repeatedly found myself unintentionally airborne and landing on my noggin. I also learned the term "Yard Sale," describing what I looked like after a fall, my equipment strewn all over the mountainside. After what seemed like at least one hundred of these painful and embarrassing accidents, I was so sore I could barely walk back to the car.

My memories of *that* day remain painful to *this* day, some fifty years later; so much so that my skis, boots and fancy Beconta jacket are permanently stored at Terry's Colorado home. I asked Terry to hold onto them because I may take up skiing once again someday, but, at this point, I doubt that I ever will. The one positive aspect of this tale is that it introduced me to the company that had provided my leather jacket, Beconta Distributors. This company was involved in another interesting legal case that saw me once again defending police officers threatened with losing their jobs.

Walter Blascoe was a German Jew who escaped the Holocaust by emigrating to the United States in 1939 and then saw service in

World War II. As part of the Tenth Mountain Division in Europe, Blascoe got to know sporting goods manufacturers in Norway, Italy and Switzerland. Once back home, he set up shop in New York City, and began importing and distributing their products around the country. He named the business Beconta and began introducing brands like Attenhofer, Henke and Nordica to American markets. Beconta soon spun off a ski equipment division that was headquartered in Vermont and that would introduce Look Bindings, Volki Skis and other well-known brands to America. In the early 1960s, the company was sold to Jim Woolner and Karl Wallach, who moved the headquarters to Elmsford, New York, a town about 35 miles south of our office. Through the acquisition of brands such as Puma, Beconta grew to become America's dominant distributor of ski equipment and apparel until its demise in the late 1970s.

Actually, the Beconta warehouse was located about five miles outside of Elmsford in an area called Greenburgh, along the banks of the Hudson River. It was in Greenburgh that a police officer that I had gotten to know during my days in the Criminal Court Bureau in the Bronx, Rich DeVito, had gotten himself arrested. He showed up at my office and explained that he admired the way I had worked when I was with the prosecutor's office and he now wished for me to represent him. Two other police officers had been arrested with him and were being represented by Arthur Spring, a veteran litigator and a former Westchester County Assistant District Attorney.

The trio was charged with assaulting a black Beconta employee outside of his workplace. Rich explained that one of the other two cops had a girlfriend who also worked at Beconta and complained to him that she was being constantly harassed by this co-worker. Her boyfriend decided to put a stop to it and enlisted Rich and the other cop to assist him in teaching the guy some manners. The three officers entered the facility and found the victim among the ski boots and poles. They frog marched him outdoors where they proceeded to deliver a serious beating. Unfortunately for the perpetrators, they performed their act of violent vengeance before the eyes of fifteen other Beconta employees.

Even though they were charged with a misdemeanor, an assault conviction would result in all three cops losing their jobs. I knew that this was a charge that should not be reduced via plea bargaining. I told Rich that our best strategy was to go to trial and that I would need $5,000 to represent him. Rich agreed.

We appeared at a pre-trial conference in the Greenburgh Town Court before Judge Ascher Katz. Judge Katz was a respected Harvard Law School-educated jurist who was a charter member of the United States Holocaust Commission, president of the Jewish War Veterans and a member of Rotary and B'nai Brith. Despite these impressive credentials, Judge Katz turned out to be a first-rate dick.

The judge made it plain that he did not like the defendants one bit and would have greatly preferred that they had entered a plea so he would not be required to try the case and tie up his courtroom with a jury trial. My co-counsel Spring and I argued that the case had to be tried. We prevailed and a trial date was set.

The first order of business in a criminal trial is the selection and seating of the jury. This process quickly became a highly contentious affair because Judge Katz constantly interrupted and interfered with our questioning of the prospective jurors.

After growing increasingly frustrated at the judge's behavior, Attorney Spring turned to me and whispered something in my ear. "Do you know what has two legs and fucks cats?"

"I give up," I replied, somewhat bewildered.

"Mrs. Katz."

That was pretty funny but I succeeded in keeping my poker face immobile and responded with only a wink to Spring. I'm not much of a comedian, but I did happen to recall that joke some years later when I was conducting a job interview with a prospective lawyer seeking to join our firm. Her name was Nikki Katz and she was the wife of a well-known gynecologist. I was hoping to hire her to take over our firm's matrimonial cases.

"Nikki," I said. "I only have one question I want to ask you. What has two legs and fucks cats?" Since her name was Katz, I should not have been surprised that she had already heard the joke. She took it well and I hired her on the spot.

I was likewise tempted to relate my "Cats" joke in 2006 when I found myself in the hospital for a quadruple bypass operation. The surgeon's name was Dr. Katz and I thought better of hitting him with the joke since I wasn't well acquainted with his sense of humor.

"What if I offend him just as he is about to take a knife to my heart?" I thought. I kept my mouth zipped and the surgery was a success (almost).

Back in the Beconta trial, I could sense the jury had little sympathy for the victim. Despite the testimony of witness after witness who recounted in detail how the defendants carried out their savage beating, the jury acquitted all three and let them walk free. Judge Katz sourly commented, after the verdict had been returned, that had there been no jury he would have convicted our clients without question.

"That's why we have jury trials, your honor," I responded.

I learned two important things from that trial. One, I now know what has two legs and fucks cats. And two, I learned to always get paid in advance. My ungrateful client refused to pay my fee and forced me to sue him in order to recover what he owed me.

This came at a time when I truly needed the money to pay for some home improvements I had ordered for our new house in Shenorock. On one side of the house, I had a small half-court basketball area installed. And on the other side, I hired a contractor to help me build a wooden deck. As we were working, the carpenter happened to mention that if I ever needed a legal secretary, he could give me the name of someone he knew from his days at Mahopac High School; someone, he assured me, who "would be great for you." As it turned out, Howard and I had talked recently about hiring a secretary, so I agreed to meet her.

Lorraine Bugg was working at a Poughkeepsie law firm and was interested in returning to her home area. I learned this during a weekend interview since she could not leave Poughkeepsie during the week. Howard and I spoke with her at some length. She informed us that she was earning $65 per week at her current job. After conferring privately with Howard, it was clear that we were both enthusiastically in favor of hiring her. I offered her $90 per week. She accepted the offer with a grin and said she could start after giving her employers two-weeks' notice. "One more question," said Howard.

"What will you say if your current employer offers you more money if you'll stay?" She answered forthrightly.

"I will tell them that my mind is made up and I am coming back to Putnam County no matter what they offer me." That put our concerns to rest, although it should not have.

The following week, I received a call from Lorraine. She informed me that her employers had indeed offered her a raise and she had decided she was going to stay with them. When I told Howard the bad news, he responded with two words: "Fuck her."

He was upset because he had specifically anticipated this possibility and had obtained her assurance that this would not be the outcome. He felt betrayed. "We don't need her," he said. But I felt differently.

"Come on, Howard," I cajoled. "We both like her and we both said she'd be a great addition to our practice. Let me try and speak with her and see if I can persuade her to join us." Howard shrugged in a way that said, *"Go ahead and try."*

I called her back.

"Listen, Lorraine, " I said after making sure she was where she could speak freely. "I've talked with Howard and we both would like for you to reconsider your decision to stay in Poughkeepsie. You really need to be thinking long-term. I don't know what sort of future you're looking at there, but we are two young go-getters and we're growing fast. I can't give you specifics, but I guarantee that if you come work with us, we will make it worth your while in every way."

145

Neither of us knew at that point, that this included someday making her my wife. She asked for a day to think about it and called me back to let me know she had reconsidered and would be happy to come work for us.

As things turned out, Lorraine was the best investment that Howard and I ever could have made. She had a sparkling personality that delighted our clients. She was unbelievably reliable and conscientious. Everyone who came into contact with her fell in love with her and that soon included "yours truly." Of course, given the fact I had a wife and two kids, this feeling presented something of a problem. During the course of Lorraine's first year of employment, I kept my secret affections in check and kept things strictly professional. Finally, after having a heart-to-heart talk with myself about the state of my marriage and my hopes for the future, I mustered the nerve to ask Lorraine to join me for lunch.

As we ate, I learned something of Lorraine's background. She had immigrated to the U.S. from Great Britain at age eleven and had settled in Yonkers where she lived with her parents and an older brother before moving to Mahopac. Her father had been a musician and a bait shop owner back in England and was now working as a carpenter.

I chose this moment to reveal that I had a great deal of admiration and affection for her that extended beyond her role as our secretary. Her response—far from being the shock reaction I had feared—was a knowing smile. I breathed a sigh of relief and suddenly felt as if a weight had been lifted from my heart.

That feeling was short-lived as I began to ponder how I would deal with the realities of our situation. How would I inform Fredda? What would I say to the boys? What would I tell my Orthodox Jewish parents about my romance with a *shiksa* (a non-Jewish woman)?

I pondered these, and a long list of other crucial questions, as I stirred my coffee and held Lorraine's hand in mine.

.

Elliot Fixler

Chapter Eight

New Horizons

"Eighty percent of married men cheat in America. The rest cheat in Europe. "

—Jackie Mason

I thought I would have some time to figure out how to tell Fredda about my relationship with Lorraine, but since I was an established "man in a hurry," fate did not afford me that luxury. As Lorraine and I pulled into our office parking lot after that fateful lunch, I spotted something that was not there when we left. Fredda's car.

Fredda was inside waiting for me as I walked into the office with Lorraine. I tried to hide my embarrassment and I, for the first time, stooped to doing something I am not very proud of. I became a liar. From that moment on until the day I found the courage to disengage from Fredda, I was living a double life, concealing my true feelings for Lorraine and lying to Fredda about my whereabouts whenever I would meet Lorraine for a tryst. I tried to justify my actions by telling myself that I was holding our family together for the sake of our kids. But I knew, deep down, that I was only kidding myself. Looking back, I recognize that making a quick break at that point would have saved both Fredda and me much anguish and pain. It also would have actually reduced the trauma endured by the children. But that's not what I did.

In the office, Lorraine and I were strictly professional. It was through her diligence that I was able to build successful relationships with the two pivotal individuals I mentioned in the previous chapter, Dick Gannon and Jay Maxwell.

Dick Gannon was the seller in a real estate deal where I represented the buyer. He was forced to back out of the deal when he learned his son had been diagnosed with leukemia. Dick was known as a collector. Not of fine art or vintage automobiles. No, Dick collected debts. He was employed full-time by the Fred M. Shildwachter & Sons Oil Company in the Bronx and handled all of their receivables. With his imposing physique and his black belt in jujitsu, he was highly effective in convincing people to pay up. Dick was also a small businessman. He owned a martial arts studio, a video rental store and a gutter installation company. He also was a capable plumber.

In his martial arts school, Dick employed men to serve as UKIs (ookies). These are like sparring partners who do combat with the students in order to train them in various jujitsu techniques. One UKI was a friend of Dick's called Billy Kemp and another was Dick's son, Bobby. I learned all this because Dick had convinced Lorraine to sign up for his classes. It was in this way that my friendship with Dick grew. We socialized often, played in the same softball league, and I even partnered with him in a number of video rental stores before Blockbuster came along and busted our blocks.

Dick had a funny moniker for everybody. He had a tough time remembering names so he would come up with a descriptive nickname instead. Lorraine was a slender gal, so he dubbed her "Slim," which stuck. I began to call her that after a while myself. My sons had their own nickname for Lorraine Bugg. They called her "Bugsy," much to my chagrin. Another person who joined Billy, Bobby and Lorraine at their jujitsu classes was my friend Stuart Myers. Let me tell you a bit about Stuart.

Not long after moving to Putnam County, Fredda and I were out on a lovely fall drive, exploring the many picturesque communities surrounding Somers. One house caught our eyes immediately because it was so out of place. Nestled among the quaint gingerbread and traditional shingle houses, was a modern glass and concrete three-story structure. As we stopped to admire the place, we were spotted by the owner who was out front clearing leaves off the driveway. He approached us with a broad smile.

"Care to come in and have a look?" he said graciously. "It's brand new. Just finished building it." Having nothing better to do, we quickly accepted his invitation, having no inkling that this chance encounter would forever change the course of our lives.

"My name's Steve Simon," said our host and we introduced ourselves as well. We followed Steve up the stairs and onto the main floor, where he introduced us to his wife, Sherry. Fredda immediately recognized her. It turns out that Fredda and Sherry had attended grade school together on Manhattan's Upper West Side. A joy-filled reunion ensued as the two women caught up on their lives. It was at this point that I realized there was another couple in the room. Sherry then introduced us to her younger sister, Nancy and her husband, Stuart Myers. The six of us hit it off and this group soon became our close circle of friends; friends we were delighted to make seeing as we were newcomers to the area and had much to learn.

It took a long while for me to fully understand what Stuart did for a living. He explained that he was an insurance adjuster and worked for his father. His clients were insurance companies and it was Stuart's job to investigate claims filed against them. After several years had elapsed—years that saw me representing numerous plaintiffs in actions against insurance companies—Stuart approached me and asked if I would be interested going to bat for the other team.

"You mean represent the insurance company?" I asked.

"Yes. They're my clients and if I explain to them that you've been successfully representing plaintiffs, they'll conclude that you'd do a great job defending them since you know all the tricks of the trade."

"Look, Stu," I replied, "I've always believed a lawyer has got to be fish or fowl."

"Wait a second," he said. "Didn't you tell me you worked as a prosecutor and now you defend the same people you used to go after? You switched sides then."

He had a point. I agreed and pretty soon Stuart sent me my first insurance company client to defend.

I found that playing defense was not that difficult. It's mostly counter-punching and reacting wisely to the plaintiff's offensive tactics. I found the work satisfying and financially rewarding, but there was one drawback. I would have to report to Stuart at various stages of each case to advise him about our progress and to assess our chances of achieving a victorious verdict. At each point, I had to also submit a dollar estimate as to how much financial exposure our client was open to. Since I had limited experience defending insurance companies, I found this task especially challenging. So, I relied mainly on my research and subscribed to legal reporting publications that allowed me look at similar cases with the same sort of injuries that had been previously tried in order to get a handle on how much a jury might award. There was a lot on the line here. The client would use my estimates to decide if it made sense to settle the case or go through with a trial. If I misjudged and the court awarded the plaintiff far more than I had projected, it would cost the client a bunch of money and could cost me a client.

Stuart kept close tabs on me. If I screwed up after he had recommended me to an insurance company client, it would reflect badly on him and might cost him an account. Fortunately, with each passing case, Stuart's confidence in me grew and he therefore kept sending me more cases. Even though defending insurance companies was now consuming a large part of my practice, I did not give up representing plaintiffs. I could see where this might lead to a serious conflict of interest if I were approached by someone who wanted me to represent them in an action against an insurer that was one of my clients. Fortunately, I was never faced with that situation.

As my practice grew, I continued to get business from clients that I had represented in real estate transactions. In addition, I was handling criminal defense cases, matrimonial and divorce cases, personal injury, and the occasional lease or contract review for business clients. I was doing a bit of estate planning work—drafting wills and trust agreements—although I left most of that to Lorraine who was, by this time, serving as my paralegal.

Lorraine also assisted me with matrimonial matters. For some reason, I had no taste for listening to a husband or wife describe the gory details of why their marriage had collapsed. So, Lorraine would conduct the intake interview and then provide me with a sanitized summary and I'd run with it.

As mentioned, another key character I represented at this time was Jay Maxwell. While I did represent Jay in a variety of legal matters, he was more of a friend than a client. Jay was a hustler and a passionately aggressive go-getter. He lived in a community called Pawling that spanned the Putnam/Dutchess county line. I first met Jay at a real estate closing when I represented the buyer of a house in Mahopac. Jay was represented at the time by his criminal lawyer, Eddie Bobick, who was totally out of his element. I wound up doing all the paperwork while Bobick merely collected his fee.

I'm not sure what Jay was mixed up with prior to our meeting, but I surmised that since he spoke so highly of Bobick, he must have had some scrapes with the law. After that meeting, we became fast friends and I became his "Go-To" lawyer. One of the reasons, I suspect, was the fact that I never charged him for my services.

At the time Jay became my client, he and his family were living on a 20-acre spread along Route 22, the main artery between Putnam and Dutchess Counties. He also owned another home along Ponce Inlet, located about ten miles south of Daytona Beach, Florida. The area was known for its massive ocean waves and for being home to Florida's tallest lighthouse. The home had a dock and was situated on an access canal. About half a mile down the road stood Jay's restaurant that also sported a dock for rentals next to the parking lot.

Jay was happily married to Jean who was ten years his senior. Jean had four children from a previous marriage plus three children with Jay. Jean's older kids became part of Jay's extended family. One of Jean's children, Billy Sanders, died due to a heroin overdose and Jay built a little memorial chapel for Jean, replete with stained-glass windows, on their property. Jay was also able to find employment for some of Jean's kids at the summer camp where he worked as director of general maintenance. Camp Ramah, in Wingdale, was operated by the New York office of the United Jewish Appeal, the major Jewish philanthropic organization at the time. Through Jay, I got to know the camp's director, Robert Fruehling, and it was through Fruehling that I was offered a seat on the UJA Board of Directors.

During my tenure on the Board, I learned that among the many worthy causes supported by the UJA, the organization provided funding for groups such as HIAS and the Joint Distribution Committee that had assisted my family in entering and settling in the United States. I soon lost interest, however, and quit the board.

Jay Maxwell's full name was Adrian J. Maxwell and it was during these years that he became a constant fixture in my office. I would handle his contract reviews and represent him in real estate transactions. He was a pugnacious fellow who was always butting heads with town officials over some types of zoning violations. I defended him in these cases and we always emerged as winners. In lieu of payment, Jay would offer to take me to dinner at a fancy restaurant, like Harold's, in Gloversville. He would typically top off the meal with a bottle of $300 Château Lafite Rothschild wine and then stick me with the check. I finally got smart and hid my wallet containing my credit cards in my shoe whenever we would go out to dine together.

This practice continued years later when I was living in Palm Beach Gardens, Florida, and Jay and his younger son, Dino, would travel south from Daytona Beach to Miami on business. Jay would insist that I meet him and Dino for lunch as they were passing through town in order for me to ostensibly review the deal documents. His choice of venue would invariably be Rachael's, a well-known West Palm Beach, high-end titty bar located just off of I-95. The food quality was great (yummy lamb chops) and the women were all sensual, but as a place to conduct business, it was challenging to say the least. The place was so dark that we were forced to use flashlights to read the contracts. That's not to mention the ongoing distraction of being hustled by strippers wanting to interest us in a lap dance. I'm not sure why this spot appealed to Jay, since he was in his 80's by this time and no doubt past the point of sexual arousal. I'm guessing it was Dino who decided on Rachel's. Dino liked to commit marriage on a serial basis. I lost track of the number of wives he hooked up with. One of them, as I recall, was actually a teenage au pair who had worked for us.

Jay kept his fishing boat docked in Montauk, along the east end of Long Island. He had christened it the Uranus (he loved puns). Lorraine would often join Jay, his son, Dino, and Jay's stepdaughter, Maggie, for wind-swept ocean pleasure cruises. On two occasions, Jay convinced me to join this jolly crew for some deep-sea fishing. Those experiences put a halt to whatever nautical desires I may have harbored.

Let me explain.

The first misadventure took place under heavily overcast skies. Nevertheless, Captain Jay decided to direct the Uranus to a fishing spot about 26 miles out at sea. In addition to me, Larraine, Jay, Dino (Jay's younger son), Maggie (Jay's stepdaughter), our crew also included a character named Frankie Garbage. Frankie Garbage was an old friend of Jay's who was in (surprise!) the waste management racket. As we set out, Lorraine was busy making sandwiches while Jay manned the helm. I was busy as well...heaving my guts out over the side of the boat. The choppy waters had started my digestive system churning and triggered a major case of *mal de mere.* I managed to make my way to the head and began praying that someone would turn the boat around and head home. No such luck.

Instead, as I sat there, I observed Frankie chumming with one hand and holding a bottle of red wine in the other as he serenaded me with a rendition of *O Sole Mio* in the original Italian. Chumming is the blue water fishing practice of throwing ground bait into the ocean to lure game fish to our fishing spot. If the fish were not scared off by his singing, I was sure his chumming efforts would be successful.

I started feeling a bit better and laid down on the deck. I quickly fell into a fitful sleep. The next thing I knew, someone was shaking me awake while screaming: "Wake up! Get up! The boat's sinking and you need to get on this life jacket."

With the taste of my own bile still in my throat and half-mad with panic, I struggled to don the orange life vest. But it was way too small and the clasps would not reach. As I looked up in terror, I detected the brazen smiles and suppressed laughter of my crew mates. I pulled off the life jacket and looked it over. It was intended for a child and it was at this point that I realized I had been the butt of a practical joke.

Did I take it good-naturedly and laugh it off? Hell no. I was madder than a hopped-up hornet and swore never to go on any more fishing trips with Jay.

Some years later, after Jay had apologized and assured me that there would be no more hijinks at my expense, I agreed, with some trepidation, to join him onboard the Uranus out of Montauk once again for some deep-sea fishing. Everything was going smoothly and I experienced no seasickness. In fact, I was starting to actually enjoy myself when a member of our crew excitedly announced that he thought he had a big Marlin on the line. Since I was the new guy onboard, they afforded me the high honor of sitting in the "fighting chair," a stool affixed to the deck where a person sits while struggling to reel in a big deep-sea fish. And what a struggle it turned out to be. I fought that brute for well over an hour under the hot sun. The others kept pouring buckets of water on me to cool me down as I did battle with what surely appeared to be the king of all deep-sea denizens. After a valiant struggle, the line broke and I wound up losing the Marlin. Or so I thought. I soon learned that there never was a fish on the line at all. My line had been tied to the stern of the boat by one of my devious crew mates, all of whom were entertained by the spectacle of watching this wet-behind-the-ears lawyer struggle with an imaginary fish. I concluded that the biggest fish on that boat that day was me. That was it. No more boating excursions for me and I have kept that promise to myself to this day.

Jay's entrepreneurial spirit saw him expanding his holdings in Florida in the 1980s. They eventually included two restaurants, a public marina and a museum in which he displayed eclectic collections of antique firearms, Native American weapons, paintings, statues and more. He told me that he owned a shipwreck off the coast of Daytona Beach that contained a sunken treasure chest and he would dive down once a year to recover some of the treasure. I was always skeptical of this claim until he gave Lorraine an actual gold doubloon as a gift. Who knows?

Dino, Jay's younger son, managed the Florida enterprises. His brother, Jay Jr., ran the New York businesses, including a machine shop and a commercial construction operation. In 1972, Jay opened the Towne Crier Café in Beacon, located in Dutchess County, New York. It became known as a celebrated music venue, attracting performers of live folk, jazz, blues, Celtic, bluegrass, Cajun, zydeco and world beat music to the Hudson Valley. It was reviewed as "First Rate" by Rolling Stone magazine. I would purchase season tickets every year entitling me to a ringside table where I could rest my elbows on the stage. The musical performances would start after dinner and we would be entertained by such outstanding singer-songwriters as John Stewart, who had been a member of the Kingston Trio, and Loudon Wainwright III. The place was eventually sold to Daryl Hall of Hall and Oates fame who changed the name to Daryl's House Club.

The last time I saw Jay Maxwell was a few months before I began writing this book. We met in Cocoa Beach for lunch. Jay arrived with his stepdaughter, Maggie, and a hefty bodyguard. I suspected he wasn't himself when I observed him pick up the check.

At our lunch, we arranged to meet the following weekend so he could show me some firearms I was interested in purchasing from him. We agreed that he would call me on Friday to set the time and place. He never called. I heard from his younger son, Dino, the following week who informed me that Jay was in the hospital in New Smyrna Beach. It wasn't COVID-19, but Dino was unclear about what exactly he was suffering from.

I later learned that Jay was told by his doctors that if he survived, he would require constant nursing care for the rest of his life. He instructed his family to take him off life support and he died the following day, July 30, 2021. He was 88, but didn't look it.

I flew up to New York to attend the memorial "Celebration of Life" put on by Jay's family at their New York estate. I extended my condolences and spent a few hours mingling with the hundreds of people who showed up. Once the rock band arrived, I saw that this was not to my taste, so I left and headed home.

Jay Maxwell was a one-of-a-kind force of nature and I consider it an honor to have called him my close friend. Perhaps someday I'll write another book just about him. On second thought, this book is probably going to be my last hurrah.

Howard and I were constantly bearing witness to the financial success being enjoyed by clients like Jay Maxwell and others. We could not resist the temptation to follow their example and so, in the late seventies, we purchased a run-down former bar located at the crossroads of two high-traffic streets in Somers. We also brought

Robert Fruehling, the summer camp director, into the deal. The three of us put up some more money and used it to fix the place up, turning it into a casual family restaurant. Both Howard and I were sporting beards in those days, so we dubbed the place Whiskers. To run the place, we hired a former member of NYPD, named Fred, a fellow that Howard and I had taken on as a client. As a bonus, Fred's brother-in-law was a talented musician named Jimmy Coyle who frequently was brought in to entertain our patrons.

Whiskers did very well at the outset, but like many such ventures, it was eventually doomed by poor management. Fred turned out to be unreliable and probably spent more time "*schtupping*" the waitresses than managing the operation. We enjoyed a two-year run and eventually closed the doors and sold the building to avoid going into the red. We took a haircut, for sure, but we did not actually suffer greatly financially. You might say that Whiskers turned out to be a close shave.

Lorraine had gone to Mahopac High School with a girl named Sharon Gorman, who was also a neighbor. Her story was rather tragic. Sharon, and her brother, Bryan, were born at Mitchell Air Force base in Hempstead, New York. They had grown up on Long Island and in the Panama Canal Zone. After their mother committed suicide when Sharon was a child, they were raised by an uncle named Jack O'Neil and his wife. Bryan had been Lorraine's high school sweetheart. Both Sharon and Bryan were very bright. Sharon wound up working for NASA and was on duty in the Mojave Desert in California on January 28, 1986, when the Space Shuttle Challenger broke apart 73 seconds after take-off, killing all seven crew members.

Sharon served as Lorraine's bridesmaid at our wedding and the two were very close. So, when Lorraine explained that one of her Uncle Jack's kids was in trouble with the law, I naturally agreed to offer my services.

Jack O'Neal had three children. Sean O'Neil, at 19 was the oldest and was a known alcoholic and substance abuser. He had been in trouble repeatedly as a juvenile but suffered few consequences because his father consistently bailed him out.

In this instance, Sean had been accused of demolishing fifteen rural mailboxes with a baseball bat. Some years later, a similar vandalism scene would be depicted in a game of "mailbox baseball," in the 1986 coming-of-age film, *Stand By Me*. The film was adapted from a 1982 novella by Stephen King, who lived in Bangor, Maine at the time. I sometimes wonder if news reports of Sean's crime served to inspire King. Sean was apprehended and charged with malicious vandalism. Not surprisingly, his father, Jack O'Neil, agreed to pay my fee to defend Sean.

When he asked me what it would cost, I answered, "$1500 sounds about right. That's $100 per mailbox."

I earned my fee by getting the court to classify the crime as a minor matter and therefore it agreed to adjourn the case for six months. If there were no further arrests during that time, the charges would be dropped. There weren't any and after six months, the case was dismissed.

It was not long afterward that Sean came to me once again and asked me to represent him in a lawsuit arising from an auto accident in which he had sustained some injuries.

Sean and another passenger were riding in the backseat of an automobile owned by a Mr. Callaghan. In the front seat were Callaghan's son and another young man named Strickland. The question as to which one, young Callaghan or Strickland, was behind the wheel became a disputed issue in the case. The four had spent the day smoking marijuana, drinking beer, and ingesting Quaaludes. Quaaludes (methaqualone), known as 'Ludes, are a synthetic barbiturate. Because of its soporific qualities, it was a popular recreational drug in those days before methamphetamine and opioids. Along a stretch of country road, the car struck a tree head on. It was presumed that the driver had fallen asleep at the wheel.

My client, Sean O'Neil, was the plaintiff seeking damages for the injuries he had sustained due to the driver's negligence. But determining exactly who was driving the car was not going to be easy. Another attorney name Richard Maher represented the other backseat passenger who was also seeking compensation for the injuries he had sustained. The most seriously injured was Strickland, represented by Bernard (Barney) Duhan. Richard Moran (not to be confused with attorney Richard Maher), represented the defendants, both young Callaghan as well as his father, who was the registered owner of the vehicle.

Moran mounted a defense based on his assertion that young Callaghan was not driving the car. It was actually Strickland and, as such, was guilty of contributory negligence and therefore not entitled to any recovery compensation. On the stand, Sean O'Neil testified that he was asleep in the backseat and did not know who was driving at the time of the accident. To settle the question of who was behind the wheel, I produced hospital records and introduced them into evidence. The records revealed that Callaghan had an imprint of a steering wheel visible on his chest, establishing that he was behind the wheel at the time of the collision. In addition, we called the ER surgeon as a witness and he corroborated that there was an injury on Callaghan's chest that was unquestionably caused by a strong impact with a steering wheel.

To counter this evidence, the defense brought in an accident reconstruction expert from Syracuse who opined under oath that Callaghan was actually not the driver but sitting in the backseat at the point of impact. How did this expert then explain the steering wheel sized imprint on Callaghan's chest when he was questioned on cross examination?

"The injury to the subject's chest could very well have been sustained due to his body's impact with the back of the front seat."

This was my first civil case trial and I was surrounded by qualified and highly experienced tort attorneys. I was expecting the trial to be a great learning experience for me and so I was paying close attention to everything that took place, starting with jury selection.

I was seated at the plaintiff's table, next to Barney, who examined each juror just before I did. I had done my homework and had read up on the art and science of effective jury selection. One of the prospective jurors was employed as an accountant and I had read accountants were a no-no for plaintiffs. Accountants and CPAs were known to be penny pinchers and not inclined to approve generous awards in the event of a favorable verdict. I whispered to Barney that he should consider exercising a peremptory challenge and remove the accountant from the jury.

Barney declined to do so and said, "Elliot, if *you* want to challenge him, it's okay with me."

"Well," I thought to myself, *"Barney's the war horse here and has been at this for a lot longer than I have, so he must know what he's doing."*

I followed his lead and did not exercise a challenge to excuse the accountant.

As things turned out, the jury awarded my client, Sean O'Neil, the sum of $10,000. Dick's client, the other backseat passenger, received $30,000. And Barney succeeded in getting Strickland, the other front seat passenger who sustained the greatest injury, exactly zero. The jury evidently bought the testimony of the accident expert who Barney referred to as the "Boy From Syracuse." I thought this was clever, but the jury evidently didn't get it. In his summation, Barney actually said that this so-called expert has brought his traveling road show to Putnam County in order present this fairy tale to the jury. This was a reference to a popular 1930's Rogers and Hart Broadway musical called *The Boys from Syracuse.* It was based on the Shakespeare play called *A Comedy of Errors.* This case certainly had its share of errors, but it was no comedy for those plaintiffs who received barely enough compensation to meet their medical bills or shut out entirely.

After the verdict was delivered, I conducted a post-mortem with Barney over lunch.

"Why did you let that accountant on the jury?" I wanted to know. His answer was cryptic and still does not make much sense to me after all these years.

"You know, Elliot, Charlie Kramer was my partner for years and he said if you don't like a juror's face, then challenge him, because chances are if you don't like his face he won't like yours. This juror looked like Charlie Kramer so I left him on the jury." So much for the fine art and science of jury selection.

I remained friends with Sharon Gorman—through Lorraine—for the rest of her life. She had married and divorced a man named Anthony and was living in Chesapeake, Virginia when she died on March 30, 2021, of respiratory failure. Sadly, she never could quit smoking.

In the following chapter, I recount some of my more fascinating cases and also describe the path that led to matrimony with Lorraine.

.

Chapter Nine

The Rocky Road to Romance

"Yes, love can be wondrously complicated, it can be confusing, and it can be terrifying. But if it wasn't all those things, then it wouldn't be love."

—N.R. Hart

I t was at about this time that both my personal and professional lives started to become more complicated. And where the two overlapped...things became intense. Our practice was picking up steam with both Howard and me bringing in new cases at a rapid clip. We enjoyed a steady stream of real estate deals, often with me handling one side of the transaction and him handling the other. We were also starting to pull in clients from nearby affluent Westchester County.

My representation of minor misdemeanor and DUI cases, as well as negligent homicide and personal injury claims, continued to expand as I often picked up clients referred by other lawyers who did not feel that such "small potatoes" cases warranted their time. My relationship with my law partner, Howard, was a solid one based on mutual respect and friendship. Like me, Howard was ambitious and sought to expand his areas of expertise. For example, he was educating himself in the intricacies of planning and zoning so as to be more of an advocate on behalf of our growing number of construction and building trade clients. I could see that this area truly appealed to Howard.

Lorraine was working out well and ingrained herself ever more deeply into our practice with each passing day. Of course, this tended to complicate matters between me and my other partner, my wife.

On the surface, our home front appeared as normal as apple pie. The kids were growing and becoming more active in athletics. Our boys made friends with the sons of one of the real estate brokers who was providing us with a stream of home sale clients. Terry Simone was a divorced father with two boys the same age as mine. We became friends and through him I gained some insight in what it would be like to be a divorced father with minor children.

Howard and I liked to tease Terry and we decided to have some fun at his expense. After a morning real estate closing that saw Howard and me on either side of the deal and during which Terry appeared to pick up his commission check, we all decided to go out to lunch at a swanky Westchester County eatery. When the check arrived after the meal had been consumed, Howard and I both pretended to search for our wallets.

"You're not going to believe this, Terry," I said straight-faced, "but both Howard and I walked out without taking our wallets. I guess lunch is going to have to be on you." As incredible as this sounded, Terry bought our story.

He became flustered and came back with, "B-b-but, fellas. I don't have any money on me. I was going to stop at the bank after lunch and cash this check. W-w-what are we gonna do?"

Howard and I sadistically enjoyed watching Terry squirm until we had had our fun and let him off the hook by splitting the check between us. Terry has never forgotten that dirty trick, but I know that he has forgiven us.

Howard and I typically would spend a lot of time with our real estate broker contacts, entertaining them and building good will. These efforts served to show our appreciation for the business they were sending our way and encourage them to keep on doing so. I refrained from pulling any more pranks on poor Terry Simone until his 40th birthday came around and I simply couldn't resist.

I had been invited to his birthday celebration being held in a private room at a local restaurant and after the meal, Terry's friends were offering toasts to "The small man with the big heart." This was undeniably true. Terry possessed a diminutive stature but was a truly generous guy. When my turn came, I pulled out a boom box from under the table that held a cassette tape I had prepared in advance.

"Rather than try to express what's in my heart about Terry at this moment, I thought I'd leave it to a great songwriter, like Randy Newman, to do the job." I then pressed the play button and the strains of Newman's 1978 hit song *Short People* filled the hall. Here are some of the tune's controversial lyrics:

Short people got no reason to live

They got little hands, little eyes

They walk around tellin' great big lies

They got little noses, tiny little teeth

They wear platform shoes on their nasty little feet

Well, I don't want no short people 'round here

© Copyright Universal Music Publishing Group

The crowd erupted in laughter and Terry took the joke with his usual tolerant nature. The composer, Randy Newman, responded to criticism about the song by explaining that the lyrics are intended to be taken as ironic. As do many songwriters, Newman often adopts the persona of an unattractive character to make a point. In this case, he was mocking the type of bigoted fool he had often encountered as a "short person" himself.

By 1973, our practice was growing so fast that Howard and I soon encountered a problem, a good problem. We agreed we needed to bring in another lawyer to help manage the workload. I mentioned our situation to Marvin Hirsch, an old friend I had first met in law school. Marvin seemed interested, but when I brought up Marvin's name to Howard, he thought that bringing in one of *his* old friends from law school—a guy named Ed Sumber—might be a better idea. I guess he thought that Stockfield, Fixler and Sumber sounded better than Stockfield, Fixler and Hirsch.

Howard pointed out that Ed Sumber was, in addition to being an attorney, a CPA, and getting him onboard would diversify the scope of our practice. I could see Howard's point and now faced the task of delivering the bad news to Marvin, who I had led to believe would be welcomed as a new partner. Marvin did not take it well. I explained that we had opted to go with someone else who had a different skillset than Marvin's. He became upset, and our relationship never recovered after that. Marvin wound up enjoying a successful criminal defense practice in Long Island and Brooklyn. I tried to get in touch with Marvin recently as I was researching this book and learned, sadly, that he had passed away in 2015 at the age of 73.

Ed Sumber joined our practice officially in 1973 and hit the ground running. He soon developed his own niche among our real estate clients including the board of the Realtors of Westchester and Putnam Counties trade association. He was a capable lawyer and plied his craft with evident skill. But sadly, we would discover a critical deficiency in the area known as loyalty.

It was a few years later that Ed called Howard on a Sunday morning and asked to have breakfast with only him (not me). He glibly informed Howard over their morning flapjacks that he was leaving the firm. He further admitted to him that he had visited our closed offices the night before and extracted the files of all the clients he considered to be his. He planned to bring these clients with him to his new practice. In those pre-computer days, a client's physical paper file was something precious. It contained all of the original documents pertaining to a given client. Not too many law firms at that time maintained off-site security back-up of files.

Howard did not need to inform Ed that what he had done was illegal. Those files were the assets and family jewels of the entire practice. His ownership was only valid to the extent he held equity in the firm. For him to abscond with a file representing a potential annual income of say $20,000 to the firm, constituted an act of theft with Howard and me as the victims.

The proper way for a lawyer to leave a practice is to inform his clients of this fact and then offer them a choice of either going with him or staying with the practice where he would be assigned to a different attorney. If the client chose to stay, and there was a pending matter involved, he would be required to execute a Substitution of

Counsel document. If the client chose to go with Ed, and owed money to the firm, Ed would be required to collect whatever was owed up to the time of his departure and remit it to us. But Ed opted to do it quick and dirty—and sneaky. His justification was that he had invested into building relationships with *his* clients and he wasn't about to just walk away leave the fruits of his labor behind. It was a specious and self-serving rationalization of a first-rate felony.

When I heard the news, I was ready go after the guy tooth and nail (knock out his teeth and nail his lying ass) and take no prisoners. Howard, always the cooler head, said to just let it go.

"We've got plenty of other clients," Howard correctly pointed out and whoever we lost to Eddie, we'll make back in no time. Besides, if we file charges it will get in the papers and the scandal will make us look bad. And that could cost us."

I saw his point. I knew how bad Howard felt since he was the one who had brought this viper into our nest, so I didn't argue with him. I cooled my heels and acquiesced.

About that time there was a popular TV mini-series being aired called *Rich Man, Poor Man.* It featured a shady character by the name of Falconetti. I adopted that moniker in all my future references to Ed Sumber, only I changed it a little. Instead of "Falconetti," he forever became "Fuckin' Eddie." It's scumbags like Fuckin' Eddie who give lawyers a bad reputation for having no scruples or moral integrity when, in truth, we often do.

Before I close the books on Fuckin' Eddie, I must point out one classic bit of irony. Not long after he was engaged in the highly unethical and illegal practices involving our firm, Fuckin' Eddie was named, in 1975, to serve as official counsel to the Westchester County Board of Realtors. It was through his work as Board Counsel that he made a name for himself by helping to launch the Westchester-Putnam County Multiple Listing Service. It was in this manner that Fuckin' Eddie got himself named to the prestigious Westchester County Board of Grievances. This is a self-regulatory watchdog organization charged with monitoring and regulating ethical conduct within the legal profession. Can you believe it?! Not since FDR appointed his stock-swindling buddy, Joseph P. Kennedy, to head up the newly formed S.E.C., had the world witnessed such an outright act of blatant hypocrisy. Of course, one could argue, under the "It takes a thief to catch a thief" maxim, that there was no one more familiar with unethical behavior in the legal profession than Fuckin' Eddie Sumber. Fuckin' Eddie breathed his last in June of 2018 and, if outliving someone is really the best revenge, then I guess revenge is mine...even if I had to wait 43 years to savor it.

In spite of Fuckin' Eddie's criminal theft of our firm's clients, Howard, through hard work and diligence, continued to grow the Real Estate side of our practice. I held up my end with personal injury work, matrimonial cases, and whatever else came through the door. Howard's years of dedication to the real estate and business communities of Carmel was not going unrecognized by the local powers that were. When an opening arose for town Justice of the Peace, Howard was asked to run. He agreed and won the election in a walk. He made a truly great J.P. His powerful combination of high intellect and cool temperament earned him the respect of the community he served.

It was while Howard was serving as J.P. that I met another unforgettable figure from that time, Bob Miller. Bob had also served as J.P. and was a member of another four-person law firm like ours that specialized in real estate work. Once we all compared notes, we realized we were sending a lot of business to local title insurance companies and all we were receiving in return was a few free lunches. So, we decided to join forces to set up our own title insurance agency and hire a manager to operate it for us. We didn't hide from our clients that the title insurance firm we always directed them to was actually owned by us, but we didn't advertise the fact, either. Clients were always free to shop around if they chose.

Bob was an amiable and outgoing lawyer. He was a Marine veteran and attended both Brown and Ohio Universities, having played basketball at the latter alongside future All-NBA forward and Basketball Hall of Famer, Wayne Embry. The friendship between the two men endured as Wayne's eleven year playing career took him from the Cincinnati Royals to the Boston Celtics to the Milwaukee Bucks. As his career transitioned from player to team executive, Wayne went on, in 1972, to become the first black general manager and team president in NBA history. This phase of his career lasted through 2008 and saw him managing the Milwaukee Bucks, the Cleveland Cavaliers and finally the Toronto Raptors. Embry was serving as senior basketball advisor for the Raptors when they won the NBA Championship in 2019. He continues in that position today.

Bob and I would play basketball in the evenings at a local church near the courthouse on a team made up of other lawyers. During the day, our court time was spent either entirely on defense or entirely on behalf of the plaintiff or the people. In the evenings, our court time would see us constantly switching between defense and offense depending on which team had possession of the ball. I liked the basketball variety better because it kept me on my toes.

Bob and I also liked to travel to the Meadowlands Arena to attend New Jersey Nets games. Because I was a season ticket holder, I eventually wound up with court side seats. At that time, Wayne was managing the Cleveland Cavaliers and when they were scheduled to play the Nets, Bob and I would try to meet Wayne after the game and we would go out for a meal together.

I'll always remember the time I was afforded the high honor of driving Wayne from the stadium to the restaurant. My car was a little Subaru 2-seater sports runabout and trying to scrunch Wayne's 6-foot-9-inch 300 lb. frame into the passenger seat was something to behold. But he managed it, leaving me with little room to maneuver in my capacity as the car's designated driver.

Another unforgettable moment took place years later, in 1999, when Bob and I were invited to be Wayne's guests and witness his induction into the Naismith Memorial Basketball Hall of Fame in Springfield, Massachusetts. Talk about a thrill. Here I was, having gone from a kid sneaking in on Saturdays, to the Pierson Layer Appliance Store on Hertel Avenue in Buffalo watching my NBA heroes like Wayne Embry do their stuff on an old black and white TV, to being a part of the ceremony that recognized him as a basketball legend.

To add icing to the cake, I was seated next to 6-foot-11-inch Bob Lanier, a 1992 inductee, who had, before playing for the Detroit Pistons and Milwaukee Bucks, graduated from Bennett High School, my alma mater, in 1966. I was on cloud nine and no matter what Mick Jagger had to say about it, I was not getting off.

Bob Miller went on to serve as a county court judge and later a supreme court judge. These days, we still manage to see each other rather often, given the fact we live on different coasts...of Florida.

One of Bob's law partners back then and one of the co-owners of the title insurance company we had set up, was an attorney named Valerie Mace. Val was as brilliant as she was tall, which is to say, "*extremely.*" Her father had pursued a hazardous occupation. He was a mob accountant and I'm guessing that somehow his numbers did not add up or he knew too much. In any case, he got rubbed out. Naturally, this event made Valerie look upon career criminals with great disfavor, and explains why our friendship was terminated in 1988, when she learned that I had taken a notorious bad guy on as client and would be defending him in court. My argument that, under our judicial system, everyone is afforded the presumption of innocence and is therefore entitled to the best possible legal representation, did nothing to convince her. She did not relent when I explained it was up to the judge or jury, and not me, to condemn this man. She accused me of taking the case only because of the generous fee.

I first met my criminal client one sunny afternoon when a long yellow Rolls Royce convertible slinked into our office parking lot and a chunky, pig-faced young man with shifty blue eyes and a mop of bright yellow hair that matched the Rolls, waddled from the back seat into our office.

"My name's Alan Ascheim and I'm looking for the Fixler. I need him to help me with a misdemeanor arrest that I got from one of the local Justice of the Peace guys around here."

I took the case and got it dismissed easily. Alan liked my swift work and started sending me other petty cases to chew on. He needed me to draft a purchase agreement for a hip-hop nightclub in York-town, for example. I complied and quickly delivered it to him.

Meanwhile, Alan was allegedly looking for a home in Westchester County and he had instructed a number of real estate brokers to show him houses in the multi-million-dollar range. This did not strike me as unusual, coming from a guy who was being driven around in a two to three hundred-thousand-dollar Rolls.

Shortly after I had drafted the purchase agreement for the hip-hop club, Alan invited Howard and me to a supposed housewarming party for a new luxury condo he had purchased in Peekskill, New York. We mingled and socialized with the other guests and, after a bit, Alan approached us.

"I need you guys upstairs for a little business meeting. Won't take long."

We obliged and made our way upstairs to a room containing a circular conference table. We were introduced as Alan's lawyers to the men seated around the table, most of whom we had seen downstairs earlier. Among them was the proprietor of the hip-hop club that Alan wished to buy. Alan whipped out the purchase agreement and a pen and slid them over to the club owner.

"These guys," he gestured towards Howard and me, "have put together a very fair offer for your club and you need to look it over and accept it...right now," Alan instructed.

The nightclub proprietor glanced at the document disdainfully and then looked up with a sneer, asking "Hey, what the hell's going on here? I'm not selling nothing."

I also was wondering what was going down. I was thinking back with trepidation to the famous scene in the *Godfather* about the nightclub owner to whom Luca Brasi explained that either his signature or his brains were going to wind up on that Johnny Fontane contract. What happened next confirmed my worst Don Corleone fears.

Which a sudden crack, a closet door behind me was smashed open and a swarthy, olive-skinned *goombah* with a slicked-back hairdo and a three-pound solid gold Hebrew Chai hanging from his bull neck emerged brandishing a very ugly submachine gun. He pointed it menacingly around the room trying to figure out who he was supposed to be terrorizing. Finally, he pointed the weapon directly at the head of the nightclub owner. After a beat, I spotted Alan giving the "convincer" a subtle nod, and the Mossad Muscle turned and walked menacingly out the door. Alan again addressed the proprietor with his very "reasonable" offer.

"I hope you will reconsider your position."

I figured by now Howard would be shitting his pants. Worse, he fell to his knees, grabbed his chest and struggled to get out "I...I...I think I'm having a heart attack!"

I helped Howard to his feet, turned to Alan and said politely, "You definitely have an unusual way of a negotiating a contract. But it's not the way we work, so good luck and we're outta here. So long."

Howard did not suffer a heart attack and Alan was eventually arrested and indicted for extortion for that incident. He asked me to defend him. I declined.

"Alan, listen. You've got to understand that I was a material witness to the alleged crime," I tried to explain to him. "I can't possibly defend you and then cross examine myself. It's a basic conflict of interest."

I informed him that I was not going to represent him in anything anymore. I thought, unless I received a late-night visit from Alan's gorilla and was persuaded to again represent Alan with the business end of an Uzi, I was done with this guy. Fortunately, that never happened. But that was not the end of the story for Alan Ascheim.

Not long after, I was reading in the papers about a string of home robberies taking place in upscale Westchester County. The perpetrators evidently were able to case their victim's homes by posing as wealthy potential buyers brought in to view the premises by gullible real estate agents. Something should have clicked when I read that. It should have reminded me about the guy in the big yellow Rolls shopping for multi-million-dollar mansions. Something should have clicked, but nothing did.

In July of 1978, one of the Pound Ridge homes, belonging to beloved award-winning husband and wife actors, Hume Cronyn and Jessica Tandy, was invaded by two men and a woman who had been brought to the home by a duped realtor. The realtor had introduced the trio as prospective purchasers of the home. Once inside the premises, the older of the two men gagged and then handcuffed 67-year-old Cronyn, then proceeded to tie up his secretary as well as the real estate broker. The younger man then threatened Cronyn and the secretary at gunpoint to reveal the location of their valuables.

The trio got away but was soon apprehended in my hometown of Somers and charged with illegal confinement and armed robbery. Although he was, at age 25, the youngest of the trio, Alan Ascheim, was clearly the one who had devised the robbery plan and had enlisted the others to assist him.

Evidently Alan was cleared of the charge, because not long afterwards, he was arrested again. This time he was accused of masterminding another home jewelry heist at another Pound Ridge mansion. Alan had allegedly solicited a young lady and her boyfriend to rob the home of a single elderly woman named Thelma Miller: no relation to Bob Miller. According to testimony provided by the young woman, Ascheim had gained entry to the home prior to the theft by posing as a prospective buyer and, during his tour of the premises, made a floor plan diagram of the place, noting the location of all the burglar alarm sensors. He used the diagram to plot the execution of the robbery with his two young accomplices.

According to their plan, the young lady, posing as a wealthy young dilettante, pulled up to the stately home in a Rolls being driven by her boyfriend, posing as her chauffeur. She knocked on the door, carrying a blank canvas, painter's easel and paintbox, and obtained Mrs. Miller's permission, via flattery, to set up her easel on the front yard in order to create a painting of her "majestic manor." Foolishly, Mrs. Miller granted her permission. Soon thereafter, the ersatz chauffeur knocked again at the front door and requested to use the bathroom. Mrs. Miller again did not object. Once both crooks were inside the house, they quickly handcuffed, tied, and gagged Mrs. Miller and then collected all her jewelry and made their getaway.

Later that day Ascheim allegedly came to the couple's apartment and collected all the loot. He came back two days later, presumably after having fenced the haul, and paid them a total of $2500 in cash for their services. In Ascheim's defense, his attorney argued that, since the witness was also a co-defendant, the young lady's testimony should not be admissible unless it was corroborated by further evidence.

The prosecution countered by citing secondary corroboration of every key point of the avaricious artist's testimony. The court found this acceptable and found Alan, as well as his accomplices, guilty as charged. The conviction held up on appeal and that was the last trace of the larcenous Mr. Ascheim in my life.

Much later, Valerie and I patched up our differences when I admitted that she was right. Yes, it's true, I conceded, every defendant deserves a rigorous defense, but an attorney can, at the same time, be selective about which cases he decides to take on. I yielded this point when she asked me the following—after learning of my family background:

"Tell me, Elliot, would you have taken on Hermann Goering as your client at Nuremberg where he was charged with leading a regime that sent millions of innocent Jews, including your family, to their deaths in the gas chambers?"

181

She got to me with that one.

"Not for all the money in the world," I muttered.

Valerie and I had been close before she got angry with me about representing Ascheim. After the reconciliation, I got to know her family. Her husband, Frank, was a lanky stockbroker who loved tennis. They had a tennis court on their property where Howard and I would play now and then. They also had two kids the same age as my Mitch and Jay who attended the same school. The older of the two was their extremely handsome seven foot tall son. Frank had groomed this towering young man for a career in sports, but, surprisingly, not in basketball. He trained in both boxing and tennis with the idea he might pursue a career in whichever sport he excelled in. Tragically, he never had the chance to find out. The very tall young man developed a lethal brain tumor at age twenty.

As my clandestine love affair with Lorraine heated up, so did Fredda's suspicions. I could feel that heat on the back of my neck as I regularly sped from our home in Shenorock to the little three-bedroom place on the banks of Lake Carmel in Kent, New York, that I had helped Lorraine purchase. Some might call it a secret love nest, but it was the one place in the world where I could truly unwind and relax. I would put the pedal to the metal in my silver 25th Anniversary high-performance Porche 911 as I hurriedly covered the 13.5 mile stretch of US 6 between Shenorock and Kent. I was still every bit a man in a hurry.

While my practice could, at this stage, have been described as something of a zoo, in the next chapter I will introduce you to some cases that made the allegation literally true. Stay tuned, folks. You ain't seen nuthin' yet!

Elliot Fixler

Chapter Ten

Darling Lorraine & Others

"The first time that I saw her, I could not be sure.
But the sin of impatience said: "She's just what you're looking for."

—Opening lyric from "Darling Lorraine" by Paul Simon
©2000 Sony Music Publishing

Those speedy summer weekend runs that saw me racing up to Kent toward Lorraine's Lake Carmel getaway would typically find me behind the wheel with the Porsche's cassette player blasting out the latest Glen Campbell or Kris Kristofferson hit—with me singing along for all I was worth. But not today. Today the onboard stereo system was turned off and I was rehearsing. As the miles flew by, I was going over each word I planned to say to Lorraine just as if I were practicing a summation before a jury. I needed to get it right.

One look at Lorraine upon stepping inside the house and I knew that this was not going to be easy. It was a beautiful sunny afternoon and she was every bit as radiant as the weather outdoors. Freshly showered, tastefully made up and coiffed, dressed in a casual comfortable "something" she had just slipped into, Lorraine looked inviting and marvelous. Nevertheless, and despite my urge to embrace her, and then some, I stuck to my guns and started my little speech.

"I told you at the beginning that I was no longer in love with my wife," I began. "That was true then and it's even more true now."

She sat down and looked at me impassively.

"But here's the thing. I do love my kids and they need me to be their father. You know what it's like at the office. I'm tied up with cases all day and at justice court at night. The only time I have to spend with Mitch and Jay is on weekends. I just got through telling them some lie about having to attend a conference in Yonkers, so I could slip away to see you. All the deception, lying to my kids, it's tearing my heart in two."

I took a deep breath and said somberly, "We've got to break this off...now."

I was expecting an emotional reaction. What I got was something else.

Not a tear. No angry words of recrimination.

Lorraine calmly stood up and said with an air of resigned finality, "Ok. I understand. So long," as she opened the door for me leave. There was a mixture of sadness and strength in her demeanor that day that I would not encounter again till many years later when I would deliver much worse news to my darling Lorraine.

That separation lasted a full week, until I found I could not stand another moment of being without her. I had to go where my heart was taking me, regardless of the pain that it would certainly cause to my family. This convinced us both that what I had with Lorraine was real and deep-rooted, not some casual fling or mere liaison. Once I understood this, I knew what I had to do.

I informed Fredda and the boys that I had decided to buy a small house near my office and that I would be living there from now on. I explained that the boys could spend the weekends with me there whenever they wanted to. Of course, on most occasions when they were with me on weekends, so was Lorraine, and this made things a bit awkward. Actually, the boys loved Lorraine, which didn't surprise me. Everyone loved Lorraine and if anyone referred to her as a home wrecker, that insult never reached my ears.

My old friend, Ray Kolkmann (more about him later), still says to this day, "The only reason a miserable guy like you has any friends at all is because of Lorraine."

He's probably right. The reason is that being able to enjoy my relationship with this wonderful woman openly brought great joy into my life. I became a genuinely happier person. People prefer to be friends with happy people—and not people constantly put out by having to hide their secrets from the world. I can't be fully objective about it, but looking back, I feel that Lorraine's positive goodness had a profound impact on my character and my outlook on the world. To put it simply, I feel that she made me a better person.

I was struck by the fact that Lorraine did not have a mean bone in her body. She never seemed to suffer from any illnesses and she had an abundant supply of smiles that she bestowed on one and all. Just one of those smiles could light up a room on the darkest night of the year. I found it astonishing how, whenever we found ourselves in public at a place with children present, the kids would always gravitate toward Lorraine and she would invariably respond to them in a loving and caring fashion. My Mitchell and Jason were no exception. This, despite the fact that, by this point, they were old enough to understand that this was the woman for whom their father had left their mother. The funny thing was that whenever Lorraine and I broached the subject, she would claim she was not interested in having any children of her own. Perhaps she was simply saying what she thought I wanted to hear.

I learned later that her high school boyfriend, Sharon Gorman's brother, Bryan, had gotten Lorraine pregnant when she was just seventeen. The pregnancy was terminated and this fact may have contributed to her antipathy toward having children.

As we prepared for divorce, Fredda and I went through the typical allocation of the financial assets of our marital estate, as well as the custody of our two minor children. We both retained independent counsel to represent us in the settlement negotiations and eventually, in court. I agreed to waive my portion of the equity in our home in Shenorock and have it titled solely to Fredda. I wasn't obstinate about the financial allocation and went along with most of Fredda's demands. My only unwavering position was in regard to child custody. I insisted that it be joint and the court granted it as such. I guess it would be considered a relatively agreeable divorce, as these things go. I agreed to give her all my assets, pay her alimony and child support and she agreed to take it.

Soon afterward, Fredda started dating and connected with a boyfriend who, in short order, moved in with her and the kids. When that fizzled, she became friendly with another guy. This one was a lawyer who she eventually wound up marrying.

Evidently, "boyfriend number two" had been shown our divorce decree and advised Fredda that the terms were categorically unfair to her. Under his counsel, she petitioned the court with a motion to increase the amount of child support I was required to pay. My reaction

was that this claim was an absurd play for more pay with no foundation in reality. My lawyer convinced me that the nuisance value of
fighting her claim outweighed any benefits I might enjoy in the unlikely event that I was successful. In other words, he said I should
agree to pay her more, and so I did. By doing so, I was finally rid of
her...or so I thought.

Lorraine and I wanted to live together, but we needed a bigger
place where the boys could feel comfortable whenever I had custody.
We found a place on Gipsy Trail Road in an idyllic area of Kent. The
home overlooked Little Buck Mountain Pond and was once part of
the Vanderbilt estate. Even though home mortgage rates were north
of 11% that year, Lorraine and I could not resist. We learned that the
home was originally built for the Vanderbilt family servants. It sat on
a verdant nine-acre plot at the base of a hill and overlooked the
scenic pond. The main residence and an ornate guest house were located across the road and were both on the market—at prices well
beyond our budget.

As things began to settle down, I saw myself becoming involved
in some rather bizarre legal cases. I was retained by a lady who sustained an injury after she had agreed to assist a dog breeder in mating
two good-sized German Shepherds. As my client was helping the
stud mount the dam, the stud turned and bit her viciously. She was
seeking to recover damages from the dog's owner. The owner
claimed that the dog was provoked because my client had for no reason grabbed the stud by its testicles and was therefore guilty of contributory negligence.

I did my homework and "boned" up on proper canine mating procedures. I learned that when a stud mounts a dam, his penis enters the vulva and two glands on either side of the shaft begin to swell. This generates a clamping response from the dam that results in what is called a "tie." Among German Shepherds, a tie typically lasts from fifteen to thirty minutes. The two dogs may remain linked together for some time after the sex act has been completed. Often dogs will become anxious when they discover they are unable to unlink and begin to whine, growl and snarl. Breeders are advised not to try to separate the dogs during this period and permit them to disengage naturally when the swelling has subsided and the penis is able to slip loose on its own. It turns out that the worst thing you can do is to forcefully remove the penis from the vulva, which will undoubtedly infuriate the dog even more and cause it to become defensive and vicious. Upon questioning, my client admitted to me that this is exactly what she was trying to do at the time she began tugging on the doggie "nuggets."

I asked her how many canine breedings she had helped with before this one. None, she answered. This was her "virginal" experience.

"Did the dog's owner provide you with any training or instructions about what you should or should not do during the mating?"

"No," came the reply. "All I was told was to hold them together till the stud climaxed and then help pull them apart so we could get on to the next pair."

I was prepared to make the case that, by instructing a novice to engage in hazardous and improper breeding procedures, it was the dog owner who compounded her negligence and was fully responsible for the injuries sustained by my client. Unfortunately, the judge, clearly not a dog lover, found our position groundless and dismissed the case before it could go to a jury. I was madder than the proverbial "junkyard dog" and immediately appealed the decision. The appellate court reversed the lower court's dismissal and ordered the case to be retried. Shortly thereafter, the Case of the "Ballsy Breeder" was settled out of court with my client receiving an equitable cash settlement.

This case harkened back to another one from a number of years earlier that did not turn out so well. I was then representing a plaintiff in Dutchess County who claimed she had been kicked in the head and had sustained severe injuries as she was assisting a breeder mate two prize racehorses. She had been guiding the stallion from the back when it suddenly kicked backwards, striking her head and knocking her to the ground.

I was beginning to get the picture that in these parts, breeding animals was a truly hazardous occupation. I felt our case was strengthened when I pointed out that the defendant had failed provide my client with a helmet or any sort of protective gear, even though she had constructive knowledge that horses kick and that people assisting with mating often get injured. Once again, the case was dismissed by the judge who felt my line of reasoning was spurious and that my client should have been aware of the risks before agreeing to participate. He did not believe that the horse owner held any obligation to provide helmets or protective gear to those who assisted with the mating.

Naturally, I was bummed out by the judge's decision and did not feel I had a strong enough case to mount an appeal. Driving back dejectedly from the Dutchess County Courthouse to my office in Carmel, I passed a new Porsche dealership that had recently popped up along Route 9 near Poughkeepsie. I decided to pull in and have a look-see. Pretty soon I concluded that the best way to overcome my depression about the horse breeding case and to best regain my equine equilibrium…was to get my hands on *some more horsepower!* I took a silver 25th Anniversary Special Edition 911S out for test drive and fell in love. Like Dean Martin used to sing, "Ain't that a kick in the head?"

When I got back, I closed the deal and purchased the 911S (with the 2.7 liter engine) for the princely sum of $14,000. Howard drove me back to the dealer the next day to pick it up. It was this baby that propelled me up and down the highway from Shenorock to Kent while I was seeing Lorraine on the sly.

There's one more case I'd like to share at this point, in order to complete this trio of tales of zoological litigation. Although I've related a canine case and an equine case, I am saddened to report that I have never had a feline case. It's a pity, because that would have afforded me ample opportunity to tell my "What has two legs and likes to fuck cats?" joke.

Nope, no felines. But I did have one unforgettable simian case. I mentioned earlier that when I was a boy, I greatly admired Clarence Darrow and would dream about someday appearing in my own version of his famous Monkey Trial case. I never could have imagined, however, that when I did, it would happen as follows:

FULL CIRCLE

It all began when I received a phone call from Tom Burke at Great Atlantic Insurance. I had been defending the insurer in lawsuit actions brought against their customers and that's what he had for me today.

"Our customer is an entertainer," Tom began. "He's being sued by an older, well-to-do Jewish lady from Westchester County who claims that our guy was somehow the cause of her having fallen down at her grandson's Bar Mitzvah party and broken her hip, requiring a prosthetic. Our guy was performing at the party and he's got professional liability coverage with us. The company and the entertainer were both named in the complaint." I agreed to meet the entertainer.

"I'll send him and his caregiver, Lee, over to your office this afternoon," Ed confirmed.

"*Hmmm,*" I thought to myself. "*Caregiver, hunh? Must be an old-timer.*" I instructed my secretary to be on the lookout for two new faces and to let me know when they arrived. I didn't have to wait long.

"There's a Mr. Ecuyer and his friend here to see you, Mr. Fixler," a few hours later, she alerted me. I figured Ecuyer was the entertainer and his friend was the caregiver. I told my secretary to send them to the conference room and I'd be there in a minute.

To say I was dumbstruck when I got my first glimpse at my new client would be a major understatement. As I entered our conference room, he was speeding at breakneck speed around the table...on roller skates! He was about 4 ft. tall wearing a large diaper and a sweatshirt with the word "ZIP" emblazoned across the chest. I no-

193

ticed he was chomping on a half-smoked cigar as he whizzed by for the fourth time. Oh. Did I forget to mention that he was a chimpanzee?

"Say 'Hello' to Mr. Fixler, Zippy," said a voice rather nonchalantly. It was the tall man seated at one end of the conference table going through a sheaf of papers. He stood and introduced himself as Lee Ecuyer and explained that he was Zippy's trainer. They had traveled from Freeport, Long Island to seek legal help. I told him that I would try, but first I needed to get all the facts. As Zippy climbed onto Lee's lap and listened intently, the trainer laid out the whole tragic tale.

"I started training chimpanzees in 1952 back in Freeport," Lee began. "This chimp is my third Zippy. Before a chimp can become Zippy and put on the trademark ZIP sweatshirt, I train him to become a world-class entertainer. He learns how to roller skate, dance, ride a bike, juggle and more. When he gets too old to perform, I donate him to a zoo and bring in a new Zippy."

I took notes and nodded as Lee continued.

"Back in the 1950's and 60's, Zippy made quite a name for himself, appearing on dozens of TV shows that aired out of New York. He was a frequent guest on Ed Sullivan's *Toast of the Town* variety show. He also appeared in a famous episode of the *The Phil Silvers Show,* where he played the part of Harry Speakup, the chimp who got drafted into the US Army. He made countless appearances on talk shows hosted by Jack Paar, Arthur Godfrey, Mike Douglas and others. That's not to mention all those kiddie shows like *Captain Kangaroo* and *Howdy Doody.* Zippy was considered the most popular chimp in America, next to J. Fred Muggs. He's even been in a couple of movies and is a card-carrying member of Actor's Equity and the Screen Actors' Guild." Lee swelled with pride at this last bit before continuing.

"Well, by the end of the 60's, things started to dry up on TV as the industry moved out to California. I wasn't about to pull up stakes and relocate, so Zippy started doing local gigs at birthday parties, supermarket openings and the like."

At this Zippy blew out a mighty puff of blue smoke from his cigar.

"Why don't you tell me what happened at the Bar Mitzvah?" I suggested.

"Glad to. It was a regular Bar Mitzvah party at a hotel in Riverdale on a Saturday night. I dressed Zippy in a little skullcap and Jewish prayer shawl. When the time came, I stepped to the deejay's microphone and introduced Zippy who ran into the hall on cue and started roller skating around the dance floor just like he had been taught. The kids were delighted, as they always are, and a whole mob of them began chasing Zippy around the room. Well, the kids got a little rambunctious and started acting wild. In all the commotion, a lady got knocked down to the floor. I learned later on that she was the grandmother of the Bar Mitzvah boy and that she had to go to the hospital with a broken hip."

Lee paused for second and then resumed.

"At that point, I stepped in and stopped Zippy and tried to get the kids calmed down. I felt real bad about what happened to his grandmother but, I swear, Mr. Fixler, it wasn't Zippy's fault. He was doing everything he was supposed to be doing. Doing exactly what he was getting paid to be doing. Zippy's been doing this same routine at parties like this for years and no one has ever been injured. If anyone's to blame for the old lady getting hurt, it's the parents of those spoiled kids who never taught them proper manners or how to behave in public."

I could tell that Lee was getting emotional and urged him to have a drink of water.

"It sounds to me like the grandmother didn't want to sue the truly responsible parties—the hosts—because they were her own son and daughter-in-law," I opined. "So, instead, she went after you because she probably learned that you carry liability insurance and she figured she could get a juicy settlement."

"Settlement?" Lee exclaimed. "I don't want to give her a nickel, the old shrew. We're not afraid to stand up to her and tell her we're ready to go to court and tell our story. We've been in court before. A comedian named Harvey Stone wanted top billing over Zippy at the Boulevard Nightclub in Rego Park, New York, and the case went to arbitration." I agreed that if we went to court with this case, we would win because the plaintiff's case was very weak.

The grandmother plaintiff, I soon learned, had contacted her nephew, who was a well-known New York personal injury attorney at a Manhattan law firm called Schneider, Kleinick and Weitz. Harvey Weitz was, at that point, the nation's leading exponent in the areas of Personal Injury, Medical Malpractice and Accident Injury representation. He was a best-selling author and a full-time law professor at Brooklyn Law School. Harvey had served as president of the New York State Trial Lawyers Association, as a Dean of the New

York State Trial Lawyers Institute, national secretary of the Association of Trial Lawyers of America, and president of the New York State Chapter of the American Board of Trial Advocates. He was a select member of the Inner Circle of Advocates, an organization of the top 100 lawyers in the country. Now, to cap his illustrious career, he was going after this poor chimp.

Lee, the trainer, kept asking me why Zippy was being sued since he wasn't the responsible party. I couldn't provide a decent answer, so I decided to do the only thing that made any sense in all this monkey business, and that was sue the Bar Mitzvah boy's parents in a third-party action. A third-party action is a legal procedure usually carried out by the defendant in a lawsuit pending before the court, to bring in a third party—in addition to the plaintiff and the defendant—to share all or part of the liability in question.

Doing this sent a clear message to Harvey Weitz that even a monkey could see Zippy was not the culpable party in this action and with the parents now brought into the case, I would be able to quickly establish the parties truly and legally responsible for the plaintiff's injuries; to wit, her own children.

It didn't take long for things to start popping. I received a desperate phone call from a distraught Harvey Weitz the day after the filing of the third-party action.

"Jesus, Ell," he pleaded. "You've got to get me out of this case. If I lose it, it will make a monkey out of me. I only took it in the first place as a favor to my aunt. We all know we can't build any type of solid case against the chimp. So just get me something—anything from the insurance company—and we'll accept it and this will all go away." This clearly gave off the smell of victory, but I played it coy.

"I don't know, Harvey," I chided him. "My client is rarin' to go to court. I'd have to discuss any sort of settlement with Zippy..."

"W-w-with the monkey?!" sputtered Harvey. "You consult with the monkey?"

"He's a chimpanzee, Harvey. A highly intelligent and very talented chimpanzee. And I don't make a move, he don't say it's okay."

"Well, I'll be a monkey's uncle," Harvey said at last.

Actually, I had called Tom Burke, the adjuster at Great Atlantic and explained the situation.

"Tom, I just talked to the plaintiff's attorney and he acknowledges they have a very weak case and would more than likely lose if it got to court. He wants to avoid the embarrassment and get the thing settled quickly, but he needs something, some token, to present to his client. I think you should consider it because to take this case to court —even if you win the case—will cost you around ten grand. Do you have any idea what it costs to depose a chimpanzee?"

"Could we settle for $5,000?"

"Make it $10,000 in 'fuck-you go-away' money and this whole thing disappears faster than a fart in a fan factory."

"Deal!" said Ed, and that was that.

I never saw Zippy again, although I do think about him every time a Planet of the Apes movie comes on TV.

Although we did, from time to time, handle unlikely cases on behalf of unusual clients like Zippy, the bread and butter of our personal injury business stemmed from standard supermarket "slip and fall cases." Unlike some firms that insist on being either fish or fowl, we represented both plaintiffs and defendants with equal vigor and dedication.

One such case was our representation of a Joan Neumann who claimed she had slipped on dirty water in the canned vegetable aisle of a Grand Union supermarket. When the case came up for trial, I was tied up on another case and unavailable. I had filed for an adjournment but was denied by the judge. I asked Howard to appear in court and he did so. To be successful in a slip and fall case against a retailer, the plaintiff bears the burden of proof. It must show that the store had actual or constructive notice of the existence of the defective condition that caused the fall—and sufficient opportunity to fix it. Constructive knowledge means that even if the store's management wasn't actually aware of the problem, they should have been.

During a preliminary hearing, we argued that since the water was dirty, that fact indicated it had been left standing for some time. If there was enough time for it to have become dirty, there was sufficient time for the store's management to have cleaned it up. Howard was unable to convince the judge of this logic, however, and the case was dismissed before it was permitted to go before a jury. The good news was that Howard and the plaintiff, Joan Neumann, became an item and, several years later, the two were married.

We appealed the case and successfully got the dismissal reversed. I now had an opportunity at the retrial to plead my "dirty water" theory before a jury. We won the case and the jury rendered a substantial verdict in favor of the plaintiff. There was a bittersweet downside to

199

this victory, however. My "dirty water" argument became well-known in the trial attorney community and I was forced to face it repeatedly in my future work on behalf of supermarket clients I defended over the years. I don't know if you call this being forced to eat my own dog food or being hoisted on my own petard, but I didn't like it one bit, because it was a compelling way to convince a jury of the supermarket's negligence and I had a hard time overcoming it whenever I was forced to do so.

It was about this time that I began attending services at Temple Beth Shalom, a Conservative synagogue in Mahopac. Lorraine was developing an interest in Judaism as a means of getting closer to me. While Conservative Judaism had not dispensed with as much traditional Jewish ritual as Reform Judaism, it was still far removed from the Orthodox practices with which I had grown up. Men and women were seated together in the sanctuary, for example, and much of the service was conducted in English instead of Hebrew. These things helped to make Judaism more understandable and accessible by Lorraine who had been raised by parents who belonged to the Church of England.

With zero prompting from me, Lorraine made the unilateral decision to convert to Judaism. Interestingly she opted to study under an Orthodox Rabbi and would travel to Brooklyn several times each week for her lessons. I think she found something she had been seeking and of value in the ancient traditions and rituals.

My mother would frequently fly in from Buffalo to visit us, usually *shlepping* two suitcases filled with enough homemade goodies to open a Hungarian *tzukrazda* (pastry shop). The subject of Lorraine being a *shiksa* was never brought up between bites of the delicious *Dobos torte* and *palacsinta*. My mother was not unhappy about Fredda and me splitting up. In fact, she loved Lorraine, just like everyone else did. Nevertheless, I'm sure that Lorraine not being Jewish weighed on her mind. I don't believe that Lorraine became Jewish because of this consideration, but it may have been a factor.

Lorraine officially became a Jewess after undergoing a ritual bath in a Mikvah (a pool of water used for immersion) and then appearing before a tribunal of three rabbis known as a Bet Din. By coincidence, Lorraine's conversion to Judaism became official on the same day, May 12, 1980, that we were to attend the opening of a Broadway production that Howard and I had invested in.

The one-woman show was called *"Lena Horne; the Lady and Her Music"* and it featured the legendary singer recounting her life's frequent run-ins with racism between renditions of the many songs, such as *"Stormy Weather"* that she had popularized. The show was a smash hit with the critics and ran 333 performances, garnering a long string of awards including a Best Musical Grammy for musical director, Quincy Jones.

The Nederlander Theater on 41st Street is usually dark on Mondays, but on this Monday it opened its doors for the show's premier performance before a select audience of Broadway critics, members of Lena Horne's family, and investors like us. After the stellar performance, Lorraine and I left the theater and headed for the lavish gala opening-night party. She stopped me for a moment and shared the following:

"You know, Elliot. Now that I'm Jewish, It feels different when Lena Horne was talking about how she was discriminated against because of her race. It's hard to explain, but it somehow touched my heart."

I had not previously informed my mother that Lorraine was studying to become a convert, but, upon hearing these words, I felt I had to share the news with her. I rushed to the nearest pay phone and right there on the Great White Way, I called my Mama Rose. The excitement of learning that our show was going to be a hit coupled with my happiness over Lorraine's conversion were evident in my voice.

"Mom, I've got two things to tell you," I blurted. "One, our Lena Horne show is going to be the biggest hit on Broadway, and two, Lorraine is now officially *halachicly* Jewish."

"Oy, Elly," she responded. "You sound so happy. I'll be there on Thursday so you two can get married."

"Mom," I said. "Lorraine and I never discussed marriage. I don't think that marrying me was the reason she became Jewish."

But to be fair, I did recall that Lorraine and I had never discussed my divorcing Fredda either, but that's what I did. Lorraine simply didn't feel like exerting any sort of pressure. After the conversion, we did start talking about marriage. I'll tell you where those discussions led in a few more pages. But first, I'd like to share some memories from this period involving my friend, Stuart Myers.

Even though I had first met Stuart through Fredda and her friendship with Stuart's sister-in-law, Sharon Simon, Stuart and I remained friends and colleagues long after my marriage to Fredda ended. The relationship with Stuart likewise included Lorraine and Stuart's wife,

Nancy. We socialized frequently and began going on dream vacations with Stu and Nancy. Of these, the greatest ones saw the four of us aboard a rented sailboat and plying the waters of the Bahamas and the Caribbean. I have nothing but the most magnificent memories of those cruises. As we sailed into the British Virgin Islands, I did as I would do most mornings in the islands: put on my running shoes while on the boat and then go for a ten-mile run through whatever island at which we were moored. On this particular day, it was the tropical paradise known as "Tortola."

As the sun emerged on a glorious Tortola morning, I meandered along a trail that led to the top of the island's central volcanic peak, Mount Sage. I recall having to run around the herds of goats that shared the trail with me along my route. Once I reached the pinnacle, I took in the breathtaking panoramic view of the Caribbean in all directions as well as the nearby Little Sisters Islands and the U.S. Virgin Islands in the far distance.

I adored island-hopping the Caribbean in our trusty windjammer, often having lunch on one island and dinner on another. One dinner that stands out in my memory took place at a RockResort called Caneel Bay on St. John in the U.S. Virgin Islands. The RockResort brand was created in 1956 by Laurance Rockefeller, a world-renowned conservationist committed to developing luxury resorts in spectacular natural environments. Our dinner was indeed spectacular, but just as it was served, our enjoyment was sullied by a fellow at the next table. He had pulled out a massive Cuban cigar and proceeded to fire it up. I have a thing about second-hand smoke and I politely and discretely asked the gentleman if he would mind smoking his cheroot elsewhere or waiting until we finished our meal. He ignored my request and not only kept puffing away, but now he appeared to be intentionally directing the smoke toward our table. I went into a slow burn myself as I folded my glasses and placed them into my pocket and then returned to Mr. Chimney's table.

"Tell me, something, sir," I asked in a calm and measured tone of voice. "Were you born an asshole or did you receive some type of special training?"

This seemed like a reasonable question to me. He stared at me and rose to get up. I thought he might be planning to take a swing at me which I welcomed, since it would afford me with an opportunity to shove that cigar into his face and maintain that I was acting in self-defense. He brought himself up to his full height and raised his right hand. But instead of punching me with it, he used it to flag down a passing waiter.

When the waiter arrived, the natural-born asshole said: "Tell the manager that this man has insulted my wife."

His wife?! This asshole couldn't even get my insult right. Nevertheless, our party was unceremoniously shown the door. Looking back, I probably should have knocked the guy's lights out and to hell with the self-defense defense.

In addition to sailing, Stuart and I used to love playing basketball together. One time, he jumped to make a rebound and came down hard on my foot. But instead of me, it was Stuart who suffered the injury. He had torn his ACL (anterior cruciate ligament that serves to stabilize the knee joint), requiring surgery to repair it. This happened in the days before laparoscopic surgery and he wound up with an angry scar.

Stuart and I also played a lot of racquetball. I recall how he used the racquetball experience to solidify his relationships with a group of four lower Manhattan insurance brokers. These relationships brought him insurance company clients interested in his company's claims adjustment services. I was familiar with this since he would often refer cases to me from clients with whom he had connected in this way. One of the broker quartet had a daughter who was a freshly minted lawyer looking for work, and so I hired her. Unfortunately, her father's insurance brokerage was at some point investigated by the FBI for irregularities in their mishandling of funds intended to go to the insurance carriers they represented. The head of the company was jailed and one of his partners committed suicide when the agency went belly up.

Over the ensuing years, Stuart continued to send me more and more cases. Many of them were tried in the various boroughs of New York City. I was grateful and worked hard to deliver my best work to those clients he sent my way. One day, Stuart asked if I would be interested in getting more NYC work from him. My answer was an enthusiastic "yes." He said he could make that happen, but it would involve my putting is sister, Zena, on our payroll to operate a remote office of our practice in Manhattan. I checked with Howard, and while he had no interest in trying cases in New York, he did not object to my setting up an office to do so. I found a small place and brought Zena on board to head our New York City office. She was a bright and capable attorney and was soon smoothly running our NYC operation. I would travel there several times each week to meet clients, and if I was appearing at trial, I would stay overnight in the city. I eventually wound up renting a small apartment near the office.

One day in the late 1970s, Stuart approached me and pointed out an ad in the Wall Street Journal promoting the sale of an entire island. The ad said that it was located in Long Island Sound off the coast of Connecticut at Bradford, a ten-minute drive north of New Haven.

When Stuart asked if I was interested, I said, "Sure!"

"Wow," I thought to myself as the daydreams came into focus. *"A private island all to ourselves."*

When we inquired, we found we were too late and the island had been taken off the market. We left our names and the broker agreed to get in touch if it ever became available again.

It did.

About a year later. We learned that the property was the furthest offshore island of the Thimble chain, made up of exposed bedrock with a thin layer of drift. The official name was Johnson Island. It had also been known as Prudden Island and Little Stooping Bush, but everyone called it Mother-in-Law Island. The reason for the Mother-in-Law moniker, according to legend, was that a young couple had once gotten married on nearby Money Island and then rowed to what was to become Johnson Island in order to spend their honeymoon camping in a tent. The young bride's mother decided to follow the couple to the island in her own rowboat. That night, the couple snuck off the island taking both rowboats with them back to Money Island, leaving the mother-in-law stranded for three days before she could be rescued. Nosy mothers-in-law, be forewarned.

The entire area of the island was only one-half acre at low tide and a quarter of an acre at high tide. Its only improvement was a ramshackle old house. At low tide we were able to walk past a large clam bed to a nearby reef named after the island's namesake and owner, Admiral Maurice Bernay Johnson. We met the irascible Admiral Johnson and found him to be a striking and very colorful figure. He was in his early 90s and had recently broken his leg while skydiving. Did you catch that? Recently!

Admiral Johnson had owned the island for decades and evidently had enough clout to have the spot named after him on all the official US Navy nautical charts. But, because of his leg injury, he found that hobbling around the island had become too difficult and reluctantly had decided to give up ownership. He said that he had tried renting it to his nephew for a year who had said he would buy it at the end of the lease term.

"Do you believe that little shithead wanted me to give him a 30-year mortgage on the place?" the Admiral confided. "No way, José. Cash on the barrelhead."

So, the island went back on the market and Stuart and I snatched it up for $40,000 each. Now came the big question:

What in the hell are we going to do with an island?!

The derelict solitary house had no electricity or plumbing. It did have a phone line, and that was it. The only way to access the island was by private boat. There was also a Thimbles Island Tours ferry boat that could take visitors back and forth from the mainland.

I owned a boat that I had been using for day trips to Lake Candlewood that I moved over to the Thimbles and Stuart did the same. We ran into a fellow from the Thimbles who owned a barge and agreed to help us deliver construction material out to our island to rebuild the house and construct a dock. He said he would also help us figure out a way to bring water as well as electric and gas service to the house.

It was while we were busy building up our island, that Lorraine and I decided we wanted to build something, too: our future together. We talked things over and, with a little push from my Mama Rose, decided that we would get married. When I asked her about it, Lorraine assured me that "I don't need no stinkin' engagement ring." I would have gladly given her one, and given her the world, too, if I could.

As we began making the wedding arrangements, we thought it would be a neat and unique idea if we held the wedding on our island. After all, Lorraine's future mother-in-law had prompted us toward matrimony, so what better place to do the deed than on Mother-in-Law Island? Stuart and Nancy, the island's co-owners, loved the idea.

The first order of business was to get that eyesore of a house brought up to snuff. This wasn't going to be easy, since, off the bat, it was covered with a fine patina of pigeon shit. Second of all, there was no water to use for cleaning. We wound up building a cistern to collect rainwater just so we could flush the toilets. This meant strict water conservation as we all worked on the massive clean-up project. Someone clever posted a sign on all the bathroom doors that read:

If it's yellow, let it mellow.

If it's brown, flush it down.

If it's red, call your proctologist.

It's funny, because this experience got me used to finding alternative places to pee and, to this day, I have studiously avoided using toilets for this very purpose, if possible. There's always a nearby tree on a golf course and when I walk my dog at night, whither he goest, I goest.

Fortunately, both Stuart and I had good friends who were willing to pitch in and help us with the Island upgrade project. I brought in my friends Billy Kemp, Bobby Gannon and his father, Dick, mentioned in an earlier chapter. They could literally do anything that needed to be done, including putting a new roof on the house. Stuart brought in a few of his college buddies to help us, Phil Rachelson and Larry Koffer. I'm sure you can guess as to what my contribution was to the project. As someone who had worked as an apprentice professional painter for my stepfather when in my teens, I was well-qualified to carry out all the interior and exterior painting. We also built a small shed to house an electric generator and I painted it to match the decor of the house. Jay Maxwell's oldest son, Jay Jr., a virtual mountain of a man, brought in the generator and successfully hooked it up.

Another of my friends whom I had invited to work on the island was David Kellogg, who owned the Tom Kat Sporting Goods Store in Mahopac, where I would buy my ski gear. David used that generator shed to generate some real excitement of his own.

Each day the Thimble Islands Tour boat—actually an old painted ferryboat—would cruise by our island loaded with rubbernecking tourists invading our sweet island isolation. And each day the captain would use his megaphone to repeat the same story about how Mother-In-Law Island got its name. After a few days of this, David had had enough. He climbed up on the roof of the shed, and just as all the passengers were being directed to look toward our island, David turned around, "dropped trou" and mooned the stunned sightseers who responded with cheers and a round of applause. The tour boat didn't come around for a while after that.

We spent the summer of 1981 busy as beavers as we scurried to get everything on the island finished in time for our September wedding celebration. As the work neared completion, we began to enjoy the island more and more. We had renovated a huge covered outdoor deck along the south side of the house where we could sit and enjoy a magnificent view of Long Island Sound. There was only water as far as the eye could see on this windward side of the island. Sitting on the porch, among the yoga mats, it felt as though you were on the deck of a ship, since the ground was not visible at all. The ocean breezes would serve as natural air conditioning on hot humid days. If you walked around to the island's lee side, the air was at least 15 degrees warmer. We also constructed a big new deck on the north side facing Money Island. From this deck you could see the dock we had built along the north shore. We had to make it a floating one since there was a seven-foot drop between high and low tide each day.

As the July Fourth holiday approached, I was tied up with a criminal case in Westchester County. My client was charged with stealing a large backhoe and I managed to deliver a favorable verdict. The client decided to celebrate the victory by sailing his boat from Yonkers to come visit us on the island. When he showed up, he presented our crew with a mountain of freshly caught lobster. We figured he had no doubt stopped to rob every lobster pot in Long Island Sound. That bit of larceny did not stop anyone from enjoying the subsequent lobster feast that day. But evidently, our guest's illegal lobster-snatching had angered the sea gods.

We had no room on the island to properly house our guest and his buddies overnight, so they anchored for the night in the water about fifty feet off the north side of the island. As twilight faded, the dusky sky filled with malevolent rain clouds. That night saw the worst thunderstorm ever experienced during our ownership of the island. The twenty-foot waves lapping over us from the southwest engulfed our new porch and swept over our newly installed roof. It was a torrential tempest that had us fearing for our lives. When the dawn arrived and found us all safe and sound, we said good-bye to our guests who sailed off, never to return.

I'm pleased to report that with the hard work and help of a great number of our friends, we were successful in getting the property shipshape in time for our wedding, scheduled for September 13, 1980.

Elliot Fixler

Chapter Eleven

Upturns & Setbacks

"Life moves pretty fast. If you don't stop and look around every once in a while, you could miss it. "
—Ferris Bueller
Popular 1980s film character

The 1980s in America saw ladies wearing shoulder pads, kids dressed in acid-washed jeans, teens in neon spandex and leg warmers, and the rise of something called "Yuppies." But I was pretty much oblivious to these fashions and cultural trends as I continued to accelerate my personal life along with my legal practice. Lorraine and I were married a few weeks before the decade was kicked off with Ronald Reagan's election to the presidency. Within two years, the economy that had suffered under Jimmy Carter had turned around and America was becoming more prosperous and productive.

Lorraine and I were also quite productive during those years. We had produced two children which, considering Lorraine's original antipathy toward having kids, was something to write home about. Our house on Gipsy Trail Road, in the Town of Kent, was now filled with the pitter-patter of little feet, as well as the barking of big dogs. Professionally, my legal practice was growing by leaps and bounds. The office I had opened in Manhattan was bringing in a bunch of new business, plus I had a steady flow of cases coming in from ShopRite, a major grocery co-op chain based in New York and New

Jersey. We had to hire additional staff for both our NYC and our Carmel offices. Our footprint in New Jersey was also growing as we took on more and more cases from the Garden State. Howard had been elected to a judgeship in the Carmel Justice Court and he seemed to greatly enjoy the experience. It certainly enhanced the stature of our law firm and got me to thinking that perhaps I could do the same thing in the Town of Kent. Hmmm.

I became friendly with our neighbor to the south of our home on Gipsy Trail Road. Coincidentally, his name was also Elliot. Elliot Michael was, at that time, a recent graduate of Lehigh University. He and I had first met at the 5K and 10K area races I had been entering. I was far from an elite runner and competed only now and then, but I always enjoyed the challenge and the excellent workout such competitions would provide. I couldn't help but notice that these races were being regularly won by some slender, six-foot, curly headed guy. Someone told me that he lived in Kent and so I made a point of introducing myself to him. And when I did, I was surprised to learn that he was actually my next-door neighbor.

I learned that EM's father (I'll refer to Elliot as EM from now on to avoid confusion) had owned a trucking business prior to his recent untimely death. EM had no interest in running the business. He preferred to be running races. So, his mother and older brother stepped in. But, according to my conversations with EM as we ran together, they were not doing very well. Even though I was ten years older than EM, we would run together most mornings and weekends and I was actually able to keep up the pace. A pace I'm sure he slowed down for my benefit. EM had been a national class runner back in

214

college, which explained his uncanny ability to finish first in every area race he entered.

Although we did not do so together, EM and I both enjoyed trail biking on the challenging pathways that crisscrossed the Gipsy Trail property. I had the honor of owning one of the very first official "Mountain Bikes." It was notable because of its very light titanium frame and its extremely fat tires. The bike had been built by a fellow named Chris Chance and it was dubbed "Fat Chance." Today Fat Chance Bikes, the company, is located in Medford, Oregon and is considered the maker of the finest mountain bikes in America.

EM was casting about for some sort of career that would keep him from getting sucked into the family trucking business. He decided he would leverage his love of running by running a shoe store that sold running shoes. Like many would-be entrepreneurs, EM found that purchasing a franchise was the easiest and quickest way to get established. He connected with a company called The Athletic Attic and signed a franchise agreement. The Athletic Attic was founded in 1973 by track and field athlete and Olympic coach, Jimmy Carnes. It was one of the first sports equipment chain stores and specialized in running shoes. At the peak of the 1980s running craze, Athletic Attic had more than 165 stores around the world. In 1997, the company was acquired by another chain called Just For Feet, that collapsed in bankruptcy only two years later.

Even though the parent company was supposed to take care of everything for the franchisee, EM was still required to secure the store's premises. He found a suitable storefront in a strip center along a main thoroughfare in Bethel, Connecticut, and decided he would be better off buying the building than renting the space. He came to me and asked if I would lend him $10,000 for the down payment. I readily agreed.

EM bought the building and opened one of the first running shoe stores in the area. After about a year, he tired of the routine and turned the operation over to his wife, Jan. Continuing with his foot fetish, EM decided to pursue his true life's dream. He packed up and moved to Chicago to become a podiatrist. Once he received his degree, he gave up the shoe store entirely and moved to Portland, Oregon where he opened a podiatry practice. EM has held on to the building in Connecticut to this day and leases it out to various commercial tenants. I'm happy to say he repaid my $10,000 loan promptly and he and I have remained friends to this day.

Another interesting neighbor was Tony Cazzari who lived across the street from our Gipsy Trail Road home. Tony held the post of Town of Kent Supervisor, which is something like the mayor. Once we got to know one another, Tony encouraged me to run for the position of Town Justice in the upcoming 1984 election. He was a Democrat and wanted me to run because he felt that my name would strengthen the ticket. "What the hell?" I figured. I decided to give it a shot.

I really did not have any party affiliation at that point. I was not a registered anything and since that unpleasant encounter with a Democratic candidate back in law school, I had consciously strived not to get involved in politics. I really had no partisan sentiments and took pride in viewing myself as an independent thinker. Now, here I was about to run for office as a Democrat. It turned out to be a bad choice. The county was almost exclusively populated with Republicans and it would have taken a very attractive and hard-working candidate to win their votes. Unfortunately, I had neither the time, the charisma, nor the stomach for the rigors of the campaign trail.

One incident stands out in my memory about that campaign. You may recall my hiring of a Mrs. Katz to take over the matrimonial cases in our practice. The incident in question is what prompted me to do so.

I found myself representing two male clients in divorce proceedings during the time I was conducting my election campaign. Interestingly, both men had wives who had cheated on them with a local tennis pro: the *same* tennis pro. Evidently, the guy had an amazing deep shot.

Both husbands were upset and deeply hurt at being betrayed by their respective wives. One of the two even wired his house with a network of surveillance cameras to keep an eye on his wayward wife while he was at work. While I represented both husbands, the two wives had each retained different attorneys. One was an aggressive sort while the other was a lying snake. Needless to say, the cases were egregious, acrimonious, and filled with animosity and belligerence. Not a fun experience, for sure. They say that hell hath no fury like a woman scorned. Well, I can attest that the fury of a man scorned is no less hellish.

One fine fall day I decided to take a break from this distasteful double divorce and go out and do some campaigning. I had gotten permission from my client, ShopRite Food Stores, to distribute promotional leaflets in the parking lot of one of their member stores.

The handout was a simple three-fold flyer that contained my photo and a list of my credentials. I was approached by a woman who asked for a brochure and, after perusing it, asked if she could have a few more. I complied and then another woman—a friend of the first —approached me and asked if she, too, could have several of the flyers. I gave her a few as well. Without uttering a word, and in full view of all the shoppers and gawkers who had gathered around, they proceeded to simultaneously tear up the brochures into little pieces that fell to the ground. They then ground their heels into the torn pieces and stomped on them vigorously with both feet. Mystified by this hate-filled behavior, I asked them calmly: "Excuse me, ladies, but do I know you?"

They introduced themselves as the wives of my two cuckolded clients, gave me the finger, and stormed off.

"Who needs this shit?" I thought to myself.

Nevertheless, I persevered and continued with the two cases until they were both settled, but I swore I would never again represent a party in a divorce proceeding. And it was that decision that led to my hiring Mrs. Katz, who got the job because she was not offended by my "What has two legs and likes to fuck cats?" joke during her job interview. By the way, that's the only joke I have ever remembered long enough to retell.

After that "ripping" experience in the ShopRite parking lot, I was more or less turned off to public glad-handing. My one sop to conventional political campaigning was ordering some garish purple and white T-shirts emblazoned with the catchy message: "Vote for Fixler." I managed to get two people to actually wear them. Both of them my children. Not too surprisingly, given my lack of ardor for being on the hustings, I lost the election. Thus ended my less-than-illustrious political career.

At this point, my neighbor, Tony Cazzari, asked if I would take the position of Kent Town Attorney. It sounded intriguing and I decided to come onboard. I was primarily charged with overseeing the town's legal activities. I attended zoning and planning meetings where I provided legal counsel for the boards. While I did an exemplary job, I found the experience of sitting through intractable public hearings to be intolerably mind-numbing. Dealing with an endless array of remonstrators, each with their personal agendas and petty grievances, was getting under my skin. I lasted two years before I simply couldn't take it anymore. If I had to listen to one more neighborhood tinhorn complain how a proposed new public lamppost would disrupt his goldfish's sleep patterns, I would be sorely tempted to shoot myself.

After my stint in the public service arena, I felt compelled to seek solace along the Vermont ski slopes. Howard and I had jointly purchased a lovely Swiss Chalet at Stratton Mountain and during the winter of 1986-87, we made good use of it. It was a gracious and spacious home that was able to sleep both of our extended families at the same time. Both of our kids, Mathew and Sarah, started skiing at age three and by this time my older boys, Mitchell and Jason, had grown into accomplished downhill skiers. And when springtime rolled around and the snow began to melt, it was back to our private hideaway on Mother-in-Law Island off the Connecticut coast.

Back at the office, Howard was devoted to his role as judge, a position that had earned him a good deal of respect in the community. He also kept busy with a steady stream of real estate transactions. On my end, I was mostly occupied with the growing number of cases emerging from our booming New York City office. My friend Stuart, who was responsible for our opening that office in the first place, continued to be a valued resource on behalf of our growing practice. He introduced me to one of his colleagues, Gene Fleisher, who, like Stuart, operated an insurance claims service called Claim and Risk Associates. Gene directed a steady flow of ShopRite Cooperative Food Store cases my way. Because of this growth spurt, we were required to increase both our staff as well as the office space at our NYC office. A good problem to have.

As mentioned, our office in Manhattan was being managed by Stuart's capable sister, Zena (Myers) Huerta. Zena was an exceptionally bright and capable lawyer, but a problem was emerging. Zena was married to a fellow named Carlos Huerta who had been raised as a Seventh Day Adventist but had converted to Judaism as an adult. Carlos, at six foot three and 250 pounds, presented an imposing figure; not your typical Orthodox Jew. But, as time went by, he became increasingly more *frum* (observant). It is often true that a convert becomes even more strictly kosher and observant than those who were born Jewish. In this case, Zena and Carlos were adhering to the Torah's first commandment "Be fruitful and multiply" by observing Orthodox Judaism's sanction against birth control. As a result, Zena was in a constant state of expectation and started giving birth to one child after another. This fact, in addition to a son from a prior marriage, was swelling the size of their household and perhaps generating more and more of a financial strain on Zena and Carlos.

At a certain point, it came to my attention that Zena was paying a significant number of her personal expenses through the firm. When I questioned her about this practice, her attitude was defiant. She was a partner, she maintained, and had the right to authorize expenses as she saw fit. I tried to explain to Zena that her position was untenable.

"You have a small minority interest in this firm," I pointed out patiently. "When you direct the firm to pay for your daycare, that means Howard and I are paying the biggest portion of that expense."

She remained adamant and insisted that she intended to continue to do as she pleased. Although it pained me to do so because of my cherished relationship with her brother, Stuart, I was left with no choice but to tell her we would have to part ways.

When I spoke to Stuart about this situation, he asked that I wait and the problem would resolve itself. He said that Zena and Carlos had purchased an apartment in Jerusalem and were planning to make "aliyah" (emigrate to Israel). I responded this way:

"Stu, I understand, but I am wondering why she failed to mention this fact when I spoke with her."

I went on.

"There was no remorse, no regret, and no recognition that she had been stealing from Howard and me. She told me, point blank, that she had no intention of stopping what she'd been doing."

Zena did not move to Israel right away. She next went to work for a competing law firm. She attempted to recruit our office manager,

Pat Gaynor, to join her at her new firm. But, to Pat's credit, she elected not to leave. Not surprisingly, the number of cases I was receiving from Stuart began to diminish appreciably. I don't think he was trying to punish me for firing his sister. It's just that the law firm she now worked for handled similar cases and Stu felt obligated to help Zena since she needed the business more than we did. Despite this, I was still galled to witness my closest friend directing business to my competitor. The impact of this loss was painful. York, Stuart's company, had evolved into our firm's biggest client and it was based on the expectation of continued business from York that we had expanded our staff and our overhead obligations. Meeting our operating expenses after Stuart staunched the flow of clients through our door became a real challenge.

So, do I regret having fired Zena? Should I have permitted her to continue embezzling in order to preserve the income flow represented by her brother? From a strictly business perspective, the answer is "yes." The amount of business we lost as a result of her departure was far greater than the unauthorized expenses she appropriated. To tolerate a partner who believes it is proper to steal from her other partners is a dangerous and unsustainable position. Nevertheless, I think I should have just let it go. I owed it to Stuart.

I did succeed in filling some of the void created by the fallout from Zena's departure by representing a new client. The client had been brought to me by a new insurance adjuster who had heard about my success in the Maguire malpractice case. I will discuss that case in a future chapter. I was contacted by the insurance adjuster who told me the following:

"This is an important case, Mr. Fixler," she explained. "It's coming up for trial in Supreme Court in New York County and we would prefer you to take it over. I just don't have much confidence in our attorney's ability and that's why I am turning to you."

There were two significant downsides to my taking the case. Number one, the time was short. It was scheduled for trial in a few weeks, hardly giving me sufficient opportunity to prepare. The case also involved significant exposure for the insurance company should I lose. Despite these reservations, I agreed to take the case.

The plaintiff was a 16-year-old girl named Cynthia Outlaw who lived in a Harlem housing complex owned by the Gold Dome Savings Bank. I was familiar with Gold Dome since their main office was headquartered in my hometown of Buffalo, New York. The bank had foreclosed on the property when the original owners defaulted on their mortgage loan. Since the foreclosure, the bank had been managing the property and served as its landlord.

The plaintiff, Cynthia Outlaw, alleged that one evening, as she was entering the building on her way home, she was brutally attacked and raped. The assailant was apprehended and received a sentence of probation. After consulting with an attorney at around the same time as seeing a doctor, Cynthia filed suit against the bank/ landlord on several grounds. She claimed that the landlord failed to properly maintain the premises and as a result, broken locks on the building's doors had been negligently left unfixed. Likewise, she claimed, the intercom used to admit entry into the building by its tenants was broken, thereby creating a security breach that facilitated entry by unauthorized parties. She also alleged that the landlord failed to provide adequate security personnel on the premises.

I didn't have much time, so I immediately reviewed the previous five years of maintenance records provided by the bank. I needed to learn if there had been a security guard on duty at the time of attack, and if not, why not? There had been an allegation made in the complaint that the landlord was intentionally failing to make needed repairs in order to induce tenants to move out. Once the units were vacated, the landlord, it was alleged, was planning to convert them to co-ops and sell them at a huge profit. This allegation also bore investigation.

After wading through twenty boxes of detailed maintenance records, I determined that both the door locks and the intercom system had been replaced the day before the incident. I also learned that there were normally two security guards on duty at all times, but on the day in question, one had called in sick leaving only one guard covering the premises. I discovered that the plaintiff lived with her parents who, like many of the other tenants, had refused to pay rent for an extended period, claiming that they were withholding payment due to the landlord's failure to properly maintain the building.

The plaintiff was claiming extensive damages due to the trauma she endured from the attack. I reviewed her psychiatric treatments as well as a medical report from a well-known neuropsychiatrist who had examined the plaintiff at the request of her attorney. Her attorney was planning to submit the report into evidence at trial and had listed the neuropsychiatrist as a plaintiff's witness to testify to the extent of the plaintiff's trauma and her prognosis for the future.

Cynthia's lawyer was a diminutive bespectacled fellow who walked with the assistance of a cane. Marty Lassoff was a Harvard Law School graduate whose stark courtroom behavior was remarkable. From the start of jury selection through the final verdict, Lassoff would sit impassively at the plaintiff's table with his hands folded in his lap. There was not a single document, not so much as a legal pad or a pencil, anywhere on the table.

Lassoff explained to the jury repeatedly that my client, Gold Dome Bank, had been negligent by failing to maintain their property in a reasonably safe condition and this negligence directly resulted in the suffering and damages sustained by Cynthia Outlaw. He pleaded the case using the argument that the building was left in disrepair intentionally to drive tenants out so a "co-op conversion" could take place that would deliver vast riches into the bank's coffers.

Lassoff's style was strictly textbook. He never altered his body language in response to what was taking place in court, always preferring to sit passively with his hands folded. He did not seem to be aware of the little subtleties that a lawyer needs to recognize in order to convince a jury of the merit of his case. For example, Lassoff did not seem to notice that a female juror sitting in the middle of the front row never took her eyes off me throughout the course of the trial. He did not see the almost imperceptible nod she offered in acknowledgement of each point I made when arguing the defendant's case.

On the other hand, I feel I perceived every nuance, every nonverbal cue issued by the jurors and adjusted my courtroom performance accordingly. And I managed to do this without the benefit of an Ivy League education. In other words, putting things poetically:

"Unlike Mr. Lassoff, I was working my ass off!"

Once both sides had rested and the jury was excused to deliberate the verdict, I approached Lassoff and inquired about his unusual demeanor.

"Do you really have a photographic memory?" I asked.

"Yes, I do," he replied dispassionately.

"Thought so," I replied.

I won't go into the details of my incisive cross examination of the plaintiff's key witness, Dr. Kaplan, the well-known neuropsychiatrist. Suffice it to say that by the time I concluded, the jury was well aware that he had been paid $5,000 by Lassoff to offer his testimony.

"And, one final question, Dr. Kaplan," I concluded.

"Had you gotten on the stand today and testified that in your medical opinion the plaintiff, Miss Outlaw, would likely suffer *no* lasting ill effects from her unfortunate experience, would you still have collected your $5,000 fee?"

He hemmed a bit and finally sputtered "I-I-I don't know."

But the jury knew, because I had delivered the message loud and clear that this guy was a medical whore and would say whatever he was paid to say.

I also strengthened the defendant's case by introducing the maintenance records that clearly established a steady pattern of ongoing upkeep of the property even though nearly half of the building's tenants were delinquent in their rent payments. I believe that the sight of me feverishly taking notes whenever a witness testified enhanced my credibility with the jurors when they compared my behavior with that of Lassoff, who sat impassively at his table staring into space.

My one vulnerable point was the matter of the sick security guard. The guard who was on duty that night testified that his partner had called in sick, was not on duty and that no one had sent a replacement to cover for him. There was no way I could get around the fact that the level of security at the building was lower than usual at the time of the incident. So, I decided to make the best of it.

"Let me ask you something, Officer Donahue," I began during my cross examination. "If your partner *had* been on duty that night, where would he have been at the time of the attack, relative to where it took place?"

"Normally, at that time, he would be walking the hallways and checking the elevator for anything suspicious," the guard replied.

So", he would not have been anywhere near the entryway where the culprit was hiding and where the attack took place?"

"That's correct."

"And isn't true that the complex has 44 entrances?"

"Yes sir. That is correct."

"And since it was you and your partner's job to check those entrances as you made your rounds, on a normal night, you each would have been responsible for checking 22 of them. Correct?"

"Yes. That's right."

"And on a normal night, how long does it take you, and how long does it normally take Officer Barnes to check all 22 of those entrances?"

"Hmm. Let's see. About two hours if I don't get interrupted with doing something else," came the reply.

"So, let's see." I said, facing the jury. "That works out to about five minutes per door. And the assailant could have entered the building through any one of those 44 doors, correct?"

"That's true."

"So, even if Officer Barnes *had* been on duty that night, and even if the attacker *had* entered the building through one of the 22 doors that Barnes normally checks, in order to have prevented the crime, Barnes would have to have inspected that entrance during a five-minute window of a two-hour patrol. Not very good odds, wouldn't you agree?"

"Yes sir. Not very good at all."

"So, Officer Donahue, as I understand your testimony, you are saying that even if Officer Barnes had not called in sick that night and even if he had been on duty, the attack, in all likelihood, would still have taken place. So, it didn't matter that he wasnt' on the job. We can all disregard that point because it's irrelevant. Am I correct?"

At this point I expected Lassoff to pop up and object to my leading the witness or to my calling for him to draw a conclusion. He did *not*. He continued to sit there with his fingers intertwined and said nary a word.

"Yes sir, that's sounds right," answered the witness.

Lassoff had only one question on cross examination:

"Officer, do you think that these housing units are a safe place to live?"

‚No" sir." came the reply. And that was it. This reply cost me the loss of a great amount of sleep over the weekend as I had to prepare for my summation on Monday,

Lorraine and the claims adjuster both came to court and sat in the gallery to observe my closing argument and hopefully learn the jury's verdict. My summation was succinct but impassioned.

I reminded the jury of all of the key points such as the "Say-for-Pay" doctor and the unwavering pattern of building maintenance exemplified by the intercom and door lock repair that took place the day before the incident. I urged them to disregard the plaintiff's attempt to confound the issue by claiming falsely that the absent security guard could have prevented the crime had he been there. Finally, I closed with my most compelling coup de grace.

"Ladies and gentlemen of the jury, it should not be necessary for me to remind you that this is a court of law, not a court of opinion. That means that in this place we look at the evidence. We do not give consideration to rumor and innuendo. Yet, the plaintiff would like for you to forget this unshakable rule. Mr. Lassoff wants you to consider as valid the unsubstantiated lies that were circulated about Gold Dome that falsely claim they intentionally allowed this building to deteriorate so they could drive out the tenants and cash in on some sort of imaginary co-op conversion deal. They expect you to swallow that lie even though they failed to introduce one shred of evidence to support it."

"But, I know something that they do not seem to know. I have observed each one of you during the course of this trial. I have watched as you have paid close attention to every word of testimony, how you have all engaged in critical thinking to determine what actually happened that night and who is really to blame. I believe that you are all too smart to fall for the sort of BS that the plaintiff's lawyers are peddling here today."

"I would like to leave you with this thought. Use your "life school." My mom, when she chose to reprimand me —something she did quite often—would say "Elly, listen to me. Don't think you are so smart because you have an education. I have life school." So do you, ladies and gentlemen. That life school is nothing more than plain common sense. I urge you to exercise the common sense that you have all learned at your own life school. I am confident that you will prove me correct by returning a verdict that is just, that is fair, and that is based strictly on the evidence and not on any unsupported rumors. And the only way to do that is for you to return a verdict of 'No Liability.' Thank you."

The jury only took half an hour to arrive at their verdict. That must have been some sort of record for cases of this sort. I knew what the verdict would be as soon as they all filed back into the jury box and the friendly lady from the middle of the front row flashed me a big smile. Sure enough, the foreman rose and announced a verdict of "No Liability."

Word of my victory soon spread around town and throughout the legal community and the subsequent impact marked a turning point in the life of our practice. As described in the following chapter, things began to take off as we began our recovery from the fallout of my having fired Zena Huerta.

There are those who believe that when one door closes in your life, another door always opens. I do not believe this to be true, but here was one case when, in fact, that's exactly what was happening.

Elliot Fixler

Chapter Twelve

Picking Up Speed

"At age 20, we worry about what others think of us. At 40, we don't care what they think of us. At 60, we discover they haven't been thinking of us at all."

—Ann Landers

Back in 1948, a writer with the British Foreign Service became alarmed at the encroaching expansionism of Soviet Russia and penned a dystopian novel depicting what life would be like in England under socialism. For the title, George Orwell reversed the last two digits of the current year and called it *1984*. It became a classic warning tale that, because of the leftward leanings of our current government and its involvement with the Deep State, *1984*, the book, is even more relevant today than it was back then. I had read the book in high school and it had made a powerful impression on me. The actual year 1984 happened to be the year that I turned 40. As the milestone approached, I recall watching the 1984 Super Bowl in late January. It featured an Orwellian commercial introducing Apple's newest computer. Something called the Macintosh. The tagline that closed the spot was: "Why 1984 won't be like *1984*." I, too, felt pleased at the time that Orwell's dark vision had not come to pass.yet...

Actually, turning 40—an age that some consider the threshold of middle age—was not a big deal for me whatsoever. When I had turned 35, five years earlier, I had gone a bit manic, obsessing about the fact that my life was now half over and I hadn't yet achieved one tenth of what I wished to accomplish in life. I recalled from my studies of Jewish history that the great King David had died at age 70 and I assumed that this would likewise be my fate (I'm 77 as I write these words). By the time David was 35, he had slain Goliath, penned all of the psalms, and become the most powerful ruler of ancient Judea. I desperately felt that I needed more time than the 35 years I thought I had left. I decided, at that point, to pick up the tempo of my life and become more productive. The first fruits of this decision? Our son, Mathew, was born in 1982 and our daughter, Sarah, came along two years later.

I spent my fortieth birthday in the company of my two older children, Mitchell and Jason, skiing the slopes on what turned out to be a sparkling sunny day. Yes, the day was fun filled but more or less routine and uneventful. Not so for the night, however.

Lorraine told me that she had invited a few of our friends over that evening to wish me a happy birthday. She said she had also spoken with an old single girlfriend a few days earlier who was coming to town and had suggested she join us as well. Sounded like a fun evening, and that's exactly what it was. Lots of laughs and friendly teasing. Nobody in our circle of friends ever took themselves too seriously. As the evening wore on, I mentioned to Lorraine that her girlfriend had not shown up yet. I was told that she was driving in from out of town and would be arriving a bit later.

At around 10 pm, Tammi-with-an-"i" showed up and I could not overlook the fact that she was a real knockout. Lorraine introduced her to everyone and when she got to me, I extended my hand. Tammi-with-an-i grabbed it, pulled me close to her and gave me a tight embrace as she whispered huskily: "Happy Birthday, Mr. Fixler."

I couldn't help but think of the time that Marilyn Monroe serenaded JFK with the words: "Happy birthday, Mr. President." What Tammi-with-an-i did next topped even that historic moment.

After planting a kiss on my lips, she turned and sashayed toward a portable boom box she had brought with her, squatted down and hit the play button causing *"Brown Sugar"* by the Rolling Stones to pulsate loudly through the room. When the vocal kicked in, Tammi seemed to explode. She executed a seductive and salacious series of bumps, grinds, and gyrations as one flimsy garment after another fell from her body and was flung wantonly into the crowd. By the time she was down to a sequined mini-G-string, things were getting raucous and raunchy as our guests offered encouraging whistles and catcalls. It was truly a WTF moment—especially for my two wide-eyed teenage sons—brought to us courtesy of "Sweet Lorraine," a lady who knew how to throw one hell of a party. This fact was reinforced six years later when she decided to throw herself a 40th birthday celebration to top mine. More about that in a later chapter.

As mentioned, one door closed after Stuart stopped sending clients my way because I had fired his sister. But, thankfully, it wasn't merely another door, but rather a floodgate that was thrown open at that point in my career. New business started pouring in from every direction: other insurance carriers, various large supermarket chains in the greater New York City metro area, and a growing number of real estate deals. What was driving this phenomenon? In all modesty, I believe it was the reputation I was developing as an attorney who wins difficult cases. Eventually, even Stuart cooled off and resumed sending us business. As a result of this spike, we had to hire in more attorneys and support staff at both the NYC and Putnam County offices.

One of my more memorable cases during this period was one that garnered a good deal of publicity and helped to solidify my reputation as "defender of the little guy." I refer to it as the "Case of the Outraged Adulterers."

I could see that Bob Falk and Marilyn Neggersmith were an attractive and personable young couple when they came to see me back in 1987. I asked if they were married and they said that they were. Just not to each other. When I asked how I could help them, Bob responded.

"We've been violated," he said.

"Really?" I replied trying to imagine the circumstances. "By whom?"

"By our church," came the answer.

"This was going to be very interesting," I thought.

The couple went on to explain that five years earlier they had both been serving as deacons at the fundamentalist Mission Church in Holmes, New York, just north of Carmel. Their friendship had led to an illicit romance and they began having an extramarital affair.

"We were in love, but neither of us wanted to destroy our families by going through a divorce," Bob explained. "I decided to go to our pastor to ask for his advice."

FULL CIRCLE

In February of 1983, Bob Falk met with their church's spiritual leader, Pastor Robert DeShea, and poured his heart out to him. His advice was deemed "not very helpful" by Bob. A short time afterward, both Bob and Marilyn moved out of their respective homes and began living together.

Meanwhile, Pastor DeShea shared the couple's story with Assistant Pastor David Stoughton who then spilled the beans to the church elders, causing a scandal. Stoughton and the church's governing council decided that the couple could no longer continue serving as church deacons. They drafted a letter exposing their sins and sent it out to the entire 220-member congregation including Bob's and Marilyn's families. Furthermore, on March 1, Stoughton read the letter aloud during Sunday morning services.

"Bob Falk and Marilyn Neggersmith have left their families," he proclaimed. "They are living together in sin. They are therefore no longer deacons at this church and should be shunned until they see the error of their ways." He went on to quote several scriptural passages about the evils of adultery.

The couple went on with their sad story.

They reported that as a result of this public humiliation, they had both suffered immensely. Lifelong friends had stopped speaking to Marilyn, and Bob had developed severe anxiety and loss of income.

Their plight touched my heart and the case intrigued me, so I decided to accept it, although I was not certain about the legal underpinnings. Does a conversation between a clergyman and a congregant enjoy the same protection of privilege as do the lawyer-client or the doctor-patient relationships? Would I be able to claim that the church or its agents acted with malicious intent? In order to prepare for the case, I turned to a source that was, up until that point, alien to me. The Bible. Although I was, thanks to my Jewish upbringing, familiar with what Christians call the Old Testament, I had never opened the New Testament. In doing so, believe it or not, I found the lynchpin upon which, I felt, I could win this case.

We filed a complaint in Putnam County State Supreme Court listing one million dollars in damages. It charged the parties with violation of confidentiality, libel, defamation of character, emotional pain and suffering, and business damage. Settlement negotiations between the church's insurance carrier, Covenant Mutual, and my clients failed to bring about a resolution. The insurance company declined to extend any offer whatsoever. So, the case was slated to be tried before Judge Fred Dickinson, a country lawyer with a solid fundamentalist Christian background. The case had received a good deal of notoriety in the local media and the fact that the courtroom was packed with reporters seemed to please Judge Dickinson. Thus, I already had one point in my favor. The clincher came when I questioned Assistant Pastor Stoughton on the stand.

"Tell me, Pastor Stoughton," I asked. "You evidently believe that sinners should not serve as church deacons and that their sins should not enjoy the confidentiality of clergy. You believe they should be exposed for all to see, correct?"

He answered in the affirmative, albeit a bit nervously.

"Then you would not object if I informed the jurors and the spectators in this courtroom about your son who is currently living in sin with a woman who is married to another man."

Before he could answer, I turned and thrust my face close to his in an accusatory stance.

"And you would not object," I went on, a bit more aggressively, "were I to expose the fact that your daughter last year bore a child out of wedlock."

Stoughton said nothing but visibly began to flush. I turned to face the jury and continued.

"Being a man of the cloth and a good Christian, I presume that you would be able to quote me the words of John, Chapter 8, Verse 7."

He thought for a moment and replied in the affirmative. I asked him to quote the passage.

"Let him who is without sin cast the first stone," he said.

"And those are the words of Jesus Christ. Am I correct?"

He nodded.

"It's clear that you chose to violate these words of wisdom when you decided to cast stones against my clients but failed to do so in the case of your own family members." I could see that I had the jury's rapt attention, so I pressed on.

"My clients turned to your church seeking guidance and counsel. Instead, you met them with condemnation, humiliation, and rebuke. A rebuke that you were all too ready to dispense in their case, but a rebuke that you withheld in the cases of your own family. You were able to quote scripture from the Gospel according to John quite accurately a moment ago. May I ask if you are also familiar with Mark, Chapter 7, Verse 6?"

Stoughton wrinkled his brow and pondered the question.

"Here, let me help you," I offered. "Isaiah was right when he prophesied about you hypocrites; as it is written, 'These people honor me with their lips, but their hearts are far from me.' "

Once I was through with the pastor, the attitude of the judge and the jury indicated they were now in my corner. More importantly, the attitude of Covenant, the church's insurance company, changed dramatically. They now were willing to talk money.

As the jury was dismissed to deliberate the amount they would award to my clients in compensation for their suffering, the Covenant people decided that they did not wish to risk it. By the time the jury returned, they were informed that their services would no longer be required, since the parties had reached an out of court settlement. My clients agreed to accept $75,000 to drop the case.

They deserved every penny since they had exhibited profound good judgement in selecting a Gospel-quoting, Bible-thumping Jewish lawyer to represent them.

A sample of the type of lurid publicity this case generated. The front page of the April 23, 1987 issue of the New York Daily News:

RACING ★ ★ ★ ★ FINAL

Shot cop's tragic soulmate
Story on page 5

DAILY ◉ NEWS

35¢   NEW YORK'S PICTURE NEWSPAPER*   Thursday, April 23, 1987

CHURCH SUED BY 'SINNERS'

Pastor rapped lovers from pulpit
Story on page 2

'LET ME DIE!'

Emergency Service cops Paul Kwiecinski (rear) and Daniel Masterson struggle to save transsexual Curz Adaibersot, 33, from the frigid waters of the East River off E. 63d St. into which Curz leaped yesterday. They succeeded despite repeated pleas to "Let me die!"

Centerfold, page 44

Shortly after the Outlaw v. Gold Dome Savings Bank case that I recounted in an earlier chapter, I received a call from Frank Gulino who was the deputy general counsel at the New York City Housing Authority. This is a massive municipal bureaucracy that manages all of the public housing in all five New York boroughs. Frank's job was to handle all litigation brought against the Authority.

"I heard how you came out in that Gold Dome rape case," Frank said. "I'm wondering if I could retain your firm as outside counsel to represent the Housing Authority in those type of cases."

"You bet, Frank." I blurted. "I'm all in with that."

So, here was another new and steady source of revenue as our NYC office set to work defending the Housing Authority in actions filed mostly by housing project tenants.

Our New York City office was now being managed by Pat Gaynor and she was fantastic. Even though I liked to kid her about the fact that I almost didn't hire her because she showed up late for her job interview, she was truly worth her weight in gold. Lorraine continued to manage the Carmel office and headed up an expanding team of paralegals and secretaries who handled the bulk of the real estate and plaintiff work.

As our staffing needs continued to broaden during this growth spurt, Howard and I found we needed to reach out and enlist more capable employees. We had known and admired Michelle Easton for years. She had worked for the Law Office of Joseph Burchetta, one of Putnam County's oldest law firms. I had heard through our secretarial grapevine that she was fed up with the way Burchetta was constantly yelling and quarreling with his son, James. She was finally ready to leave the firm. As we discussed her salary requirements and moving over to our firm, I thought back to my first encounter with her boss.

I had first met Joseph Burchetta early in my own career when he asked me to try a case that he had passed on. I knew he had plenty of capable attorneys on his staff, including his son, James, so I presumed he wanted to give it to me because there was not enough money involved and he didn't want his own lawyers wasting their time on a small case they were unlikely to win. It turned out to be a rather interesting case for several reasons. For one thing, the entire trial—from jury selection to the announcement of the verdict—was conducted in just one day. That was unheard of then and it is certainly unheard of today.

My client had caused a rear-end collision and that was considered to be an almost automatic defendant liability outcome. Yet, I pulled it off and managed to win the case by demonstrating that the plaintiff contributed to her own damages by recklessly pulling out from a side street without stopping, making it impossible for my client to stop his vehicle in time to avoid the collision. In those days, before the concept of comparative negligence had been introduced (a principle that allows for an allocation of culpability in negligence cases between the plaintiff and the defendant) if the plaintiff was found to have contributed to any degree whatsoever to her own damages, she was barred from receiving compensation.

What added to my joy at this outcome was the fact that I had invited Lorraine's mother, Isabelle, to come to court for the day to watch me work. She was able to observe an entire case, from start to finish, all in one day. I came away from that case thinking that my victory surely must have impressed Mr. Burchetta and the others at his law firm. So, it roiled me that I never got another case from him. But, in the end, many years later, I did manage to get Michelle Easton.

Michelle turned out to be every bit as awesome as we anticipated. She and Lorraine became fast friends and wound up taking trips together to places like Ireland and other far-flung ports of call. Michelle stayed a part of my team for years until in 2004, I learned she was planning to escape to Florida. Something I did as well not long afterwards. Today, Michelle lives near me and we have remained good friends. In 2014, Michelle opened the Trilogy Title Services company in Wellington, a successful venture driven by the area's booming real estate sector. Her success didn't surprise me one bit. I always regarded her as smarter than most lawyers I came across.

On the home front, my older boys were moving from high school to college and Lorraine and I felt it was likewise time for us to move on. So, it was a stroke of good timing when I got a call from Michael Barile. Mike owned a local construction company and was one of our firm's primary Putnam County clients. He had become a close friend of both mine and Howard's. Mike mentioned to us that one of the houses down the road from his place on Lake Mahopac had just gone on the market. We decided to have a look and Lorraine fell in love with it, despite the fact that it was an older home and the appointments were somewhat dated. The home sat on the largest lot on the lakefront—four wooded acres—and offered 400 feet of unrestricted shoreline. Our Carmel house sold quickly and we immediately purchased the house on Lake Mahopac.

The picturesque hamlet of Mahopac encircles the lake's scenic four miles of shoreline. There are dozens of hiking and biking trails and the lake is stocked with both largemouth and smallmouth bass. We learned that the actor Henry Winkler spent his childhood summers at Lake Mahopac and taught water skiing at a nearby Jewish summer camp. Winkler's mother, Ilse, still spent her summers on the lake when we were living there.

The pine trees on the property served to keep the air fresh and aromatic. But the place was so heavily overgrown with them that it was impossible to get a decent view of the lake from inside the house. We wound up paying a tree removal service to turn a swath of them into pine lumber thereby providing us with a window onto the lake. We soon learned that there were other problems. The existing well had run dry and we were required to drill a fresh one. Again, we brought in a professional. When he had finished the well, we then discerned a particularly unsavory aroma wafting our way from the newly dug well. We soon learned that the well-digger had not applied for a permit before commencing his excavation. Had he done so, he would have learned that his proposed well was much too close to a septic line. Yuch!

I had no choice but to bring in a new well-driller to do the job properly. I felt that since I had paid the original driller, and since he screwed up the job, he should help bear the cost of the new well. He did not see it that way and refused to pay me. I knew that I was in the right, so I filed suit against the guy. This action on my part did not sit "well" with my client and neighbor, Mike Barile. Mike regularly employed the driller in his construction business and was the one who had recommended him to me.

"You've got to drop this suit, Elliot," Mike stated firmly. "I use this guy all the time and need his good will. If you go ahead with your lawsuit, he'll be pissed off at me for referring him to somebody that hauled him into court."

"I'm not going to drop it, Mike," I replied with just as much determination. "He should have filed his plans with the town and gotten a permit. His stupidity cost me. It forced me to pay twice for a new well. Anyway, he's got insurance to cover situations like this."

Still, Mike had his mind set and there was no way I could reason with him. He did not understand that there was more involved here than merely money.

In the end, the driller's insurance company settled with me and the matter never wound up in court. But I wound up losing a friend and estranging a neighbor. Looking back, I probably should have just given in since the amount of money involved was minimal compared to what was lost.

This was the second time—the Zena Myer episode being the first — that my standing on principle had wound up costing me more than the money in question. But I was young and mule-headed in those days. Even at forty, I had not begun to mellow in the slightest. I didn't understand at the time that suing the contractor would jeopardize my friendship with Mike Barile. And I certainly had no inkling, at that point, that doing so might actually cost me my partnership with Howard. I'll tell that story a bit later.

Chapter Thirteen

A Fork in the Road

"Sometimes good things fall apart so that better things can fall together."

—Marilyn Monroe

By the late 1980s, I had been lulled into a false sense of stability when it came to our successful law practice. I was unprepared for the shifts and shocks that were to soon rock my life. Frank Gulino had for several years been sending our NYC office a steady stream of business from the New York Housing Authority. But one fine day, Frank announced that he was leaving his post there. I felt I owed him a debt of gratitude and so, when I learned he was looking for a place to land, I unilaterally offered him the opportunity to join our firm. I knew that Frank was bright and felt he would provide some guidance and leadership to the cohort of young lawyers we had recently taken on board. My expectations were fulfilled and Frank stayed with our practice for 13 years, eventually receiving a small partnership interest in our NYC operation.

During the summer of 1989, Howard came into my office and sat down. I could tell by his expression that this was going to be a serious chat.

"You know, Ell," he stopped and let out a sigh. 'I"ve been at this for more than twenty years and I'm just plain tired."

"What are you trying to say, Howard?" I asked, although I already knew the answer.

"I'm getting out. I don't want to keep practicing law till I get so burned out, I'm not able to enjoy life and my family. I'm leaving the partnership.."

"I thought we made a damn good team," I replied, "but it's up to you. What are you going to do next?"

Howard explained that he was joining the real estate development and construction company owned by Mike Barile and his partner, Tom Boniello. They were going to make him a partner and he would serve as their in-house lawyer. The news broke my heart. I loved Howard like a brother—actually, since I never had a brother, I can't really say that. Like the brother I imagined that I never had.

I recognized that Howard was operating in his own best interests, but I couldn't help but feel that his departure was precipitated by my dispute with Barile over a stupid hole in the ground. I could not prove it, but I suspected that had Barile and I remained on friendly terms, he would not have lured Howard away from our firm. I understood Howard's thinking and his stated reasons for wanting to move on, but I didn't like it one bit. I was hurt by his willingness to split up a team that had proven so clearly successful. I'm pleased to say there was no rancor or animosity over the break-up. Unlike Fuckin' Eddie, Howard did not make off with any clients when he exited. He was a true mensch. But it still took me a long time to get over the pain.

Our separation was unusual in several respects. Most such break-ups occur due to financial disputes or personality clashes. Neither was the case here. Even though my end of the practice always generated far more revenue than Howard's work, I never thought about it in those terms or made an issue of it. We had made a handshake deal at the outset that called for all profits to be split 50-50 between us and we stuck to it without question over the years. We genuinely liked each other and we remained on friendly terms after the break-up.

Years later Lorraine and I began socializing with Howard again. By this time, he was divorced and was deeply involved with Joan Neumann. You may remember Joan as the plaintiff in the ShopRite slip and fall case that Howard and I had litigated, described earlier. You might say that Joan had slipped and fallen in love. After living together for many years, the two finally tied the knot in 1997.

Howard died in 2012 and it was his business partner, Mike Barile, who handled the funeral arrangements. Despite our long-ago dispute, he chose to honor me by asking if I would deliver the eulogy. I gladly agreed.

As I said in my remarks, "Our years of partnership were the best of my professional life. There will always be a special space in my heart where Howard resides."

I kept the name of our practice as Stockfield and Fixler for a while after Howard's departure. We had invested a great deal in building a brand in our community and I was not anxious to simply dispose of it. I eventually changed it to Fixler and Associates which is how it remained until I closed the practice in 2006.

I also decided to move our offices after Howard left. I purchased a building across the street from the Putnam County Courthouse right on Main Street. It had previously served as a hardware store and sat right next door to a busy bank. I hired Jay Maxwell, Jr. to carry out the renovations and he did a great job. We ended up with a brand-new two-story office in a prime location.

I also decided to move our New York City office. I entered into a lease agreement with Merrill Lynch brokerage house to occupy the 16th floor of a building they owned at 199 Broadway, two blocks east of the World Trade Center. After building out the space, we were able to start work there in 1990. With a stroke of good fortune, we moved out of that location eight months before the September 11, 2001 terrorist attacks.

At this point, Frank Gulino was managing our team of lawyers who operated out of this location. Like Frank, I also needed a private office for those times I was trying cases in New York. When it came to deciding who would take which office, I thought back to the time that Howard had offered me the choice of offices when he and I were first starting out. I graciously stated then that Howard, being the more senior partner, should take the larger office. I expected a similar response when I now offered Frank his choice of offices. But I was disappointed when Frank immediately opted for the coveted corner office with its views overlooking Broadway on one side and the Twin Towers on the other. It was a petty matter like this that marked the beginning of my discontent with Frank that would eventually lead to his departure.

Meanwhile, back on the home front, Mitchell and Jason were both off to college. Mitchell, at his mother's insistence, went to Brandeis University in Waltham, Massachusetts. I had suggested that he go to

UVM, the University of Vermont in Burlington instead (UVM stands for Universitas Viridis Montis or the University of the Green Mountains) where he could put his outstanding skiing skills to good use. But, at this point, Mitchell remained very much under his mother's thumb.

Jason was off to Widener University in Chester, Pennsylvania. He loved the school and received a first-rate education. Both young men obtained post-graduate degrees. Mitchell attended the College of Insurance (part of St. John's University in NYC) and, after that, both he and Jason earned law degrees from Yeshiva University's Benjamin N. Cardozo School of Law, also located in New York City. I was happy to subsidize the associated costs, making it unnecessary for either one to take out a student loan. Jason is today a practicing attorney who, unlike his law partner who is still paying off his student loan, is not burdened by any such debt. Mitchell is a lawyer and presently serves as the Chief Operating Officer at ResolveStar which is discussed in a later chapter. Lorraine and I underwrote the costs of his undergraduate, College of Insurance, and law school education. Like his siblings, Mitchell has not. been burdened with loan repayments.

Both Mitchell and Jason moved to New York City in 1992. Both initially found work in the insurance industry. Jason spent three years working for AIG before deciding he wanted to go to law school. Mitchell, upon graduation from Brandeis, attended the College of Insurance for several years after which he, too, decided to enroll in law school. Interestingly, their mother chose this time to pursue a late-in-life law career and enrolled in law school along with Mitchell.

A few years before, my own mother had lost her balance as she was descending the front steps of their home in Buffalo. She fell and was hospitalized with assorted contusions, including several head injuries. Her recovery was complicated by the fact she suffered from diabetes. Upon receiving the news, I rushed to Buffalo and spent the night in the hospital fearful that she might not make it. But Rose was a survivor through and through and managed to pull through. She spent the following year in and out of the hospital and each time they would amputate another portion of her leg.

Lorraine and I, along with the kids, would drive up to Buffalo often during those days. We would take Mom out in her wheelchair and spend the day in her company. Prior to the fall, she had been in good shape mentally, but afterwards, things began to deteriorate. I found that watching her personality dissolve as her condition worsened to be heartbreaking. By the time she died on March 10, 1990, I had cried so many tears that I had very few left to mourn the passing of this woman who had valiantly carried me from the horrors of the Holocaust to safety and a new life in America.

Chapter Fourteen

Some Consequential Cases

*"Justice has nothing to do with what goes on in a courtroom;
justice is what comes out of a courtroom."*
—Clarence Darrow

A t this juncture, I will take a break from the chronological narrative and share my memories of a few notable cases drawn from my legal career. But first, a disclaimer. I have tried to avoid technical language to make these descriptions accessible to all readers. Nevertheless, I understand that reading about lawsuits and court battles is not for everyone. So, if this sort of thing is not your cup of tea, then feel free to skip this chapter and move on to the next one. I won't feel a bit offended.

Kahill v. Kingston

Know when to hold 'em; know when to fold 'em.

During the mid-1980s I was retained by one of the insurance adjusters I worked with to defend their client, Kingston Labs, in a medical malpractice case. The lab was being sued by a Mrs. Kahill who had checked into the Ulster County General Hospital to undergo hip replacement surgery. Prior to the operation, an employee of Kingston Labs was instructed to draw some of Mrs. Kahill's blood to determine its type. The purpose was to make supplemental blood available should it be needed during surgery. The lab employee entered Mrs. Kahill's non-private room and bungled the blood draw, collecting the sample from Mrs. Kahill's roommate by mistake. As a result, Mrs. Kahill received mismatched blood during surgery and nearly died from renal failure.

Not long before meeting with the plaintiff's lawyer to discuss a settlement, I had attended a continuing education lecture by a leading medical malpractice attorney named Richard Shandel, author of the highly respected "The Preparation and Trial of Medical Malpractice Cases" (Law Journal Seminars-Press, 1980). Shandel opined that if a client almost dies as the result of malpractice, then the case is worth at least $100,000 in damages. So naturally, I was pleased to learn during the meeting that the plaintiff was willing to settle the case for $35,000.

When I presented this offer to the claims adjuster, he said he would agree to it as long as the hospital would pay a portion of the settlement amount. He felt that they had contributed to the negligence by permitting untrained non-hospital personnel to enjoy unrestricted access to patient rooms.

"If Ulster General had not let that inexperienced Kingston Lab gal waltz into the patient's room, this never would have happened," he maintained. "They've got to eat part of this. If they come up with five, I'll approve the thirty thousand." I did not think this was a very persuasive argument and neither did the hospital. They denied any responsibility and said they would not pay a penny. So, the case went to trial.

I tried the case and, to my surprise, the jury accepted my argument that the hospital share in responsibility for what had happened. As Shandel had predicted, the jury came back and awarded Mrs. Kahill $100,000. They held that 40% of the award should be paid by Ulster General and the balance by Kingston Labs. I immediately phoned the claims adjuster.

"I have good news and bad news," I told him. He asked to hear the bad news first.

"The jury awarded her $100,000." I heard him moan.

"What could possibly be the good news?" he said dejectedly.

"The hospital has to pay 40% of the award." His mood changed dramatically.

"See, I told you," he exclaimed. "I told you they were partly responsible. Great work, Elliot."

I couldn't believe my ears. This guy was delighted that he had been proven correct. This despite the fact his company would be shelling out $60,000, plus my fees, when they could have paid only $35,000 had he agreed to settle in the first place. He would rather be right than rich. The hospital came off even worse. Instead of agreeing to pay $5,000 to make this case go away, they were now stuck with eight times that much in damages. Both were stupid stubborn idiots in my book.

Lesson? Like the Kenny Rogers song I quoted in Chapter Six says: "You gotta know when to hold 'em. Know when to fold 'em. Know when to walk away and know when to run."

Black v. Major Muffler

"I'm your lawyer. I'm here to defend your ass, not kiss it."

In the legal business there is often a thin line between winning and losing a case. I always saw it as my job to give clients my best advice about which side of that line they would likely come down on. Based on that information, I would then advise the client about whether or not to settle, how much to settle for, or if they should insist that the case be tried in court. This would enable my client to make an informed decision about how to proceed. Of course, all of my great advice is for naught whenever the client chooses to ignore it—as was the case of the unfortunate Mr. Black of Alameda, California.

"Discover how you can translate your love of cars into your own business by owning a muffler shop franchise." Lured by this come-on, Mr. Mitchell Black took out a second mortgage on his home and ponied up the franchise fee being charged by Major Muffler, a national concern operating automotive service centers in several states. Black was drawn to Major Muffler by the fact they provided their franchisees with a hydraulic self-contained pipe-bending machine. With such a device, Black judged he would not need to stock a large inventory of muffler parts since the machine promised to enable him to make his own custom exhaust pipes for any type of vehicle as needed. This, he felt, would give him an advantage over his competitors.

Within a year of opening his muffler shop, however, Mr. Black's business failed and he was forced to close its doors. More misfortune followed. He was unable to maintain his heavy mortgage payments and lost his home when the lender foreclosed. Black also suffered a heart attack that he maintained was caused by the stress of losing his business and his home. His protests that Major Muffler was to blame for his misery could not be muffled. He filed suit against the company demanding restitution of his franchise fees, start-up costs, medical bills and assorted other alleged damages. Major Muffler's sole shareholder, Nat Shapiro, was a client of ours and asked if I would represent the company even though the complaint had been filed in California. I agreed.

My first step was to hire local counsel in Alameda County to handle all of the pre-trial paperwork. I next applied to the California Bar Association to grant me a Pro Hoc Vice admission. This entitled me to practice law and appear on behalf of my client in California Superior Court—but only in connection with this particular case.

Mr. Black's complaint alleged that Major Muffler was guilty of interstate fraud and breach of contract. After reviewing the facts, I felt I could mount a strong defense by demonstrating that the plaintiff was incompetent and never learned to properly operate the pipe-bending machine. I explained this to Nat and also pointed out that I could effectively challenge the plaintiff's allegation of medical causality between his business failure and his heart attack. Nat was fine with my analysis and I was certain that if the plaintiff was reasonable that this case, like most others, would settle. And, if not, we stood a good chance of achieving victory in court.

Shortly before we received notice from California of a trial date, Nat died. He had two sons from whom he had been estranged for twenty years and were now the beneficiaries of his estate. I quickly brought them up to date on the case. Unlike Nat's view that he was fine with trying the case if necessary, and despite my optimistic outlook regarding the likely outcome, Nat's sons would have none of it. They had someone on the hook to buy the company but they could not go through with the deal with a pending lawsuit hanging over their heads. They needed a quick resolution.

"Go to California, Elliot," I was ordered. "and do whatever you need to do to get this case settled." I disagreed with this decision, but I nevertheless caught the next flight to California with Lorraine and Mathew in tow.

My marching orders soon became moot, however, by something I had never seen happen in a lawsuit, either before or since. As the parties convened for the pre-trial hearing, the presiding magistrate, as a matter of course, asked the plaintiff's attorney how much money it would take to settle this case and avoid going to trial. Even though I preferred to try the case, I was obliged to carry out my client's instructions. So, I waited to hear the proposed amount so I could plan my settlement negotiation strategy.

But much to my surprise, Black's attorney rose and brazenly announced: "This case cannot be settled, your honor. It must be left up to the jury to put a number on it."

The plaintiff's attorney was pompous and arrogant. I felt that he was so sure that he would wind up with a huge verdict that he had no doubt persuaded his client to agree to this gambit. My clients wanted to settle but they never received a number. Fortunately, they had a great lawyer.

As I strode into the courtroom on opening day and looked over the prospective jurors, most of whom were black, I made sure they were all looking my way. I then opened my briefcase and pulled out a well-worn baseball mitt and laid it on the corner of the table. I said nothing about the mitt in my questioning of the jurors, nor in my opening statement, nor at any point during the course of the trial. At the end of the day, I would pick up the mitt and return it to my valise. The next morning, I would pull it out again and place it in the same spot, only to again ignore it all day and put it back in my bag when court was adjourned. I repeated this process daily. I did not even tell my co-counsel, Schickman, who owned the mitt, why I was doing this. I could sense, with each passing day, the jury members' swelling curiosity about the meaning behind this leather fielder's mitt. That was exactly my intent.

It was a complex case and the trial took a full week. In support of his claim, the plaintiff called in other Major Muffler franchisees to testify how they too had been defrauded by the company's unfulfilled promises and about the poor quality of the support they had received. I countered his claim by demonstrating to the jury that Mr. Black had not bothered to undergo the required training and therefore did not know how to properly operate the pipe-bending equipment. I cited numerous examples of other franchisees who had gone to the trouble of being trained and were now successfully operating the same equipment. I further argued that it was, in fact, Mr. Black's incompetence and unprofessional sloppiness that contributed most significantly to the failure of his business. I then brought in medical evidence establishing that Mr. Black had a history of cardiac issues long before he became a Major Muffler dealer. This served to undermine the medical records his lawyer introduced to document the linkage between his heart attack and his business failure.

In civil cases, the jury is required to consider a "preponderance of the evidence." I was able to add to that preponderance during my questioning of Mr. Black.

"Isn't it true that at the time you suffered your heart attack, you were also a part-time employee at the hospital where you received treatment?"

"Yes," he answered somewhat nervously. "That's right. I had to take another job because I wasn't making anything to speak of at the muffler shop."

"And as a hospital employee, isn't it also true that you had access to patients' medical records?" He nodded.

"Let the record show that the witness answered in the affirmative." I said. "And isn't it true that you had the opportunity to alter your own chart to make it appear as though your heart attack was the result of so-called 'business stress'?" Not surprisingly, Black vehemently denied this allegation and his attorney objected to the question, which I withdrew—but not before a seed of doubt had been planted in the minds of the jurors.

It was my habit to write out my summation in advance, but in this case I didn't do that. Up until the moment the plaintiff's attorney rose to make his final argument, I was unsure about how I would present my side of the case. I wondered if using the baseball glove schtick to discredit his case was going to be necessary. After all, I had already established my case and things were going pretty well. Maybe it wouldn't be necessary. But then he wound-up and delivered his final pitch. And he aimed it right across my strike zone.

"Ladies and gentlemen of the jury," he concluded after reviewing the key points of his case. "The defendants think they can waltz in here to Oakland and hire some big-gun New York City lawyer to fool you into letting his client off the hook. But what he doesn't know is that you fine folks are no fools and you're not going to let him get away with his big city lawyer tricks. Let's show him together how we do things here in Oakland and send him back to New York City with his tail between his legs."

That did it. It all came together for me and I decided to go gonzo and take no prisoners.

I started by calmly reviewing the facts about the pipe-bending machine and the hospital records and the rest. I then went silent and walked over to the table and dramatically picked up the baseball glove that had been sitting there all week.

"You've probably been wondering why I've been bringing this old baseball mitt with me to court each day. Let me tell you why." You could have heard a Post-It note drop.

"If you've ever watched a baseball game, you've probably seen an outfielder make an error, like dropping an easy fly ball or letting the ball bounce through his legs. And then what does he do? He stares at his glove as if there was a hole in it, right? It couldn't have been *his* fault. No, it must have been the glove." I detected several of the jurors nodding slightly. They were with me, and so I continued.

"Or have you ever seen a tennis player look at his racket after missing a shot as if it had a hole in it? Or a golfer angrily throw his club to the ground after missing a putt?" At this point, I pulled the mitt onto my left hand and held it aloft.

"You see that glove? That's me. I'm here to offer some protection to my client. If a player drops the ball, you don't blame the mitt. That's the easy way out. If Major Muffler dropped the ball, blame them. Don't blame the lawyer. But why does Mr. Black's lawyer want you to blame the mitt? Why does he want you focus on me and not the facts of the case? Because he knows, and you know, that Major Muffler did NOT drop the ball. They did everything they promised to do. So, since he cannot expect you to blame the player for Mr. Black's problems, he wants you to blame the mitt. Well, ladies and gentlemen, if that's the way the plaintiff and his lawyer do business here in Oakland—and if you buy into that—then I'm on the first flight out of here back to New York City. At least there they don't ask you to blame the mitt when they can't blame the player."

Actually, I did catch a flight back to Buffalo right after I finished my closing summation. I needed to meet Lorraine and Mathew there to attend the Passover Seder at my mother's house. There's a custom that's observed as part of the Seder that involves opening the door to permit entry to the prophet Elijah, so he may "bring the promise of relief, to lift downcast spirits and to plant hope in our hearts." It was at this point, just after we had opened the front door, that the phone rang. It was Mark Schickman, the California lawyer who had handled the preliminary paperwork and had sat with me during the trial. I had left Mark behind in Oakland to take the verdict. The good news he delivered most certainly did provide the promise of relief.

Mark reported that after a relatively brief deliberation, the jury had returned a verdict in favor of my client and, in addition, we were awarded court costs. The decision was never appealed and as a result,

Mr. Black received nothing, nor did his clueless attorney who had accepted the case on a contingency fee basis.

As we concluded the Seder, several of the family members inquired about the case. I explained how I had used an old leather fielder's mitt to help me win an important case.

Had I been able to carry out my clients' instruction to "settle at any cost," I explained to the group, their company would have been out far more than the attorney's fees I would charge. Likewise, had Mr. Black and his lawyer agreed to a negotiated settlement, Black would have walked away with enough money for a down payment on a new house.

The lesson? Humility is a virtue and don't underestimate your opponent.

Maguire v. Columbia Medical
Either toss out the one bad apple or prepare to make applesauce.

Bill Maguire felt pretty good when he checked into New York City's Columbia Presbyterian Hospital to undergo another corneal transplant on his right eye. He did not feel that way when he checked out, however. That's because he was dead.

Just as he had done the previous year when he underwent a transplant on his left eye without any problem, he now opted to again have it done on his right eye under general, rather than local, anesthesia. As before, the anesthesiologist used Halothane to induce and maintain unconsciousness during the procedure. Popular as a general anesthetic agent in those days—the 1980s—Halothane reduces blood pressure, pulse rate and respiration. It induces muscle relaxation and dulls pain by altering tissue excitability. Its use has been discontinued because of the potential for causing fatal hepatitis. It has been supplanted by newer safer agents such as Sevoflurane.

As dictated by medical protocol, Mr. Maguire again underwent a battery of liver function tests prior to undergoing surgery. Unfortunately, the ophthalmologist, a Dr. Frank Hoefle, as well as the anesthesiologist, both failed to wait for those test results to be returned before proceeding with the eye surgery. Had they done so, they would have observed that the patient had an abnormally functioning and diseased liver.

As the old adage goes: "The operation was a success, but the patient died." Mr. Maguire contracted hepatitis, became completely jaundiced and hallucinatory, but managed to cling to life for another six weeks. I was retained by his estate in a wrongful death action brought against the ophthalmologist, the anesthesiologist, and the hospital in the Supreme Court of Manhattan.

The voir dire, or jury selection process, was a grueling grind that stretched over three days. Each of the three defendants had retained their own attorneys, each of whom was permitted to question every prospective juror making the process a lengthy ordeal.

By the close of the third day, we had the six-member jury empaneled and were in the process of selecting an alternate before we could call it a day and start the trial the following morning. As the very last of the fifty prospective jurors took the stand, I had one peremptory challenge left. As I questioned her, I could tell from her attitude that she was not likely to be sympathetic toward the family I was representing. But it was late in the day, I was exhausted, and had I rejected her, that would have meant another fifty prospective jurors would need to be brought in on the following day, further delaying the trial. "After all," I thought. "What's the harm? She's only an alternate and will most likely not be deciding the verdict." I opted not to exercise my challenge and permitted her to remain on the jury as an alternate. Bad decision.

I could not help but observe, throughout the trial, how the unfriendly alternate's expression would change to one of disdain whenever I was arguing a point or presenting evidence. I felt as though every time I came near her, she was giving me the "*ayin ha'ra*" or the Jewish "evil eye" (something my mother used to ward off by saying *"ke'nina ha'ra* and spitting three times). As luck would have it, one of the actual jurors—my favorite juror, who came from my own hometown—asked to be excused because she had plane tickets to go to Buffalo for Thanksgiving. The judge excused her and—wouldn't you know it—Ms. Evil Eye, the annoying alternate, was thus promoted to a full-fledged juror.

As the trial wore on, I explained to the jury that the anesthesiologist had improperly administered general anesthesia to a patient with a diseased liver, and by using Halothane, had chosen the wrong agent. In addition, the surgeon had performed the surgery without first waiting for the results of the laboratory liver enzyme tests which clearly indicated the existence of liver disease. Dr Hoefle, as the surgeon, was the captain of the ship and I maintained that both of the doctors were negligent and had directly caused the patient's death.

I then pointed to a large body of medical literature that supported the warning that one needs to avoid the administration of any general anesthesia if the patient suffers from liver disease. In addition, I claimed that it was improper to use Halothane in this case since it had been administered to the patient the previous year for a similar surgery and the medical literature cautioned against using Halothane twice within a two-year period.

In order to prepare for this case, I could not rely solely on expert medical testimony. I had to become something of a medical expert myself. Hence, I had conducted a substantial review of the medical literature, educating myself in the fields of gastroenterology, ophthalmology and general surgery. I would soon learn if my efforts were to be rewarded as the jury adjourned to decide their verdict.

In a rather unusual move, the court had ordered a bifurcated trial. This meant that the jury would first need to rule on the question of the defendants' liability. If any of them were found to be liable, the jury would then reconvene to hear evidence, decide on the amount of the damages, and render a verdict.

After a considerable time spent in deliberation, the jury returned a five-to-one verdict in our favor. A unanimous decision was not required of juries in tort cases like this. The hospital was exonerated, but both doctors were found liable. I had no question as to which of the jurors had voted "No Liability." At this point, the jurors were instructed to return to the jury room consider the evidence relating to the damages suffered by the plaintiff.

After a few hours, a message was sent from the jury room to the judge. The jurors wished to know if a juror who had voted "No Liability" the first time around could now be excluded from deciding the amount of the damages. The answer was 'no." All jurors, regardless of how they voted on the question of liability, were entitled to vote on the amount of the award. This question told me that Ms. Evil Eye was being troublesome in the jury room and the other jurors wanted to restrict her ability to influence the damages.

Finally, the jury returned with a verdict of $150,000 to be awarded to the Maguire family by the two doctors. On my way out of the courtroom, I passed by the jury room and spotted the ophthalmologist's attorney, Bob Deutsch, under the table on his hands and knees going through a waste basket. I walked in and asked, "What are you doing, Bob?"

He stood up with the contents of the wastebasket in his hands. There were six slips of paper, each one bearing a dollar amount inscribed by a different juror. One of the slips read "$0." All the rest contained substantial dollar amounts. It was obvious that the jurors had each written down the amount of the settlement they thought was fair and then the resulting average of the six numbers was the amount they had declared.

We did the math and determined that had Ms. Evil Eye, who had certainly cast the zero dollar amount, not been permitted to vote, the average of the sums submitted by the five other jurors would have been $180,000, not $150,000. By failing to reject that troubling juror when I had the chance, I had cost my client $30,000. Naturally, I did not share with my clients what I had learned from that jury room dumpster dive. And while no amount of money could replace the unnecessary loss of a loved one, they were gratified to receive vindication and the $150,000 award.

Lesson? Always go with your gut. Even if you're tired and it's late in the day. When your inner instincts tell you that a juror is not going to be good for your client, then turn her loose and move on.

Burke v. Kodak

Research is formalized curiosity. It is poking and prying with a purpose.

In the days before iPhones and digital cameras, the Eastman Kodak company loomed large as the nation's major purveyor of all things photographic. During the 1980s, Kodak was also deeply involved in scientific research and often purchased highly technical measurement equipment from a company called Brookhaven Instruments, located in the Long Island hamlet of Holtsville in Suffolk County, New York.

On a clear day in 1987, a Kodak employee, driving a light truck, was leaving Brookhaven after having picked up a piece of equipment. On his way back to Kodak headquarters in Rochester, the driver ran into a Mr. James Burke,...literally. Mr. Burke, a fifty-year old school psychologist traveling from one of his assigned schools to another, was stopped at a red light in Holtsville when the Kodak truck failed to halt in time and rear-ended Burke's car.

The minor collision resulted in $3,500 in damage to Mr. Burke's car plus, according to him, a litany of medical complaints that became the crux of a major lawsuit he filed against Eastman Kodak. Kodak was being represented by an attorney who lacked the necessary experience in actions of this scale. Based upon my reputation for success in this arena, I was brought in and took over the file before the case was docketed.

In reviewing the complaint, I learned that Mr. Burke was claiming the accident had caused severe head injuries, traumatic encephalopathy (brain damage), encephalitis (inflammation of the brain), as well as aggravation of preexisting cervical conditions, such as ankylosing spondylitis (stiffening of the spine), and additional subsequent fallout from these conditions. The complaint went on to claim that Mr. Burke, due to his injuries, had been rendered permanently disabled and, as such, was incapable of working at his job. In order to calculate the damages, Burke's attorneys had retained an economist to place a dollar value on his loss of income for the remainder of his working life. It was in the millions.

My first task upon taking over the case was to depose Mr. Burke. At the deposition, he arrived in what appeared to be a "virtual vegetative" state. His attorney showed me photos of his client before the accident. They depicted a spry, athletic and healthy fellow in the prime of life. Was this shell of a man before me really the pitiful figure he appeared to be...or was this an act intended to soak millions from a Fortune 500 company?

The central issue in this case was causation. How could a minor collision like this be capable of causing such devastating injuries? I had to start digging to get at the answer. The first place I decided to search for answers was in the field of biodynamics. I contacted an accident reconstruction expert and provided him with the deposition transcript, police report, repair estimates and other relevant documents. Based upon this information, he was able to accurately calculate the change in velocity (known as the Delta-v) of the Kodak vehicle at the time of impact. Between seven and nine miles per hour was his expert opinion. He further opined that it was impossible for a vehicle traveling at such a slow speed to cause such permanent injuries to Mr. Burke.

Yet, Burke had lined up a contingent of physicians who would swear that his conditions were real and legitimate. How to explain this was my next task. If his condition was real and they were not caused by the accident, then what had caused them? I realized I had to do a deep dive into the plaintiff's medical history. I was able to obtain numerous hospital records relating to admissions dating back to when Burke was in his teens. My careful review of these voluminous records revealed many of the same symptoms: seizures, headaches, confusion, neck pain and diarrhea that he was now listing as being attributable to the accident. In his deposition, Burke had denied having any such pre-existing conditions, but the medical records proved he was lying. Lying *under oath*, no less.

In my quest for answers, I learned all that I could about Burke's alleged conditions by studying medical journals and literature. In those pre-Google days, this type of research was difficult and time-consuming; many attorneys dispensed with it. But in my frequent role of representing plaintiffs in personal injury cases, I had become convinced of the value of making myself knowledgeable about my client's medical condition. I felt that this practice was every bit as true in the current case where I was representing the defendant. Knowledge is power.

Based upon my research, I arrived at a surprising conclusion. I discovered that Burke had been suffering from a lifelong undiagnosed gastrointestinal condition known as Celiac Disease, a chronic digestive and immune disorder. The disease causes long-lasting digestive problems and deprives the body of needed nutrients. This conclusion was supported by a physician who had treated Burke years before the accident and whose notes indicated that he suspected Burke was suffering from Celiac Disease. I deposed the doctor and he delivered his professional medical opinion that Mr. Burke's symptoms were in no way connected to the minor accident in question.

In reporting the results of my research to my client, I advised the Kodak people of the following realities:

- The case would probably boil down to a contest between their expert witnesses and our expert witnesses. It's anyone's guess as to which experts the jury will find more credible.
- According to my best estimates, I evaluated a potential awarding of damages as coming in between seven and ten million dollars.
- I felt that, based upon my findings, I would be able to successfully undermine the plaintiff's contention of causation between the accident and his current medical condition. I rated my chances of winning the case at 70%. Of course, that meant that there remained a 30% chance that Kodak would be forced to pay upwards of ten million dollars in damages.

Based on my advice, Kodak decided to pursue an out-of-court settlement. The good news was that Burke's legal team had become aware of my success in destroying their causation arguments. Hence, they were likewise inclined toward reaching a settlement agreement.

The case, which had a potential eight-figure downside for my client, settled out-of-court with Kodak paying only $750,000. This outcome was regarded as a major victory by me and my clients.

Lesson? Do your homework. Justice resides in the details.

Fast Eddie v. Durante

The case of the forgetful fireman.

Fast Eddie had been represented by Howard on several real estate transactions, but when he decided to file a personal injury lawsuit, Howard referred him to me. Eddie explained that he worked as a fireman in New York City and that he had already made the rounds to several law firms and could not find one that would take his case. Not being quite as choosy as some of my colleagues, I decided to listen to Eddie's story.

"It happened when I was standing in the street in front of the fire-house," he began. "We had just received a report of a fire and I had stopped the oncoming traffic so the big hook and ladder truck could pull out. I was in uniform and when I saw a car approaching, I held up my hand for him to halt. He slowed down and I told him he had to stop and wait. He didn't like that and shouted 'Fuck you' as he hit the gas, slamming into me as he drove by. I was knocked to the ground, but I got a good look at his face and his license plate. I didn't want to forget the number, so I scrambled around in the gutter and found a small piece of sharp glass. I used it to scrawl the license number right into the asphalt."

Eddie reported that he had injured his right knee when he was knocked to the ground and this had resulted in a permanent injury.

He could not continue his duties as a fireman and was forced to give up his livelihood. He wanted to sue the driver to recover his loss of potential income over the remainder of his working life.

"Did you file a police report?" I asked.

"I sure did," he answered. "I was able to give them a description of the car—a white little sports job—and the license plate number. I also gave them a good description of the driver. He was about my age, Caucasian, half-bald and with a huge schnozz."

"A what?"

"You know. A big nose." This smelled like a promising case so I decided to take it.

I first had Eddie examined by a competent physician who would be able to convincingly testify that Eddie would never be able to work as a fireman again. I next obtained the police report and learned that they had tracked the license plate down to a man living in New Jersey named Durante. Mr. Durante claimed he was innocent and was back in New Jersey at the time of incident. I filed our pleading in civil court and Durante's lawyer filed a response denying the charge. We exchanged discovery responses, such as consents to obtain medical records, and we were asked to submit a Bill of Particulars. A Bill of Particulars is a detailed, written statement of claims given upon the defendant's formal request to the court for more detailed information.

My next move was to depose Durante. I did so and that's when I ran into some serious problems. The license plate was registered in New Jersey to a small sports car, but it wasn't white. It was bronze.

273

"Well," I thought to myself, "maybe he had it painted after the incident."

Durante's lawyer then deposed Eddie.

"Is this the driver of the car that struck you?" asked the lawyer, pointing to Durante. Eddie studied the man's face, and while it did sport a good-sized proboscis, Eddie appeared to be uncertain.

"I'm not sure," he finally said. I nearly fainted at this response.

"Shit!" I grumbled to myself. "This case just went belly up."

But I could not simply walk away. I had already invested a good deal of time and effort into this case and wished to avoid taking a loss.

My hope was that Durante's insurance company would still come through with some sort of settlement offer rather than go to court. No way. They felt confident we would not be able to pin this on their customer and opted to have the case tried. In their shoes, given the circumstances, I would have done the same.

The judge we drew was Richard Daronco, whom I considered to be generally friendly toward plaintiffs. In 1987, he would be appointed by President Reagan to the U.S. District Court for the Southern District of New York. Sadly, he would be assassinated one year later by a disgruntled plaintiff whose sexual harassment case against her employer had been dismissed by Daronco for lack of evidence.

Once we had a court date, I ran into another snag. My client, Fast Eddie, had picked up and quickly moved to Colorado. He told me that he did not wish to come back for the trial. I had taken the case on contingency and since he had no money invested at this point, he felt rather indifferent about whether he won or lost. This guy was really starting to grate on my nerves.

"Look, Eddie," I let him know forcefully over the phone. "If you don't show up, the judge will dismiss the case and I'm out my time and the tab for the doctor and the economist I hired to figure up the damages. So, unbuckle your skis, get on a plane and get your ass to the courthouse next Tuesday. Got it? "

He reluctantly agreed.

Once in court, my strategy was to overcome the discrepancy about the color of the vehicle that appeared in the police report. I never put the question about re-painting the car to Durante because I knew he would deny it, even if it was true. So, I tried a different tack. I introduced a color chart into evidence. It had been provided by the manufacturer of the vehicle and had samples of painted metal strips for every color that they offered. I had established that the incident took place around noon on a sunny day and then pointed out how, due to the high reflectiveness of the material, many of the color strips appeared to be white when they were struck with bright light. This seemed to resonate with the jury.

When Eddie took the stand, he was still unable to positively identify the defendant. I had not "coached" him on this issue and he responded just as he had done during the deposition.

The defendant then took the stand and, as expected, claimed to have been in New Jersey on the date in question. The defendant's attorneys were so confident that the case would be quickly disposed of that they did not bother to provide any alibi witnesses. Big mistake. This conspicuous absence caused the jury to conclude that there were no such witnesses, causing them to question the defendant's alibi. The next step was my summation.

"So, it is entirely possible," I argued to the jury, "that if you are lying injured in the street trying to catch a glimpse of a vehicle speeding off in the bright sunlight, you might mistake a bronze paint job for a white one." I recognized that this argument was tenuous at best and I had to go for a clincher if I was to have any hope of victory.

"Ladies and gentleman, you have read the police report which was introduced into evidence. It documents that the plaintiff identified the driver of the car as a man with a huge nose. It listed the defendant as the owner of a sports car whose license plate matches the one my seriously injured client carved into the pavement that day. I ask you to now give the defendant a good hard look and determine if he was or was not the man my client identified as the driver of the car."

I then turned from the jury box and pointed at the defendant.

"Look at his nose," I admonished them. "It's *huge*. Just as described by my client in the police report. Your decision to find for the plaintiff should be as plain as the nose on *his* face."

I felt it was a positive sign when Judge Daronco agreed to allow the jury to take the paint samples into the jury room with them. I was right. They returned a unanimous verdict in favor of Eddie, determining that the defendant had full liability. The jury was then instructed to reconvene in order to set the amount of the damages.

Since the judge had not permitted me to call the economist I had hired to testify about how much in lost wages Eddie would suffer over the course of his life, the decision about damages was entirely in the hands of the jury. In my summation, I pointed out that, at my client's age, he would have been capable of working for at least another 20 years and, at his current salary, his lifetime loss of income could easily amount to one million dollars. Add to that the cost of his medical bills and his pain and suffering, and his total damages were double that sum.

In those days, it was not necessary to disclose to juries how much a winning plaintiff was to receive from other sources—such as disability insurance and pension payments—when setting the size of an award. We had won the hard part of the case, so by my reckoning, I was fully expecting the jury to award my client at least two million dollars. But that did not happen. Fast Eddie did me in once again.

Before the jury had a chance to set the award, Durante's insurance company finally decided to start making settlement offers to Eddie. Typically, at this point, the client and I begin the process of dickering for a much larger amount. In a move that is rather unusual, Eddie opted to grab the first amount they offered him, $150,000.

It is likewise unheard of for a client to accept the first settlement offer presented. But that's exactly what Fast Eddie did. I was flabbergasted when he informed me that he wanted to take it and I tried to get him to understand what his ill-advised decision to settle would cost him.

"The hard part—establishing liability—had already been accomplished and at this point we could have gotten a lot more," I pointed out in exasperation.

"No, Ell." Eddie responded. "I'm done and I want to go home." I was forced to settle the case for a fraction of what I knew it was worth. I was sickened in doing so but I could not go against my client's wishes.

"Why did you accept it, Eddie?" I asked him again afterward. "The jury would have given us a hell of a lot more."

"Maybe," he said, "but I didn't really care about this case beyond establishing the extent of my disability. Once it became part of the record that I'm fully disabled, I qualify for lifetime disability payments through the fire department at 75% of my annual salary—tax-free. Why take a chance on the jury?"

After the decision, I questioned members of the jury as part of my routine follow-up. I learned that they did actually play around with the color chart in the jury room and were able to manipulate it in the light so that certain colors appeared to be white, just as I had claimed. This served to enhance my credibility and so, when I argued that the defendant had to be guilty, they believed me. One juror, I learned, joked that the reason the defendant's nose was so big was that it, like Pinocchio's, grew longer every time he told a lie.

As it turned out, Mr. Durante was not the only one guilty of having stretched the truth in this case. After all the shooting was over, Fast Eddie admitted to me that things did not happen exactly as he had reported them to the police. The driver had gotten him so angry by ignoring his order to halt and then cursing at him, that Eddie decided on the spot to make him pay. He went on to admit to me that he had struck the car hard with his hand as it drove by and then intentionally fallen to the ground. He did not have to fake his injuries, however, because he actually did mangle his knee when he fell.

Despite my disappointment at the outcome, this case taught me a valuable lesson. Take everything your client tells you with a grain of salt.

The handful of examples described in this chapter represent a mere sampling of the many fascinating cases it has been my good fortune to litigate. While not every outcome was in my clients' favor, I can honestly say that there were understandable reasons behind each of the cases I lost. If you are a young person considering a legal career, it is my hope that these cases will give you a flavor of the excitement and satisfaction—as well as the hard work—that comes with being an active trial attorney.

Thank you for taking this side road down memory lane with me. The following chapter picks up the narrative and explores my and my family's love of athletics and competitive sports. So, if you're ready to go from civil courts to basketball courts, please do read on.

.

Elliot Fixler

Chapter Fifteen

Full Court Press

"The only place that success comes before work is in the dictionary."
—Vince Lombardi

ymnast Mary Lou Retton once observed, "Trophies collect dust, but memories last forever." In this chapter I'd like to share some of my favorite memories from a time when I had the ability to engage both in athletics and work with my kids as they developed into outstanding athletes.

My law practice appeared to be doing fine despite Howard's departure. I spent most of my time bouncing back and forth between our Carmel and NYC offices monitoring cases and supervising the topflight team I had assembled. The firm's reputation as winning attorneys continued to grow and we were attracting clients from all sorts of new sources. Thanks to the outstanding work being performed by our attorneys, office managers and staff, I actually found myself with more free time than before Howard had left the practice. This free time allowed me to concentrate on raising Mathew and Sarah, something I was not able to do fully with Mitchell and Jason.

After moving into the Lake House, we conducted a nearly total renovation. When we removed the old asbestos ceiling tiles in the living room, we were delighted to discover beautiful wood planking that only needed some minor restoration to look like new. Part of the renovation involved planting pillars and building an outdoor deck overlooking the lake. For safety reasons, we surrounded it with a ten-foot-high fence. The deck included a fantastic "sports court." This consisted of a full basketball court plus facilities for tennis and volleyball. The court flooring was made up of plastic tiles laid atop the wooden decking. It was a truly spectacular addition to the house and got a lot of use over the years, particularly by Mathew and his basketball buddies. Mat enjoyed a decided home court advantage whenever he and his pals played on our sports court thanks to Finster, our Rottweiler. I'll explain.

One of my clients, Tony Provenzano, had a girlfriend who decided to raise Rottweilers. Tony honored Lorraine and me by offering us the pick of the first litter. How could I say no?

We brought home a pup who I named Finster after my first wife. Finster means "darkness" in Yiddish. Finster and Mathew developed a special bond as they grew up together. This bond resulted in Finster being highly protective of Mat. So, whenever Finster observed one of Mat's friends guarding him a little too closely during a basketball game, the pooch would run onto the court and nip at the kid's butt. This canine consideration provided Mat with some extra breathing room whenever he had the ball.

The sports court was not only for the kids. I likewise often invited my basketball buddies over to play. Sunday morning games were the best. Lorraine would prepare a spread of bagels and lox for the members of the "tribe" and fresh doughnuts for the others. As I kicked back after a grueling game, I would savor each sweaty moment. Biting into a luxurious sesame seed toasted bagel topped with a slab of Philadelphia cream cheese, sliced smoked nova, a slice of tomato, red onion, capers and crumbled hard-boiled egg, I could not help but reflect on how far I had come from my teenage pickup basketball games back in Buffalo.

In my mind's eye, I envisioned how we would quickly shovel the snow off the driveway at Snip's house (Snip was my friend, Richard Polisner's nickname), and play half-court using the backboard affixed above the door of his family garage. We would play to the point of exhaustion and then dig into the snacks. It wasn't bagels we snacked on in those days, however. Snip's mother would serve us pepperoni pizza; I did not hold back. It was the first *trafe* (non-kosher) food I had ever eaten and I recall marveling at how good it tasted since I had been raised to believe that only kosher food was fit to eat.

As mentioned, our daughter Sarah Beth was born in 1984 and by the time she was three years old, she was up on skis instructed by her brother, Mat, who was an old pro by then at age five. We often traveled to our ski chalet in Vermont that we continued to own with Howard even after he and I ended our professional partnership. When Mat and Sarah became active in school sports and were no longer available for ski weekends, we decided to sell the place. We were striving to simplify our lives and would conduct our skiing out west in Colorado.

As part of this simplification process, we had to give some consideration to our island retreat. It was by all means a very special place and a cherished getaway destination for us, but maintaining it involved a lot of work that became more and more of a burden as time went by. Just bringing groceries to the place by boat was an on-going challenge. And cleaning up at the end of a fun-filled weekend amounted to a lot of plain old drudgery. Lorraine and I started to feel as though we were operating a bed and breakfast, except at the end of their stay, our guests only paid us with kisses and handshakes. We finally came to the conclusion that it was simply more trouble than it was worth and I sold my interest to Stuart Myers. Farewell, Vermont; adieu to Mother-in-Law Island. Time to move on.

Without these obligations I was able to devote more attention to Mat and Sarah and help them develop into fine little athletes. What with baseball, soccer, basketball and cross-country running—both at school and at various community sports programs—I could visualize our kids becoming Olympic athletes at some point in the future.

I continued to keep myself in good shape physically as well. I would run with Mat and Sarah and also on my own. I played basket-ball regularly, both at home and at the Jefferson Valley Racket Club where I joined a league and made many new friends. Some of these friends would wind up playing a major role in my life and I continue to count them as friends up through this day.

When I first joined the Jefferson Valley Racket Club, located six miles southwest of Mahopac, it was primarily a tennis and racquet-ball facility. On one of my early winter visits there to practice my backhand with some friends, I discovered racquetball. It was love at first swat and I never went back to tennis. My frequent matches with Stuart Myers were exhausting, but exhilarating. Our love for the game carried over to our time working on cases at our NYC office.

We sought out a nearby racquetball court in Manhattan and visited there whenever our workload permitted us to break away.

Jefferson Valley eventually expanded by adding a full court basketball area. This was great because it allowed me to engage in my deep-seated passion for the game of hoops and hustle. I immediately signed up to play on a team in the leagues they were setting up. It was through those leagues that I got to know some of the most interesting and colorful characters I have ever had the pleasure of meeting. This rogue's gallery included Bobby Dellangelo, Jay Paldin, the Tully brothers, Frank Reynolds, and perhaps the most outrageous character of them all, Raymond Kolkman.

It was with members of this hearty crew that I would retire to the club's second-floor lounge after a round of racquetball, where we could look down and watch other games in progress. Paul Iacuone owned a nearby pizza joint and we would often head there afterwards for a slice and a beer. Paul's partner in the restaurant was a basketball buddy of mine and a client of Howard's from Syracuse named Mike. Eventually, Mike and Paul's partnership ended and Paul, with whom I by now had become good friends, expanded the pizza parlor into a full-blown Italian restaurant. It became our "go-to" place not only after racquetball, but also after basketball games and other events.

Paul and his wife, Terry, got out of the restaurant racket and went into the dry-cleaning business, but he held on to the building and leased it out to other operators over the years.

In 2007, Paul and Terry came to me and asked for my guidance in helping them adopt a baby girl whose birth mother was a drug addict. I told them the hard truth that it was probably not a good idea since addiction can be passed on to the fetus and they would be letting themselves in for a lot of future grief. They ignored my advice and proceeded with the adoption; it turned out to be the right decision. That baby became the fourth child of the Iacuone family and he turned out to be a true jewel in every way. As of this writing, he has accepted a lacrosse scholarship at Monmouth College. I have never been so happy about being so wrong about something. The lesson here is that if a child has great parents like Paul and Terry, they will most likely turn out okay.

I love Paul dearly but he is such an assiduous friend, it can become annoying. Every time I feel like picking up the phone and checking in with him, he invariably calls me first "just to see how you're doing."

And I feel like a schmuck whenever I say, "I was just about to call you."

I have recently received a "Save The Date" postcard from Paul announcing the wedding of one of his sons on May 28, 2022. I was forced to tell him I would not be able to attend because that date corresponds to the day that I married my first wife, the "Wicked Witch of the West." It is a day of mourning for me, not celebration. He thought I was joking and laughed it off. He was right. I was kidding.

Another member of our racquetball gang was Bobby DellAngelo who knew everyone in Mahopac not only because he was a mail carrier, but also because of his dynamic personality that endeared him to one and all. Like the attorney I had faced in the Outlaw v. ShopRite case, Marty Lassoff, Bobby had a photographic memory. But in addition, he also had a "phonographic" memory. He could recall and recite back verbatim anything and everything he heard with the accuracy of a court stenographer. He possesses an infuriatingly accurate and encyclopedic knowledge of all sports trivia and was often called upon to arbitrate disputes over certain athletic statistics. I also played basketball with Bobby and he could be every bit as pesky whenever he would be required to guard me as I tried to make my way down the court.

Jay Paldin, another member of our intrepid crew, would certainly endorse my opinion of Bobby's basketball skills. Jay and I were pals for a long time until we had a falling out, which I will explain.

These days, Jay lives nearby in Florida, but he avoids me as though I had tested positive for not only COVID-19, but also the Bubonic Plague. Like me, Jay played basketball in the Jefferson Valley Racket Club league, although the two of us never played on the same team. He stood 5 foot 8 and was fast and feisty. Also, like me, Jay hated to lose, so when our team beat his team for the league basketball championship, it was a sweet victory that I have savored for years, and one made sweeter by affording me the many opportunities to never let Jay forget it.

Jay was a gifted athlete in other sports as well. He had played shortstop on the University of Kentucky varsity baseball team during his college years. He had taken a job as a gym teacher at Mahopac High School. Jay was a terrific coach of the girls' basketball team. He was able to motivate his not-particularly-talented collection of teenage girls to work hard and become over-achievers.

My disaffection with Jay began long after we had played basketball against each other at the Jefferson Valley Racquet Club. My daughter, Sarah, was in the eighth grade and a rising star on the Mahopac High School Varsity girls' basketball team. Jay Paldin was their coach. Despite the fact that Sarah was clearly the team's best shooter, Jay kept her almost permanently glued to the bench. Whenever he did allow her to play, he took heat from parents who complained that he was letting an 8th-grader play instead of their own upper grade daughters.

I can still recall the big game between Mahopac and their in-town rival, Carmel High School. It was a close contest as the clock approached half-time and Jay finally decided to put Sarah in the game. She wasted no time in making three 3-point shots to end the half. Jay put her in again near the end of the third quarter and she amazed the crowd by sinking a three-pointer from mid-court right at the buzzer. Yet, despite Sarah's impressive display of shooting prowess, Jay refused to put her in at all during the fourth quarter and Mahopac went home a loser.

Jay was simply not inclined to put younger players into the game, preferring instead to give more court time to the upper grade girls. He stubbornly stuck to this this practice even if it meant losing the game. Even the local newspaper reporter, Mark Alan Tierstein, who covered girls' high school basketball for the Putnam Daily Voice, noted this fact in his coverage that appeared in the paper's January 8, 1998 issue:

> Mahopac eighth-grader, Sarah Fixler, had scored 10 points in the second quarter, including three 3-pointers, and she added a half-court 3-pointer at the third quarter buzzer.

"We had to adjust on Fixler and we went into man-to-man defense to break up their rhythm," said Carmel coach Dan O'Hare whose team finished with at 49-44 victory.

Carmel's switching to man-to-man defense (actually, girl-to-girl, to be politically correct) to thwart Sarah on the court made no difference. She was still able to break down their defense with her deft ball handling and precise passing skills.

What was infuriating about Jay's unwillingness to play Sarah was the fact that he was fully aware of her skills and would speak about them publicly. On December 10, 1997, Coach Paldin was interviewed by a reporter for the North County News newspaper during which he was asked about the eighth grader who would be playing on his team during the upcoming season.

"Sarah is an extremely good ball handler and has an extremely good shot from the outside," he replied. "I think she's going to fit in and complement our team nicely as an outside threat."

I guess he meant "fit in" on the team bench.

I had first met big (six foot four) Ted Tully when Mathew began playing soccer in the fourth grade on the same team with Ted's son, Ryan. Our friendship was cemented on the basketball court at Jefferson Valley Racquet Club as well as on the sports court at our home. Ted coached MSA basketball and did so for Sarah's fourth, fifth, and sixth grade teams. Ted's son, Sean, also played on those teams. It was during those years that, working with Ted, Sarah further developed her skills on the court. She matured into a great shooter and ball handler and her passing was nothing short of brilliant. Sean was the team's tall center and, thanks to him and Sarah, they won the championship every year.

Sean played basketball, football, and lacrosse for Mahopac High as did Ryan Tully. Ryan and Mathew were in the same grade and best friends. Ryan stood six foot five while Sean was six foot seven.

Ted's brother, Pete, stood 6 foot 3, had a wonderful personality that was, at times, enhanced by the fact that he suffered from alcoholism. At one time, I represented Pete and helped him beat a drunk driving arrest. As some cynic once said, "A good lawyer knows the law, a great lawyer knows the judge."

I was successful in getting his case dismissed and, as was my usual practice in the case of friends, I did not charge him a fee. At the conclusion of the trial, Pete convinced me to loan him $10,000 which he promised to pay back in two weeks. He never did, claiming that I had actually loaned the money to a corporation that had gone belly up.

There were a few more members of our court-side cadre I could mention, but my fear of making this book too long prevents me from doing so. There was one figure, however, who stands out in my memory so strongly that he simply cannot be overlooked.

Ray Kolkmann was a one-of-a-kind piece of work and a true force of nature—and not because he possessed any great basketball abilities. He loved to shoot but lacked the skill to do so accurately. Ray loved to coach MSA basketball and did so on teams that his sons, Timmy and Ryan, played on. Timmy was in the same grade as Sarah and they often played on opposing teams. Ray's team, it seemed, was never able to beat Sarah's team, no matter what he exhorted his son and the other players to do to stop her. She was simply unstoppable. Ray remains one of my best buddies to this day but still whines about the way Sarah's team would consistently beat the pants off him and Timmy. There is more about Ray beyond basketball that needs to be told, but I will save that for later.

While my law practice continued to do well, it was during this period that I thought it might be a good idea to engage in some more marketing to promote our practice's personal injury services. Like many P.I. lawyers at the time, I looked into running TV commercials. These would appear during daytime TV on local cable channels when the demographic profile of viewers aligned with that of our preferred personal injury plaintiffs.

One of the lawyers working in our Carmel office, Kent Benziger, had a background in Radio and TV advertising and offered to assist in putting together an ad campaign. He felt that most attorney TV commercials were too stiff and formal, resulting in intimidating rather than attracting potential clients. Kent advised that we produce a spot that would "humanize" me and thereby make me appear more accessible and friendly. He suggested that we enlist members of my family to appear in the TV spots.

I persuaded Mat, who was ten at the time, to appear on camera to promote "the Law Offices of Stockfield and Fixler." He did a first-rate job and showed some true acting skills as he introduced me to the audience as "that distinguished lawyer who will separate his firm from the rest." After starring in a few such spots, Mat tired of the repetition of having to shoot take after take and begged to be released from his contract. I agreed to do so if he promised to devote his energies toward achieving excellence in his schoolwork and athletics. I'm proud to say that Mat kept his promise. If you care to view these TV spots starring Mat, they are available online at https://youtube/ wIEjv1vf6Yc.

Yes, Mat kept his promise to work hard...and then some. His grades and scores were off the charts. He was ranked either number one or two in his class every year while his test scores consistently placed him in the 99th percentile. Sports, however, was a different story. Student athletics in our community were run by the Mahopac Sports Association (MSA) and they sponsored a soccer league for elementary school kids for which Mat was signed up. He would come home unhappy after every game because he was being given a hard time by the other kids on the team. I suspected it might be because he was one of the few Jewish kids in the community, but I told him to tough it out. He did. As time passed and his teammates got to know him, the problems abated. In fact, he was eventually held in such high esteem by his classmates that he was elected class president in the 4th, 5th and 6th grades.

The MSA offered baseball, soccer, and basketball programs. The elite basketball program was sponsored by the Catholic Youth Organization (CYO) and held yearly try-outs. Only top players qualified for the Mahopac CYO team. Mat tried out for it and performed very well. Yet, he was cut from the team. I was outraged at this blatant favoritism being exhibited toward Christian children who were members of the Catholic Church where the games were held. Mat then tried out for a different CYO team in an adjacent community and made the team. In fact, he was skilled enough to play in games with kids above his age level.

Some parents hold their children back a grade level so that they will be more developed than their classmates and therefore competitively advantaged when it comes to athletics. We thought this practice to be unfair and actually harmful to a student's athletic and academic development. In fact, we always encouraged our kids to compete against others who were better and stronger than they were. "That's how you get good," I advised.

Mat came face-to-face with this issue when he was on the track and field team at school. He frequently competed in two-to-three-mile foot races and would usually finish first. Whenever he finished second, he invariably lost to another student named Matthew (with two T's) who had been held back a year. Mat's nemesis, Matthew, was a year older and a head taller than Mat. Allowing Matthew to compete against younger students was clearly unjust and presaged today's environment in which we see athletic officials sanction unfair competition between transgender males and females.

Both our kids, Mat and Sarah, excelled at athletics because they worked hard and played hard. They did not seek out any unfair advantages. Mathew played basketball at Yorktown, Shrub Oak and Mahopac as did Sarah. Sarah qualified for the Mahopac CYO team while Mat played for the one in Shrub Oak. He did great there although he missed not being able to play alongside his classmates.

As a sixth grader, Mathew played AAU basketball on a travel team. The team was composed mostly of seventh graders, but Mat held his own alongside the older boys. Mat was a tenacious and skilled player. I still recall his one-on-one game on the sports court on our deck against his cousin, Chris Bugg. Chris was the 16-year-old center of his high school basketball team at the time and stood 6 foot 6. He beat Mat, but not by much. Final score: 15 to 14. Mat had scored all those points without anyone setting up a screen (protective wall of offensive players) or a pick (an offensive player blocking an opponent seeking to guard a teammate).

That sports court would see both Mat and Sarah practicing their shots and moves day and night. I likewise worked with them putting them through a variety of drills, having them run around the perimeter of the court, switching hands as they dribbled the ball. I had them run the length of the court passing to one another until one would execute a lay-up shot with first the right hand and then the left. When it got too cold to practice outdoors on the deck, they would retire to the basement and keep up the drills. Sometimes they would watch basketball instruction videotapes produced by basketball pro "Pistol" Pete Maravich.

The dynamic between Sarah and Mat was amazing. She idolized her older brother and sought to emulate his athletic abilities. As for Mat, he wanted her to be as good as he was and devoted himself to her training. As a result, Sarah was able to join the local girls' basketball league in the third grade, even though she was playing alongside fourth graders. She was selected to play on an MSA team coached by Ted Tully (more about him later). Sarah's team managed to win the MSA championship every year through sixth grade.

Sarah went on to play basketball in the Shrub Oak Boys' League where, in sixth grade, she made the All-Star team and was voted the

MVP (most valuable player) in the big All-Star game. She never ran into any friction due to her being the only girl on the team. Sarah played the point guard position and although she had control of the ball most of the time, she was never selfish about it and would frequently pass to another player. Probably a bit too often to avoid charges of "hogging" the ball.

Sarah was a double threat in that she also played baseball in the Boys' League. She played shortstop and also pitched. This fact, at times, posed a problem whenever she struck out a batter. The player would invariably be teased by his teammates for being "struck out by a girl." They would sometimes get angry and exhibit poor sportsmanship directed at Sarah.

Sarah likewise followed in her brother's footsteps academically, turning in exemplary grades and test scores. Just like Mat, Sarah was elected president of the student body in the fourth, fifth and sixth grades. I was extremely proud of both kids; not only for their achievements in the classroom and on the court and field, but also because of the kind of people they were becoming: caring, bright and self-reliant. They both made a father's heart swell with pride.

.

Elliot Fixler

Chapter Sixteen

Party Time!

"Trust me. You can dance."

—Vodka

T he number one hit song in America in July 1990 was *She Ain't Worth It* by Bobby Brown. It was playing on the radio when Lorraine informed me that she wished to throw herself a 40th birthday party. After some quick private deliberation, I wisely came to the conclusion that "She IS Worth It" and said, "That's fine, dear."

After the terrific shindig she had put on for my 40th, how could I say otherwise? I did lay down one condition, however, "Don't ask me to dance."

I had observed that most white people look rather stupid and awkward on the dance floor. The well-known Seinfeld TV series episode called *The Little Kicks* in which Elaine Benes displays her painfully inept and comical dance moves, comes to mind. While I do appreciate professional choreographed dancing and have even sat through a ballet or two and enjoyed the experience, I feel that most amateurs engage in dancing for two reasons:

- As a poor substitute for sex, or
- Because they believe it to be a way of getting some exercise

297

In either case, sex or fitness, I prefer the real thing.

I am not one who enjoys all the work and preparation necessary to put on a social event like what Lorraine had in mind, so I was comfortable in the knowledge that she would handle all the details. I just had to show up. We did not discuss budget because, by this time, I had come to know that Lorraine was not a frivolous spender. She managed our family's finances with deft skill and her only fiscal weakness was her willingness to loan people money without my prior approval. So, when it came to putting on this grand event, Lorraine had carte blanche.

While I thought the guest list of more than 100 "intimate" friends was a bit heavy, I appreciated that she decided the venue would be the outdoor areas of our home on the lake, instead of some lavish catering hall. As mentioned, we had built a huge deck along the lakefront side of the house that contained a central stairway down to a 60-foot walkway that led to the water. There was a gazebo on one side of the deck that could be used as a bandstand by the musicians that Lorraine had hired. And, of course, there was the sports court that could be illuminated at night.

Lorraine decided that since the deck was not covered and we did not want our guests inside the house, we would need to rent a tent in case of rain. It was erected on the lawn that sloped from the deck down to the water and featured tiled flooring that allowed for tables to be set up, as well as a good-sized dance floor (which I would NOT be seen on). Lorraine wanted to hire some roving entertainers to keep the guests feeling jolly. She wound up hiring a few excellent celebrity impersonators who delighted our guests by greeting them as an ersatz Clark Gable and Marilyn Monroe.

I realized, shortly before the July 13 party date, I really ought to do more than merely show up. I felt I should reciprocate for the strip-tease surprise that Lorraine had arranged for *my* 40th birthday. I knew that she and her girlfriends occasionally traveled into the city to catch a Chippendale male stripper show, but bringing in a hunky beefcake bump-and-grinder would not be too original. That had already been done.

I was pondering this as I drove home from the office while listening to Howard Stern on the radio. Looking back, I'm embarrassed to admit I enjoyed listening to that crude cretin. I'm happy to report that my tastes have grown more sophisticated since then. Actually, Lorraine and I both preferred listening to the "I-man," also known as Don Imus. That got me thinking about an entertainer that appeared regularly on his "Imus in the Morning" radio talk show, a comedian named Rob Bartlett. Bartlett had a recurrent bit during which he hilariously impersonated Panamanian dictator Manuel Antonia Noriega. He also performed ingenious voice impersonations of the Godfather, Dr. Phil, Rush Limbaugh, Larry King, Bill Clinton and Bob Dylan. His most outrageous character was a long-running fictitious old blues musician known as the "Blind Mississippi White Boy," Pig Feets Dupris.

I tracked down Bartlett through WNBC-AM in New York and hired him for the reasonable sum of $5,000 plus a limo to deliver him to and from the event. It was worth every penny just to see the look on Lorraine's face when he made his entrance and planted a birthday kiss on her lips. Evidently Bartlett had conducted a little homework about me by consulting with my friend, David Kellogg (the fellow known to enjoy mooning passing tour boats from Mother-in-Law Island). Hence, Bartlett was able, in addition to his usual routines and impersonations, to deliver some "custom-crafted" jokes, all at my expense.

All of my kids were in attendance and they had a blast. They particularly appreciated the fact that we had invited one of their beloved schoolteachers, John Scaglia, who evidently did not share my opinions about dancing. He was a good ol' country boy and spent the evening "dosey-do-ing" all over the dance floor.

Lorraine was particularly pleased that her parents, Bella and Bob, were able to attend and celebrate her big milestone. Shortly after their granddaughter, Sarah, was born, Bob retired and they decided to buy an RV and see the U.S.A. They made it as far as St. Augustine, Florida, and loved it so much they decided to stay and put down stakes.

During the party and afterwards, I could sense that there was some tension between Bob and Bella. She seemed short-tempered and would often snap at Bob. I finally was able to corner my father-in-law and he opened his heart to me.

"I don't know what to do with her, Elliot," he bemoaned referring to Bella. "She thinks I'm cheating on her and I swear to you, it's not true. At my age, I don't even look at other women."

"Well, you two are together all day and night, right?" I pointed out. "When does she say you're doing all this fooling around?"

"That's just it," he said shaking his head. "She talks about the time I was a saxophone player with a band back in London like it was yesterday. That was 40-some years ago!"

Lorraine's parents went back to Florida a few days after the party, and we didn't see too much of them for a while. Then we got the news. Isabella had been diagnosed with Alzheimer's Disease. It was what had accounted for her erratic behavior. Although Lorraine and I, along with our kids, visited them several times in St. Augustine, we never really witnessed all the suffering that both she and Bob endured as victims of this devastating disease.

Eventually, and tragically, my mother-in-law succumbed to the illness and passed away at age 74.

As a result of losing Bella to Alzheimer's, I read up on the disease. I learned that although it was still not fully understood whether Alzheimer's is caused by genetic or environmental factors, having a first degree relative (parent or sibling) with Alzheimer's increased a person's likelihood of contracting the condition. Was there a chance that Lorraine would be afflicted? I dismissed the thought because she was so much more like her father—who lived to age 100 with his mental faculties intact—than her mother.

As you will discover, I was to pay the price for this cavalier attitude. Let me just say I was dead wrong, not only about the chances of Lorraine escaping the ravages of Alzheimer's. I was also dismissive and callous about the safety of my children. One reason for writing this book is for me to be able to declare "Mea Culpa." I was wrong, terribly wrong, about so many things.

Elliot Fixler

Chapter Seventeen

Mathew

"There is no footprint too small to leave an imprint on this world."

—Anonymous

As I discussed in Chapter Fourteen, during the first half of the 1990's, I made it a point to avoid being an absentee father. Perhaps I was overcompensating because when the boys from my first marriage were growing up, I was, as often as not, simply not present. I was busy building my practice and developing my legal career and, like many men during that stage of life, I had become a part-time father. This became dramatically true after my separation from their mother with the boys no longer living with me full-time.

Yes, I played ball with them when they were little and showed up at their games as they got older. But I was not fully engaged. I bought them trail motorcycles and went riding with them. I took them skiing and shushed the slopes with them. I accompanied Mitch to Europe and took both boys on a wild west vacation. In the 1970s, Howard and I had bought Yankee season tickets and we often took the boys along to Yankee Stadium. In fact, those season tickets were passed down and are being shared these days by Jason and Mitchell along with Stuart Myers' son-in-law. But, when you add it all up, I still did not spend the proper amount of time needed to be a guiding influence in their lives.

I have always been haunted by the dysfunctional relationship I endured with my stepfather—a fraught family connection that I described earlier in this book. I had long before committed myself to not replicating the sort of emotionally detached parenting practiced by Sam Fixler. So, in taking stock, I felt as though I had fallen short when it came to Jason and Mitchell and had not invested myself fully in their lives. I had not lived up to the goal I had set for myself. And I vowed to do better.

Raising Mathew and Sarah was an all-consuming passion. I was fortunate that I had the time, the financial ability, and the inclination to spend a generous amount of time with each of them. As described earlier, a lot of this "together time" was devoted to athletics. There were cross-country races, gymnastic competitions, soccer matches, baseball games, and, of course, basketball tournaments. As mentioned, our weekends were so full of sports activities that we no longer were able to get away and go skiing in Vermont and, as a result, wound up selling our ski lodge. Lorraine and I made no weekend plans for ourselves during those years. We were totally committed to participating in all of our kids' activities and we were loving it.

Mat was a member of three different in-town basketball teams. It was the CYO league in the winter and the AAU basketball league in the summertime. Sarah followed dutifully in Mat's sneaker steps and used his life as a template for her own. As mentioned, she played brilliantly in the boys' basketball leagues. She gave up on girls' softball after a short time because she found it was not challenging enough for her. Sarah moved over to boys' baseball through sixth grade. She joined the girls' High School Junior Varsity basketball team when she reached seventh grade.

The last day of school, in May of 1994, was a particularly lovely late spring day. The weather matched Mat's mood. He had just graduated from sixth grade and was as happy as I had ever seen him. His good looks were already beginning to emerge as he stood on the threshold of puberty. On top of that, he was extremely eloquent and well-spoken. These attributes had contributed to his being elected class president three years running. He was also consistently voted top athlete of his class and finished each year either in the top or number two spot academically.

I mentioned earlier that Mat did a fantastic job as an actor in our firm's TV commercial campaign, but that he quickly begged off claiming he had grown tired of the repetitive nature of the work. It was at this point I learned the truth. The real reason Mat wanted out of his acting contract was that the commercials were making him something of a local celebrity, resulting in his attracting a good deal of embarrassing attention from the many girls who now recognized him whenever he went out in public. This undue adulation was making Mat's young girlfriend jealous and upset.

Mathew's life was about as perfect as any 12-year-old red-blooded American boy could hope for. He was a champion baseball, soccer, and basketball student athlete. His gorgeous lakefront home sported a nearly full-size basketball court with a regulation batting cage located behind the four-car garage. And to top it off, he had a sweet little girlfriend and a bunch of great buddies and pals.

What he was lacking, I'm grieved to report, was a father who was smart enough to protect him from the dangers that lurk in this world.

July 19, 1994, was a picture-perfect, cloudless mid-summer Tuesday on Lake Mahopac. I was working from home and Mat had invited over one of his classmate buddies for some fun on the lake. Mat came to me and asked if he and his friend, Riley Quinn, could take our two jet skis out on the water for a spin around the lake. I didn't think twice about saying "sure."

While the current New York statute states that anyone operating a "personal watercraft" must have a boating safety certificate and be at least 14 years of age, I was not aware of any such restrictions in place at the time. In any case, Mat had driven these recreational "water hogs" often and was highly experienced in their proper use. The thought of any imminent danger never entered my mind.

You might well ask how this could be so. How could an attorney who has spent his career representing both plaintiffs and defendants in personal injury and negligence cases not consider the risk of allowing children to operate these powerful motorized devices unsupervised? I know it's hard to fathom. It's a question that has haunted my every waking and sleeping hour from that day to this.

I watched from the deck as the boys took off across the lake and I then rose and walked up to the house to do some work at my desk. About fifteen minutes after I sat down, the phone rang. It was Mike Barile's daughter, Nicole.

"Elliot, there's been an accident," she blurted with a clear sense of urgency. "It's Mat. He's had an accident with the jet ski. He's been taken to Melchner's Marina." I jumped in the car and drove like the wind halfway around the lake and screeched to a halt outside the marina. I ran up the steps and spotted Mat, lying inert on the wooden deck planking. There did not appear to be any visible injuries. The paramedics arrived and transported Mat to the Putnam Hospital Center in Carmel.

I phoned my friend, Dr. Janus Rudnicki, a local Ob/Gyn who worked at the hospital to alert him that they were bringing Mat in to the E.R. When I arrived at the hospital, a grave-faced emergency room doctor delivered the news that I had been dreading.

"He's gone," is all he said. There was nothing he or anyone else could do. Mat was gone and gone with him were all of our hopes and dreams for his future.

I don't recall much about my emotional state at that painful moment, except I knew what I had to do next. And it was something I dreaded beyond words. I had to tell Lorraine.

For some reason, she and Mitchell had travelled to New York City that day. Telling her that Mat was gone was undoubtedly the most difficult thing I had ever done in my life. She did not cry when I gave her the sad news. She was every bit as stoic as she was on the day I had told her I had to break off our relationship. She did not condemn me. There was no recrimination, no anger directed at me for my negligence. Sometimes I wish she had lashed out at me. It might have helped to expiate my guilt. But all she said was "How did it happen?"

It took a while to put all the pieces together, but we eventually learned that Mike Barile's eldest daughter, a classmate of Mathew's, was out on the lake piloting her father's boat. A girlfriend of hers was also onboard. They witnessed Riley drive his jet ski directly into Mathew's. What caused him to do this? Was he distracted by the girls in the boat to the point that he lost sight of where he was going? Did the girls on the boat somehow trigger the accident? Did Mathew? We'll never know. I did not have the heart to dig into the details. I never questioned Riley or the girls. I didn't care. All the investigating in the world would not bring Mathew back.

I had, in the past, represented families in two cases that involved losing a child due to an accident. One was a 16-year-old who had died in an auto accident and the other a 12-year-old boy who was killed in a school bus collision. I had, in those two cases, and in other similar ones, prided myself on being empathetic toward my clients who had lost loved ones. I would offer palliative comments such as "I understand how you're feeling." But these were lies. As I discovered the hard way, I did not have a clue about the depth of their pain nor the expanse of their grief.

My next chore was perhaps even more onerous than breaking the news to Lorraine. We gathered up Mitchell and Jason and drove up to Sarah's summer camp to pick her up and bring her home. Telling her that the big brother she worshipped was permanently gone was perhaps the most horribly heart-wrenching experience of my life and I know it wasn't one bit easier for Lorraine. The car trip home was a nightmarish blur. I was devastated by Mat's death and my feelings of guilt for letting it happen. I was hardly able to look at the faces of my children and my wife and bear witness to their grieving over the sudden loss of their beloved brother and son during that long ride home.

Lorraine handled all the funeral arrangements. I told her that I wanted only immediate family to be there and after that, I just shut down. I spent the next three days huddled on the floor of our walk-in bedroom closet. After the funeral, my family engaged in the Jewish memorial ritual of sitting Shiva. This is a seven-day observance that involves the immediate family of the deceased sitting low to the floor and wearing clothing that has been rent. They carried out the Shiva on the first floor while I remained in bed upstairs. I could not bring myself to face anyone.

About a week later, Ted Tully, my friend, and Mat and Sarah's athletic coach, organized a meaningful memorial service that took place by the lake. A large contingent of Mat's many friends and classmates attended. Ted told me that the kids needed this way of expressing their grief. He told me that he understood if I was not up to attending, but he would like it if I showed up. So, I did. One of Ted's sons, Ryan Tully, had been Mat's best friend and I know that Ted put the memorial service together for him as well as for our family to try and find some closure. I was deeply touched by this gracious and good-hearted gesture.

At a certain point, both Lorraine and I felt like our world had come to an end. She was devastated and could barely put together a coherent sentence. I went to work but found I could not really function. I had the feeling that my associates and partners were going to have to take over all my cases because I was simply finished, kaput, done. I became anhedonic—unable to experience any sort of plea-sure. My friends convinced me to play some golf to help me get over my grief. No dice. Even my early morning runs failed to give me the adrenaline boost I was used to.

I read every book on the subject of losing a child and learned about the Kubler-Ross model of the five stages of grief. I read and re-read Harold Kushner's *When Bad Things Happen to Good People*. I even tried reading "comforting" poetry collections. But, as they say in Yiddish: *Gournisht helft.* Nothing helped.

I finally decided to look into grief counseling which only served to deepen my despair. I attended group therapy sessions under the supervision of a shrink who asked each of us to tell our story. The others were mostly women who suffered miscarriages and a few who had lost children to suicide. All I could do was compare my enormous loss to what seemed like trivial matters to me. How could you begin to compare the loss of a fetus in the womb with a 12-year-old superstar, full of promise and so much talent, being deprived of his bright future? It didn't make any sense to me, so I said good-bye to all that.

In all my reading on the subject, one statement above all rang the truest. It was uttered by Dwight Eisenhower who, in 1921, lost his 3-year-old son, Icky, to scarlet fever.

"There's no tragedy in life like the death of a child," he said. "Things never get back to the way they were." Truer words were never spoken.

Chapter Eighteen

AfterMat(h)

"It has been said that 'Time heals all wounds.' I do not agree. The wounds remain. In time, the mind, protecting its sanity, covers them with scar tissue and the pain lessens. But it is never gone."
— Rose Fitzgerald Kennedy

Now what? After Mat's death, Lorraine and I were left groping in the dark. Our perfect little world had fallen apart and we had no clue as to what we were supposed to do next. I felt as though I was a leper, not fit to be in the company of decent people. Although such feelings eventually subsided, it took a long while before I again could feel comfortable in the company of my old friends.

I appreciated the way that Snip flew in from Florida during that period to try and console and comfort us. Stuart Myers was likewise always there to offer support as was his colleague in the insurance industry, Barry Persofsky. Stuart had introduced me to Barry, and we hit it off and become friends. I recall how Barry invited me to play a round of golf as his guest at the secretive and highly exclusive AIG links, Morefar Back O' Beyond. He did so to lift my spirits, although I'm sure I was lousy company. Even being afforded the privilege of teeing off on the 15th hole—said to contain the buried ashes of AIG founder, Cornelius Vander Starr—did little to alleviate my detached and despondent disposition.

I likewise appreciated the fellowship of my running buddies like Michael Spain, who stepped up to the plate to do what he could to ease my pain. Years earlier, Michael had asked me to represent him when he and his brother, attorney Bill Spain, were arrested on trespass and assault charges arising from an altercation that took place when a representative of the Homeowners' Association that managed Lake Mahopac had asked the brothers to cease playing hockey on the ice. It could not have been easy for Michael to put up with my moodiness during our runs together. He was a good listener who patiently allowed me to verbalize my angst which served as a valuable cathartic and helped me to expiate my demons. At work, I was more or less a basket case. Unable to focus and easily distracted. I simply could not bear to be around people due to the guilt and shame I felt at having contributed to Mat's death.

Over time, I increasingly came to depend upon my friendships to preserve my sanity and allow me to again become functional. A key player in this process was the aforementioned Raymond Kolkmann.

During the 1990s, the Jefferson Valley Racquet Club merged with a similar facility in nearby Briarcliff Manor and both began operating under the name "Club Fit." They continued to offer basketball league competition in which I now participated with a vengeance. In addition, I'd often join in spontaneous pick-up games and it was there that I first spotted another player whose hunger to win was almost as voracious as my own.

Ray Kolkmann loved to shoot. He was a real chucker. The fact that his success percentage was rather low did not deter him one bit. I guess he believed that old adage, "100% of the shots you DON'T take will fail to go in." Ray was about two inches shorter than me, although, if you look at photos of the two of us taken at the time, we appear to be the same height. That's because Ray would always stand on his tiptoes if he knew he was being photographed. What a poser.

I guess we all have our foibles. For example, Ray liked to make fun of the fact that I wore two wristbands, a headband, and a protective guard for my glasses whenever I was on the court.

"Who is that guy with all the paraphernalia and why does he always grab my jersey when he's guarding me?" Ray would ask his teammates.

"Oh, he's just some lawyer from Carmel," he was told. 'Don"t pay him any mind."

This allegation of "shirt-snatching" had gotten back to me and so when I ran into Ray at Paul and Terry's pizza parlor after a game, I approached him and tried to straighten him out.

"I don't need to hold on to your jersey or anything else to defend against you, fella," I told him directly. But I was not able to disabuse him of that notion and to this day, Ray maintains that I was a chronic jersey grabber.

Professionally, Ray is a successful optometrist and operates a large number of optical stores in Westchester, Putnam and Duchess counties. I learned that Ray and his wife, Mary, had four kids. The two boys participated in all the MSA sports programs and then went on to play high school sports. Both had attended the same schools as Mat and Sarah. Ray coached his son Tim's MSA teams that often played against Sarah's teams. Sarah became something of Tim's archnemesis. Neither he nor his teammates were able to contain her and they wound up losing every year to Sarah's team.

Shortly before the tragedy, Ray took Mat—along with Ray's other son, Ray J—to the Manhattan College basketball camp in Yonkers. Manhattan College is a private Catholic liberal arts academy located, paradoxically, in the Riverdale section of the Bronx, New York. The school had moved there from Manhattan in 1922 but decided to retain the name. The camp is tailored for boys in grades seven through twelve, although they did allow entry to younger boys like Mat who demonstrated they had the requisite skills. The facility primarily prepares young basketball players for collegiate level competition. Each camper is taught basketball fundamentals along with college-level drills such as passing, rebounding, defense and ball handling. The camp's mission is building leadership skills in a competitive environment. Mat loved the camp.

Thanks to this experience, Lorraine and I got to know Mary and Ray and began socializing with them as our two families grew closer. I recall the weekend that Sarah invited their son, Tim, to join us at our Vermont home for some skiing. It was a great weekend for all of us and I still recall how Tim tried to pay for ski lift tickets, equipment rentals, meals and the like all weekend long.

"You're our guest, Tim. Relax," I finally advised him. But his father had loaded his pockets with cash and warned him about not being a "*schnorrer*" (a freeloader). Ray reciprocated for the generosity I extended to his son that weekend by making it impossible for me to pay for a pair of glasses ever since then. Considering the cost of eyeglasses over the past 25 years that I was not required to pay for, I guess I came out "lookin' pretty" on that deal. But the real benefit was that Ray, Mary and their kids became our best friends, something that is simply priceless.

Over the ensuing years, we spent a good deal of time with the Kolkmanns. We particularly enjoyed going on cruises with them across the Caribbean and the Mediterranean. I recall how the Kolkmanns accompanied us on a quixotic quest aboard the good ship Norwegian Pearl. It happened like this:

In 2011 I was watching an episode of *Boardwalk Empire* on HBO. As the closing credits scrolled, the soundtrack featured a mournful Irish ballad called *Carrickfergus* that, for some reason, reminded me of Mathew. I saw that it was being performed by an artist I had gotten to know back in the 1970s at Jay Maxwell's Town Crier Café. His name is Loudon Wainwright III, Grammy-nominated and GLAM Award-winning recording artist Rufus Wainwright's father. I did some digging and discovered that Wainwright, the elder, was slated to soon appear at a musical event known as Cayamo which is a seven-day "Journey Through Song" holiday cruise that takes place each year aboard a ship called the *Norwegian Pearl*. As they sail off to exotic ports of call, such as St. Thomas and St. Kitts, guests enjoy an entertainment line-up of stellar singer-songwriters and recording artists such as Emmy Lou Harris and John Prine.

"Why not try to catch his act and listen to Wainwright perform 'Carrickfergus' in person?" I thought.

So, Lorraine and I booked passage aboard the *Norwegian Pearl's* Cayamo cruise and we invited the Kolkmanns to come along. On our third night at sea, we caught Wainwright's act and it was terrific...except he failed to sing *Carrickfergus*. We booked that same cruise twice more and caught Wainwright's act each time. Still no *Carrick-fergus*. After the third time, I approached Wainwright after his set and politely asked if he would mind performing the song because it had a special meaning for my wife and me.

"I'd love to, man," he replied. "but I don't think I can remember all the words. Sorry."

What he said was believable because there were several instances during his performance when Wainwright was struggling to recall a tune's lyrics and he was forced to rely on the audience to help him out.

I was none too happy with this response and felt like saying "Oh, really? The hell with you. Van Morrison sings it better than you do, anyway."

But I decided that sounded petty and childish, so I held my tongue and grumbled in silence.

It was shortly after losing Mat that my friend, Stuart Myers approached me with a proposition that truly helped to bring some sunshine into my life.

"I've got just the thing that will help you get over your misery, Ell," he said.

Stuart had recently gone back for an advanced degree at Harvard Business School. While there he had become friendly with a Louis Weisman, he explained. Louis lived in Palm Beach Gardens, Florida, and had invited Stuart to come visit him for some golf in the sun.

"Why not come with me. We can check out Florida and see how we like it."

I agreed. I was happy to escape and put some distance between me and the scene of my crime.

Stu was right. The Florida sunshine served to help disperse some of the darkness that had been shrouding my spirits. We both loved the area and I enjoyed getting to know Louis and his wife Bonnie. We would play golf together regularly, along with Stuart and other new friends we made at the PGA National. We became so enamored of Palm Beach Gardens, which, at that time, was home to PGA headquarters, that both Stu and I put down deposits on houses being built in a new section of the PGA National Golf and Country Club development. A side benefit was getting to know our realtor on the deal, Jan Burke and her husband, diagnostic radiology specialist, Dr. Robert Burke. Rob I and became golf buddies and continue to play together often these days.

My place was a 1,600 square foot, two-bedroom home with a tiny pool. It was not lavish, but it was quite adequate as a getaway home for Lorraine, Sarah and me. Stuart's place was a few doors down and considerably grander. It was a two-story job with four bedrooms that he wound up sharing with his York business partners. Our place became our prized vacation getaway home until we sold it in 2004.

Ray and Mary also owned a vacation home. Theirs was located in Scottsdale, Arizona, and they would make a pilgrimage there at least once a year. Eventually, they bought another home near us in Palm Beach Gardens. This was great because it meant we were able to see them and enjoy their company far more frequently. As mentioned, Ray is a one-of-a-kind character with a larger-than-life personality and an even bigger heart. I'll never forget how he and Mary helped

Lorraine and me make it through that very fragile and fraught period of our lives.

One of the things that makes Ray so colorful and, at times, infuriating, is his penchant for pulling pranks and practical jokes. An example:

During one of our weekends in Vermont, the snowfall was insufficient for decent skiing, so Lorraine and I traveled to nearby Manchester for some shopping. While browsing through an art gallery, I spotted a nude painting that reminded me of Rembrandt's famous Baroque masterpiece, "Danae." I fell in love with it, quickly purchased it, and brought it with me to Florida. After placing it into a decorative frame, I hung my masterpiece in a prominent place of honor in our living room. One evening, as Lorraine and I were heading out for dinner, we stopped at the Kolkmann home nearby to pick them up. Ray insisted that we come inside for a drink.

Once indoors, I could not believe what my eyes beheld. Right there, hanging on his living room wall was my pride and joy. My pseudo-Rembrandt! My Danae! I went ballistic and began to call him every name in the book. He reacted to my fury by trying to conceal his laughter. Finally, he just burst out. The more steamed I became; the louder Ray would laugh.

"When did you steal my painting, you lowdown son-of-a-bitch?!" I bellowed.

"It's not yours," he got out between fits of laughter. "It's mine."

After he tired of watching my apoplectic reaction, he came clean and revealed the truth. Ray admitted that he had snuck into our home while we were out. It was easy to do since we seldom locked our doors. He snatched my painting off the wall and had it precisely re-produced. After replacing the original, he then found an identical frame and mounted the forgery in his living room. Can you imagine going to all that trouble just to savor the reaction on my face when I saw what I thought to be my painting hanging on his wall? Well, I must say that I did not find this prank to be too amusing at the time, but I'm happy that my enraged reaction did not disappoint. He couldn't stop laughing for the rest of the evening and still cracks up every time he tells the story.

It was another one of Raymond's little jokes that finally convinced us to start locking our doors. This happened in the Jefferson Valley condo where we lived just prior to moving full-time to Florida. Our bedroom was on the second floor and one night Lorraine and I had gone to bed and were just dozing off when we both felt something large and strange under the covers. She screamed and I tried unsuc-cessfully to grab my pistol from the nightstand. I had recently watched the *Godfather* on TV and my first thought was that someone had placed a decapitated horse's head in our bed. I was wrong. It turned out to be Raymond himself who had snuck into the house without our knowledge and was now snuggling in bed with us. Had I been successful in grabbing my gun, my days of free eye care would have been over for sure.

While I appreciated Ray's generosity in providing me with optical care at no cost, at times I wondered if it was worth it. This because he seemed to give my needs a lower priority than that extended to paying customers. For example, his store advertised that customers would receive their glasses within 24 hours. Yet, in my case, it usually took two weeks (if I was lucky). Sometimes, I wouldn't get them at all. Once I dropped off a high-fashion pair of gold Serengeti sunglasses and asked Ray to replace the standard lenses with corrective ones. Two weeks later he informed me that he had misplaced my glasses. They eventually turned up...two years later! By then my prescription had changed. Oy!

Although Ray's kids, all of whom today work in the business, have been urging him to retire, he refuses because he loves running Raymond Opticians. The namesake of the business, by the way, is not Ray himself, but his father, who founded the company and was also named Raymond. So, despite the downsides, Ray continues to provide me with eyeglasses to this day. I'm reluctant to quit him for fear of offending the guy. After all, who am I to look a gift like free glasses—or Raymond—in the mouth?

Unfortunately, assuring me as to when I will get my glasses back is not the only thing that Raymond was untruthful about. He tended to shade the truth when asked about why he failed to return my phone calls, for example. Responding with some concocted white lie still does not seem to register as improper behavior in his eyes. My guess as to the reasons behind his ability to dance lightly around the truth has to do with the fact that he is a devout Roman Catholic. Some members of the Catholic church, I have observed, feel that once they have confessed to the sin of spreading lies, and have received a dispensation, are free to go at it again with a clean conscience. I would love, just once, to be a fly on the wall inside that confessional booth each Sunday when Raymond reveals his sins to his priest and to his God.

In fairness to Raymond, he is patently ecumenical. I have convinced him that he should support Chabad, a movement sponsored by the Jewish chassidic sect known as Lubavitch. I suspect that Raymond has some sort of Jewish ancestry that accounts for his affinity for Jews and Jewish traditions. In addition to providing financial support, Raymond agreed to attend one of the Rabbi's classes being offered at the local Chabad synagogue where I am a member in good standing, despite the fact that I am the token atheist.

I had convinced Ray to attend this particular class because it dealt with the shortcoming I mentioned earlier. I had not told Ray the topic beforehand, so he was taken aback when, upon arrival, he discovered it was, "When Is It Alright to Lie?" Ray was not a bit happy about this, since he immediately understood why I had brought him along. The Rabbi passed out textbooks and directed us to the passage that listed the ten times when it was not considered sinful by Judaism to prevaricate. With each instance, Ray's mood improved so that by the time the class was over, he was actually beaming with joy.

"You see?" he pronounced proudly. "I told you that those little lies I sometimes tell were okay."

I groaned.

"You know Ell," he said as we were leaving. "I'm going to think about becoming a Jew." Nice sentiment, but probably a lie.

I will introduce you to my association with the Palm Beach Gardens Chabad and its dynamic spiritual leader, Rabbi Dovid Vigler, in a forthcoming chapter.

Raymond also participated in a Chabad-sponsored golf outing not long after that where he could not refrain from engaging in some of his malicious mischief. He and I were in the same foursome and he observed that, hole after hole, I was having a tough time with my putting. Instead of rolling smoothly toward the cup when I tapped my ball, it would fly up in the air and bounce around wildly. After enduring this all the way to the 18th hole, the other fellows finally clued me in as to what was going on. Ray had been secretly stepping on my ball at each hole, pressing it into the turf. To add insult to my injuries, Ray was now gloating, laughing and expressing pride in his devilish ingenuity. I was so angry, I felt like smashing *his* balls into the turf as well.

I could go on sharing some of the endless outrageous stories about Rainman (my nickname for Ray from the 1988 Barry Levinson film, *Rain Man*, starring Tom Cruise and Dustin Hoffman in the title role of an autistic idiot savant), such as the time he buried his brother-in-law's toilet in the guy's backyard. Or the time another friend, Tom Stern, had stocked his new fishing pond with little baby Choi fish and Ray snuck in during the night and replaced them all. The fellow found his pond the next morning filled with fully grown Choi fish and was left scratching his head about his pond's miraculous growth properties. I could go on, but I'll stop here. After all, this book is supposed to be about me. If Raymond feels his childish antics are so damned funny, let him write his own book!

There were two athletic events that were established after Mat's death that served to commemorate his memory during the years we continued to live in New York before moving full-time to Florida.

The first was a golf outing that had originally been organized by my friend, Jay Paldin, who was Sarah's basketball coach as mentioned in Chapter 14. Jay had introduced me to one of his buddies, Ed Sonnenberg. Ed had attended the University of Texas where, as a freshman, he had played against "Pistol" Pete Maravich, whose basketball instruction videos Sarah and Mat used for training purposes.

I had faced Jay and Ed in basketball league games at Jefferson Valley Racquet Club in the early 1990s. I recall how, during one of those games, Ed was absolutely ferocious during an intense first half. When he sat down on the court during the half-time break, he told his 11-year son, Brett, that he didn't feel well and had decided not to play during the second half of the game. Ed died of a heart attack that night.

Ed's teammate and close friend, Jay Paldin, put together an annual golf outing and dedicated it to Ed's memory. The event was held each year at the Mahopac Golf Club or some other public golf course and featured a banquet where Ed's legacy would be invoked. All the work was done by volunteers with 100% of the proceeds going to a college scholarship fund to benefit Mahopac students.

After Mat's death, I approached Jay and asked if he would consider adding Mat's name to Ed's for the upcoming golf outing. Jay graciously agreed. In fact, he thought doing so would increase participation and he was right. With the addition of Mat's name, the outing became a major community fundraising event. During the first few "Ed Sonnenberg and Mathew Fixler Memorial Golf Outings," in the late 1990s, more than 200 golfers would sign up each year, raising tens of thousands for the scholarship fund.

In order to manage the contributions, I set up a 501(c)(3) charity called the Matshtick (pronounced matchstick) Foundation. Matshtick is a Yiddish pun that referenced the fact that athletics was Mat's *schtick* or avocation. The golf outing was such a success that Jay and I decided we would expand and have the Foundation sponsor a girls' basketball tournament. And so, the Fixler/Sonnenberg Memorial Friendship Tournament was launched in the fall of 1994.

By 1998 the tournament had grown in popularity to the point that it, too, was generating sizable sums for the scholarship fund. Interest was particularly high that year because Sarah was now a high school freshman and was playing on Jay's team, the Mahopac Indians. Here is a quote from the sports page coverage of the big game between Mahopac and Ossining, written by Stuart Lederer in the September 28, 1998, issue of the *Putnam County Courier:*

> But this year was different in many respects. For one, Sarah Fixler is now a freshman and she is also the starting point guard. Sarah is the sister of Mat, the 12-year-old boy the tournament is co-named for, who was killed in a boating accident on Lake Mahopac four years ago. Sarah and Mat were very close growing up and this would be the first time she would be able step onto the court and play in her brother's name.
>
> As a starter and a point guard, she would be the one to control the tempo of the game against Ossining and be responsible for distributing the ball and finding the open player. She succeeded on all accounts—and then some. Fixler scored 24 points as Ossining simply couldn't stop her unbelievably accurate outside shot while also leading an offense that played completely as a team.

As we moved into the 2000's and I saw my law practice go into a slow decline, participation and revenue from these events likewise diminished since many of the people attracted to them were my clients and contacts. By 2006, fewer than 100 golfers showed up for the golf outing. But it was at this event that something took place that would trigger an entirely new chapter in my life.

After the golfing had concluded and we were about to sit down for the evening's banquet, I spotted my cousin from Buffalo, Aaron Heisler, enter the hall. Aaron was my late Uncle Bernie's son whom I had known since childhood. By this point his health was in decline and I could see as he approached me that he was using one hand to pull an oxygen tank connected to a nasal cannula. In the other hand he held a book that, after extending his greetings, he presented to me.

The book was called *Not to Forget, Impossible to Forgive; Poignant Reflections on the Holocaust.* It was written by eminent Torah scholar and author of numerous books about the Holocaust, Dr. Moshe Avital. As was the case with our family, Dr. Avital's original home was the town of Bilke, and in this book he describes the destruction of Bilke's Jewish community at the hands of the Nazis.

"Have a look, Elliot," Aaron urged me. "They're in there. Our grandfather and his brother. It tells who they were and what happened to them. Have a look."

I took the book from Aaron and thanked him for making the effort to attend this event held in the memory of my son. I rushed home afterwards and spent the entire night going through the book's pages; pages filled with ghost memories and trainloads of tears.

Reading Avital's book was a true epiphany, a turning point in my life every bit as profound as the moment I discovered the truth about my real father. By the time Aaron died in 2009, I had begun my quest to discover and unearth my family's history, a process that continues to this day. I was struck by the impact on a person's life that a single book could produce. This book is a part of that process. It is a quest that has taken me back to my birthplace in Budapest, and to the modern-day town of Bilke in search of my identity and my heritage. I describe that ongoing quest in an upcoming chapter.

Chapter Nineteen

Call Me Bwana

"Until the lion tells his side of the story, the tale of the hunt will always glorify the hunter."

—Zimbabwean proverb

I t should be evident by now that for my entire life I have had the uncanny tendency to attract the friendship of slightly kooky and colorful characters. Perhaps none fit that description more aptly than Rodney Huebers who, despite his antics (or maybe because of them) has remained my friend for lo, these past 25 years.

You might recall David Kellogg as the co-owner of the Tom Kat Sporting Goods store and the fellow who enjoyed baring his backside to passing tour boats from our island retreat. It was Dave's brother, Jeff, who first introduced me to Rod Huebers. Jeff was, in the 1990s, serving on the board of the Putnam County Hospital Foundation. The hospital had recently hired Rod to serve as its administrative CEO. After getting to know Rod, Jeff thought it would be a good idea for him to meet me. He was right. We hit it off immediately. As Jeff had anticipated, it was a case of two characters sharing a common kindred spirit.

At a certain point, I was surprised to be invited to join the Foundation's Board of Directors. I surmised that Jeff and Rod were under the impression that I had a good deal of money and would be willing to part with some of it once I had been bestowed with this honor. What they didn't know was that I spent every dollar as soon as I earned it. What with alimony payments, college tuition fees, and similar expenses, I was not in any position financially to become a serious philanthropist.

I enjoyed my tenure on the Board. The meetings were interesting and the annual Gala was fun, but my involvement was mostly hinged upon my friendship with Rod that I very much cherished. In 2000, however, Rod decided to move on to the verdant pastures of Virginia where he accepted a position as CEO of Loudon Healthcare and Wellness.

After his departure, Rod and I would still get together for some golf and the occasional Thanksgiving dinner which always involved a lot of laughter and jolly good times. Rod continued his wandering ways by accepting gigs in far-flung locations like Texas, Michigan, and Louisiana. While in Shreveport, Rod asked for my legal help with a project he was working on. I agreed to fly down and help him out. I was picked up at the airport by Karen, Rod's girlfriend and future wife. I was somewhat stunned when we reached her car with my bags. It was an old broken-down army Jeep that looked like a refugee from a jalopy junkyard.

"What kind of way is this to welcome your lawyer?" I chided Karen. "You know, I'm used to getting picked up in a limo." This elicited a chuckle as she slid behind the wheel and began struggling with the well-worn floor-mounted gear shift handle. Rod, after moving to Florida a few years later, had that Jeep completely restored and added it to his eclectic car collection. He turned it into a true work of art that became Karen's car. His other motorcar masterpieces include a completely restored Model A Ford and a rebuilt1940s Chevy pick-up truck.

Rod, and his car collection, finally landed in Lake Worth, Florida, some fifteen minutes from my home, and thus we have been able to once again enjoy frolicking on the fairways and enjoying the occasional turkey drumstick. Even today, Rod is able to propel a golf ball off the tee for a country mile, and occasionally succeeds in making it fly straight! In addition, his many talents include being a world-class gourmand and a distiller of fine moonshine whiskey. A true Renaissance Man, I consider Rod to be one of my most intelligent friends. This is proven by the fact that whenever I'm concerned about a medical issue, I call Rod before I call a doctor.

Among the many things for which I remain in Rod's debt, the most significant was his introducing me to Dave Festa. Dave was the IT guy at Putnam County Hospital and a brilliant computer engineer. He and I discussed launching a company that would offer online insurance claims settlements. Dave was a gifted programmer and developed an amazing product that we hoped to bring to market. I will discuss more about that venture in a later chapter.

About the same time that Rod Huebers introduced me to Dave Festa, my friend and associate, Stuart Myers, connected me with another influential person in my life, Stan Long. Stan was from Oregon and had been recruited by Maurice Greenburgh, the chairman of AIG, the world's largest insurance company in 1992, to serve as the company's president of their newly established Claims Services Division in New York. Prior to that, AIG had, for many years, been using Stuart's company, York Claim Services, to handle a portion of their claims activity. AIG now wished to employ its own division to handle their claims. Stan thought that AIG buying Stuart's small claims company, which serviced a niche market aimed at self-insured clients, would benefit AIG, and he facilitated the sale.

Stuart generously split the proceeds of the sale equally four ways. He gave each of his associates in the business, Fred Schiller and Eileen Rachelson (his office manager) a quarter share of the proceeds. He split the remaining balance equally with his wife Nancy. Before joining up with Stuart, Eileen had worked as a dance instructor and Fred had been the manager of an upscale restaurant in Boston. I'm sure that neither anticipated receiving such a windfall. This act of generosity on Stuart's part convinced me that he truly was a *mensch* (a decent principled person).

In addition to the purchase price, Stuart received a three-year employment contract with AIG where he continued to work with Stan as Stuart ran York Claims. Stan continued as AIG president until being lured away by Travelers Insurance in the late 1990s.

Stan had come from a workers' compensation insurance company in Oregon, the SAIF Corporation, where he had served as its CEO. His impressive résumé also included a stint as the Director of Oregon's Department of Commerce, his role as City Attorney for the City of Eugene, deputy State Attorney General, and chairman of the Oregon Land and Conservation Development Commission. Except for his contention that presidential candidate, George W. Bush was a highly intelligent political leader, I found Stan to be one of the brightest people I had ever met. For some reason, we hit it off and became friends despite the fact I was far from being his intellectual equal.

Stan fervently enjoyed hunting and fishing. He said the outdoor life was part of his family heritage; a family that traced its roots back to the gamblers and gunslingers who settled in Oregon during the wild west era. He and his wife, Rosie, purchased a home near ours and so Lorraine and I got to know them as friends as well as neighbors. It was in this capacity that we were invited to join them aboard his boss, Maurice Greenburgh's, impressive yacht for a fun-filled and unforgettable weekend cruise in 1996. It was just the four of us—along with a skipper and a chef—sailing around scenic Long Island Sound aboard a 60-foot Absolute Flybridge yacht that easily slept eight. I recall feeling like a *gantzeh k'nocker* (Yiddish for big shot) as I looked down and waved to the other boaters below.

It was a few years afterwards that Stu, Stan, and I started planning an African safari that would take us and our wives to Tanzania's bush country. Stan, who had previously hunted with a company called Robin Hurt Safaris, opted to hire that company once more. It was a great decision and truly was a trip of a lifetime. I wound up paying less for the adventure than the other two because I had agreed to do all of my shooting with a camera. Stu and Stan both had to pay triple because they opted to use rifles in order to become actual big game hunters. I could somewhat understand Stan's lust for stalking wild animals given his background as an Oregonian outdoorsman. But Stu? Stu was a Brooklyn-bred guy who played stickball as a kid. The closest he had ever come to an elephant was when Barnum & Bailey came to Madison Square Garden. What was he doing with a rifle instead of a camera? I guess he harbored dreams of being the Great White Hunter; perhaps the result of seeing too many Tarzan movies.

Once we arrived, we were connected with the Robin Hurt people who provided our supplies, our guides, and set our course. The scenery of the African veldt was lush and spectacular and during our three weeks on safari we visited and hunted in three different regions of Tanzania, each featuring different topography and indigenous game. We enjoyed hunting for animals to shoot (me with my camera, they with their rifles), but just about everything we approached ran away from us before we could press a shutter or pull a trigger. One highlight (actually a lowlight) was the time Lorraine and I played a round of golf on a derelict course that hadn't been maintained since the British had abandoned it decades earlier. In preparation for our game, a crew of local women were dispatched to the greens using tree branches as brooms to brush away the accumulated brush and debris.

A true high point was a morning run through the bush accompanied by a spear-toting Masai warrior who was assigned to deploy the weapon should a lion, or some other attacking beast, decide I might make a good breakfast.

In addition to the native guides, our group was assigned three professional game hunters: one for each couple. Since we were only shooting photos, we wound up with the least experienced guide. Stuart was assigned the second most experienced, a devilishly handsome, English-speaking chap who went by the name of John. I would often ride with John in the Land Rover as we drove across the countryside. When I commented to him that the vehicle had no side mirrors, he explained that they had been knocked off while driving through the bush and they were of no use anyway. He was wrong.

Whenever we came upon a herd of elephants, John enjoyed tormenting them with a game he had devised. He would position the Land Rover in the path of one of the elephants and drive straight at the animal, forcing it to move backwards. He would do this repeatedly until the animal became frustrated and gave up, running off in another direction. Lorraine and I were stunned by this behavior and asked that John discontinue his little game of "Annoy the Elephant," but, he persisted. He would soon come to regret not heeding our request.

The following day I was riding in the Rover's passenger seat with John behind the wheel. Lorraine was back at the camp. We entered an area marked by exceptionally high grass—some as tall as our vehicle—and soon found ourselves approaching a small herd of elephants. Since Lorraine was not in the car, John felt unhindered in engaging in his favorite game of torment. But this time things were different. Instead of meekly backing off, the bull elephant came lumbering directly towards us at high speed. John swiftly turned the wheel and sped off into the tall grass. This maneuver did little good as the giant beast continued its pace as it persisted in chasing after us. John, hunched over the steering wheel, gave it the gas to accelerate but we were hampered by the tall grass that was slowing us down. There being no side mirrors, John was required to furtively sneak glances over his shoulder to judge if the elephant was gaining on us. It was during one of those backward glances that he nearly drove us directly into a tree. I could tell from John's facial expression that he was petrified.

I thought to myself, "If this guy is scared, I should be panicking!"

Just as the massive, tusked leviathan began gaining on us, and as I coincidentally broke out in a cold sweat, imagining what it would do to us when it caught up and began extracting its revenge, the grasses parted and we found ourselves on a clear path that allowed the Rover to pick up speed and leave "Dumbo" in the dust.

As we sat around the dinner table that evening recounting our near-death adventure, I turned to John and asked him, "Tell us the truth, John. Were you frightened?"

He gave a condescending smile, shook his head and said, "Nah. No way."

What a lying piece of shit. But aside from that one character flaw, John was an overall great guy and a lot of fun to be around.

I thought my days of confronting wild animals were over once we had returned home to New York. That was not to be the case. Not long after our expedition, I was driving somewhere when I received a call from Lorraine on my flip phone.

"You've got to turn around and come home right away," she pleaded. "Hurry up. I'll explain when you get here."

All sorts of unpleasant thoughts from a few years earlier crossed my mind as I made the U-turn and headed back home. By this point, we had sold the lake house with all its unbearable memories and had moved into a home near Jefferson Valley. As soon as I walked in the door, Lorraine pointed me towards the garage.

"There's a skunk in there," she informed me. "It's living in there and I'm afraid to go and get in my car. You've got to get it out of there."

Back in Africa, every creature big or small, would run the other way as soon as they got a scent of us. But here in civilized New York, this little fucker was somehow attracted to us.

"He must be rabid," I told Lorraine. Grabbing my trusty broom handle, I faced down the vicious beast and beat him out the door with a few good swats. Afterwards, I put the broom back on its hook as I told Lorraine: "That's it. I'm hanging it up. I'm done with hunting forever."

Of course, that statement did not apply to fishing. So, a few years later, when Stan invited us to come to Oregon for some fishing on the Mackenzie River, I took the bait. It was an unbelievable experience. To this day I recall our lunch of freshly caught trout, prepared and eaten along the riverside, as the finest fish meal of my life. Stuart and his wife, Lida, were slated to join us on the fishing expedition, but cancelled at the last minute. Something Stan was none too happy about since he had hired guides and purchased provisions.

The Longs lived in a stylish home in Eugene's central district. In addition to the fishing trip, Stan and Rosie treated us to a tour of Oregon's finest wineries that saw us finish the day at their other home along the magnificent Pacific coast.

In addition to enjoying some great runs through picturesque Eugene, I appreciated Stan teaching me the fine art of fly fishing. But I definitely did not enjoy shelling out $1000 for two Orvis Mirage fishing reels since I haven't used them since. I guess I fell for the allure of fly fishing "hook, line, and sinker."

As I discussed in the previous chapter, I had met Barry Persofsky back in the 1970s in the same way that I had met so many of my friends, through Stuart Myers. Barry had invited me to join him at the exclusive AIG golf course known as Morefar Back O' Beyond shortly after Mat died. Our friendship has endured despite the fact that Barry has moved on to pursue different ventures in various parts of the country over the years.

His experience of working with Stuart at York Claims was not a particularly good fit and Barry soon moved on to accept a position as CEO of Phico Insurance. Phico was Pennsylvania's third largest insurer of doctors and hospitals before it collapsed in 2002 under a mountain of claims that it was unable to pay.

Barry, who had moved from New York to Harrisburg when he took the job, invited me to serve on Phico's Board of Directors, which I did for several years. When the Pennsylvania Insurance Commission took over control of the company after it went belly-up, they sued the Board for $25 million in an effort to raise funds with which to pay off claims by policy holders. I felt I had done nothing improper and therefore was reluctant to settle. I had come onboard long after the policies that led to the collapse had been put into place. Also, this all occurred in the middle of a devastating medical malpractice crisis that was engulfing the entire industry. Nevertheless, a settlement was reached that saw the Insurance Commission receive $10 million, all of which was, ironically, paid by Phico's D&O (Directors & Officers) insurance carrier.

The final years of the 20th century found me engaged in a fascinating and unusual experience that was marked by my return to the land of Israel for the first time since leaving it at the age of seven—shortly after the century's midpoint.

My stepfather, Sam Fixler, passed away on February 1, 1999, almost nine years to the day after his wife, my mother Rose, had died. Living to age 90, Sam enjoyed a remarkably long life, given what he had endured in the numerous concentration camps and forced labor prisons that he had miraculously survived during the Holocaust. At the end, he was residing in an assisted living facility in Buffalo where I would visit him as often as I could. Although we were not at all close, I still respected the man in several ways. Unlike my biological father, Sam had managed to survive the flames that consumed one third of the world's Jewish population. While his survival back then was mostly a matter of luck, his success in building a new life in America was strictly the result of hard work. He never accepted a dime from the government and never whined that antisemitism or racial prejudice were responsible for his station in life. And mostly, I was proud of the sanctuary and opportunity to live and prosper that our country extended to this this survivor of man's brutality to others.

As recounted in the early chapters of this book, my relationship with my stepfather was not what anyone would consider close or loving. We continued to keep our distance emotionally, even after my mother died and he really had no one else nearby. That's why I was surprised, during one of my visits, that he asked me to make him a promise.

"Elliot, maybe you don't remember," he began somberly, "but my brother and I both bought burial plots on the Mount of Olives in Jerusalem. Please promise me that after I'm gone, you'll take me there and see that they bury me properly."

I was speechless.

I was not surprised by his desire to be buried in this holy spot favored by observant Jews who adhere to the Talmudic belief that when the *Mashiach* (Messiah) arrives, he will do so at this place and then miraculously bring about the resurrection of the dead. What surprised me was the fact that Sam had selected me to carry out this mission. Whatever meager estate he had at the time he had bequeathed to his nieces who lived in California. I had always imagined that they would look after this matter. As I considered my reply, I thought back to the fact that, despite our bloodless relationship, Sam had more or less raised me as a son. I recalled how he had loaned me $10,000 with no questions asked, enabling me to purchase my first house. And, of course, he had been my mother's constant companion for close to 50 years.

"Okay," I said finally. "I'll do it."

When the time came, I coordinated with the funeral home in making the necessary arrangements to transport his remains to Israel. Stuart, good-hearted fellow that he is, offered to accompany me and the casket "in my time of grief," as he put it. It would give him a chance to see his sisters and other family members who lived in Israel.

"Thanks for the offer, Stu, but it's really not necessary," I told him. "I'm not experiencing a lot of grief here at all." But he insisted and so I gained a traveling companion as the casket and I winged our way across the Atlantic.

When we deplaned from the El Al flight at Ben Gurion International in Tel Aviv, we searched for the driver who was supposed to meet us and drive us to Jerusalem. He was nowhere in sight.

"Maybe he's waiting for us outside," I suggested to Stu. "Why don't you check down at one end and I'll go to the other end and let's see if one of us can find him."

Stu agreed and took off while I stepped outside and began my search. It was not too long before I found our driver. He had been in the cargo area where he had already loaded the casket into his mini-van.

I hopped into the front passenger seat and tried to explain to the driver that I was with a friend and we needed to locate him before leaving the airport. This communication was made difficult by the fact that he did not speak English and I had forgotten whatever Hebrew I may have known as a child.

As the sun began to set and as we cruised back and forth searching for Stu, the driver became increasingly agitated. He kept urgently pointing to his watch and repeating "Yerushalayim, yerushalyim!" (Jerusalem). He kept gesticulating with his hand towards the exit and I understood that he wanted me to know that we, along with the casket, needed to be in Jerusalem by a certain time and we had to leave immediately. In those pre-international cell phone days, I was left with no choice but to head to Jerusalem without Stu. I was comforted in this decision by the knowledge that, once he realized that I had left the airport without him, Stu would be able to contact his family who lived in Tel Aviv. They would certainly be able to pick him up and get him to our Jerusalem hotel where I would hopefully find him after the burial ceremony, and that's exactly what happened.

The driver made quick work of delivering me to Jerusalem, arriving there in less than 45 minutes. He pulled to a halt at a vacant bus stop, although I had no idea why or what was going on. As I stepped out of the van, I spotted a young, bearded fellow standing on the curb. I approached him and asked, "Do you speak English?"

"Yes, I do," he replied.

"Do you have a phone I may use? I need to call my friend's relatives in Jerusalem and tell them to pick him up at Ben Gurion."

His response surprised me. "Are you Mr. Fixler?"

Hunh? How did this guy know my name?

I confirmed that I was Fixler and asked him how he knew who I was and could he explain why I had been brought to this spot. I was expecting to be taken to a synagogue or a mortuary, not a street corner.

"My father is the rabbi at your father's shul in Buffalo," he explained in perfect English. "I am studying for the rabbinate myself here in Jerusalem."

The yeshiva *bochur* (rabbinic student) then proceeded to explain that we were now awaiting the arrival of another van containing a group of additional students who would comprise the *minyan* (minimum quorum of ten Jews) that was required in order to conduct a ritual burial.

"Once they arrive," the young man went on, "they will remove the casket and take it to the gravesite for burial."

"Tonight?!" I interjected. It was nearly 11 pm. Who conducts funerals at night?

Before he could answer, the other van pulled up behind the one in which I had ridden. A bearded gentleman, dressed in the black garb favored by Chassidic men, jumped from the van and approached me.

"Are you Fixler?" he asked somewhat abruptly.

I said that I was.

"I am in charge of the local *Chevra Kedusha* (Jewish burial society) and our boys will be taking your father's casket up to the Mount of Olives where we will conduct the burial. Do you wish to join us?"

"Well, of course," I replied, somewhat annoyed. "That's the reason I travelled here from New York."

Without uttering another word, the burial leader grabbed the left lapel of my brand-new sports jacket and, in accordance with Jewish tradition, ripped it, leaving a six-inch tear in the very expensive fabric. After he was assured that I was not a *Kohane* (a member of the priestly tribe whose members are forbidden to come into contact with a dead body), the fellow then ushered me into the second van. As I peered inside, I could see that they had already transferred Sam's casket. Seated around the pine box was a group of nine identically dressed young men, all sporting black hats and beards. Counting the driver, they constituted the required minimum number for a minyan (10).

The van followed a serpentine path up to the very top of the Mount. The atmosphere was made eerie by the absence of any sort of

341

lighting. The only illumination was provided by the vehicle's head-lights. As we reached the top, some of the men hopped out carrying lanterns to light our way to the gravesite. These cast spooky shadows everywhere, giving the entire scene the appearance of an old-time gothic horror movie.

Some of the men were assigned to be the pallbearers. They carried the casket up a short flight of stone steps to the top level where I could see, by the shaky lantern-light, that a hole in the ground had been prepared in advance. The whole situation was giving me the willies as the casket was placed next to the opening.

Without preamble or fanfare, the box was opened and Shmuel Fixler's earthly remains, wrapped in a white linen shroud, were re-moved by the young men and unceremoniously dropped into the gap-ing grave. A few words in Hebrew were mumbled quickly by the leader as his young charges wasted no time in using their shovels to fill the grave with dirt from the nearby mound. On the ride back down to the street, I asked the leader about the practice of nighttime burials.

"It is considered customary," he replied in his best pedagogical manner, "to bury the body as soon as possible after death occurs. So, we don't waste any time. If that means we need to bury at night, we bury at night." He said this with a sincere sense of pride, as though he were an auto mechanic boasting about his garage's 24-hour ser-vice. Once we had reached the street, I was instructed to get out of the van.

There I was, alone in Jerusalem, City of Gold. But it did not look golden at all in the middle of a pitch-black night. I was in such profound despair over the manner in which the so-called funeral was conducted, that I wandered the streets aimlessly trying to collect my thoughts and gain control of my emotions. Yes, Sam Fixler was a cold, unpleasant and thoroughly unfriendly person. But he deserved better than this short shrift, midnight express burial that I had just witnessed.

Somehow, I managed to get myself to the King David Hotel where, as I had hoped, I reunited with both Stuart and my luggage. Stu explained that once he realized I had gone off without him, he had called his family and his nephew came to the airport to pick him up, after which he arranged for a taxi to bring him to Jerusalem.

That same nephew was a terrific guy who would, over the following days, serve as our very capable tour guide. He showed us many of Jerusalem's timeless treasures and then guided us southward to the ancient fortress of Masada, site of a mass suicide by Jewish zealots at the time Judea was being conquered by the Roman Empire in the second century C.E. It is at this site where all IDF soldiers swear an oath of allegiance to the Jewish State upon completion of their basic military training. As we surveyed the broad vistas from atop this incredible historic artifact, I concluded that Masada was truly one of the wonders of both the ancient and the modern worlds.

At that moment, I promised Stu—and myself—that I would return. As to be recounted, I fulfilled that pledge a number of years later on a mission to Israel led by Rabbi Dovid Vigler, the spiritual leader of the Palm Beach Gardens Chabad synagogue. It would be a trip of true discovery, during which I would get to know fellow travelers with whom I have remained friends ever since.

Elliot Fixler

Chapter Twenty

Sarah

*"Whoever said 'It's not whether you win or lost that counts,'
probably just lost."*
—Martina Navratilova

As devastating as the trauma of Mat's death was for Lorraine and me, it was many times more so for our daughter, Sarah, who was ten years old at the time and idolized her older brother. Yet, it would be Sarah who would become the shining light that illuminated the path through my own personal darkness over the coming years. Lorraine's stoicism and refusal to issue a single word of recrimination against me were certainly admirable, but in some ways, they were equally infuriating. If she would only express her anger or disappointment at my failure to prevent what had happened, perhaps I might have felt I could somehow and to some degree expiate my guilt. A guilt that was an incessant throb in my heart and a constant presence that would keep me awake at 3 am, lying in bed and replaying all the things I had not done right.

If you are familiar with the Kessler-Ross model that identifies the five stages of grief, you know that the fourth one, extreme sadness and depression, is the most difficult. It was in this stage that I found myself with little chance of ever reaching the salvation of the fifth stage, "acceptance." It was when I began to feel that my soul and spirit could no longer hold up under the gathering weight of remorse that a redeeming angel appeared who figuratively saved my life; an angel named Sarah.

Like Mat, Sarah had been an enthusiastic athlete since childhood. I had trained and worked with both kids and shared their many moments of victory. If you think I was one of those fathers who lives vicariously through the accomplishments of his kids, you're correct. There's some justification for this, I feel. Growing up in an immigrant community, raised by parents to whom American sports were completely alien, getting switched from one school to another during my high school days and, most significantly, coming from an observant Jewish family that made playing sports on the Sabbath an impossibility, combined to restrict my development of any sort of athletic career during my youth. Yes, I felt I had been denied the chance of becoming a star athlete, and this fact no doubt contributed to my desire to make sure my kids were afforded every available opportunity. I believed that the pride I experienced at their achievements on the basketball court or the baseball diamond was justified by the fact I had contributed to their success. And I don't believe they resented this in any way.

By the time he was twelve, Mat had already racked up an impressive string of successes in multiple sports, academics and school politics. For this reason, and for so many others, his death created an enormous void in our home and in our hearts. Lorraine and I sought out grief counseling and I spent the next several years being treated by a psychiatrist for depression. I sometimes wondered if our marriage would survive and I today believe that, had it not been for

Sarah stepping up and filling the void left by Mat's loss, our marriage would not have endured.

Sarah demonstrated enormous drive and she clearly hungered to figuratively fill her late brother's sneakers. These traits gave her enormous potential that over time would see her blossom into an extraordinary competitor, beginning in fourth grade and extending through some of her college years. Did losing Mat and her desire to live up to his legacy account for Sarah's eventual athletic excellence? In all honesty, I don't think so. We'll never know, but I firmly believe that her career would have been just as spectacular had Mat lived. In this chapter, I'd like to present you with some of the highlights from those halcyon days that saw Sarah deliver healing sunshine into our tattered lives as she grew into an amazing athlete in her own right.

Sarah began playing competitive basketball, soccer and softball in local girls' leagues as a third grader. She found softball boring, however, and opted to play baseball on boys' teams through the sixth grade. She found she was every bit as talented as the boys on her team. Sarah likewise played on boys' basketball teams in Mahopac and in the Yorktown area through the sixth grade.

Starting in fifth grade, Sarah began playing basketball on a Hudson Valley AAU (Amateur Athletic Union) girls' traveling team. Lorraine and I had a grand time following the team from town to town and cheering Sarah on. They were a decent team that, during the summer before her sixth-grade year, provided Sarah with the opportunity of competing in the girls' basketball national championships held that year in Lafayette, Louisiana. That was a long way to go, but Lorraine and I used the experience to enjoy some of what that region of the country had to offer. Perhaps the most memorable local custom we encountered was the prevalence of drive-thru cocktail lounges. We could drive up to one of these joints and order a margarita just as if we were ordering a Big Mac.

I was delighted when I learned the town of New Iberia was located nearby. New Iberia is the family home of noted author, James Lee Burke, and is the setting of many of his Dave Robicheaux books. I had read just about all of them at that time, and it was a real kick when we visited the town to see many of the places I had visualized only in my imagination now come to life.

Those days of traveling to watch Sarah play were a truly special time in my life. The enthusiasm and excitement I experienced during such games were like a release valve that enabled me to let off some of the pressure that had been building up inside me. At times, I became a bit overly zealous, I'm afraid. I mentioned earlier that neither Mat nor Sarah ever seemed to object to the fact that I was vicariously experiencing the joy of competition through their exploits. The following episode was, perhaps, one instance when that did not hold true.

When Sarah was in seventh grade, I was sitting in the bleachers attending one of her basketball games. As I watched her repeatedly bring the ball down the court, I observed that, instead of taking a shot, she would invariably pass the ball to an open teammate, thereby sacrificing a scoring opportunity. I began shouting instructions to her from my seat in the middle of the bleachers. I felt that these were offered as constructive criticism intended to improve her game. I kept urging her to shoot the ball more often since she was clearly the best shot on the team. But she persisted. After seeing her pass the ball to a teammate who, as usual, missed the shot, I was so incensed that I shouted, "Shoot the damn ball, Sarah!"

Sarah called a time out and walked over to where I was seated. I could tell by her expression that she was annoyed at my trying be her "bleacher teacher." She pointed her finger at me and said in a calm measured tone that reminded me of her mother's manner.

"Dad, the next time that you shout instructions to me from the bleachers, I will walk off the court and I will not be playing basketball anymore."

I knew this was no idle threat. She meant it. So, thus ended my court-side coaching career and I never did anything like that again. I did, however, continue to offer my helpful recommendations and trusted tips to some of the referees and officials who obviously needed my "assistance" in properly calling fouls, for example. On one such occasion, a humorless striped shirt told me to shut-up or else leave the gym. That cured me of this obvious exercise in futility. There is no percentage in trying to teach the unteachable.

I was really at a loss to understand why my suggestions were met with such harsh rejection. By comparison, I found that NBA refs and coaches were much more open to my guidance. After all, my clients willingly paid me for my advice and here I was dispensing it for free. You'd think they'd be grateful. I had first become an NBA season ticket holder in 1981 when the Long Island Nets moved to New Jersey. Traveling all the way to New York City to watch the Knicks play at Madison Square Garden had become a real pain, so I readily became a Nets fan. At the Meadowlands, the Nets new home in New

Jersey, I had two season ticket seats in the 13th row with a clear view of the foul line. After a few years I decided I wanted to get a better view of the games and I bought two additional courtside seats. By this time, the Nets were playing at the Izod Center. I held on to these four seats until I moved to Florida in 2004. Our seats were opposite the foul line and this was the spot where one of the refs would stand while officiating along the side of the court, placing me within easy earshot.

I made it a practice of pointing things out to the various refs; things they should have properly observed themselves. These tips were always accompanied by my (usually) respectful admonition to hone up on their officiating skills. One such referee who benefited from my guidance was Joey Crawford, who was regarded as one of the finest, albeit strictest and most controversial, officials in the NBA. He had a reputation for assessing technical fouls against coaches as well as players. By the end of his career in 2015, Crawford had worked more playoff games than any other referee in the league. He was frequently selected to ref the NBA All-Star Game which indicated the high regard he enjoyed within the sport. I like to think that my steady stream of instructions from the sidelines helped Joey to attain his exalted stature. I would, from time to time, run into Joey when Sarah's AAU games took us to Pennsylvania. He would be there watching his own daughter play. Joey would invariably thank me for my willingness to extend my advice during Nets games. He felt it helped him to do a better job. It was a pity that the AAU refs did not share Joey's attitude and instead looked at every suggestion as unwanted criticism.

FULL CIRCLE

My motives in offering advice to Sarah from the parent gallery were not entirely altruistic, of course. I understood that if Sarah stood any chance of getting noticed by college recruiters, she would need to start scoring more. She was an outstanding defender and a brilliant passer, but scoring is the ticket to superstardom. There is today a banner in the Mahopac High School Gymnasium, recognizing the 1000 plus career points scored by Sarah Fixler.

Sarah was, in all fairness, an excellent team player and was never guilty of hogging the ball. Some might consider this a shortcoming, but I can't point a finger because she probably inherited this trait from me. I was notorious for giving up scoring opportunities by passing the ball to a teammate who was open and closer to the basket.

Sarah gave up playing basketball with the boys when she went into the seventh grade. She was then allowed to play for the Mahopac High school girls' junior varsity basketball team. As an eighth grader, Sarah made the MHS varsity squad, where she was played sparingly because, as explained earlier, the coach preferred to play upperclassman.

When Sarah became a freshman at Mahopac High School, she again joined the school's girls' varsity basketball team. Her presence, based on her reputation earned while playing on the team the prior year as an eighth grader, generated a storm of excitement and interest in girls' high school basketball throughout the community. Two of the Town of Mahopac councilmen, Tim Wilson and Jim McDonough, who both were avid sports enthusiasts, thought it would make sense to cover the games on the local cable TV network, and they proceeded to make it happen.

351

This exposure helped to boost interest and soon the stands were overflowing at every girls' basketball contest. By comparison, the boys' basketball games were hardly drawing anyone. After a few years of this, the boys' coaches and players began to complain. They thought the girls were getting an unfair advantage by having their games broadcast. They requested that the boys' games be likewise covered in the hopes that doing so would serve to boost attendance. Tim and Jim agreed and soon Mahopac citizens were able to view both boys' and girls' high school basketball on TV. But it didn't help attendance for the boys one bit. Their teams still looked anemic and amateurish compared to the skills on display by Sarah and her fellow distaff dribblers.

Sarah's team racked up an unparalleled record during her five years as point guard and team leader of the Mahopac Indians. She led them to victory in 50 straight regular season games. Their only losses came at the hands of state playoff rivals who were able to defeat them because Sarah's team lacked the height enjoyed by other contenders. I'm proud to report that Sarah was voted to receive a coveted All-Section designation at the conclusion of the basketball season during all four years of her high school career.

During her high school summers, Sarah played girls' basketball for a Rockland County AAU team as well as in various other locales and in a number of tournaments. We all hoped that with this much exposure, she might land a Division One college scholarship. We learned that Princeton's coach was interested in recruiting Sarah and she had prepared to commit to that school when the Princeton coach took a job elsewhere and that opportunity vanished.

FULL CIRCLE

When as a senior, Sarah found herself waiting for college basketball offers to reach her, she became increasingly impatient. She disliked the uncertainty of not knowing where she would be going to college. Then one day, out of the blue, she received a call from the head coach at Northwestern University in Evanston, Illinois, offering her an athletic scholarship.

"That's fantastic," I said when Sarah broke the news to me. "Northwestern's got a great women's basketball team."

"But, Dad," she said baring a broad grin. "It wasn't the basketball coach who called me. It was Kelly Amonte Hiller, the new girls' lacrosse coach."

Lacrosse?! Yes, lacrosse. In addition to basketball, Sarah had also played lacrosse in high school. She had joined the newly formed JV girls' team during her freshman year where she learned the game and became a fierce competitor. She continued to play on the varsity team during her sophomore and junior years, earning All-Section honors in the sport both years. Early in the season of her senior year, Sarah sustained an injury and was forced to suspend active play.

During those years, the New York State Department of Parks and Recreation sponsored an annual event known as the Empire State Summer Games. The games were patterned after the Olympics and saw amateur athletes compete, representing their region of the state, in a variety of sports, including basketball and lacrosse. While the Empire State Winter Games are still being held each year at Lake Placid, the summer games saw their last in 2014. Sarah qualified for the Empire State basketball team during both her freshman and sophomore high school years. In her junior year, she switched and decided to go out for the lacrosse team and made it. As far as I know, Sarah is the only athlete who ever competed in the Empire State Summer Games in two different sports.

Now, with this time-sensitive offer from Northwestern on the table, Sarah had to make a decision. Should she continue waiting for an offer to come through from a college basketball program or should she accept Northwestern's offer and go off to play lacrosse in Chicagoland? It did not take her long to decide. Like her old man, Sarah prefers the fast lane and is always in an impatient rush to get where she wants to go. Her decision to accept the offer from Northwestern was influenced by the fact that the school is one of the nation's top academic institutions.

Sarah went off to Northwestern in the fall of 2002, where she was a starter in most of the school's women's lacrosse games during her freshman year. As she was preparing to return to Evanston just before her sophomore year, Sarah came to me with some news.

"I've decided I'm not going to be playing on the lacrosse team this coming year," she informed me.

"I see," I replied, taken aback by this unexpected decision. "So, are you thinking of going out for basketball?"

"No, Dad," she stated firmly. "I'm done. My career as a student athlete is over. I plan to focus on getting the best education I can at Northwestern."

"You know what this means, don't you?"

She nodded.

"Bye-bye scholarship," I said with a sigh.

But the loss of Sarah's scholarship was not the most egregious aspect of Sarah's decision to hang up her long stick. Her team, the NW Wildcats, would go on to win the Division One National Championship the following year...and win it again during each of the next four consecutive years! Both of Sarah's college roommates were members of the team and both were named All-Americans. Did Sarah ever express any regrets about her decision not to play basketball in college? Not once. Was she ever dismayed about exiting a soon-to-be legendary lacrosse team? Same answer. She never looked back for a second.

After graduating from Northwestern, Sarah worked in the wholesale insurance industry as a broker. She did that in both Florida and Georgia and then decided to follow her brother's examples and further her education by obtaining an advanced degree (just when I thought I was finally done paying tuition fees!). Sarah enrolled at UCLA's Anderson School of Management in Los Angeles and within a few years had earned her MBA. She then pursued a career in the sports health field, working for several companies before deciding to found her own business, called "Juna." Juna supports a community of strong pregnant and postpartum women and produces a highly regarded fitness and nutrition app for "this special part of life."

Sarah is married to Eric Kuhn, an executive with RingSmart Home Security Systems. He works closely with law enforcement in the area of crime prevention. Eric and Sarah live in Westlake Village in Los Angeles County, California and are the parents of three of my wonderful grandchildren: Luca, Kyla and Levi. Sarah remains athletic and is an outstanding snow skier and snowboarder. Watching her as a mother interact with my grandkids is a new joy in my life and one that I savor enormously. Although we are on different ends of the country these days, I thank goodness for FaceTime, Zoom and the modern technologies that make it possible for me to stay in touch with Sarah, Eric and the kids.

At times, I still get nostalgic for the days when Lorraine and I would *shlepp* around the country watching Sarah play basketball and lacrosse and cheering her on to victory. I am comforted at such times by the knowledge that I feel I have done right by all of my children. Once Sarah got her MBA, I felt I was at last done with my filial obligations. I have helped all three of my surviving kids get a good head start in life. I have assisted them in avoiding crippling long-term student debt and I have supported each one in purchasing their first homes, just as Sam Fixler did for me. I have even helped finance honeymoons and provided start-up capital for their own enterprises. I feel that things have come full circle and now, during their prime earning years, it is the time when each will be focused on helping their own kids get the most out of life.

Before closing this chapter, I want to express my gratitude to Sarah for two important items that she has done on my behalf.

First, Sarah is the one who encouraged me to write this book. It was really her idea, so if you don't like what you're reading you can contact her for a refund. You certainly won't get one from me.

On a more serious note, I want you, dear reader, to know that I will forever be in Sarah's debt for helping me and her mother survive the loss of Mathew. She made our lives worth living again and I will always be grateful to her for that.

Chapter Twenty-one

The New Millennium

"The illiterate of the 21st Century will not be those who cannot read and write, but those who cannot learn, unlearn, and relearn."
—Alvin Toffler

O nce the Y2K hysteria subsided and the dot.com bubble popped, I had the opportunity to examine where things stood for me professionally in this brave new century. My lease on our office space in lower Manhattan was up. The landlord was selling the building and the new owner wanted the space. I determined that our firm's cash flow had, at this point, diminished to the point that operating a law firm in three different locations was no longer necessary for me to run my practice. It had always been a challenge, but when there's a steady flow of clients coming in the door, you rise to the occasion. But now, I felt, was the time for consolidation.

Elmsford is a lovely village in Westchester County located in the town of Greenburgh, not far from Carmel and within the New York City greater metropolitan area. I felt this would be an ideal spot from which I could conduct my practice and remain in proximity to all my current clients. After a brief search, I located and purchased a two-story building not far from an I-287 highway exit. At the same time, I sold the Carmel building and moved the staff into the second floor of the new Elmsford location. I leased some of the first floor space to a private investigator who did a good deal of work for our firm. Another portion of the first floor space was devoted to the new business venture I had established with Dave Festa, while the remainder was left vacant until I could decide what to do with it. I later rented it to a company that manufactured backyard play equipment and used it as showroom space. Dave Festa, as you may recall, was the IT guy at Putnam County Hospital whom I had met through Rod Huebbers. He was a gifted programmer who had developed an amazing product for processing insurance claims online that we had hopes of bringing to market. I'll go in to that subject a bit later.

We, at this point, began transitioning my NYC office to the Elmsford building. I offered all of our New York staff members the opportunity of moving to our new location. Some accepted, others opted out and by the end of 2000 we closed up shop. As mentioned earlier, the timing of our firm's departure from our lower Manhattan office, located in the shadow of the World Trade Center, turned out to be propitious. The twin towers were destroyed by the 9/11 terrorist attacks nine months later.

At one point, both my my sons were working in the New York City office. Mitchell had started as an associate there after finishing law school. He had been given a caseload that included maintaining a relationship with an insurance company that was providing us with a sizable number of defense cases. Jason, likewise, joined us upon graduation and was working diligently on the cases he had been assigned. The management of our legal team at our new digs was effectively handled by one of the top attorneys from our NYC office,

Jim Skelly. The administrative staff was placed under the supervision of Michelle Easton whom, you may recall, came to work for us in Carmel after leaving the Burchetta law firm. Michelle was ably assisted in her new duties by her good friend, Lorraine Fixler.

At some point before the move to Westchester, I sensed that Mitchell was not happy with the practice of law and might consider making a change. I spoke to him and suggested that he perhaps would enjoy working with Dave Festa in our fledgling business venture. Mitch seemed open to the idea. So, I spoke with Dave Festa about having Mitch join us and Dave agreed. We dubbed our company EDM for Elliot, David, and Mitchell. We now felt that our team was properly poised to launch our new start-up.

Our first product was an online claims settlement platform that would streamline the process for insurance claims adjusters. We attempted to pitch it to a number of insurance carriers but were unable to generate much traction. We next developed a voice recognition program for radiologists. It would automatically transcribe their verbal analyses of X-ray and other diagnostic images and attach those as notes to the image file. It worked well and we attracted a lot of lookers, but insufficient buyers to make the venture financially viable.

During those early development days at EDM, I was paying Mitchell and Dave's salaries, as well as footing the bill for all operating expenses and equipment purchases out of my own pocket. We needed to find a viable and marketable product quickly. Fortunately, we found one.

Our next product came at the suggestion of a Mahopac neighbor whose company handled insurance claims management for hospitals. He suggested that if we could come up with a program that would monitor and control a hospital's legal expenditures, he might be able to get some of his clients to have a look at it. Hospitals and physician groups were constantly employing lawyers to defend them in medical malpractice cases. These lawyers would submit invoices for their services to the hospital's insurance carrier. The insurance company's claims examiners would then review the invoices and if they seemed to be okay, they would authorize payment in full. If, however, the claims examiner discovered any discrepancies, the invoiced amount would be reduced and the lowered amount and then paid. It was a tedious and labor-intensive process that required the examiner to go through the often massive files of each case to determine if the charges being billed were legitimate.

The insurance companies were willing to bear the expense of this ongoing due diligence because they recognized that by deploying claims examiners to serve as watchdogs, they would force the attorneys to be more accurate and scrupulous in their billing practices. The process worked and served to reduce the legal expenses that insurance companies were required to underwrite, although it was hard to determine if those savings exceeded the cost of the watchdogs.

Dave went to work in an effort to streamline this invoice review process and came up with a program we labeled ResolveStar. Eventually, we changed the name of the company from EDM to ResolveStar. ResolveStar was pitched to insurance companies as a single, powerful web-based solution that would provide a comprehensive and uniform platform for monitoring and controlling legal expenses. We touted it as a seamless, end-to-end pipeline for invoices and receipt submission, review, approval and payment.

The product did not actually conduct any claims examinations. It worked by preparing guidelines for lawyers and then training them to submit their invoices directly to ResolveStar. The bills would hit our servers where our algorithms would go over each one. If an invoice was found to deviate from established guidelines—guidelines that stipulated what could be charged for and how much could be charged —it would get kicked back to the lawyer. The lawyer could then recalculate the invoice, bringing it into compliance, and then resubmit it. Alternately, the lawyer had the option to provide an explanation for the deviation. This "explanation" option would necessarily result in a delayed payment as the claim was further evaluated. Hence, lawyers were provided with strong incentives to comply with the guidelines and in this way, our clients enjoyed significant savings. And by using our product, the cost of achieving those savings was now a fraction of what it had been when they were doing such auditing manually.

Our first contract was with a company called the CCC (Combined Coordinating Council). This was a hospital management group that serviced about 20 area medical centers. They had a robust manual invoice auditing system already in place. They, therefore, had little expectation of ResolveStar having much of an impact. They believed that their in-house examiners had already succeeded in bringing down legal costs as far as possible. Their interest in ResolveStar was for us to serve simply as a watchdog to keep the lawyers on the straight and narrow path of continued compliance. They held zero expectation that we would be able to reduce their legal costs any further. Were they ever shocked when they looked at the first year's results after deploying ResolveStar. They found that their legal expenditures had been lowered by several million dollars! As you may imagine, they were overjoyed.

The program that Dave Festa had created turned out to be an unequivocal success and ResolveStar was off and running. From there we began attracting clients primarily by word of mouth. The hospital administration and insurance industries are relatively inbred and news of this nature spreads quickly. Over the ensuing years ResolveStar has provided a decent livelihood for both Dave and Mitch, who still serves as its Chief Operating Officer. It also provides me with an income which has come in very handy now that I don't practice law or mediate lawsuits.

While back at my law firm on the second floor, Jason and the other attorneys were working their tails off, somehow my enthusiasm for the practice had started to wane. I tried a few cases, but I could tell I wasn't up to par and at times, even floundering. Although I was not yet 60, I began to wonder if age was catching up with me. Fortunately, my friend, Stuart Myers came through for me again and rescued me from my sea of self-doubt.

Stuart's company, York Claims, did business from coast to coast and enjoyed relationships with law firms in most major cities. In Miami, Stu used the services of attorney Manny Diaz. Manny became well-known when he represented Lázaro Gonzalez in the celebrated custody case involving his grand-nephew, Elián Gonzalez. Manny was present at the Gonzalez household on April 22, 2000 when the home was raided by immigration agents. As a result, Manny was propelled into national prominence.

The following year Manny leveraged that fame and decided to run for mayor of the city of Miami and was easily elected. He found himself as the chief executive of a city near bankruptcy. The state of Florida had imposed a financial oversight board that closely monitoring the city's spending. Mayor Diaz got to work immediately implementing a vast overhaul of the entire administrative structure. Doing so, he correctly understood, would result in financial stability and I'm happy to say, thanks to Stuart's assistance, I became part of that positive process.

One of the most devilish areas that Manny had to deal with upon taking office was the city's risk management department. This department is responsible for managing a city's insurance contracts as well as its workers' compensation claims. These duties include conducting claims examinations, arranging medical exams for claimants, setting up monetary reserve funds for payment of claims against the city, oversight of the lawyers retained by the city, and authorizing legal settlements with claimants.

Manny quickly recognized that the head of the risk management department was incompetent and needed to be replaced. The mayor confided in his friend and advisor, Stuart, about this problem and Stu suggested that Manny bring me on board. At least temporarily, until he could locate a permanent replacement.

Stuart called and set up a meeting between me and the mayor. The outcome was that I agreed, strictly as a favor to Stuart who I held in high regard, to run the department for three months. Three months, as things turned out, that stretched into six. I packed my bags, said good-bye to Lorraine and headed south to the sunshine state.

I found, once I began my duties, that I was in charge of a team of 30 city employees. I enlisted their aid as I began reviewing the worker's comp claims and then made myself familiar with all the pending lawsuits against the city. I soon discovered that I enjoyed the job and felt as though I was making a difference in helping to control costs for the city. I also discovered that the City Attorney had been approving the settlement of claims without first obtaining approval from my department—which was a no-no. I soon made sure that all such settlements were reviewed by us and if they were too generous, they were rejected. I brought in an expert named John Petillo, who was an old friend of Stuart's and mine, to assist me in the review of all outstanding insurance contracts held by the city.

Although I really relished the work and the fine weather, it was a rather lonely time for me. I grew tired of living in a hotel and eating all my meals in restaurants. I was simply no longer cut out to be a bachelor. Even in swinging Miami with all its vice.

Manny introduced me to Richard Lydecker who had worked in the mayor's law firm and had run his successful election campaign. Richard now had his own small firm and he and I discussed the possibility of merging his firm in Miami with mine in New York. We soon realized that neither of us knew how to manage the logistics of such a merger and the opportunity soon dissolved. Actually,

Richard's Miami law firm began to thrive and saw Mayor Manny join the firm after he had termed out as mayor.

Upon returning home after my stint in Miami, I came to the conclusion that it might be time for me to pack things up and make the move to Florida. After discussing my thinking with Lorraine, she fully agreed. I then embarked on the process of disconnecting myself from my New York activities in preparation of the move. I describe that process and our move to Palm Beach Gardens in the following chapter.

.

Elliot Fixler

Chapter Twenty-two

Escape from New York

"Fantasy is not an escape from reality. It is a way of understanding it."

—Lloyd Alexander

I n Texas, or so I've heard, they say you're not a man until your daddy says you are. I was thinking about this and asking myself if my kids were prepared to face life without me nearby as I began making plans to leave New York and head south. Mitch was situated, however tenuously, working with Dave Festa at ResolveStar. Sarah was in California, working on her degree. That left Jason, who had established a law partnership with his friend Paul LaGattuta and set up shop in the Equitable Life Building in lower Manhattan, not far from where my New York office had been located.

I was worried about whether or not Jason would make it on his own. I had never been easy on him when he worked at my firm and I was afraid he might have inherited some of my less attractive personality traits. My mind was set at ease about Jason a few years later when he invited me to join him at a father-son golf weekend. As mentioned, not spending more time with Jason when he was growing up had always been one of my life's regrets. So, when this opportunity came along, I jumped at it.

The three-day event was held at Connecticut's Foxwoods Seminole Casino and brought together a circle of friends (and their fathers) that Jason had made through the Brae Burn Country Club in Purchase, New York. After I had been introduced to only five or six of Jason's buddies, I could not help but be impressed with the esteem in which they seemed to hold him. Several of the guys were top level corporate execs with Fortune 500 companies and used the occasion to garner some free advice on the fairways from Jay. He graciously responded with both legal and strategic business guidance. His golf buddies, as well as their dads, seemed to pay rapt attention to his every word.

It was not solely for professional advice that they turned to Jay. They were also intently interested in his opinion about more mundane matters such as their club president's job performance. These were members of New York's business elite, several of them among the city's super-wealthy, who were turning to my son with questions about how to structure their next mega-deal. I couldn't help but feel a sense of paternal pride. It was similar to that old E.F. Hutton commercial, "When J.L. Fixler talks, people listen." Actually, these days I think he would be called an "influencer."

I'm pleased to report that Jason has leveraged the leadership skills I witnessed on display that day into building a solid practice through his hard work, diligence, and commitment to his craft. I feel that Jason's success is something to which I may have in some ways contributed, although I'm certain his mother would take full credit for it all.

So, with my kids well-situated, I began laying the foundation for our move to Florida. As mentioned, I had sold the Mahopac lake house with all its memories and moved into another home during Sarah's final high school years. When Sarah had gone off to college, Lorraine and I lived in a condo that had been built by city councilman and radio broadcaster, Jim McDonough, who had covered many of Sarah's high school basketball games. Although the unit contained a suite for Sarah, she came home infrequently, so it got very little use.

I was still in my early sixties and figured there was no reason why I couldn't practice law after moving to Florida. Of course, that required that I pass the Florida bar exam. So, I devoted a good deal of my time holed up in my Palm Beach Gardens winter home studying for the exam. I sat for the exam and managed to pass; despite being distracted by the buxom babe who was seated across from me. I certainly do not recall seeing anyone like this amply endowed aspiring attorney back when I sat for the New York bar exam. I guess one must stay abreast of the times. I originally had hoped to start practicing law in Florida once the right opportunity came along. Well, if opportunity knocked, I was too focused on other matters to go and open the door. And, of course, my advancing years did not help matters.

One of those other matters was finding a bigger house. The place in PGA was okay for a few weeks of winter getaway, but if I was going to put down stakes here among the swaying palms, we would need a bigger place. I imagined that our home would become "Vacation Destination #1" for my kids and their families. Things did not turn out that way, however.

Our realtor directed us to a luxury gated community in Palm Beach Gardens called Mirasol. Our house hunting took place in May of 2004, in the midst of a frenzied housing boom that eventually led to the collapse of the housing market in 2009. At this point, just about everyone in South Florida who could say "credit default swap," was taking advantage of low no-money-down mortgage terms and snatching up all the homes they could lay hands on. With area home prices rising at more than 17% per year, people who had been flipping burgers not long ago were now flipping houses and cashing in as the bubble expanded. Once again, my lamentable bad luck in financial matters came through and I wound up paying top dollar for a home in Mirasol just before the market crashed. Once again, I had arrived to the party just as everyone was going home. More about my memories of Mirasol in the following chapter.

I had finally gotten all my ducks in a row—or so I thought—back in New York, and was poised to finally disconnect, despite the fact I still had an active business interest in ResolveStar. Regardless of the fact I had two adult children living in New York and even though we would be leaving behind most of our friends and social contacts, I felt I could manage all those relationships remotely and I was ready to make my Great Escape, except for one nagging bit of unfinished business.

It seemed that my friends, Janusz and Anna Rudnicki had a legal problem. They had asked for a helping hand and I had agreed to extend mine. I simply could not run out on them, so I put my relocation plans on hold until their case was resolved. Jan and Anna had been Cold War refugees who had made a genuine Great Escape across the Iron Curtain from Communist Poland in the 1970s. Before emigrating to the U.S., Anna had been a psychiatrist and Jan, an OB/GYN. Jan, with unparalleled tenacity, had passed his Foreign Medical Graduate exams, undergone a medical residency, and became a licensed, board-certified gynecologist. He formed a partnership with Dr. Marcel Goldberger and the two had together built an extremely successful medical practice in Carmel.

Jan's success had enabled the couple to realize and fulfill the American Dream, a quest that had propelled them, like my own family and like so many others, to find political freedom and economic opportunity in America. They owned a magnificent mansion in Westchester County, but by 2005, they had become empty-nesters and decided they wanted to downsize. The couple placed a bid on a pricey smaller home, a bid that was quickly accepted by the seller. The bid was contingent upon the Rudnicki's being able to secure a mortgage commitment for a particular minimum amount from a lending institution. Jan put up $100,000 in earnest money that was placed into escrow by the seller's attorney. According to the contract agreement, if the mortgage loan was granted and the deal went through, the money would be applied toward the purchase price. If they were not granted the loan, the money would be returned to the Rudnickis.

The bank refused to grant them a mortgage. The problem was that the bank's appraisers affixed a market value to the home that fell below the amount of the mortgage loan. That would leave a portion of

371

the debt unsecured and therefore the deal wouldn't fly. Evidently, the Rudnickis had agreed to an inflated purchase price. I counseled my friends that it made no sense to proceed with this house. They should get their earnest money out of escrow and start looking for another home to purchase. They agreed, but, guess what? The sellers refused to turn over the dough.

Their refusal placed the sellers clearly in violation of the terms of the sales agreement. I wasted no time in filing an action against them that would bring the force of law to bear and compel them to return the deposit money. As was my practice, I did not charge my friends for representing them. In any case, I assumed it would be a simple matter since both the facts and the law in this case could not be any more clearcut. Wrong again, hotshot.

The sellers took the position that the Rudnickis should find another lender to provide them with a mortgage loan. This was patently absurd, since any other bank would likewise appraise the property, find it to be insufficient collateral, and also decline to grant the loan. The simple fact was that the sellers had placed an outrageously high price on the house, found two doctors who didn't know much about real estate negotiating who foolishly had agreed to pay the price being asked. We were under no obligation to scour the countryside looking for some other lending institution that would agree to grant my friends the loan. And that's exactly what I wrote in the pleadings I filed in the case.

Of course, after the pleadings, there were to be depositions, and motions and pre-trial conferences and endless client meetings. I had soon invested nearly $30,000 worth of my billable time into this "open and shut" no-brainer of a case. And, meanwhile, my flight to Florida freedom was getting pushed further and further down the road. After a good deal of laborious haggling, I convinced the sellers to agree to a refund of $90,000. I took the offer to Janusz and he was *livid*.

"How can he screw us out of ten thousand like that and get away with it!?" he bellowed. "No way. Tell him he gives back every penny or we go to court."

Janusz, of course, was right. If he accepted the offer, he was getting held up for $10K that was rightfully and legally his. Yes, I was sure we would have no trouble convincing a court to compel the seller to pay back the full amount, but, at what cost?

It was at this point I began to regret providing free legal services to my friends. By doing so, they attached no monetary value to my work and therefore it did not come into play in deciding whether or not to accept a settlement. I decided to lay it on the line.

"Look, Jan and Anna," I patiently explained. "I need to wrap up my New York affairs and get on with my life. A trial will not be docketed for six weeks and then another week to get a judgement. If you decide to reject the $90,000, you're going to have to find yourselves another lawyer."

Anna gave Janusz one of those looks and they agreed to accept the $90,000.

It was finally "Florida, here I come!" time...or so I thought.

There's a Yiddish expression that goes, "Man plans. God laughs."

Well, perhaps it's because I'm an atheist, but I did not find my inability to carry out my relocation plans one bit funny. I was, in fact, quite frustrated. Just as I had successfully extricated myself from the Rudnicki real estate matter, I was faced with yet another case that would once again cause me to postpone my southbound sojourn.

Jason and his partner, Paul, had by this time launched their law firm in lower Manhattan. Among the cases that Paul had taken with him from our firm was a dispute involving a client named Sari Miller. Sari was a partner at Stuart's company, York Claims Services, and was something of a real estate entrepreneur. I had gotten to know her from the time that I had been an investor in one of her ventures. It was not a particularly complex case and although Paul was handling it and was certainly capable of doing a first-rate job, Sari had been advised by Stuart that she should insist that she be represented by me. While I appreciated Stuart's high regard for my expertise, the case, at this point, was a major nuisance as I was trying to wrap things up and get out of New York. Perhaps Stuart just wanted me to stick around a little longer.

The lawsuit, filed by Sari, sought the recovery of $500,000 that she had loaned to a former business partner named Shapiro for which he had signed a promissory note. The sum represented Shapiro's capital contribution toward a new venture that Sari had put together. He was to repay the note from his share of the profits from the enterprise. Shapiro made no payments and had defaulted on the loan. Sari wanted it repaid in full, with interest. The case was to be tried before the highly regarded Commercial Division of the Manhattan Supreme Court, before renowned Justice Ira Gammerman. Gammerman most

FULL CIRCLE

often presided over medical malpractice cases. This loan dispute, which he had somehow gotten stuck with, represented a minor pain in the ass. As stated, it was a *major* pain in the ass for me.

Problems began popping up from the very first day as we embarked on the jury selection process. Paul had been handling all the pre-trial aspects of this case, so I had not had the opportunity to meet the defendant's attorney, Victor Gerstein. As I addressed the potential jurors for the first time, I introduced myself and went on to explain the role of each party in this action.

"The defendant, Mr. Shapiro, is being represented by his attorney, Mr. Gerstein, and he...."

I was interrupted immediately by Gerstein who popped to his feet and accused me of mispronouncing his name.

"Ladies and gentlemen. My name is not pronounced Ger-STINE as Mr. Fixler would have you believe. It is pronounced Ger-STEEN. Just like Bruce Spring-STEEN."

"Jesus!" I thought to myself. *"Is this what this case is going to be like? If he's going to jump on every word I say, we're going to be here till the cows come home."*

The defense attorney's demeanor was so condescending and pompous that I determined his attitude might be used to my advantage. I responded by pointing out the absurdity of his words to the potential jurors. I turned and addressed him directly.

"Mr. Ger-STINE," I said, intentionally mispronouncing his name. "I'd like to suggest that it is impossible for your name to be pronounced as you allege since it not spelled in the same manner as Mr.

375

Spring-STEEN's name. The last syllable of his name is spelled S-T-E-E-N while yours is spelled S-T-E-I-N." The jurors got the point and I reinforced it by intentionally mispronouncing Gerstein's name during the entire trial.

Gerstein continued his antics by constantly objecting to trivial and irrelevant matters. His clear intent was to annoy and unnerve me, but I could tell that he was actually succeeding in annoying the judge and the jury. So, his objections wound up having the opposite effect. Instead of irritating me, his petty outbursts boosted my confidence since I felt they were helping my case and hurting his.

A key issue in the case was the admissibility of testimony from a defense witness. The witness was a lawyer called to support the defendant's claim that he was not required to repay the loan. The problem was that the witness had been retained by the business that was, at the time, owned by both partners, the plaintiff, Sari Miller, and the defendant, Mr. Shapiro. Therefore, he had represented both parties to this lawsuit and this fact indicated a clear conflict of interest. Judge Gammerman found this troubling and said so. He further stated that this matter might need to be sent to the New York Bar grievance committee once the trial was concluded.

Based on the judge's favorable comments and other indicators, I felt rather certain that I was going to win the case. The calculation of interest, however, was uncertain, since this would be carried out by the judge as he saw fit. This positive attitude on the part of the judge gave me the impetus to put on the pressure.

When it was my turn to cross-examine the aforementioned lawyer, I went after him hammer and tong, peppering him with a constant barrage of questions about his suitability as a witness.

"Weren't you hired by the company owned by both Sari Miller and the defendant? Wasn't Sari Miller the president of that company? So, isn't it true that my client was once your client? She trusted you and the advice you provided. And here you are on the witness stand testifying against her. How can this jury, or anyone for that matter, consider you a credible witness when you are willing to stoop to such unethical and unprofessional tactics?"

My aggressive cross-examination, not surprisingly, prompted Mr. Gerstein to pop up from his chair frequently to object. It didn't matter even if the judge sustained the objections, since I was effectively getting the point across to the jury.

I next asked the witness a long and detailed question. It didn't matter what he answered because the question itself made the point I wanted the jury to understand. As I expected, Gerstein objected.

Before the judge could rule on the objection, I turned to the bench and asked, "Is he objecting to my question or the way I'm pronouncing his name?"

"Objection sustained," declared Judge Grammerman. "Ask your next question." I paused for a moment, pondering my next move. I then proceeded to repeat the exact same question, in the same precise detail, that the judge had just disallowed. Gerstein shot up like a jack rabbit and objected mightily. At this, the judge turned to me.

"Mr. Fixler. Did I not just sustain the objection to that very same question two minutes ago?"

"Yes," I replied. "Yes, you did."

"Well, then. What are you doing?"

'I"m giving you another chance," I said with a wink in my voice. The judge did not appear to be amused.

"You don't need another chance," he said rather gruffly.

"Not me, your honor. I was giving YOU another chance to correct your previous ruling." At this, Judge Grammerman was forced to cover his mouth with his hand to conceal a chuckle from the jury.

"Move it along, please, counselor," he said, shaking his head in disbelief.

I wound up winning the case, although we did not collect as much as we had hoped for. At the charge conference, the judge said he would not permit the jury to consider awarding the treble damages we had asked for. He also rejected the plaintiff's desire to have the interest calculated on a cash-on-cash compounded basis. Once we had calculated what the anticipated award would be, I advised my client to settle for that amount rather than wait for the outcome and appeal the decision if it came back lower than anticipated. I explained that such an appeal would only further delay the repayment of a note that should have been paid off years ago. *"And further delay my departure to the sunny south,"* I thought to myself as I observed a fresh layer of snow accumulating outside the window.

Sari wisely agreed to accept the settlement sum that equaled the principle amount of the note plus simple interest and attorney's fees.

The settlement agreement was reached just before the jury was to start their deliberations. No one was more pleased than me since I finally put the last obstacle to my escape from New York behind me.

Once we got ourselves moved and settled in Palm Beach Gardens, I reached out to the contacts I had made during my six-month stint as head of Miami's Risk Management Department. I informed them that I was now living in south Florida and available for service. As a result, I was offered an opportunity to serve as the assistant director in the same office that I had previously and temporarily headed. I was assigned to monitor and try to resolve the most troublesome workers' compensation cases the city was facing. I also was tasked with working with the City Attorney's Office to supervise, as necessary, cases that were being litigated against the City of Miami.

It was at this time I underwent an annual physical exam at my cardiologist's office. He had me undergo a treadmill stress test and the outcome turned out to be highly disturbing. He discovered I had a significant blockage in several of my arteries and that one was so close to the heart that inserting a cardiac stent was not an option. He explained that my left anterior descending artery or LAD was almost completely blocked. If it became fully obstructed, it would stop all blood flow to the left side of my heart, causing it to stop beating. This made me a prime candidate for a "widow-maker" heart attack that was most often fatal. If his intention was to scare the shit out of me, the water in my bowels demonstrated that he had succeeded.

On a bright sunny Tuesday in 2006, I was admitted to the Palm Beach Gardens Medical Center on Burns Road to undergo quadruple bypass surgery. I first met the anesthesiologist and then the surgeon dropped by to introduce himself, explain what was to happen, and answer any questions. His name was Dr. Arthur Katz and I had checked him out in advance and learned that he was considered the best in his field.

"So, Mr. Fixler," Dr. Katz said genially, "do you have any questions?"

"I have two," I answered. He told me to go ahead.

"First, am I the first surgery on your schedule today?"

He assured me that I was.

For the second question, I was tempted to ask Dr. Katz if he knew what had two legs and liked to fuck cats. But I thought better of it and could not summon the guts to ask it. After all, this guy was about to open my chest cavity and would be literally holding my life in his hands. I had no clue about his sense of humor, so I didn't risk the joke. Instead, I asked him how many of these types of surgeries he had performed. He said that he had stopped counting after hitting one thousand. That sounded good to me and I guess he did a commendable job of it since I'm still walking around and no widows have yet been made. I recovered quickly and was able to return to work at the Miami Risk Management Department a few weeks after surgery.

While I was certainly enjoying the south Florida lifestyle and found my work challenging and meaningful, the daily commute up and down I-95 was becoming more and more arduous, especially during "The Season" when the population of Palm Beach County doubles each year between November and May. I decided I had had enough and I believe the City of Miami felt much the same way. The

City Attorney regarded me with increasing animosity, since it was my job to look over his shoulder and monitor the way he defended the city's interests in court. At the end, we mutually agreed it was time for me to move on.

I wanted to keep busy, so I enrolled in a program that would enable me to become certified as a civil mediator. Once I received my certification, I contacted attorney Richard Lydecker who instructed his growing team to direct mediation cases to me. It turned out that I had a knack for the fine art of mediation. Of my first five cases, I succeeded in getting all five settled so they need not be tried in a civil court. Actually, I realized that I had been conducting mediations for years whenever I negotiated an out-of-court settlement on behalf of a client. I tended to look at any dispute from both the defendant's and the plaintiff's points of view. I was then able to build a compelling case to convince the attorneys as to the many merits of reaching an out-of-court settlement, benefits that would be enjoyed by the attorneys, and their clients, on both sides. While I enjoyed the work, I soon realized that in order to keep a steady stream of cases coming my way, it was necessary to spend my time hustling judges and lawyers and motivating them, by whatever means available, to refer cases to me. This I was not willing to do, so my career as a mediator eventually went into decline.

While we had made many new friends in Florida, especially after moving into Mirasol (see next chapter), our social life also involved old friends like Stuart Myers and his wife, Lida, who had moved to Florida not long after we had. Stuart had divested himself of his interest in York Claims Services and initially was living in PGA National. He and Lida eventually followed our lead and moved into Mirasol. John Petillo and his wife, Sharon, also had a place at PGA National and he, along with Stu, would often join me on the fabulous fairways of Palm Beach Gardens. Our wives, likewise, became golf buddies and it was on the links that Lida brought up an idea that Stuart had suggested.

The idea was that the three ladies would leverage their expertise in the insurance business and set up an insurance agency. With contacts provided by the three guys, they could quickly launch the agency and begin making some money and keep busy at the same time. They decided to do it and I did not object. I should have.

Supposedly John D. Rockefeller once astutely observed that "A friendship based on business is far better than a business based on friendship."

How right he was.

As you will read in the forthcoming chapter, it was this venture that, more than any other factor, led to the end of friendships that had endured for more than forty years.

Chapter Twenty-three

Sweet Lorraine

*"You have not lived today until you have done something
for someone who can never repay you"*
—John Bunyan

T he real estate mania that had gripped South Florida was in full swing as we began seeking larger quarters. I recall visiting a newly constructed home for sale that I had located on the internet. It was situated in an upscale gated community called Mirasol. As we were leaving after having toured the house, a man approached us and without a word of introduction began trying to dissuade us from buying the house.

"Listen, you don't want to buy that place," he blurted and then proceeded with his rapid-fire pitch. "I've got a much nicer place down the street and I'm asking a lot less money. Especially if you can pay me cash. Plus, there's no golf equity involved. I can sell to you for less 'cause it's not listed. No agent's commission, see?"

I realized that the fellow was one of the many people seeking to make a "quick buck" in this overheated market by buying homes and quickly flipping them. I told him I wasn't interested and wound up buying the place that we had come to see; not one of my best decisions. Within two years, the housing market was in shambles and our new home's value had diminished by 35%.

Once we were settled in at Mirasol, we began making new friends and were warmly welcomed by the community, until we met Jeanne; Hurricane Jeanne—one of a trio of tropical storms that ripped through our community shortly after we had moved in. I was instructed by the civil defense network to cover all my windows with the heavy metal shutters that had come with the house. This was before the building codes were changed requiring that all new home construction be CBS (concrete block structure) and all windows be able to withstand hurricane winds up to 150 mph.

I was struggling to get those panels screwed into place when I was approached by a neighbor who asked if I could provide the crew he had hired to put up his shutters with the installation instructions. He pointed out that his home was identical to mine and needed the written instructions to help guide his crew since he would not be around to supervise them. I replied that I did not have any written instructions and asked why he couldn't oversee the work himself.

"Are you kidding?" he replied. "I'm getting the hell out of here. Going to Tampa where it's safe."

We were complete virgins when it came to dealing with hurricanes, and that first one was quite an adventure. Several of the shutters could not be secured properly and blew off, turning into deadly flying missiles. Also, our huge sliding glass doors were not covered because they could not be secured, so we spent a good deal of time and effort barricading them from the inside—at times using our own backsides—so they would not implode.

After it was all over, we got to know the neighbor who had hightailed it to Tampa. Mike Nicklous was, and remains, an en-

trepreneurial type of guy primarily involved in the elevator maintenance industry. He had paid a lot less for his house than I had for the
exact same model. And when Mike decided to sell and move to another gated community up the road, Ibis Golf & Country Club, he
sold his Mirasol house at the height of the market. I sold our identical
home just a year later for $500,000 less than Mike had received. I
remained friendly with Mike after he had moved out of Mirasol. He
was a big-hearted guy and, like many of my friends, something of a
character.

I had been formally introduced to Mike after his return from Tampa by another neighbor, Donna Demato, who, along with her
boyfriend (and later husband), Tom Noonan, had moved in across the
street from us after relocating from another nearby Mirasol home. I
became friends with Donna and enjoyed enough fun-time exploits
with her and Mike Nicklous to fill another book. I might just write it
if I ever finish this one.

After a few years, I determined that the cost of maintaining our
Mirasol mini mansion was becoming a real financial burden. In addition to the POA (Property Owners Association) fees, there was also a
monthly HOA (Home Owners Association) fee, plus golf member-
ship and greens fees, plus landscaping and pool maintenance fees
and if I didn't agree to replace my roof every five years, I would be
pilloried by the petty neighborhood kingpins who ran things at Mirasol. So, I decided to sell the place and move on.

After my miserable track record, I had no stomach for again getting mixed up in the local real estate market, so I decided to take a
break from home ownership and became a rental tenant in a house

located back at PGA National. I asked my buddy, Ray Kolkmann, if he wanted to rent his house to me for one year. He and Mary weren't using it that much anyway and they agreed. The home was big enough to accommodate all of us whenever they would come down to spend a week in Florida. Lorraine and I actually stayed in the home a while longer than a year until I once again got the urge to move on.

As discussed in the previous chapter, Lorraine, along with her friends, Lida and Sharon, had assembled some refurbished office furniture and file cabinets and proceeded to open an insurance agency. It seemed that over time Lorraine was spending more and more hours each week at the agency office. I also noticed that whenever I would drop in to visit her there, she was the only one doing any actual work. The place was peppered with pastel Post-It notes, each one reminding her to carry out some chore or another.

Lorraine was handling the least profitable area of the business, homeowner's coverage, while her partners focused on the more lucrative business casualty insurance. When I pointed this fact out to Lorraine and questioned it, she explained that Sharon had a lot of experience in that area and was not willing to take the time to train her. This seemed odd, since I observed Sharon playing a lot of very time-consuming golf. As far as Lida was concerned, I had no idea how she was spending her time, but it sure wasn't being spent at the office.

Not being shy about such things, I let my displeasure be known to the hubbies, Stuart and John. I told them that I didn't think it was fair that Lorraine was saddled with all the grunt work while Lida and Sharon were off doing other things.

Stuart's reaction was immediate. He wanted out and said he wished for us to buy out his interest in the business. John took a bit longer, but his reaction was similar. They both wanted to abandon the business. Stuart and Lida got out immediately, selling their interest to John and Sharon and Lorraine and me. A year or so later, John said he had a friend who owned a similar agency in the area who might be an interested buyer. It turned out he was indeed interested and our agency was sold. By coincidence (?), Sharon soon went to work for the agency that had bought ours. In any event, that ended Lorraine's career as an insurance agent. But the sale also represented the beginning of the end of something else, my long-standing friendships with Stuart Myers and John Petillo.

Actually, over the previous five or six years, there had been a growing and gnawing feeling of discontent regarding my relationship with Stuart. He would often call and invite me to join him for dinner at the Flagler Steak House or some other swanky Palm Beach eatery. But, as time went by, I was less and less inclined to accept. He had somehow become a different person from the great guy with whom I had traveled the world and shared so many memories. Of course, in all honesty, perhaps it was me who had changed. Whichever way it was, there came a point when it seemed that all the joy had drained out of our friendship. I could sense that Stu felt the same way.

This realization brought on a profound sadness. I thought back to our younger days when I would listen to that Simon and Garfunkel tune called *Old Friends* and imagine that we would become those bookends on the park bench someday:

> Old friends, winter companions, the old men.
> Lost in their overcoats, waiting for the sunset.
> The sounds of the city sifting through trees
> Settle like dust on the shoulders of the old friends.
> Can you imagine us years from today
> Sharing a park bench quietly?
> How terribly strange to be 70.
> ©Paul Simon Music

Sadly, it was not to be. It did indeed feel very strange and we were not even 70 yet.

From my vantage point today, I now understand that the problems I perceived at the insurance agency were to some degree attributable to Lorraine's encroaching Alzheimer's' Disease. She was, by that time, experiencing limitations in what she could do, even though there were no obvious changes in her personality. But I was blind to that possibility at the time because I was clearly in a state of denial. I had witnessed Lorraine's mother, Isabella, fall victim to the disease and I believed Alzheimer's to be a hereditary condition. As a result, I had made up my mind that Lorraine was like her dad who lived to be 100 with a clear mind to the end. She would never fall victim to Alzheimer's, I told myself constantly. And if *I* was engaged in such self-inflicted blindness to the truth, how could I have reasonably expected more from Stuart and Lida or John and Sharon?

Once Lorraine was out of the insurance business I decided that we had lived long enough in someone else's abode and I again began looking for a home to buy. I located a lovely community called Ironhorse that contained more moderately priced homes than did Mirasol. I identified two houses that I thought would work for us and I submitted an offer for one of them at the full asking price. The realtor informed me that there were other buyers who were strongly interested and it might require going higher than the asking price to seal the deal. I really did not wish to get into a bidding war so I turned my attention to the second Ironhorse property and was able to purchase it easily at slightly below the asking price.

For once, I had made the right real estate decision. Had I decided to go for the first house, I would have had to pay a huge premium or certainly lost the bidding war. I learned that it sold to a former West Palm Beach fireman who had been struck by a city vehicle while on the job. He had retained a slick personal injury attorney who aided him in recovering $3 million in damages plus a full lifetime disability pension. The fireman evidently had money to burn at this point. He waltzed in and offered $80,000 over the asking price and paid for the place in cash. To add to my aggravation, I would frequently see my fortunate fireman neighbor cruising the community in his new snow-white Mercedes SL convertible. The exact same car that I had been lusting after. All I can say is, "Only in America."

I recently learned from Sarah that Lorraine was strongly against our moving into Ironhorse. Her objection was that it was downwind from the open city dump and when the winds shifted, the area would be permeated with a foul odor that upset her. I was oblivious to so much at that time, I didn't wake up and smell the dumpsite. In actuality, that problem had mostly dissipated by the time we moved in, but the stench of bad reputation lingered on. There were other storm clouds gathering on the horizon as well that I likewise chose to ignore.

Sarah, to her credit, did not engage in the same sort of denial that blinded me to Lorraine's deteriorating situation. Sarah recently told me that her mother was aware of what was happening to her but tried her best to conceal things so as to not become a burden on me and the rest of the family. When Sarah expressed concern about her own future risk, given how the disease seemed to strike female members of our family, Lorraine tried to comfort and reassure her.

"Oh, don't worry, honey," she told her. "By that time new medical discoveries will be able to save you from all this."

Sarah shared with me that Lorraine's biggest fear was being remembered not as the friendly outgoing capable woman that everyone fell in love with, but instead as what she has ultimately become, due to this terrible disease. A few years after that conversation, and after Sarah had her first child, Lorraine and I visited Sarah and Eric in California. Sarah became heartsick observing her mother transformed into the very thing she dreaded most.

Before Sarah and Eric moved to California and were still living in Colorado, I had offered a suggestion that it might be good step to get Lorraine a therapy puppy. Sarah thought it was a great idea and said she would start looking right away. Shortly thereafter, we received a video from Sarah of an adorable Cavalier King Charles Spaniel puppy whose eyes bore a lost and forlorn look. I suggested that maybe we should get him a companion from the same litter. "I'll take two," I said. Not long afterwards, our two playful pups arrived and we named them Oliver and Apple. Lorraine adored them and it seemed that bringing them into her life was a great joy...for a while.

Lorraine's decline began to accelerate toward the end of 2011. She had been advised to keep challenging herself with cognitive brain games like Luminosity and daily crossword puzzles. She did these assiduously at first, but soon she could detect that she still was slipping. I found that I was increasingly needed at home to help carry out more and more ADLs (activities of daily life), such as caring for our new puppies. I started taking over the domestic chores like meal preparation, laundry and cleaning. At this stage, Lorraine was still able to walk the dogs around the neighborhood. We were actually able to take them with us on bike rides around Ironhorse with one pup seated in each of our handlebar baskets.

Once I was finally able to admit that Lorraine was afflicted and becoming more and more impaired, I started looking for therapies and/or pharmaceuticals that would delay the progress of the disease. I learned about an anti-Alzheimer's drug trial and I enrolled us both. I had to be part of the program because the study's researchers tracked Lorraine's progress and my reporting was vital to get a clear picture of where things stood. They explained that it was a double-blind study and half the subjects, selected randomly, will be receiving placebos instead of the actual medication.

Not long afterward, Lorraine voluntarily stopped driving after a harrowing incident. We had been out with friends in Wellington, an upscale community west of West Palm Beach. I asked Lorraine to drive us home since I had consumed too much liquor to pass a breathalyzer test should we get stopped. Lorraine had always acted safely and responsibly behind the wheel and would most often be selected as the designated driver whenever she went out for an evening with the girls. I had observed that over the past few years, however, Lorraine had exhibited difficulty carrying out simple tasks whenever I was driving, with her in the passenger seat. I would, for example, ask her to take out my iPad and locate the nearest Star-bucks, a task she was unable to complete. I am ashamed to say that I would become frustrated and reacted with anger. Now I understand that she was experiencing early stage Alzheimer's. Despite my reser-vations that night, I proceeded to give her the car keys. She tried to drive us home but became lost and disoriented within a few minutes. This was the watershed point when I finally began to get it. We man-aged to make it home safely, but, at her own choice, Lorraine decid-ed to never get behind the wheel again.

As discussed in a previous chapter, Lorraine's parents had settled in St. Augustine, Florida, where her father became her mother's caregiver for as long as he was able to do so. Her father, Bob, had retained the services of a permanent home health care provider named Kathy who became almost like a member of the family. Bob was a highly active octogenarian, playing tennis and riding his bike almost daily into his early 90's. This ended when he was involved in an auto accident and suffered permanent disabling injuries that even-tually confined him to a wheelchair.

After Bella's death, Kathy continued her services, now providing care for Bob. The relationship bloomed into a romance and Kathy became Bob's life partner and cared for him for the rest of his days. Lorraine and I were quite pleased with this situation. We enjoyed peace of mind knowing that her father was being well-cared for in his dotage. We also realized that if it weren't for Kathy, the responsibility for Bob's care would fall on us or on Lorraine's brother, Robert Bugg, Jr. who went by Rob.

For most of his professional life, Rob had worked in the banking business but at some point, broke out of that role and become an ex-patriot and a "citizen of the world." His life was spent traveling from one exotic location to another. I recall an amazing vacation that Lorraine, Sarah, Grandpa Bob, and I took to Hong Kong where Bob and his wife, Barbara, gave us the grand tour from the night market of Kowloon to the casinos of Macao.

Eventually, Rob and Barbara moved back to the States and settled in scenic North Carolina. At this point, Lorraine and I had moved to Palm Beach Gardens and his father, Bob, was living with Kathy in St. Augustine. Rob would constantly complain to us about Kathy. He accused her of stealing from his father, although Bob was not a wealthy man and I couldn't imagine what he owned that would be worth stealing. Rob suspected Kathy of trying to swindle Bob out of his house and other such treacherous deeds; all of which seemed un-founded and presented without a shred of actual evidence.

Lorraine and I couldn't understand Rob's animosity toward Kathy. Didn't he realize that Kathy was providing his dad with the type of care that would cost a fortune if he had to hire a private caregiver? Didn't he understand that if it weren't for Kathy, it may have been he and Barbara who would be charged with looking after his aged father? Lorraine did not agree one bit with her brother's constant criticism of Kathy. She had a liking for Kathy and thought that her presence was good for her dad and contributed to his longevity. Bob and Kathy were together for more than 30 years.

We got to know Kathy and, at times, we would arrange to meet her and Bob in Cocoa Beach, which was halfway between St. Augustine and Palm Beach. Kathy would do the driving and put in the effort required to transport Bob on such a road trip. This involved handling the transfers from the car into his wheelchair and back, assisting him whenever we would visit a restaurant, helping him go to the bathroom and so on. Kathy carried out these duties with a smile and without a word of complaint. And it was clear from her demeanor that she was not extending this high level of care because she was being paid, but rather because she loved the man she was looking after.

By way of contrast, complaining about Kathy seemed to be Rob and Barbara's favorite indoor sport. I finally got fed up and decided I had listened to just about enough of their whining and constant bellyaching. I told them to just let it go and stop their incessant bitching. I guess that Rob figured I no longer wished to hear what he had to say, because that was the last conversation I had with him, ever. Despite the fact his sister is suffering with the most devastating disease imaginable, there has never been a phone call, email, or note inquiring about her welfare since that day. Lorraine's niece and nephew, by contrast, regularly send her greeting cards on her birthday and on holidays. The fact that Lorraine is no longer capable of reading them doesn't diminish the value of the gesture. But from her brother? Nothing but the "Sound of Silence."

I find this sort of estrangement to be disappointing and hard to fathom. I genuinely liked Barbara and Rob and always enjoyed their company. Even if they now dislike me, how could they act this way to Lorraine?

For a while, Lorraine's condition appeared to stabilize—or so I thought. I was able to leave her home alone while I went out to the store and even long enough for a round of golf. Our next-door neighbor was a lovely lady who loved Lorraine (as did all who met her) and would frequently drop in and visit with her. I also felt comfortable going on bike rides around the neighborhood with Lorraine until she began doing strange things. For example, she would suddenly speed up, ride alongside me and then act as though she was about to cut me off. The bike rides stopped since I could not be sure that she would always act safely.

Our vacation travels together likewise soon came to a halt. Our last such trip was a Colorado visit to my old Copper Mountain ski instructor buddy, Terry Simone and his wife, Christina. Skiing became impossible because it was too difficult keeping track of Lorraine's whereabouts. She would wander off aimlessly along the slopes and I was constantly afraid of losing her in a snowdrift.

Shortly after returning home, Lorraine and I attended the regular drug trial session in which we had been now taking part for several years. I had come prepared to pull the plug. I did not see the point of subjecting either of us to further participation since I could see no benefits coming our way. Lorraine's deterioration was progressing steadily and the medication seemed to be having zero effect. Before I could say a word, we were told that the program was ending since the pharmaceutical company that was sponsoring the study was likewise seeing no positive results. It's possible that we were in the placebo control group, but in either case, our participation amounted to a frustrating waste of several years' time and effort.

To add to our daily challenges, I learned that both of our adorable dogs had serious heart conditions that required my giving them medication both day and night. From time to time it was necessary for me to rush one or both Oliver and Apple to the animal hospital for emergency treatments.

Of course, I also was kept busy administering medications to Lorraine while taking over more and more of the household duties. My hopes of one day practicing law in Florida soon vanished along with my ability to continue my work as a civil mediator. My passing the bar, getting licensed to practice law, and becoming certified as a mediator now all appeared to have been wasted efforts on my part. I saw myself as reduced to being a caregiver for my ailing wife and my canine cardiac patients. I couldn't believe it. I barely had the ability to take care of my own needs and now this. What a crazy mixed-up world this was.

Chapter Twenty-four

Flyin' to Zion

"A journey is best measured in friends, rather than miles."
—Tim Cahill, founder of OUTSIDE Magazine

Noted Holocaust author and Nobel Peace Prize laureate, Elie Wiesel, would often point out that a Jew does not simply travel to Jerusalem, he *returns* to it—even in the case of a first visit. My long-awaited return, slated for 2012, would be both physical *and* spiritual; well, with as much spirituality as an atheist like me can muster. Little could I have imagined, back when I began planning this voyage to the land I had left when I was seven years old, that I would be bringing along my sweet Lorraine, whom I had by now come to admit was an Alzheimer's victim, living under the shadow of a terrible death sentence. I could not possibly have conceived of the challenges she and I would face over the coming decade; rewarding at times, yes, but mostly days filled with heartache as I tried to understand what was going through Lorraine's mind, a mind that was inexorably wasting away before my eyes.

The trip was being organized by Chabad of Palm Beach Gardens under the leadership of Rabbi Dovid Vigler and his wife, Chana. I had connected to the shul thanks to Lorraine. When Rabbi Vigler first arrived in Palm Beach Gardens as a Chabad ambassador, he established a presence in the Jewish community via a popular radio talk show and podcast called the *Sunday Schmooze*. One of the first sponsors of the program was Compass Insurance, the agency that Lorraine was running with her two associates. She was impressed by the dynamic and charismatic young Lubavitcher and helped him along by becoming a sponsor of the golf outings he would organize to raise money for his fledgling congregation. Lorraine had helped to put together the golf outing fundraisers we had put on back in Mahopac and she offered to lend her expertise to the rabbi, who readily accepted it.

I recall how, when Lorraine first introduced me to her new friend, Rabbi Vigler, I felt an instant attraction and a sense of connecting with something deep in my psyche. Perhaps it was merely nostalgia for my early Hebrew school days when I was tutored by another young Lubavitcher rabbi back in Buffalo, New York. Or maybe it was something more profound. In any case, we hit it off and I suggested we hit a few golf balls to get him ready for his golf outing.

I gave the rabbi an old set of my golf clubs and off we trekked to the "green pastures and still waters" of the Mirasol links to play a round. He played gamely, but I would be surprised if he has picked up a golf club since. His golfing experience has been limited to riding in a golf cart during his regular fundraising outings, dispensing good cheer, in the form of vodka, scotch and a hearty *L'chaim* to the participants.

When Rabbi Vigler announced he was planning a congregational mission to the Holy Land, Lorraine told me that she wanted to go. Given the uncertainty of her condition, I was torn by doubt. On one hand, I disliked denying her anything she asked. Not only that, but the trip perhaps could prove therapeutic. At the same time, was it safe for her to take this on? What if she wandered off at the airport and wound up delaying the whole trip? In the end, and after looking into the details, I determined we would constantly be shepherded by tour guides, security officers plus the rabbi and rebbetzin (rabbi's wife) themselves. I decided that we would go ahead, which turned out to be one of my best decisions ever.

Before we joined the synagogue, Lorraine had come to me with a request. She wanted me to accompany her to one of the rabbi's classes that he had told her about. The course was developed by the Rohr Jewish Learning Institute, the adult education division of the Chabad-Lubavitch Orthodox Chasidic movement. It consisted of six classes that met on Tuesday afternoons. The class was called "Mindful Awareness and Divine Spirituality to Help You Think, Feel, and Live More Deeply." It purported to reveal the meditative tools needed to help us open up and see more, tools that were given to Moses and the Jewish people via divine revelation at Mt. Sinai. Not exactly the kind of stuff known to warm the cockles of an atheist's heart (whatever cockles are).

Hence, I responded to Lorraine's entreaty with two words, "Absolutely not."

I explained to her that she was welcome to attend, but that after my two doomed tours of duty at high school yeshivas, I had consumed all of the Jewish learning I could stomach. My thirst for "*Yiddishkeit*" (Jewish culture) had been fully slaked and I had no desire to drink another drop. I didn't say a word, I reminded her, when she loaned money to people who never paid her back. I did not object whenever she extended her generous help to staff members who appealed to her for financial assistance because they knew she was a soft touch. I didn't complain when she took off with her girlfriends, headed for destinations that did not involve traveling with "the boys." But this time, I was putting my foot down.

"No way, José," I told her firmly. "I mean it, Slim. I'm not going to that class with you."

Yet, she persisted.

"Look, honey," she said sweetly. "the rabbi told me the course is about how the ancient Talmudic law compares with modern civil law and he wants an expert like you in the class to provide appropriate context. Besides, I want you along to keep me company."

"Which part of 'No way, José' don't you understand?"

"But, honey, think about it. You can receive CLE (continuing legal education) credits for taking the course."

I thought about it and replied with, "Can I get a blow job for taking this course?"

"Sure," she said with a grin. And as it says in the 34th Psalm: "I shall bless the LORD and his praise shall continually be in my mouth."

She had her way with me, and that's how I became the sacrificial lamb being led to Rabbi Vigler's altar.

I soon realized that I had been grossly mistaken about the course and found it utterly fascinating. When it was completed, I asked Vigler when he was planning to offer it again since I would have loved to take it a second time. This course created a connection between me and Rabbi Vigler that resulted in my joining Chabad of Palm Beach Gardens and signing up for the Israel Mission.

Looking back, I recall experiencing regret over some of the financial commitments I had invested in over the years. For example, I'm not convinced that NBA and Yankee season tickets were worth the money I spent on them. But I'm pleased to report that I have yet to experience any such buyer's remorse regarding the money I spent supporting Chabad. I have received value for every penny.

I am considered something of an anomaly by my fellow congregants, many of whom have become close friends. This is because I have two life rules: I never pray and I never dance. Among Orthodox Jews, both activities are conducted on a gender-segregated basis. Pundits say that the reason Orthodox Jews frown on premarital sex is that they are afraid it might lead to mixed dancing.

I remain thankful there is no prohibition on drinking, however. I would hate to have to sit through some of those lengthy religious services stone sober. And, although I remain a devout and pious atheist, I have, now and then, invoked the words of Burt Bacharach and asked Rabbi Vigler to "Say a little prayer for me." I made similar such requests in behalf of my daughter, Sarah, when she was facing hospitalizations and childbirth issues. He graciously did so in the hopes that by witnessing God's power through prayer, I will somehow abandon atheism and embrace what I consider to be the myth of divinity.

Has that happened? Not yet, I'm afraid.

I turned to Sarah to discuss the advisability of Lorraine traveling to Israel. Sarah agreed that since her mom was only in the early stages of dementia, the trip could bring her some joy before she lost the ability to appreciate it. Sarah seemed to have such a good understanding of her mom's condition that I decided it would be helpful to have her join us. So, I invited her, along with her future husband, Eric, to come with us to the Holy Land. Happily, they agreed. I also invited one more pilgrim to join our mission, my childhood best "bud," Richard Polisner, aka "Snip." He jumped at the chance and pretty soon Fixler Family & Friends were all Flyin' to Zion.

It was during this extraordinary journey that new friendships were forged with members of the congregation. Friendships that have endured and become a vital part of my life as well as Lorraine's; friendships with people like Mickey and Cookie Gottlieb, for example. Mickey was and remains the dedicated Congregational President. Some of the others in this group include Michael and Shelly Paolercio, as well as Odette Schwartz and her partner, Irv Sparage. I can honestly say that, were it not for the comfort and companionship we have enjoyed from this outstanding group since coming home from that 2012 Israel trip, I don't think we could have made it through the stress-filled nightmare that was to come. Another Chabad couple, Rob and Jan Burke, who did not participate in the Israel trip, have likewise extended their hands in friendship and warmly welcomed us into the growing Chabad family.

The trip itself was an incredible journey of discovery and learning thanks to the outstanding guidance of Rabbi Vigler and Chana. I won't run through the entire itinerary, but instead focus on a few shining and memorable moments. Of course, no one forgets their first visit to Masada, the first century desert fortress built by King

Herod and the site of a heroic, but doomed, last stand by Jewish zealots who committed mass suicide rather than surrender to the invading Roman legions that were besieging their mountaintop stronghold. It is the place where every IDF inductee is today sworn into the Israeli military with this solemn oath: "Masada shall not fall again." *My* first visit to Masada had taken place a few years earlier, after I had buried my stepfather in Jerusalem as recounted in Chapter 18. It had made such an important impression on my heart that had a visit to Masada not been on our itinerary, I would have returned there on my own.

Our group arrived at the base of the massive prominence, in the heart of the Judean desert, at around noon, when the blistering sun had pushed the temperature close to 100 degrees Fahrenheit. It was too hot by then to risk walking up the serpentine path to the mesa-like mountaintop, so we were bundled into a gondola and rode swiftly up the cable lift. When we disembarked, I could not believe the first thing I saw. It was a tiny Chabad House.

To appreciate the significance of this sight, you need to understand the reputation that the Chabad movement has earned over the years. They see themselves somewhat like evangelicals. But, unlike classic missionaries who seek to bring non-Christians to Jesus, the Lubatichers work to bring Jews closer to Jewish tradition and to spread thriving Jewish culture to remote drought-ravaged areas of the world. Fulfilling this mission has made Chabad outposts ubiquitous in every Jewish community, no matter how small. But, to find one here? It was like finding a Starbucks at the North Pole.

The place was no bigger than a Mirasol home's walk-in closet, but we could tell instantly that it was air-conditioned. Those clever Chabadniks knew how to lure Jews in through the doors. I stepped inside and approached a bearded man seated at a table, holding an ink-stained white feather. I identified him as a *sofer*, a creator and inscriber of Torah scrolls.

As the members of our group were trying to wedge themselves into the tiny (but heavenly cool) enclosure, our progress was stopped by the rabbi in charge. He held up his hand and pointed to his wrist-watch saying, "I am sorry, but we close at 13:00," which means 1 pm in Israel.

He held the door open and indicated that we should make our exit. Rabbi Vigler explained that we had traveled from Florida to be here and exerted all of his considerable charm to cajole his Chabad colleague to let us stay for a bit, to no avail. When the two rabbis spoke to each other in Yiddish, Rabbi Vigler detected an accent.

"Zent ir italyenish? (Are you an Italian?) Vigler asked. When the rabbi replied that he was, our rabbi introduced him to his wife, Chana, who spoke fluent Italian. Chana and the Masada Rabbi began conversing in Italian and she explained that her grandparents had come to the U.S. from northern Italy before World War II. This common ethnicity seemed to please the fellow, but did not cut the salami. He still insisted we had to clear out. Until, that is, Chana told him about her *other* grandfather, also a rabbi, she explained. A rabbi by the name of Reb Chaim Yehuda Krinsky, known as Zayde Yudel by his many grandchildren.

Rabbi Krinsky, at age 88 as of this writing, is one of the most revered figures in the Lubavitch movement. He was the trusted personal secretary of the renowned Lubavitcher Rebbe, Menachem Mendel Schneerson. He was held in such high regard for his rectitude, that when the Rebbe's wife, Chaya, died in 1988, Rabbi Krinsky was named as the new executor of the Rebbe's estate. He today still serves as the chairman of the movement's main institutions, including all outreach facilities...*like the one in which we were standing!*

In other words, the Italian Rabbi suddenly realized he had nearly ejected the granddaughter of his boss out of his Chabad House and into the blazing heat.

The Masada rabbi's attitude reversed in the blink of an eye as he now rolled out the red carpet and welcomed our group inside with open arms. We were treated like royalty, which is not surprising since Chana actually was regarded as such by the Rebbe's devout followers. Once we were settled and refreshed, the typical Lubavitch mantra kicked in.

Snip, my Buffalo buddy, was approached by a young Chabadnik who asked in a heavy Yiddish accent, "Ist you Yooish?"

Snip nodded and before he knew what was happening, the fellow rolled up the left sleeve of Snip's sun-protective long-sleeved shirt, whipped out a pair of *t'fillin* and began attaching them to Snip's arm and head.

T'fillin, known in English as phylacteries, are small sacramental black boxes containing tiny scrolls of parchment inscribed with scripture. The boxes are worn by observant Jewish men during the daily morning prayers known as *Shachrit*. They are affixed to the forehead and to the upper left arm with long strips of black leather that are wrapped in a proscribed ritual manner.

T'fillin are donned to fulfill the Biblical commandment found several times in the Torah, including this passage from Exodus 13:9: "And it shall be for a sign for you upon your hand, and as a reminder between your eyes."

They are intended to remind the wearer that the Lord took the Jews out of Egypt "with a strong hand and an outstretched arm."

The wearing of *t'fillin* during prayer is considered by observant Jews to be the fulfillment of a *mitzvah,* a Biblical commandment. The Lubavitchers believe that every time a Jew fulfills a mitzvah, such as donning *t'fillin*, it hastens the arrival of the *Mashiach* (messiah) who will usher in an age of universal peace and happiness. Hence, young Lubavitcher men compete with one another to see who can convince the most non-observant Jews to put on the boxes and straps and recite a Hebrew prayer. Today, it was Snip's turn. He was persuaded to "lay" *t'fillin* and then recite a Hebrew prayer for the first time in his life.

After succeeding with Snip, the young man started in on me. I replied that yes, I was Jewish, but I respectfully declined his offer, explaining that I had laid *t'fillin* every weekday for years as a teenager and so I felt I had done my part toward heralding in the *Mashiach*. Actually, I felt I was done with such foolishness and was not about to abrogate my personal sanction against praying just to satisfy this eager fellow.

After our respite in the Chabad House, we emerged with body and soul refreshed, ready to tour the ancient ruins of the fortress. We were shown the remnants of the massive ramp used by the Romans to gain access to the mountaintop as well as the many archeological artifacts of what was once a "city on a hill." At a certain point, Rabbi Vigler explained that we were now in the remains of a *mishkan* or tabernacle, used for prayer by the Jews who occupied Masada during the first Jewish-Roman War.

At this point, the rabbi made an announcement. He informed us that Shelly and Michael Paolercio were traveling with their son, Jeremy, a young man about the same age as Sarah and Eric. Vigler explained that Jeremy had never celebrated a Bar Mitzvah and that he wished to do so here, albeit belatedly, in this spectacular and highly meaningful setting. As Rabbi Vigler provided him with a *kipa* (skull-cap) and *tallit* (prayer shawl), Jeremy was led through the requisite prayers. A small Torah scroll was produced and the rabbi guided the young man in reading a part of the weekly portion in Hebrew, thereby officially inducting him into the ranks of the community of Israel. It was clear from their beaming expressions, how much witnessing their son carry out this ancient ritual meant to Shelly and Michael. I don't know if it was due to the dust from the blowing sand, but I could feel tears welling up in my eyes as well.

At the conclusion of the ceremony, Rabbi Vigler did something unusual. He presented Jeremy with a traditional gift. It was a prayer book called a *Siddur*. But before handing it to him, the rabbi pulled out a container of glue from his pocket and began applying it as a border around the edge of the book's cover. He next bent down and picked up a handful of sand which he then dribbled onto the book. The particles clung to the glue, creating a permanent border of sand that would serve as a tangible reminder of this major Masada memory. It was truly a moving moment for us all.

As our mountaintop tour wrapped up, we were again guided back to the cable car lift. But our group of mavericks—Sarah, Eric, Snip, Jeremy, and me—preferred to climb back down along the serpentine footpath. We couldn't allow Lorraine to go down alone in the gondola, so we asked her to join us and she, being a real trooper, agreed. When we reached the entry to the trail, however, we found that it had been blocked with a chain bearing a sign that read, "Closed due to the heat." Of course, we weren't going to let a little thing like a chain deter our intrepid crew. Although it was steep and we were required to make a few stops along the way, we all arrived at the bottom safe and sound and were greeted with the admiration of our fellow travelers.

As tradition dictates, our next stop was at the oasis and waterfall known as the Ein Gedi Nature Preserve. It is Israel's largest desert oasis, featuring cool freshwater streams fed by underground springs. The spot has made nearby settlements possible going back to pre-Biblical times. While the waterfall was no Niagara, it still felt great to jump in and cool off in this lush natural spa.

Our next obligatory stop was at a Dead Sea beach where we were invited to have a float. I say float because swimming or submerging your body in the dense mineral-rich water is impossible. While many find it soothing to simply and effortlessly float on the surface, I actually found it painful. The waters irritated my sunburned skin and I quickly headed for shore. Slapping handfuls of the supposedly medicinal black mud that covered the bodies of my companions did not serve to soothe my burning flesh. This visit to the lowest spot on Earth (1,412 feet below sea level) certainly did not turn out to be one of the high points of our tour as far as I was concerned.

An actual high point was the Shabbat dinner our group enjoyed high upon the rooftop of a Chabad rabbi's home in Jerusalem. The vantage point provided an outstanding nighttime view of the Kotel, known as the Western Wall. As worshippers gathered at this holiest spot in all Jewry, we fell in sync with the rhythms of Shabbat as we lit candles, blessed the bread and wine and enjoyed the camaraderie of our new-found friends. Afterward, we joined the throngs in the Kotel plaza as some members of our contingent eagerly joined in the Shabbat celebration by dancing with the many IDF soldiers (not me, of course). The sight of hundreds of Jews, joyfully singing and demonstrably connecting with our common heritage, filled me with a sensation beyond description. As anyone who has experienced this sense of peoplehood arising from a Friday night Shabbat celebration at the Kotel will attest, Jerusalem truly is an eternal city.

Many other sterling moments stand out in my memory from that trip. Among them was our visit to the ancient Roman seaport of Caesarea along the Mediterranean coast between Tel Aviv and Haifa. We were escorted to the ruins of the Hippodrome where the Roman occupiers of Judea once enjoyed watching chariot races. We were shown an inscription at the entry, discovered in 1961. It mentioned Pontius Pilate, the governor of Judea who served under Tiberius at the time of Jesus. As recorded in the New Testament, Pilate was the

official who presided over Jesus' trial and then ordered his crucifix-
ion.

This inscription is the sole known reference to Pilate that appears
on an artifact created during his lifetime. This intrigued me, since I
had recently read a book that investigated the historical evidence of
Biblical events. The book had raised the question of why there were
no historic records documenting the life and acts of Jesus. I raised
the question with Rabbi Vigler and asked about the Jewish position
on the existence of Jesus. He replied that there was no question about
Jesus' existence. He is mentioned extensively in the Babylonian Talmud, which is the central text of Rabbinic (post-priestly) Judaism
and the primary source of Jewish law and theology.

The belief in the divinity of Jesus Christ is the fundamental de-
marcation line between Judaism and Christianity, he went on to explain.

"Other than that one point," he commented. "There's not a great
deal of difference in the basic theology. We both believe in the coming of the Messiah. It's just that Christians believe that when he arrives it will be for the second time."

I recall how the late Israeli Prime Minister, Menachem Begin
would minimize this difference, "You know what?" he would often
say with a smile. "When the *mashiach* gets here we'll ask him if he's
been here before and that will settle the matter."

By coincidence, I had read in the Jerusalem Post that evening that
a newly discovered archeological artifact from the same time period
had been located. It was a first century ossuary box used for storing
the bones of the dead. It allegedly bore an inscription that read:

"James (Jacob), son of Joseph, brother of Jesus" cut into one side of the box. According to the article, the authenticity of this relic, known as the James Ossuary, was questioned. The box itself was later determined to be authentic, but the inscription was declared to be a modern forgery by the Israeli Antiquities Authority.

The single most significant factor in making this trip so unforgettable was, of course, the leadership of Chana and Dovid Vigler. They blessed us with their profound knowledge of the region's history and allowed us to benefit by meeting many of their valuable contacts. I would never consider a return trip to Israel without them along.

Lorraine, thank goodness, was never a burden nor a problem. Physically, she was in great shape and handled the rigors of the journey without a hitch or complaint. She was just not the same open-hearted and gregarious person she had once been. While this fact saddened both Sarah and me, we agreed that the trip had done her a lot of good. She had been afforded the opportunity to view the Holy Land at a time when she was mentally still capable of appreciating the many wonders we encountered. Our decision to travel to Israel with Lorraine, we concluded, had been the right one.

Stimulated by the exposure to our people's long heritage provided by this journey and prompted by the book given me by my cousin Aaron Heisler at the golf outing in 2006, *Not to Forget, Impossible to Forgive; Poignant Reflections on the Holocaust,* written by eminent Torah scholar and author of numerous books about the Holocaust, Dr. Moshe Avital, as described in Chapter 17, I developed a renewed interest, upon our return, in getting to the bottom of my disjointed family history.

As in my mother's case, the book's author, Dr. Avital, likewise had come from the town of Bilke. I had learned very little about our family history from other relatives I had contacted over the years, so this book proved to be a revelation. I had, at some point, come across an article written about my Uncle Eddie who was an Auschwitz survivor. I figured he must remember certain facts and be able to fill in the gaps in the tattered knowledge of my family background..

Ever since that day when I discovered, as a 14-year-old boy back in Buffalo, that Sam Fixler was not my biological father, I had been haunted by how little I knew about such things as how and when my mother had met my real father. Why did my mother leave her hometown of Bilke? How, when, and why did my parents wind up in Budapest where I was born? Where did we live? How had my father died? The only thing I had to go on was an old photograph. According to my mother, it depicted my youthful biological father, Marton Adlersheim, standing in front of his Budapest grocery store where I had entered the world in 1944. I was not convinced that this was actually him. Like so many aspects of my spotty knowledge about my own past, this, too, was shrouded in a fog of uncertainty. I decided I needed to know more and that the first place to go was Phoenix, Arizona, to visit my 85-year-old Uncle Eddie who I hoped could provide some answers.

I made arrangements to fly to Phoenix and meet with Eddie in April of 2014. I enlisted the aid of my friend, Mickey Gottlieb, to help plan a trip of discovery to Europe where we would explore some of our ancestral towns in a quest to learn more about our respective family histories. Mickey made all the flight and hotel arrangements. We were scheduled to leave at the end of May. I hoped to be armed with more knowledge after my meeting in Phoenix with Uncle Eddie in April.

There was no need for Lorraine to accompany me to Arizona and, of course, she could not be left unattended in my absence. I was fortunate to be able to enlist the aid of Lorraine's long-standing childhood friend, Sharon Gorman, who was living in Houston at the time. I phoned Sharon and explained the situation. Sharon graciously agreed to come to Florida and stay with Lorraine while I was gone on my first journey of discovery.

After speaking with Sharon that morning and reviewing the travel arrangements that Mickey had accumulated, I felt everything was now in place. I headed out for a round of golf, leaving Lorraine home alone. This was something that I had been doing with no problem in those days, so I didn't think much about it. I should have. While I was out hitting golf balls, the proverbial shit was hitting the fan.

Elliot Fixler

Chapter Twenty-five

Gone Girl

"Until you see Alzheimer's firsthand, you have no idea how brutal it is."

—Seth Rogan

I covered the mile from our home to the Ironhorse clubhouse, riding my Club Car golf cart, in about four minutes. It was a glorious sunny morning as I greeted my regular foursome partners and headed off toward the first tee. I had told Lorraine before leaving home that all the arrangements for my trip to Phoenix to see Uncle Eddie were set and that Sharon would be coming to stay with her while I was away. I gave her a kiss as I headed out the door and told her I'd be home by noon.

As I was waiting to tee off at the third hole, I received a call on my cell phone from Ann Blanchard. Ann was our wonderful next-door-neighbor who would look in on Lorraine from time to time. I could tell from the tone of her voice that she was agitated.

"I just went over to your house to see Lorraine," she said hurriedly, "and there's no one home. I went inside and searched the whole place."

"Maybe she went for a walk?" I suggested.

"No, I looked for her in the cul-de-sac and up and down the entire street. There's no sign of her."

I decided I had better head home. I said good-bye to the guys and drove off in my cart at top speed.

Ann was right. After searching the house from top to bottom, I concluded that Lorraine was definitely MIA. Trying to reach her on her cell phone was not an option since she could no longer use one and had given it up. I got back in my golf cart and began the process of driving it up and down every street in the development. After fruitlessly covering about nine miles, I pulled up to the clubhouse and enlisted the aid of a staff member to help me search for her in the dining room, the beauty parlor, the pro shop, the fitness center and everywhere else—all to no avail. By this point, I was beginning to get anxious. Horrific thoughts kept popping into my head, thoughts that took me back twenty years to the time I was frantically searching for Mathew and finally found him as he lay dying on the dock at the marina. I redoubled my efforts to locate my missing wife.

I retraced my steps. This time I drove my car up and down the palm tree-lined lanes of Ironhorse. I felt it was unlikely that she would have wandered past the manned security gate but I still questioned the guard, who reported he had not seen her. There was no contiguous fence surrounding the neighborhood, so it's possible, at certain spots, to get through to a neighboring community by cutting through the landscaped vegetation. But that, too, seemed unlikely.

In desperation, I phoned the West Palm Beach Police Department and reported the situation. They quickly dispatched squad cars, ambulances and two helicopters to comb all of Ironhorse and beyond. As the minutes turned to hours, I began to imagine some rather frightening scenarios. Our property, and those of our neighbors, backed up to a lake that was home to an abundance of alligators. I tried to drive such thoughts from my head and started looking around the house for some clue that might explain Lorraine's disappearance.

Other than a silverware drawer that was sitting open, everything in the house was in perfect order, just as I had left it that morning. There were no suitcases missing and no evidence that she had packed a bag. I placed a few phone calls to her girlfriends, asking if they had heard from her and advising them of the situation. I next printed some photos of Lorraine to give to the police who were planning to conduct a house-to-house search.

By the late afternoon our property was filled with police and emergency vehicles. Curious neighbors milled about and a few offered words of assurance and consolation.

The sun was hanging low on the horizon when a police officer approached the assembled onlookers and me. He was holding Lorraine by her right upper arm.Lorraine's clothing and hair were completely disheveled and there was blood pouring from numerous cuts covering her arms and legs.

"My God, Lorraine!" I exclaimed upon seeing her. "What happened? Where have you been? What in the hell is going on?"

She stared at the ground and slowly shook her head back and forth.

"I don't know," she whispered. "I don't know."

The police officer informed me that he had spotted Lorraine hiding in the bushes next to one of the homes in the cul-de-sac. He explained how he had extracted her from the shrubbery and recovered a kitchen knife that he found on the ground nearby. He believed she was trying to commit suicide.

Was she?

Or was she engaging in this self-destructive behavior only to attract attention? I suspected that somehow my informing her of my intention to fly to Phoenix and leave her at home might have triggered this bizarre reaction. But I never received a coherent answer from Lorraine and, to this day, still do not know the reason behind what happened.

Lorraine was transported to the hospital by ambulance where she was examined and her wounds were treated. Then she was "Baker Acted." Since 1972, the state of Florida has had on its books a unique law introduced by State Representative Maxine Baker of Miami. The Baker Act was touted by its advocates as a means to strengthen due process and the civil rights of people in mental health facilities. In reality, it gave law enforcement and medical providers the emergency power to temporarily detain someone whom they observe as impaired due to mental illness and whom they deem is likely to pose a danger to him or herself or to others. Hence, Lorraine was remanded to a mental health treatment center for 72 hours for observation. I was told that if, after that time, an evaluation indicated she was not likely to pose any further danger, she would be released.

I did not care to wait that long to bring Lorraine home. I felt the best place for her right now was to be with me, but I couldn't pull it off. I contacted everyone I could think of: doctor friends, politicians, law enforcement officials—all to no avail. The problem was liability. If she should be released early and then proceeded to harm herself or someone else, whoever authorized the early release would be on the hook.

Finally, three days later, Lorraine was released. The medical staff at the facility said she was doing well and was not likely to pose a threat either to herself or others. I could tell from speaking with the team that had cared for her, as well as with some of her fellow patients, how much affection they had all developed for Lorraine after only a few days with her. Like I have said: Everybody loved Lorraine.

Once we were home, I decided not to press her about what had happened. She was clearly embarrassed and almost obsessively apologetic. She still did not appear to be aware of exactly what she had done and certainly had no idea of why she had done it.

"I'm so very sorry," Lorraine kept repeating. "I just don't know what happened."

She seemed genuinely mystified.

Suspecting that it was my plan to leave her alone when I traveled to Phoenix that might have blown her fragile psyche off the edge, I tried to comfort her and reassure her that I wasn't going anywhere without her.

"While you were in the hospital," I told her, "I canceled my trip to see Uncle Eddie and I called Sharon and told her we did not need for her to come."

I now understood that whatever happened, I would never be able to leave Lorraine alone again. This represented a fundamental and tectonic shift in both my life and Lorraine's. Things had permanently and inexorably changed, and not for the better. My wife may have been found crouching in the bushes, but my sweet Lorraine—the woman I loved—was gone for good.

As far as the search for my family's history was concerned, I never did get to Phoenix to interview my Uncle Eddie Heisler, who has since passed away. I didn't wish to ask him personal questions over the phone, so I kept putting off the trip until it was too late. I had really blown it. I had again missed a golden opportunity to acquire knowledge about my own family background.

I also considered canceling my plans to travel to Prague and Budapest with Mickey but decided against it. While I realized that I would not be able to make the trip without Lorraine, I held out hope that she may, by then, be in sufficiently sound shape mentally to accompany me. Holding out such hope may be viewed as an act of denial on my part, but that was not the case. I was completely clear-eyed about the situation and was relying upon the professional advice of medical specialists as the basis for my hopes. But it's definitely true to say that I was using hope to fill the holes of frustration in my heart.

Chapter Twenty-six

The Search Begins

"The best time to learn about your roots is twenty years ago. The second-best time is right now."
—Chinese proverb

Lorraine arrived home from the treatment center for the most part unaffected by the traumatic episode that had sent her there. This could have been due to a certain degree of "flat affect" that prevents a person with Alzheimer's to openly express emotion. They may internally feel elated or depressed, but others cannot tell since there is little smiling, frowning or raising of the voice. I could not even be sure that Lorraine remembered the incident at all.

After giving the matter much thought and discussing it with Mickey and Cookie Gottlieb, I decided that Lorraine's cognitive issues would not negatively impact our planned trip to Europe in search of our respective family heritages. There would, at all times, be three pairs of eyes keeping watch over her. In any case, bringing Lorraine with us was by all means preferable to leaving her at home. I recalled how much she had benefited from our trip to Israel two years earlier and had no reason to believe her mental health would in any way be compromised by such a journey.

We could not have asked for better traveling companions than Mickey and Cookie. Mickey had handled all the travel arrangements, including flights, transfers, tour guides, and hotel accommodations, down to the last detail. He guided us to comfortable airport lounges whenever we had a lengthy layover. The hotels Mickey had booked were all terrific, especially the charming boutique establishments he arranged for us in Prague and Budapest.

In the weeks leading up to our departure, I busied myself assembling what little documented material I could lay hands on about my family's history.

Here is a collection of some of the items I was able to put together in advance:

A Czech transit document dated May 12, 1948, listing when Sam Fixler was at Mauthausen, which was at the same time as Marton Adlersheim.

This document, to some degree, helped me answer the question of how my mother could possibly have known how my father had been murdered by the Nazis. *(see the following chapter)*

A document written in either Hebrew or Yiddish that was issued by a Jewish religious tribunal court known as a Bet Din. I wasn't sure, but I suspected it was a *"Ghet"* or a bill of divorcement issued to Orthodox widows whose husbands had perished under unknown circumstances during the Holocaust. Such a document was needed in order to allow a Jewish widow to re-marry:

Photos of my great-uncle, Samuel Heisler and the Berger brothers taken by the Nazis at Auschwitz as the three men waited in line to be gassed, presumably a few hours after these photos were taken. The left photo depicts Jacob Berger (left), Samuel Heisler (center), and my grandfather, Meier Berger (right). The right photo shows Jacob Berger and his brother, Meier Berger, behind him.

These photos were discovered, among others, by Bilke-born Holocaust survivor, Lili Jacob Meier in a Nazi officers' barracks at the time of her liberation from a slave labor camp in Dora-Mittelbau, Germany. This collection of photos was later published in *THE AUSCHWITZ ALBUM* (1981, Random House), one of the 20th century's most powerful and unique historical records. Harrowing, eerie, immensely poignant, these pictures of the German death factory and of the pained and bewildered faces of people "selected" for either slave labor or the gas chamber, form what has been called "a holy document."

Somehow, these two photos from the Lili Jacob Meier collection wound up in my mother's portfolio that I discovered in 1958. How had they gotten there? Did Lili Jacob distribute the photos to the families of those people depicted in them? I wish I knew.

A photo I discovered in Moshe Avital's book, *Not to Forget...* It depicts my mother (circled) at the Bilke train station in 1937. She is shown with a group of townspeople saying good-bye to my mother's best friend, Lea Peltz, who was leaving for the United States. I recall going with my mother to visit Lea Peltz and her children in New York City. My mother explained that the reason Lea had come to America before the war was because she was to be married in Bilke and the groom had left her at the altar. Lea then decided to join a sister who was living in New York. This turned out to be a stroke of luck for her since had she been wed and stayed in Bilke, she would have certainly been deported to Auschwitz along with the rest of the town's Jews:

An undated wedding photo of my mother and biological father in formal attire. This was the photo I discovered in the closet when I was fourteen, as recounted in Chapter One. As with so many of the details of my parents' lives in Europe, I do not know and can only speculate as to the date of their wedding.

I did not know, for example, how and why my mother went from Bilke to Budapest at some point between 1937 and her wedding. Why did she leave behind her sister and her parents who would fall into the clutches of the Nazis? While I did know that my father was 46 and my mother was 38 years old when she gave birth to me in

1944, I did not know how or when they met and got together. All I knew was that my father was from a neighboring village, some three kilometers away from my mother's hometown of Bilke. So many questions I could have asked, should have asked my mother and others when I had the chance:

A small (1 in. x 3 in.) black and white photo of a man standing in front of a grocery store mentioned in the previous chapter. My mother had given me the photo, but I am uncertain as to whether or not she had correctly identified the man as my biological father.

Was the man in the photo actually Marton Adlersheim? Was this his store? Was this the building where my mother had lived with him above the store before the war and where she had given birth to me after my father had been taken away? These were only a few of the many questions I was hoping to resolve during my journey back to Europe and back in time, in search of my roots.

This was another example of my many missed opportunities to learn more about my past when I had the chance. I could have easily questioned my mother at the time she gave me this photo and learn more about it. But I didn't. I accepted the photo passively and said not a word. There was, at that point in my life, a certain distaste about digging through the ashes of memory. This reluctance was due to a feeling that by questioning my mother, I would cause her pain, something I did not wish to do merely to satisfy my own curiosity. By the time I was ready to start digging, my mother had died and it was, by then, too late. This is another example of my regrettable failure to raise such questions when I had the chance.

I also brought along a January 2016 printout from *ancestry.com* documenting my biological father, Marton Adlersheim's, date of birth as July 18, 1898. His birthplace is listed as "Unleserlich," which is not a town but the German word for "illegible." It also shows his Mauthausen prisoner number and his date of death as February 21, 1945.

◈ ancestry

Marton Adlersheim

in the Austria, Mauthausen/Gusen Concentration Camp Death Record Books , 1938-1945

Name:	Marton Adlersheim
Birth Date:	18 Jul 1898
Birth Place:	Unleserlich
Mauthaus #:	115179
Nationality:	Ungarn (Hungary)
Arrest Reason:	Jude (Jew)
Night and Fog:	No
Profession:	Kaufmann (Merchant, Dealer)
Death Date:	21 Feb 1945
Arrival Date:	1945
Source:	AMM Y/36; (E/13/1)

Source Information

Mauthausen Gedenkstätte. *Austria, Mauthausen/Gusen Concentration Camp Death Record Books , 1938-1945* [database on-line]. Provo, UT, USA: Ancestry.com Operations Inc. 2008.

Original data: This data is provided in partnership with JewishGen.org.

🔶 JewishGen

As recounted in Chapter Two, after I learned that Sam Fixler was not my real father, my mother informed me about her first husband and my biological father, Marton Adlersheim's, death. She said that he was, while interned at Mathausen, part of a labor detail being marched into the cold in February of 1945. As the prisoners were lined up and about to depart on foot through the snow, the commandant in charge announced that anyone who had difficulty walking should take two steps forward. My father suffered from arthritis and had trouble walking long distances. He stepped out of line and was immediately shot and killed by the commandant.

When my mother recounted this story, I simply accepted it and remained silent. How I regretted my failure to question her when I had the chance. After her death, I visualized how I would have employed my finely-honed cross-examination skills to pose such questions as, "But Mom, you weren't there. How could you have possibly known that's how my father died?"

It would take two trips to Europe and a lot of digging before I could even formulate a speculative answer to that question.

I had held out some hope of finding the answers to some of these and other questions during my planned visit to Phoenix to meet with Uncle Eddie in May 2014. But, as explained in the previous chapter, that trip was canceled because of the incident involving Lorraine's disappearance and self-mutilation. And by the time I was in a position to travel without Lorraine along, Eddie had passed away.

I explained my reasons for wishing to return to my place of birth to Mickey and Cookie. They were intrigued by my story and were happy to accompany me as I searched for answers about the fate of my family. To tell the truth, I don't think I could have made the trip without them. There was no way I could have put together the incredibly complex itinerary we experienced.

Upon occasion, Cookie would jokingly pretend to complain that Mickey was that "good for nothing" husband of mine.

I would correct her.

"No, Marlene," I pointed out, using her actual first name. "He's good for *one* thing. He puts together one hell of a travel itinerary."

I assure you you'll never in your life meet a warmer, kinder and more generous-hearted person than Cookie (Marlene) Gottlieb. At that stage of my life, it wasn't particularly easy making new friends, and thus I consider myself to be lucky indeed to have found such dear companions as Mickey and Cookie Gottlieb.

My friends decided they would likewise use this opportunity to locate and visit their own family's ancestral hometowns. Both Mickey and Cookie are avid students of Jewish history and wished to explore sites about which they had read. They were interested in both historically significant places as well as those involved with Jewish myth and folklore. For example, they were intent on visiting the Czech Republic, home of the Prague Golem. According to the legend predating the story of Dr. Frankenstein, the Golem was a 16th century creature, fashioned from clay and brought to life by a Kabbalist rabbi who used it to protect the Jews of the city's ghetto from persecution.

Mickey also wished to visit the Prague Jewish cemetery as well as the nearby Terezin concentration camp, established by the Nazis as a propaganda exhibit to deceive the Red Cross and others into believing that incarcerated Jews were being will-treated, when in fact almost all Jews interned there were murdered at Auschwitz. Mickey had also prepared a list of local Chabad Houses in the cities we visited. As we made our way to each one, Mickey would invariably ask if the local rabbi knew our Rabbi Dovid Vigler. Many of them did and all of them knew his wife, Chana's, grandfather, Rabbi Yehuda Krinsky, who was (and remains) the head of the worldwide Chabad movement.

Cookie expressed a desire to visit her family's hometown of Lviv, or as known in Yiddish, Lemberg. Both Lviv and my family's hometown of Bilke were now located in Ukraine. Unfortunately for us (and even more unfortunately for the Ukrainians) Russia was, at this time in 2014, in the process of invading the Crimea, making travel to Ukraine unfeasible. It is interesting to note that as I write these words in 2022, Russia has invaded all of Ukraine and world attention is once again focused on this troubled area.

The first stop on our journey brought us to Prague, the capital and largest city in the Czech Republic. From there, we traveled by car to the town of Terezin, the site of the notorious Nazi concentration camp known as Theresienstadt. Converted from a military garrison into a walled ghetto, the facility was initially used as a transit camp for western Jews enroute to their deaths in Auschwitz, Sobibor and other extermination centers. It was later used as a propaganda tool by the Nazis who publicized the camp as a "retirement settlement" for elderly and prominent Jews. While deceiving the Red Cross and much of the world via such bogus films as *Hitler Builds a City for the Jews*, the Nazis deliberately engineered conditions at Theresienstadt to hasten the death of its Jewish prisoners. More than 33,000 Jews died there, mostly due to malnutrition and disease.

After our lunch in the town of Terezin, we headed back to Prague and our boutique lodgings at Hotel Residence Agnes. The hotel was situated in the heart of the city's Old Town district, just a few steps from the Jewish Quarter known as Josefov. This noted tourist area contains synagogues, Hebrew street signs, and other artifacts of Jewish life, all preserved as museum pieces. While it was a fascinating and educational way of learning about pre-Holocaust Jewish life, it was, nevertheless, disconcerting to note the absence of any actual Jews living in Josefov. It felt as though Hitler's dream of relegating Judaism to nothing more than an extinct culture, existing only in museums and history books, had been fulfilled here in Prague.

Mickey had done an excellent job by booking us into the Agnes. The breakfasts were delicious and the staff were all friendly and eager to insure our comfort. We got to know the owner of the hotel, a successful builder who also owned a vineyard in the South of France, as well as a vacation home in Sarasota, Florida. He saw to it that upon each day's return from our sight-seeing excursions, we would be met with our choice of vintage wines from his vineyard. It was a great way to close out the day, seated in the hotel's lobby, sipping fine wines and reliving the day's adventures.

I won't go into detail about our sightseeing, other than to say the hills were steep, the people friendly, and the experience so memorable that we would return two years later and again stay at the Hotel Residence Agnes. As you will read in a forthcoming chapter, at that time I would bring along the Czech travel documents I held in my collection of family artifacts. I presented them to a member of the hotel's staff for translation and was greatly surprised to learn what they contained.

Stay tuned.

Our next destination was the place of my birth. Budapest, the capital of Hungary. The city spans both sides of the Danube River that flows in front of several notable monuments of classical architecture, including the Hungarian Parliament (the world's third largest) and Buda Castle. The city is also home to the world's second largest synagogue (the Dohany Utca) and around 80 geothermal springs.

Mickey again outdid himself in making our travel arrangements. He had retained the services of an excellent guide who spoke perfect English. We were booked into another outstanding boutique hotel that was located within the walls of Buda Castle. Located on the Buda side of the Danube, it is called the Baltazar Budapest. Containing only 11 suites, the Baltazar is a luxury hotel that sits on a quiet street within the historic city center in the middle of Budapest's Gastronomic Quarter, filled with unique and world-famous eateries.

This is not surprising, since the Baltazar is owned by Zsidai Hotels, whose CEO is Zoltan Zsidai (*zsidai* means Jewish), a well-known and award-winning Hungarian gastronomist. The hotel is perched on the edge of the castle grounds, high above the Danube, and afforded us with spectacular views of the river and the Pest (pron.: pesht) side of the city. An outdoor elevator would deliver us to a sidewalk promenade below that offered access to the landmark buildings as well as to a shopping mall and a broad esplanade. We also toured the central area which serves as a transportation hub. We would not realize the importance of this location until we returned to Budapest in 2016.

We would travel from our hotel on the Buda side of the river to the city center on the eastern Pest side; a ride of less than 20 minutes by metro or taxi. It was from here that we conducted most of our sight-seeing, visiting the former Jewish Quarter and the Dohany Utca Great Synagogue. We also visited the site of the notorious Budapest Ghetto where, as described in Chapter Two, the city's Jews, including my mother and me, were herded to await being transported to our deaths in the gas chambers of Auschwitz.

It was difficult to fathom how the wonderful Hungarian people we met at every turn could have been made accomplices of the Nazi death machine. As we strolled the area, occasionally stopping at cafés and pastry shops, we were deeply moved by the monuments memorializing the victims of the Hungarian fascists known as the Arrow Cross. Especially heart-wrenching were the bronzed shoes, taken from Jewish victims before they were killed and dumped into the Danube. The shoes, exhibited along the sidewalk next to the river, stand as silent reminders of the atrocities committed there.

One of my primary purposes in making this journey was to learn what I could about the lives of my mother Rose and her first husband; my biological father, Marton Adlersheim. I did not come armed with much background information, but I did have the small photo of the man standing in front of a store that my mother had given to me. I showed the photo to our guide, Gabriella, and explained that I believed the man in the photo was my father and this was his grocery store. She was well acquainted with every byway of Budapest, and I asked if she could tell from the photo where the building might be located. After studying it, she sadly reported that she could not identify the location. She did, however, point out that the photo must have been taken in Buda since the slope of the sidewalk suggested that it was located on a hill; total dead end, I'm afraid.

Gabriella suggested that we visit the offices of the local Jewish Agency since they were likely to house the records of Holocaust victims. Unfortunately, by the time we reached the building, it was Friday afternoon and the office was closed for Shabbat. It would not reopen until Monday morning, by which time we already would be en route to Vienna. It was frustrating to realize that the central purpose of my visit to the place of my birth was not being realized. I left Budapest knowing no more about my family's history than when I had arrived.

In Vienna, our accommodations did not match those we had been enjoying to that point. The hotel was nothing to write home about and the famed Viennese cuisine (including their Wiener Schnitzel) left us unimpressed. Mickey and Cookie agreed with my impression of Vienna. We could not shake the feeling that we were not wanted there. I, for one, could not overcome the reality that this nation and its people were complicit participants in Hitler's genocidal Final Solution. I made up my mind never to return.

As far as Lorraine's mind was concerned, who knows? She had proven to be no problem whatsoever during our travels. She had always been an easy-going person, willing to go along to get along, and that had not changed. She was never demanding during our many exploits and seemed happy just to be part of our group and be included in everything we did. But her flat affect rendered her something of a non-entity, almost like a phantom image of the person she used to be; no joy, no emotion. She was just there.

When it came to being a great travel agent, Mickey was two for three. A .666 batting average like that would have gotten him into the Baseball Hall of Fame. As a trip planner, I gave him a B+ and advised him to stick with it. No need for him to return to his legal career or chasing deadbeat creditors. Despite his less than perfect performance, I love him dearly for his efforts and decided to ask for his help again in arranging for my next European quest of discovery.

Chapter Twenty-seven

Circling Back to Budapest

"Yes, the past can hurt. But you can either run from it or learn from it."

—Rafiki,

the mandrill shaman in The Lion King

I returned home in a blue funk. Actually, it was a Boeing 767, but even the in-flight movies could not help me shake off my feelings of frustration and regret. These emotions only served to fuel my obsession to learn more about my origins. Unfortunately, I had gathered pitifully little information about my forebears during our sojourn in Eastern Europe. How much easier it would have been to question my mother about her past when I had the chance. I likewise failed to discuss such matters with my stepfather because I somehow feared that he would feel slighted if I expressed too much interest in my real father. If I were somehow ever granted a "do-over," I swore that I would overcome such hang-ups and encourage them both to openly share the events of their early lives.

Not long after our return, I was able to connect Lorraine with a new physician, Dr. Jack Waterman, who treated her along with a neurologist, Dr. David Silvers. Although neither were qualified to provide a differential diagnosis, both physicians felt that she was suffering from a moderate case of Alzheimer's Disease.

We both got back to our mundane and routine activities. However, with each passing day, more and more of those activities fell to me, as my role as Lorraine's sole caregiver continued to expand. She had a healthy appetite but had to be reminded that it was time to eat. She was no longer capable of food preparation, basic housekeeping, or using the simplest devices such as the TV or the telephone. It was up to me to make sure she took her meds, remind her to bathe and deal with her occasional incontinence. Eventually, even the most rudimentary tasks, such as ordering food from a menu or selecting what clothes to wear, required my intervention.

By 2016, I found myself a prisoner in our own home, afraid to leave Lorraine unattended, and utterly exhausted physically and spiritually. This situation was not sustainable, I concluded, and proceeded to consult with Sarah and various memory-care professionals about seeking the services of an in-home caregiver.

While I was busy searching for someone to help me look after Lorraine, I was, at the same time, making travel plans with Mickey for another European "In Search of our Heritage" mission. He suggested that we include Alaska in our itinerary, but I demurred.

"Alaska's in the opposite direction," I pointed out. "And besides, this is probably the last trip I'll be able to make with Lorraine. She would not do well in Alaska."

Mickey, to his everlasting credit, understood completely and was a real *mentsch* about it.

"Okay," he said. "Let's go back to Budapest and Prague and search some more for your family. Maybe we can even make it to Ukraine this time and search for Cookie's."

In the intervening weeks prior to our departure, I contacted a number of home health care agencies and started screening a succession of unqualified, unprofessional and unappealing so-called care providers. Some quit after one day, others I told not to return after a less than a week on the job. As I shared my frustration with a neighbor, she told me that she was friends with a professional caregiver and suggested I call her. Jeane Mongrain was a certified HHA (Home Health Aide) caregiver and after a positive interview, I decided to give her a try. We worked out her schedule and salary and decided she would start full-time once we got back from Europe. Jeane turned out to be absolutely outstanding at the outset and wound up being Lorraine's primary caregiver for several more years.

We proceeded with our travel plans. I was comfortable that between me and the Gottliebs, Lorraine would be well looked after. Plus, the knowledge that once we returned I would be getting a portion of my life back thanks to Jeane, improved my attitude considerably and allowed me to relax and enjoy the experience.

Our first stop this time around was Amsterdam. This was my first time in the Netherlands and I arrived knowing only three things about "the Venice of the North."

1) Amsterdam was the site of the Anne Frank House, where the noted Jewish teenager and her family had hidden from the Nazis for years in a secret annex, as chronicled in one of the world's most widely read books, *THE DIARY OF A YOUNG GIRL.*

2) A lot of the local citizens rode bicycles.

3) The city had a notorious red-light district where the sex providers displayed their wares in storefront windows.

Our primary reason for including Amsterdam in our itinerary was that I needed to meet with an attorney regarding an investment I had made in a company that was headquartered in the Netherlands.

I had little interest in visiting the Anne Frank House. I had my own Holocaust story on which I was focused and would soon be seeking the Adlersheim House in Budapest. We did take the obligatory walking tour of the Red Light District one afternoon and that turned out to be an utter waste of time. I learned that the Happy Hookers of Holland really were "Ladies (and gentlemen) of the Evening." Like the stars and grandma's false teeth, they only came out at night. And we had been warned that touring these bay window bordellos past sunset was not particularly safe. After failing in our quest for some cheap carnality, we decided to grab a bite, but could not find anything to eat other than street food fare. We quickly made our way back to our hotel. By this stage of the game, I had adopted a philosophy learned from my dog, "If I can't play with it or eat it, then piss on it."

As far as the bikes were concerned, they were everywhere and coming at us from every direction. There were no set bike paths and the cyclists seemed to have universal right of way, especially on all the narrow bridges that crossed the city's many canals. Obviously, this country did not have a high density of personal injury attorneys ready to seek damages caused by reckless two-wheeled hooligans. My apprehensions, sadly, were proven to be justified by what happened next. As Mickey and I were crossing the street, with Cookie and Lorraine following about six paces behind us, a well-dressed fellow on a racing bike came barreling through the intersection. He plowed directly into Cookie, knocking her to the ground...hard.

Cookie landed on her shoulder and suffered injuries that have persisted to this day. Had this happened back home, I, as an experienced personal injury attorney, would have had this guy in front of a judge before his wheels stopped spinning. But this was not America and I had no idea what to do next. I felt like punching the idiot right in the nose but calmed down when he began apologizing for his actions. It's a good thing, because had I punched him, I would probably have been arrested and charged with assault—even though I would have pleaded that my actions were a justified reaction to the biker having recklessly injured my friend. Anyway, it should have been up to Mickey, not me, to stand up for his wife's honor and go after the guy that had violated her person. But Cookie didn't see it that way.

To this day, whenever her shoulder gives her trouble, she'll turn to me and say, "My shoulder's killing me today thanks to that stupid Dutch biker who knocked me down. And you let him get away with it!"

The whole incident left a bad taste in my mouth and I decided to add "Revisiting Amsterdam," alongside "Revisiting Vienna," to my "Fuck-it" List; not a Bucket List, which contains those things you wish to do before kicking the bucket. A Fuck-it List is the opposite. It is a collection of those things you *never* wish to do again for as long as you live.

After getting Cookie patched up, we next headed back to Prague in the Czech Republic. This time, we actually felt as though we knew the city and enjoyed visiting some of the same sites as before, as well as some new ones. We stayed in the same boutique hotel and again connected with the very genial owner. After a sumptuous breakfast one day, we asked the proprietor about how we could make our way to a castle we wished to visit. Instead of permitting us to hire a taxi, he directed one of his employees to drive us and then return later to pick us up. What a prince of a guy!

Once again, we would return at the end of each day and retire to the lobby where we would sit and partake of the owner's fine quality wine—on the *house!* It was during one of those late afternoon grape guzzling sessions that I asked an English-speaking hotel staff member to help me translate some of my stepfather's travel documents that I had brought along with me. In the case of one such document, a visa application, she translated the Czech text and revealed that it asked the applicant to list all the places he had lived since 1941.

Sam Fixler had listed all the concentration camps where he had been interned. The last one listed was Mauthausen, where he was a slave laborer until the camp was liberated by the Third U.S. Army on May 5, 1945—one of the last concentration camps liberated by the Allies. Wait a minute. Mauthausen? That's where my real father was imprisoned. Eureka! Suddenly, the pieces started to fall into place.

Sam Fixler had been my mother's brother-in-law during the time she was married to my real father, Marton Adlersheim. Sam Fixler's first wife was my mother's sister. So, Sam had to know my mother, Rose, and therefore knew her husband, Marton. The two men, both married to one of the Berger sisters, were interned at Mathausen at the same time. I concluded that if Sam had not been on the same forced labor detail at the time Marton was killed, he had at least heard about how he had met his fate. This explained how my mother was able recount to me in detail how my real father had perished. She had no doubt been told the tale by her brother-in-law and future husband, Sam Fixler, who survived and managed to come back from the ashes of the death camp.

It amazed me that simply by translating the words of a 70-year-old transit document, I was able to find the answer to a question that had been plaguing me for years. Although I had more recently obtained a document recording my father's death prepared by the Nazi administrators of Mauthausen, I did not understand, until this moment, that my stepfather, Sam Fixler, was also interned there at the time my father was murdered.

This revelation now explained how my mother was able to obtain a *"Ghet"* in 1947, documenting that she was a widow, thereby freeing her to remarry under Jewish law. A Jewish court (*Bet Din*) will not issue such a document unless they have convincing testimony corroborating the death of the woman's husband. This was no doubt provided by Sam Fixler, who was able to affirm that he had witnessed (or had heard about from reliable sources) the death of my real father at Mathausen.

Our next destination was Ukraine and I must admit that the place did not impress me that much. Deplaning in Lviv, we were met by an expansive modern airport, nearly devoid of any travelers. Locating the rental car desk, we immediately drove south for 170 miles to the village of Bilke, my mother's hometown. I found it to be a pleasant but primitive place, not unlike the numerous other little towns we had passed through on the road from Lviv.

As we walked the narrow streets, I could not shake off the realization that it was from this village that two thousand Jews, parents, brothers, sisters, children—the town's entire Jewish population—had been rounded up by evil forces and with great suffering and torture, sent off to their deaths. All of the town's Jewish institutions, the synagogues, the schools, the mikvah, the youth clubs, hundreds of Jewish homes and businesses, all destroyed, eradicated in the blink of an eye. Jews had lived beside their 10,000 or so non-Jewish neighbors for more than 300 years and now, more than 70 years after they were all deported, not a Jew in sight.

I know this because we asked each of the townspeople we met: *"Jsou tu nějací Židé? (Are there any Jews here?)."* In this way, we discovered that there was a widow who lived on the outskirts of town who had been married to a Jew. We trekked to the house, knocked on the door and an elderly woman let us in. With our guide serving as translator, we learned that the woman's husband had survived Auschwitz and returned to Bilke. He was the only Jew in town and so could find no Jewish woman to marry, she explained. After a few years she and the Jewish man were wed. He never became a Christian since they lived under Soviet rule which frowned on *any* sort of religion. Although he no longer did anything "Jewish," he was nevertheless known as "the Jew" till the day he died some ten years earlier. After sharing her story, our hostess graciously served us tea and biscuits and brought out several family photo albums. I leafed through them, hoping to spot a familiar face, but no such luck.

With the death of "the last Jew of Bilke," the Nazi dream of making the world "*Judenrein*" was fulfilled in my family's hometown. *Judenrein* was a term favored by the Nazis to describe an area that has been "cleansed" of Jews. The term perpetuates the Nazi stereotype equating Jews with rats and cockroaches, requiring extermination for the sake of achieving social "hygiene" in the Reich.

Of course, the overwhelming question that haunts everyone who tries to imagine what it must have been like during those dark times is, "What would I have done, if I had been a Jew living here then?"

Of course, in my case, I was actually living not far from here at that time, but I was an infant. What if I had been a Jewish adult back then? Would I have heeded the prophetic words of Revisionist leader, Ze'ev Jabotinsky when he warned the Jews of Europe to either arm themselves or flee? "Jews must put an end to the diaspora," he implored them during the 1930s, "before the diaspora puts an end to the Jews." Who knows?

With these thoughts inhabiting my head, we made our way back to the center of town where I pulled out the hand-drawn map I had brought along with me. I had found the map in the pages of the Avital book *Not to Forget*.... It depicts the town's main drag and identified the houses that lined the street and listed the owners' names in Hebrew.

My grandfather, Meier Berger's house (No. 9) is clearly shown as being next door to his brother's house (No. 10). Both were located near the town's main synagogue. Moshe Avital's house is also shown as being close to the synagogue *(see following page).*

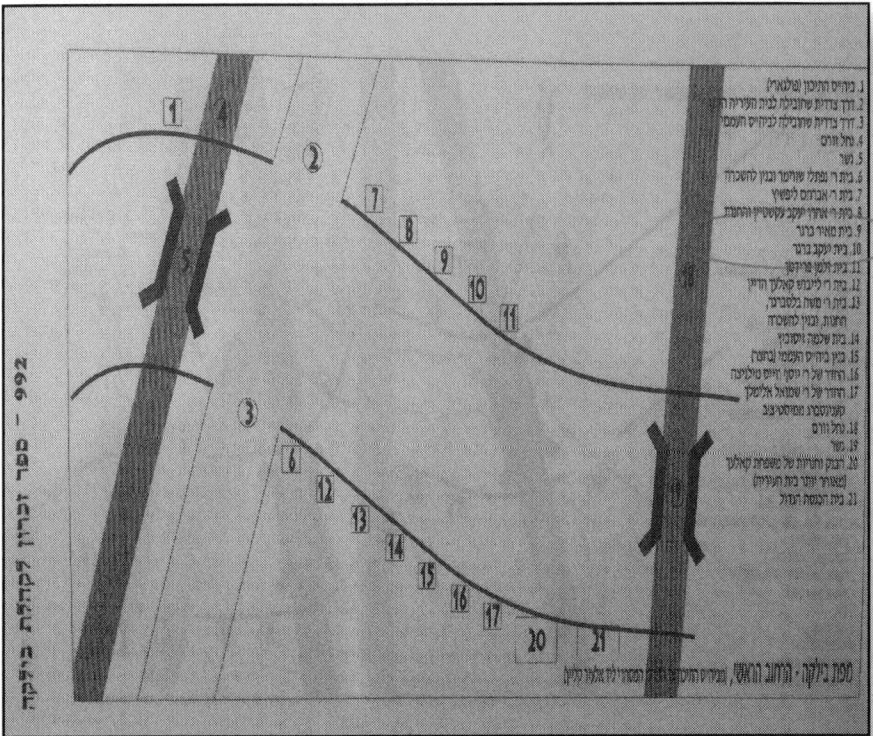

Going by the maps and asking residents, we arrived at a pretty good approximation of where these houses and the synagogue would have stood. They had all been replaced by newer homes and commercial shops.

Evidently getting rid of all the town's Jews had not done much to improve the local economy. Bilke still had the general appearance of a poverty-stricken backwater hamlet, with street vendors hawking consumer goods on blankets laid down on the sidewalks. We came upon a bronze monument on one end of main street. It was a four-foot-high replica of a cattle car of the type that was used transport the town's Jews to Auschwitz. This memorial tribute to the two thousand murdered Jews of Bilke was dwarfed by a far larger memorial dedi-

446

cated to the memory of the two dozen soldiers from Bilke who had died during World War Two.

Thanks, Bilke. Thanks for nothing.

We next made our way to the Jewish cemetery. Not surprisingly, we could tell as we approached that it was in disarray and horribly overgrown. After all, if there were no Jews in the town, who was there to maintain the graveyard? We wished to nevertheless go through the rows of crumbling grave markers looking for Heislers and Bergers and perhaps even an Adlersheim. Unfortunately, our entry was blocked by a solid wooden gate. The hasp of the gate was secured with a rusted combination lock.

"Let me take a crack at it," Mickey volunteered. Within ten seconds he had opened the lock.

"How in the fuck did you do that!?" I marveled.

"The result of a misspent youth breaking into school lockers and my extensive knowledge of Judaism."

I urged him to explain.

"You see, I recognized this as a primitive padlock with a three-digit combination. You spin right to the first single digit number, left to the second, right to the third number and left to open. That meant there were exactly 1000 possible combinations ranging from 0-0-0 to 9-9-9."

"But how did you know which one it was? You didn't try all 1000 combinations, did you?"

"I didn't have to," Mickey replied with a grin. "I asked myself, who puts a lock on a Jewish cemetery? Probably a rabbi or maybe a *gabbai* (sexton). What 3-digit number would a rabbi choose? 6-1-3. That's the number of *mitzvot* (commandments) in the Torah. Got it on the first try."

"Mickey!" I exclaimed, "You're a genuine Jewish genius!"

Once we got the gate unlocked, we found no reason to enter the cemetery which was completely overgrown with weeds and wild vegetation. So, we got back in our car and bid farewell the "boulevards" of Bilke. We headed six miles due west to the nearby municipality of Irshava. This is the town that was listed on my biological father's Mathausen death record as being the place of his birth in 1898. We spent the night in an inn and left the next morning after breakfast. The town appeared to be equally as primitive as what we had seen in Bilke. I asked a few members of the hotel staff if they had ever heard the name Adlersheim and was met with empty stares. Our next stop was the place I was anxious to visit once again, Budapest—once known as the Paris of Eastern Europe.

Arriving back to the Baltazar Hotel, we quickly unpacked and began to once again take in the stellar sights of the city. We walked the short distance to two of Budapest's world class historic attractions: the Buda Castle and the famous Fisherman's Bastion. The 13th century castle was the ancient seat of government and one of the locations from which the Habsburg monarchy ruled the Austro-Hungarian Empire. The Bastion was completed in 1902 to mark the 1000th anniversary of the Hungarian state. After the day's drive we were too tired to actually tour these sites, so we caught a glimpse and headed back. We were glad to hit the hay back at the Baltazar.

We rose the next morning and enjoyed a delightful breakfast of Hungarian crepes in the sun-drenched courtyard. Taking a taxi across the Danube via the Chain Bridge, we arrived at the Pest side of the city to resume our sightseeing. We again visited some of the city's memorials to those Hungarians lost during the 1940s and we toured the magnificent Dohany Utca synagogue, located next door to the birthplace of Theodor Herzl, the father of modern Zionism. The *shul* boasts splendid gothic architecture and is the second largest Jewish house of prayer still existing in the world. We toured the outdoor Holocaust museum located in the *shul's* courtyard. It was certainly impressive, but the thing that impressed me the most was brought to mind by that child's nursery rhyme: "Here is the church. Here is the steeple. Open the doors. *Where are the people?*"

Yes, while the place was filled with tourists from all over the world, the Dohany Utca synagogue had no congregation, no rabbi, and no regularly scheduled religious services. In other words, it was yet another artifact of a lost world. I understand that the local Chabad does conduct high holiday services there every year, but nine months of German occupation in 1944 followed by 45 years of Soviet domination has not left much of a viable Jewish community in Budapest, I'm afraid. The good news is that thanks to Chabad and others, several synagogues are being rejuvenated and Jewish life, little by little, is being restored under the Orban regime.

As we made our way through the bustling boulevards and grand plazas of Pest, we could not help but feel the energy level constantly buzzing around us. We stopped into bookstores, libraries, and found a kosher deli that offered some mouth-watering traditional Jewish fare like *cholent* and braised beef short ribs. The peasant market, as it was called, is an outdoor exotic bazaar offering esoteric delicacies and finely crafted products from around the world. Eventually, we again made our way to the Jewish Agency office that we were unable to visit during our previous stay in Budapest.

We were directed to the room containing the archives of the Jews of Budapest. These consisted of large docket-style books that were brought out to us, one at a time, by the helpful curator. We spent more than an hour poring over these typed pages of names and addresses, searching for any mention of my parents, Marton and Rose (née Berger) Adlersheim and came up empty. Discouraged, we picked up our shopping treasures from the marketplace, thanked the lady in charge, and headed for the door. Just before we reached the exit, we heard the lady give a shout.

"Come back. Come back. I just thought of something. Let's try one more book."

We shrugged and turned around, not expecting much at this point. The lady walked over to the bookcase and pulled out a small and relatively thin volume. It was labeled with the words *Zsidó túlélők*. My Hungarian language skills were not adequate to translate the book's title.

"This book," explained the curator, "lists the Jewish survivors of the Holocaust who had come from Budapest." Once we had the book opened before us, we could see that, like the others, the names were listed, directory-style, alphabetically. Skipping to the page that began with the name Adler did not take long. Here is what I saw on that page:

After looking at the text carefully, I could only echo the immortal words of Yankee Hall of Fame shortstop, Phil Rizzuto, whose hallmark expression was, "Holy Cow!"

I was not stunned to see my own name and birth year listed in the Hungarian fashion as Adlersheim Illés in the second from the top position. Included next, as part of the same listing, was my mother's maiden name, Berger Rozsi. My mother's name appeared again in the subsequent third listing, this time as Mrs. Marton Adlersheim along with her birth year of 1906. Next came the maiden name of her mother, Heisler Fanny (aka Faige). In keeping with the Jewish genealogical practice of matrilineal descent, only the mother's maiden name—and not the father's name—of each entry was listed.

Finding our names included in this listing of Jewish survivors from Budapest did not really surprise me, since I had to some degree expected us to be there. But what I saw next floored me, because it was the bit of information that I had been fervently seeking for years. There it was: Ostrom u. 29. The house where I was born. Seeing that address is what caused me to shout out that joyous Rizzoto-ism.

The address was listed after my name while the following listing, containing my mother's married name, showed no address. Only a cipher (—). I concluded that this symbol meant Ibid or "the same as the address above." The lower-case "u." following the name of the street was an abbreviation for *utca* (pron.: OOT-tsah) which means "street." Once we all realized what this find meant, all four of us exclaimed in unison:

"How do we get there?!"

The very helpful curator directed us to the Central Station and instructed us to get on a number 11 bus. We thanked the lady profusely and explained that she had helped us find what we had traveled all the way from Florida to discover. After jotting down the precious address, we decided against the bus ride and instead headed back to our hotel to drop off our packages and get freshened up. I had waited 58 years to find this house. I could wait a few hours more.

We rushed back, got changed and quickly reconvened in the lobby, excited and anxious to finally find the building on Ostrom utca that had eluded me for so many years. I approached the desk clerk and showed him the slip of paper containing the address.

"Where do we need to go to catch the bus to get to this address?" I inquired.

"*Nem, nem*," he replied shaking his head. I knew enough Hungarian to understand that this meant "No, no."

My heart fell to my feet. I was sure he was going to tell us that this address no longer existed. "What do you mean by 'No'?" I asked.

He responded to my worried expression with a smile. "No, no," he repeated. "No bus needed. No taxi either. Just go down the outside lift (elevator) at the end of the courtyard. When you get to the street level, make a left and walk about 200 meters (about a block) and you'll be right there."

You could have knocked me over with a Hungarian paprika. Mickey and Cookie couldn't believe it, either.

"You mean after all this searching, all the disappointments, coming back here twice, we were less than a block away the whole time?"

Mickey looked astonished.

It was like the penultimate scene in the Wizard of Oz when the good witch informs Dorothy that she had the ability all along to go back home—just by clicking her ruby slippers three times and saying, "There's no place like home."

Well, I had found my ruby slippers and was more than ready to see my original home. I describe what we found in the following chapter. Please read on.

Elliot Fixler

Chapter Twenty-eight

Anti-Climax

"Guilt is simply God's way of letting you know that you're having too good a time."
—Dennis Miller

I t seems unbelievable to me now, but it's a fact that during our trip to Budapest, and during the previous one as well, we completely failed to explore the Buda side of the Danube, particularly since all the major attractions were within walking distance of our hotel. While we did do some touring of the area by car—driving by some of the splendid country villas once owned by the Hungarian aristocracy (some Jewish)—we had not yet experienced Buda's famous hydrothermal spas, visited the Buda castle or toured Fisherman's Bastion. Instead, we had traveled each day to the cosmopolitan Pest side to explore, shop and dine. Had we simply done some freestyle exploring around our hotel, we might have come across my childhood home much sooner.

Armed finally with the correct address, we now emerged from the hotel and walked briskly to the outdoor elevator that would lower us down to street level. Turning left, as instructed by the hotel clerk, we quickly came upon Ostrom Utca as we made our way down the street. Literally down, since the street was situated on a steep hill. After ten minutes, we found ourselves standing in front of a stunning multi-story building. The number 29 was emblazoned over the resident entrance of what was still a residential structure housing a street-level storefront. While in my father's day the store was a grocery that no doubt sold apples, on the date of our discovery the store was home to a business that repaired Apples. Apple Computers, iPhones, iPads, Apple watches, etc.

Such is progress, I guess.

As we stood on the sidewalk, marveling at the building's classic elegance, I guess we looked a bit lost. A good-looking gentleman stopped and as asked us, in perfect English, if he could be of any help. He verified that the building was a protected historic landmark and therefore could not be altered or demolished. I thanked him and he agreed that there would be no reason for anyone to modify such an attractive edifice. Although I thought about entering the place to see if I could determine exactly where we had lived and the spot where my mother had given birth to me, this was not an option since the Apple repair store was closed for the day and the entrance to the apartment units was only accessible to residents.

We decided to conduct some exploration of the neighborhood and continued downward about another 300 feet until we reached the end of Ostrom Utca. By this point our thigh muscles were feeling the stress and I thought back to the comment made by our guide during our prior visit to Budapest when I showed her the photo of the building and asked if she could identify it. "It must be on the Buda side of the city because it looks like the street is on a hill."

I now understood how she came to such a conclusion.

As we reached the bottom of the hill, we were met by a vast open area that looked like a terminal point for buses and trams. As we surveyed the area, I spotted something that is almost as ubiquitous as Chabad Houses: a Starbucks. Even from my vantage point all the way across the plaza, I could see that this was, without a doubt, the largest Starbucks I had ever seen.

After picking up our mocha latte grandes, we pushed on towards the enormous shopping mall across from the Starbucks. We soon arrived at a lovely esplanade surrounded by tiny eateries and designer brand shoppes. It was definitely an upscale and bustling area that we had completely overlooked even though it was only a short walk from our hotel. We promised each other that we would definitely spend more time in Buda on our next visit to the city.

We bid "*szerbusz*" (good-bye) to Budapest in high spirits, feeling as though we had managed to fulfill our mission and have a fun time in the process. Next destination: Lviv, Ukraine, Cookie's ancestral hometown. Unlike me, she knew the address of the house her family had once owned, and we located it easily. We discovered it was now a dental office. During our tour of the city, our guide pointed out the one remaining synagogue in Lviv, a city that boasted more than fifty Jewish houses of worship before the second world war.

Learning from our experience in Budapest, we decided to explore the area within walking distance of our hotel. Taking a side street as we departed Rynok Square, we came across a store that looked like any of the others except that it had a life-sized bronze statue erected by its door. And I do mean "erected." The store, we learned, was a sex shop and the bronze statue was the image of Leopold von Sacher-Masoch, author of the erotic classic *Venus in Furs* and who lent his name to the sexual deviation known as masochism.

The friendly sex shop clerk informed us that many visitors like to put a hand into the statue's left pocket for good luck.

"Why the hell not?" I thought and inserted my hand into the pocket, only to find I was groping Mr. Masoch's male member. I'm sure I disappointed the store clerks who were hoping for a shocked reaction, but I stayed calm and nonchalant. I did not reveal to my companions about what I found in the pocket and suggested to Mickey that he give it a go.

He declined at first, but after much prodding, Mickey agreed and the sex shop staff got the reaction they were hoping for.

Once again, Lorraine was a pleasant non-entity who only once caused us some distress. Our Lviv hotel did not offer electronic key cards, but instead provided old-fashioned metal keys. As we were preparing to leave, we found that our room key was missing. We searched for it high and low, but it was simply gone. The desk clerk said that they did not have a duplicate. We continued our search and finally found the key behind the toilet tank. It seems that Lorraine had hidden it out of fear that we would leave her behind. We reassured her that this would not happen and our trip continued without further incident.

Our last stop was in the Donbas region of Ukraine, where Mickey's family originated. We saw nothing exceptional to report. As of this writing, in 2022, the Donbas has frequently been in the news. It is Ukraine's most highly pro-Russian population center. It is the site of Donetsk and Luhansk, both of which were recognized as independent nations by the invading Russian forces during the 2022 Russo-Ukrainian conflict.

We arrived back home safe and sound and were not required to face down any savage skunks as we had upon our return from Africa. I was soon back to the regular rhythms of my life, thanks to the respite offered by Lorraine's caregivers.

Jeane Mongrain turned out to be every bit as capable as I had been led to believe. She was a tireless workhorse and a terrific cook, feeding and clothing Lorraine and, at the same time, helping to look after our two dogs. Lorraine was left in my sole care from after dinner to the next morning when Jeane would arrive to work. When it became clear that Lorraine required such care seven days a week, Jeane recruited Patty Melcarek to assist her. Other temporary home health care providers came and went, but Lorraine's care was left to Jeane, Patty and me.

This set-up lasted for several years. Years that saw Lorraine's dementia grow progressively worse. She was becoming fully incontinent which was problematic for me to deal with when Lorraine was solely in my care. Eventually, her verbal skills were lost and she had difficulty expressing herself. I had started noticing, about this time, that whenever I left Lorraine in Jeane's care, Lorraine would become highly agitated. I recall coming home at such times and being greeted by Lorraine rushing to the door and visibly upset. At first, I could not understand her reasons and of course, she was unable to tell me. I then noticed that on those days when Patty was working, Lorraine was calm and seemed like an entirely different person.

I came to the conclusion that as Lorraine's Alzheimer's got progressively worse, Jeane's level of care likewise worsened. I knew I would have to do something soon before things got out of hand. I dreaded firing Jeane. She had been a loyal and devoted member of our household for several years at this point and she continued to be a very hard worker when it came to doing chores around the house. But I could see the trend. As Lorraine became more needy, Jeane became more detached and distant. I was also concerned about whether or not I could locate anyone suitable to replace her.

I did not have to make the decision about letting Jeane go. She departed on her own. She admitted that she was having an increasingly hard time coping with Lorraine and she felt I should find someone more fully trained in Alzheimer's care. I thanked Jeane for her honesty and for her years of dedicated service.

I turned to Patty who was not surprised by Jeane's departure. Patty had worked with Jeane before in other caregiving assignments and Alzheimer's care was always a problem area for her. Patty agreed that Lorraine would be better served by someone more tolerant and accepting of her needs. Patty stayed on and helped me locate several more qualified caregivers and the situation seemed to grow better. Unfortunately, Lorraine's condition continued to grow worse.

I wish I could conclude things with a Hollywood happy ending, but that's not the way Alzheimer's works; no happy ending, only the intractable descent into oblivion, as first the mind, then the body are incrementally demolished. And the inevitable ending, as we know, is always the same.

FULL CIRCLE

When I realized that I could no longer care properly for Lorraine during my assigned 12-hour shift, I had to consider transitioning her into a memory care facility. At this stage of the game, Lorraine no longer understood what her condition was and I had no stomach to continue trying to live in our home as the normal couple next door. The house was getting older and so was I. I was simply worn out and knew I was no longer able to give Lorraine the care she now required.

I was fortunate that, with help of a doggy adoption agency, I was able to locate a couple who would adopt both Oliver and Apple, even after they had been told about their tenuous medical conditions. Their new owners seem to be giving them excellent care and occasionally send me photos. Although the pictures may cause me to miss them a bit, I certainly don't miss paying their ongoing medical bills.

When it came to selling the house, I again turned to Jan Burke. She helped me do the staging and prep the house for sale. With her help and guidance, we found a buyer within two hours of the house appearing on the Multiple Listings website. The buyer agreed to the asking price with zero negotiation, making me think we probably set the price tag too low. They say that the worst thing you can do to a Jew is accept his first offer. Actually, I was happy to sell the place so quickly so I could start searching for a suitable new home for Lorraine...and a new place for me as well.

A few months earlier, I had looked at a memory care facility near our Ironhorse home. But at that point I found I was emotionally incapable of institutionalizing Lorraine. But as her condition declined and once I had a sales contract in place for the house, the reality of

461

the situation took hold. I located a nice townhouse-style apartment for myself in Palm Beach Gardens and signed a one-year lease agreement. The leasing agent suggested that I look into a memory care facility across the street from the apartment complex. I did so.

At this point I was still using Patty's services on a part-time basis. She was helping me find a suitable facility for Lorraine and had agreed to stay on to help Lorraine get accustomed to her new surroundings. The facility across the street from my apartment complex is called HarborChase and, after checking it out, Patty and I both agreed that it would be a good fit. HarborChase is a luxury retirement community that offers assisted living and memory care services. And with me living right across the street, it would be convenient to visit frequently and make sure she was being treated well.

Unfortunately, HarborChase did not live up to the hype. In the beginning, Lorraine was able to attend and enjoy the resident events and entertainment offered by the facility. I would visit frequently, joining her for lunch or dinner as well as the Sunday brunches. But, as her condition continued to worsen, so did the level of care she was receiving. The onset of the COVID-19 pandemic in March of 2020 only served to exacerbate the deteriorating situation. The place soon turned in to a first-class shit hole. For example, Lorraine's diaper was not being changed as needed and her appearance began looking disheveled and seedy. Whenever Patty or I would visit during those days, we would invariably find Lorraine curled up on her bed in a fetal position, so heavily medicated that she was oblivious to our presence.

I decided to move Lorraine to the Morse Life Memory Care center in West Palm Beach and it appears, at this writing in early 2022, to have been the right choice. I had chosen Morse Life after having been highly recommended to me by my friend and Ironhorse golf buddy, Neil Buchwalter. Neil's wife, Gail, was a resident at Morse Life enjoying exceptional care. Over the prior few years, I had noticed some signs of dementia whenever we would get together with Neil and Gail at their home for dinner. Gail's deterioration took place very quickly and Neil had placed her at Morse Life and was very pleased with the level of service.

So that brings things up to date. Lorraine is now at Morse Life and wheelchair bound. She is no longer ambulatory and has suffered a series of falls that landed her in the E.R. She no longer recognizes me, Patty, Sarah or anyone else. Her nurses report that they like Lorraine—as I've said before, "Everybody loves Lorraine."

They tell me that, unlike some Alzheimer's patients, she is never the source of any problems. I continue to visit her although at times it seems pointless. I do it out of a sense of Jewish guilt, I guess. Like my own Jewish mother used to say, "It doesn't matter what you do, as long as you feel guilty about it." Actually, Patty visits Lorraine more often than I do, a fact that only adds to my guilt.

Elliot Fixler

Chapter Twenty-nine

Parting Shots

"We know we've come full circle when we stand at a very similar crossroad where we made such a mess of life before, but this time we take a different road."

—Beth Moore, Author & Evangelist

W riting this closing chapter has turned out to be the toughest task of this book project. I had feared that the retelling of my son's death would be emotionally challenging. It certainly was that, but writing it took less time, and less struggle, than did this chapter. I now find myself almost unable to finish what I started. Is it really finished? I have such profound feelings of relief that I really am finally done with it. I feel moved to express my gratitude to anyone who has read this far. Believe it or not, I still feel there are more memories that are worthy of inclusion, but my editor has already expressed his concern that the book has grown too long. Proofreading, inserting photos, designing the cover are among the tasks that now lie ahead. Foremost, of course, is selecting a suitable title.

When I started writing this book I thought that a good title might be, *From Budapest to Palm Beach; My Life's Journey*. My editor, who is experienced in such matters, suggested *Full Circle*. I questioned that choice. I asked my daughter, Sarah, and her husband,

Eric, what they thought of the title and, to my surprise (and chagrin), they both thought that *Full Circle* would be more appropriate. I thought about it further, and, although it took me several days to recognize the circular patterns of my life, I finally got it. My life started in Budapest and it wasn't until I returned to the place where it all began that I was able to better understand where I came from, who I am, and where I now stand. I have actually come "full circle."

A similar circle may be discerned in my connection to Judaism. My earliest instructors were members of the Lubavitch movement, people who dedicate their lives to bringing Jews closer to our traditions. And now, after decades of distance from that heritage, I am again making connections, thanks to the Lubavitch Chabad movement and my teacher, Rabbi Dovid Vigler.

It must be understood that in the realms of discovering my family background and redeveloping ties to my heritage, both must be regarded as works in progress. The publication of this book does not signal the end of my searches. On the contrary, it is intended as a chronicle of these quests and, more importantly, as an inspiration for others to pursue a similar path.

As you have read, my life's journey has been marred by some soul-crushing challenges. The loss of a young son left me broken and wondering if I would ever smile again. Caring for my wife and watching her decline into the darkness of dementia continues to be a challenge and a daily reminder of the fickle finger of fate.

At the same time, one cannot observe the larger landscape of my life without realizing the overwhelming number of blessings and "against all odds" good fortune I have enjoyed. Of all the babies born to Jewish mothers in Budapest in 1944, I was somehow one of the few who survived. Of all the Jewish children who were forced to grow up as orphans after having lost one or both parents in the flames of the Holocaust, my mother managed to keep me alive with the help of her brother-in-law, whom she eventually married. Of all the displaced families dreaming of coming to America after the war, ours actually did so, thanks to the kindness of relative strangers.

The good fortune continued as I completed my studies, found a wonderful law partner, established a successful legal practice, married a wonderful and sweet woman (on my second try), collected an army of dear friends, was blessed by some great children and grandchildren as well as a new life partner who enabled me to enjoy the best of what life has to offer every day. My only regret is that I did not embark on these journeys of discovery any sooner. If I had, I am certain that the feeling of being grounded in my family structure and, as an active member of the Jewish people, would have benefited me greatly during the challenging situations I mentioned.

As I have explained, making sure that my children and grandchildren do not experience the regret that I feel at failing to question my forebears about their lives is my primary purpose in writing this book. It is intended to outlive me and, after I'm gone, should someone further up the family tree wish to know about my life, it's right here between the covers.

So, at long last, that brings me to the point I'd like to close with. Whoever you may be, an heir, a family member, a friend, a colleague, or someone I've never met, I urge you to consider doing what I have tried to do. Get connected. Learn from my mistakes. Do not do what I did. Do not wait until your family members are gone before deciding you would like to hear their stories. Talk to your older relatives…now. Listen to their voices. Find out about their early lives and discover how you fit into the scheme of things. The same goes for connecting with your heritage. There's no reason to wait until you retire before you start making those connections. In both cases, gaining an understanding of how you are linked to those who came before you—either in terms of family or your cultural heritage—will serve as a tremendous comfort should you, at some point, find yourself facing one of life's challenging situations.

You may find, as I did, that once you start on this path, you will experience the very satisfying feeling of having come full circle. While I do not believe in the existence of a supreme being, I do nevertheless feel there is much to be gained by recognizing that you are a part of something greater than yourself.

Thank you for taking this spin of the wheel of life with me. I hope you found it a worthwhile ride and that it will encourage you to also consider recording your own life history in some fashion. If I have inspired you at the end of this story to embark on the beginnings of your own story, that represents once again having come full circle. That will convince me, beyond a doubt, that writing this book was truly a worthwhile undertaking. Thank you.

—Elliot Fixler
March, 2022

Photos

Elliot Fixler

My maternal grandparents
Faige (née Heisler) Berger, Meier Berger. c. 1920

My uncle, Maurice
Berger; my aunt,
Rose (née Heisler)
Berger.
c. 1935

My biological father, Marton Adlersheim. c. 1935

My mother, Rose Berger. c. 1935

Berger Family Portrait.
(standing, l-r) Raise, Maurice, Rose (my future mother).
(seated, l-r) My grandmother, Faige; my grandfather, Meier.
c. 1935

(l-r) My uncle Jacob Berger, my great-uncle Samuel Heisler, and my grandfather, Meier Berger on the train platform at Auschwitz shortly before they were murdered. 1944

(center) My uncle, Jacob Berger; *(behind Jacob)* my grandfather, Meier Berger on the train platform at Auschwitz. 1944 The two brothers lived next door to each other in Bilke. They remained together as they faced death.

474

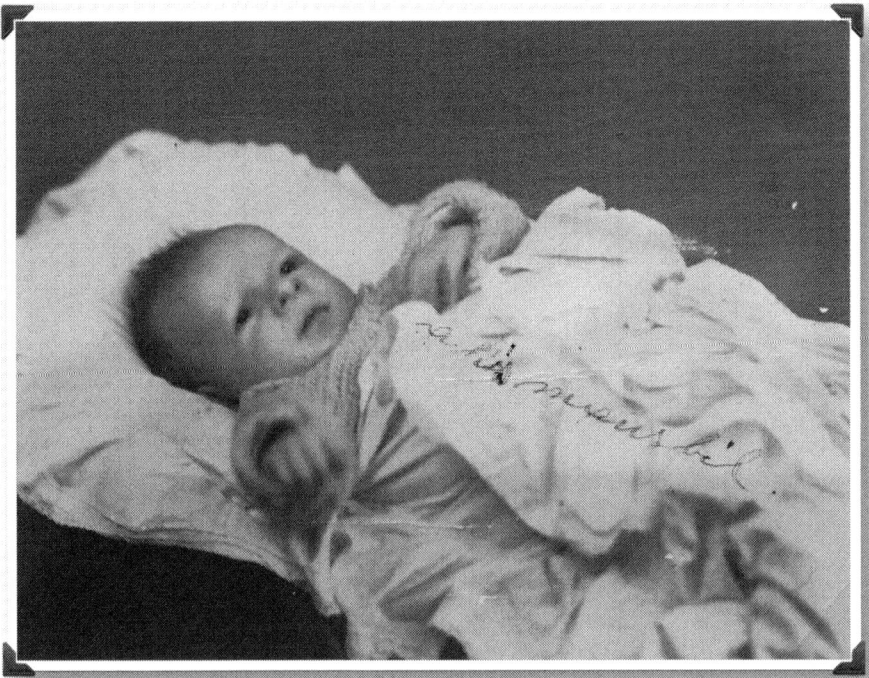

Budapest Baby.
Illés Adlersheim (as I was then known) at age 2 months.
1944

An 18K gold Omega
pocket watch belonging
to my biological father,
Marton Adlersheim,
given to me by my
mother, the only artifact
I own from the father I
never knew.
Note the engraved MA
monogram in the center
of the watch cover.

My first of many bicycles. In Usti
Nad Labem, Czechoslovakia. 1947

476

(l-r) My mother, Rose Berger; me; my stepfather, Sam Fixler in Usti Nad Labem, Czechoslovakia. 1948

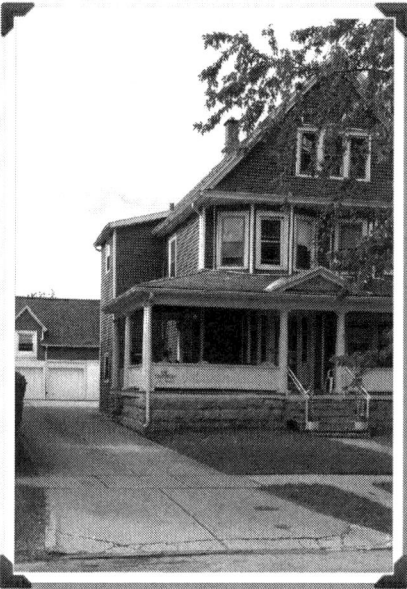

My childhood home at 196 North Park Avenue, Buffalo, New York. c. 1955

My mother's well-worn valise in which I discovered a trove of photos and documents that revealed a number of shocking secrets. 1958

College kid. c. 1965

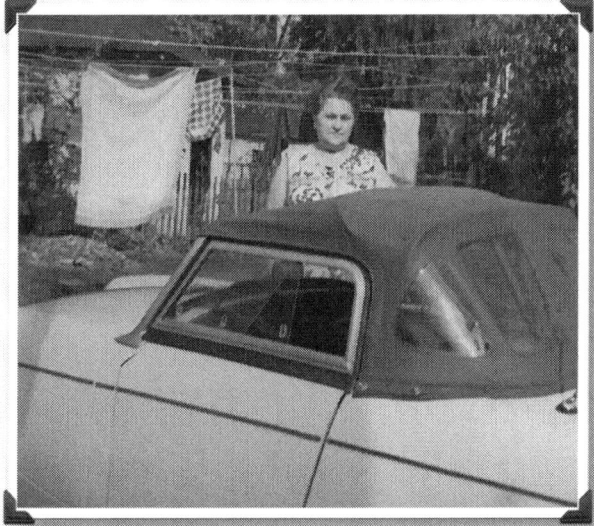

My mother and my first
MG sports car.
Buffalo, New York.
c. 1965

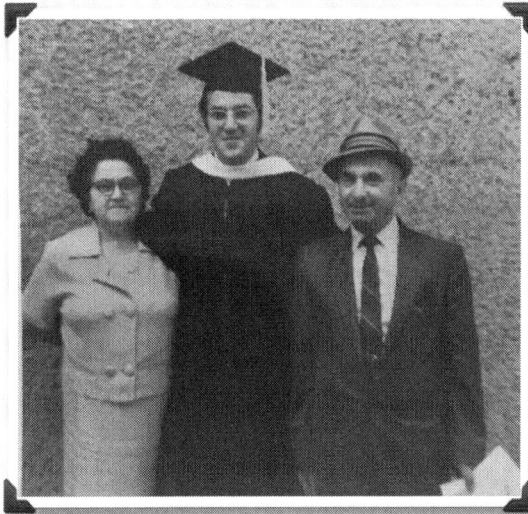

Graduation from Law
School with my parents.
1970

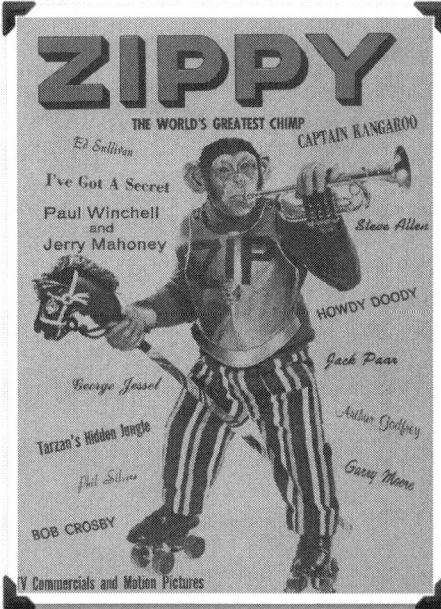

A flyer promoting one of my early clients, Zippy, the world's greatest chimp.

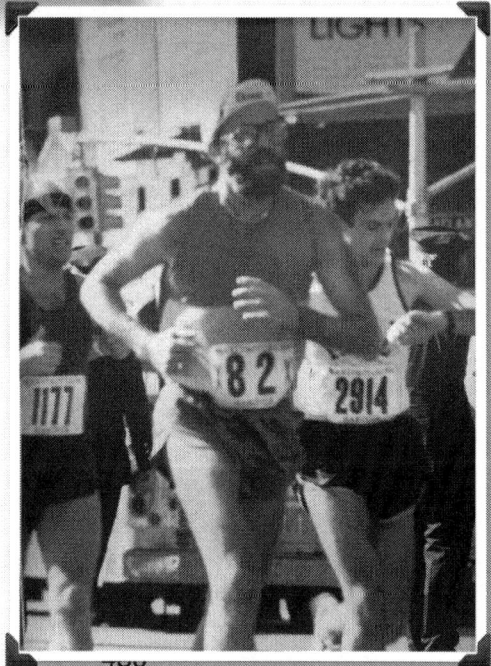

My second (and last) New York Marathon in 1977 which I finished in 2 hrs. 58 min., qualifying me to compete in the Boston Marathon.

Island Wedding Day. September 13, 1981

Sweet Lorraine

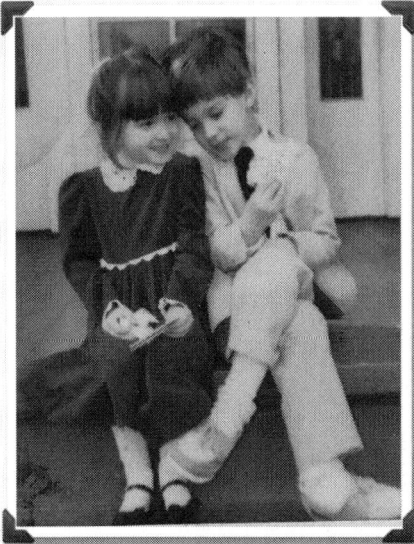

Sarah and Mathew at my parents' home in Buffalo.

With Jason, Sarah, my mother Rose, and Mathew in Buffalo.

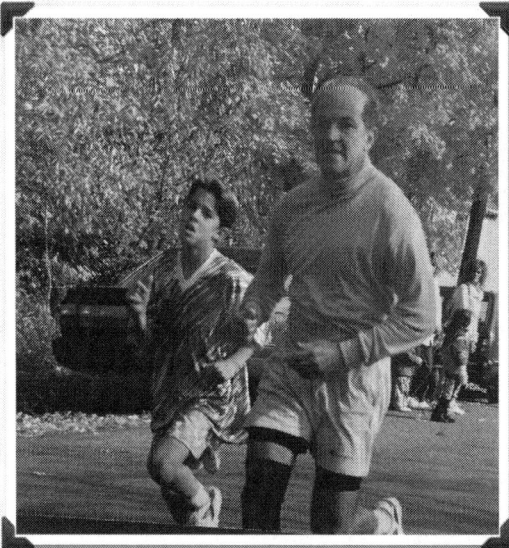

Me running with Mat in a school race, which he won as usual.

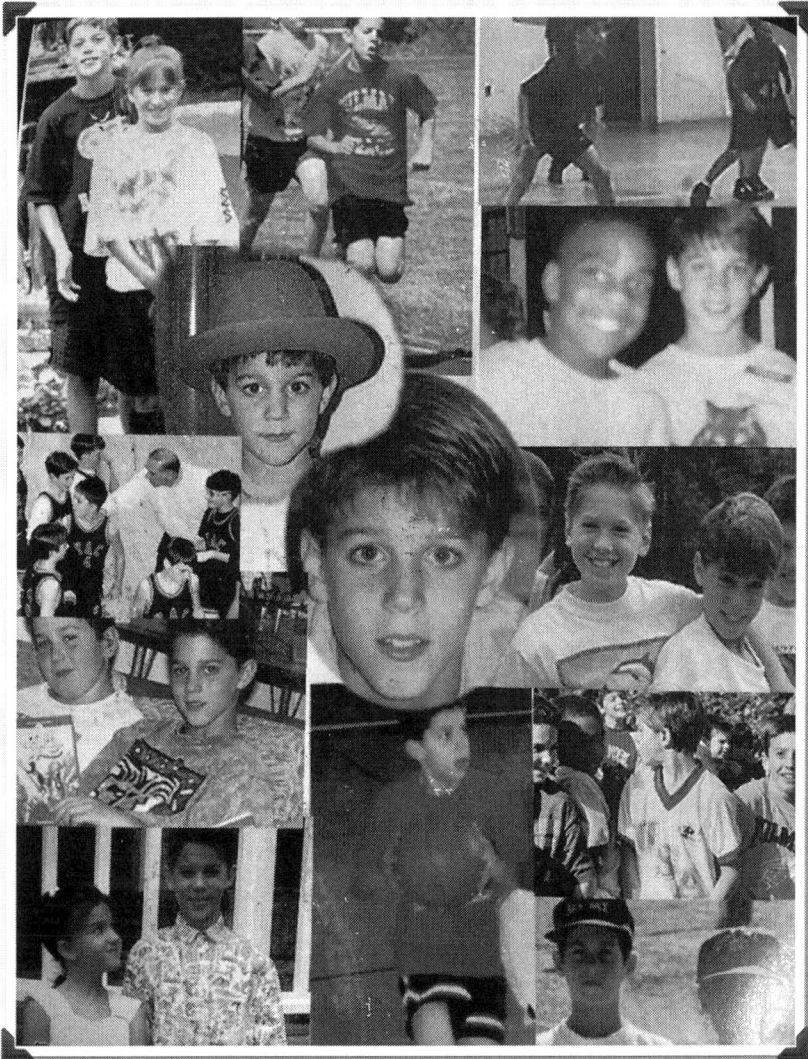

Mathew Collage

Mathew

Sarah (circled) at the opening ceremonies of the Empire State Games.

Sarah, the basketball star athlete playing at the Westchester County Center in the playoffs for the state championships.

Aerial view of the Lake House.

Our Stratton, Vermont ski lodge.

The good life on our island.

(l-r) My partner, Howard Stockfield; friends Gene Fleischer;
Gene's wife; me; friends Elliot Michael; Dick Gannon, and
Janusz Rednicki.

Our island getaway.

Bare-assed beach boy wind surfing au naturel.

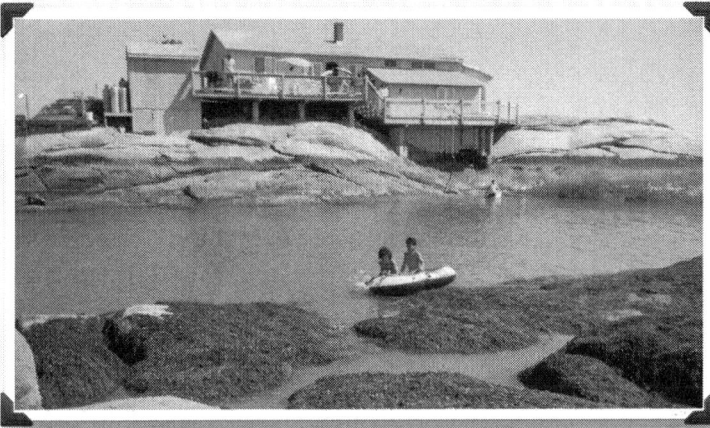

South view of our island at low tide.

The Fuji Blimp getting a south view of my friend, David Kellogg
extending his usual greeting to sight-seers.

The surprise stripper Lorraine provided at my 40th birthday party.

Lorraine, at her 40th birthday party, dancing with our friend and kids' grade school teacher, John Scaglia.

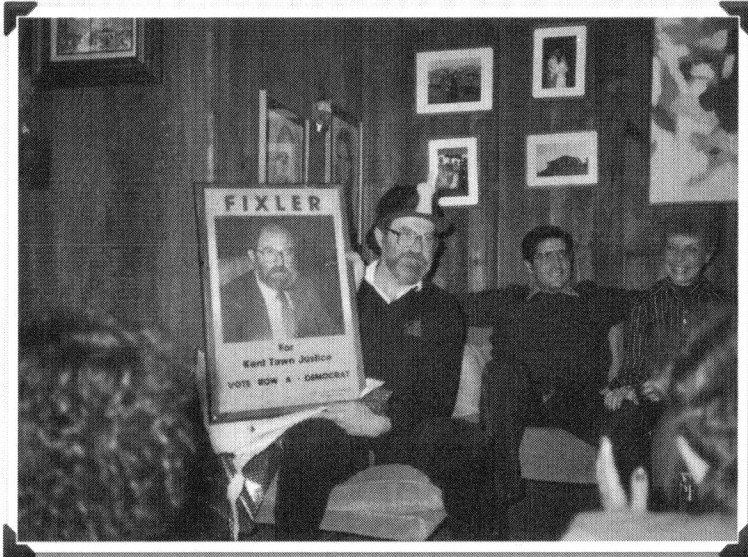

My ill-fated attempt to run for office and the end of my political career.

On the slopes with
Mathew, Sarah,
and Lorraine.

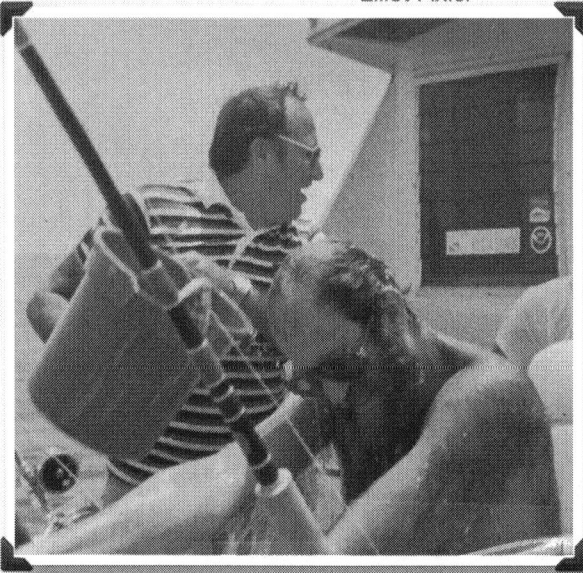

Jay Maxwell dousing me with water as I struggle to reel in what I thought was the "Big One."
It actually turned out to be a prank that I fell for hook, line, and sinker.

Jay Maxwell's other boat, his schooner, moored in front of his home in Ponce Inlet, FL.

Paying close attention court side at a Nets home basketball game
at the Meadowlands. This image appeared on national T.V.

With All-NBA forward, the first black NBA General Manager,
Wayne Embry at his induction into the NBA Hall of Fame.

With the Fixler and the Myers families in the Cayman Islands.
1992.

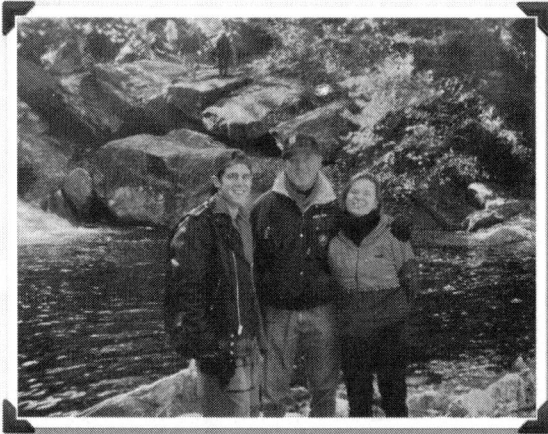

With Jason and Lorraine, hiking near our home in Stratton, Vermont.

Painting that Raymond Kolkmann secretly had reproduced and hung in his home to prank me and make me believe he had stolen my original.

Our African Safari crew and two of our professional guides.

(l-r) In Africa with Lorraine, Rosie Long, Stan Long, Stuart Myers, and Lida Myers.

496

With Miami mayor, Manny Diaz.

Our grade school through high school crew that has managed to get together every year. *(l-r)* Me, Richard Polisner, Jim Smolev, Ron Diner, Barry Warner and Stu Alexander. Drinking and dining in Ponte Vedre, Florida. Richard, Stuart and I live along Florida's east coast. Barry is from Houston. Ron is from the west coast of Florida and Jim Smolev hails from Maryland.

An alligator consuming a fish near our home.
I feared Lorraine may have met a similar fate when she disappeared.

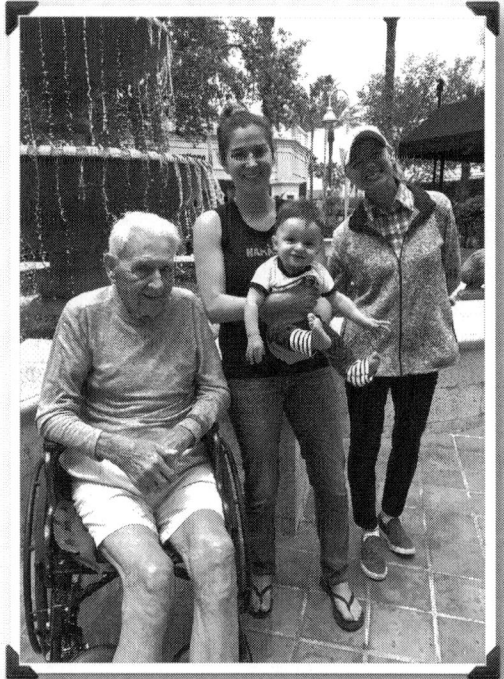

(l-r) Gramps (Lorraine's father); Sarah; my grandson, Luca; and Lorraine at our rendezvous spot in Melbourne, FL

498

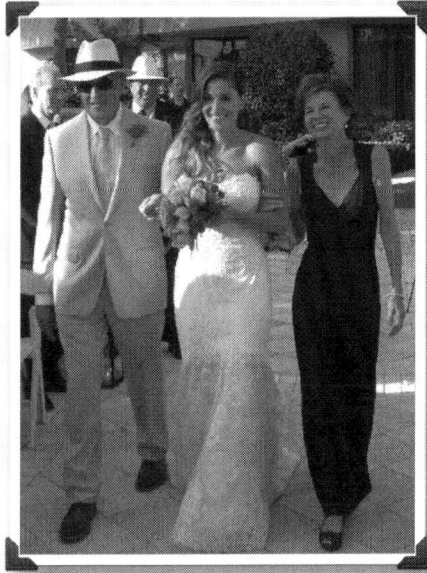

Lorraine and me walking Sarah down the aisle.

With Rabbi Dovid Vigler and his grandfather-in-law, Rabbi Chaim Yehuda Krinsky, the head of the worldwide Chabad movement.

The Fixler Israel Travel Crew
(l-r) Sarah, Eric, Snip, me, Lorraine and the rabbi stopping on
the way down from Masada.

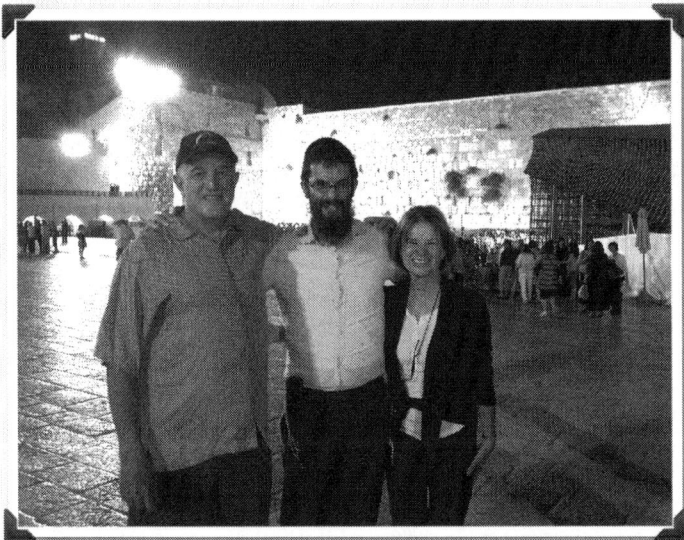

With Rabbi Dovid Vigler and Lorraine at the Western Wall
(Kotel) in Jerusalem)

Sneaky Selfie

This photo was featured in a 2015 *Send In Your Selfie* article from the Palm Beach Post. It was taken at the Temple Mount in Jerusalem. Our group was attempting to visit the site, but the entry was guarded by a Palestinian Authority officer. He was armed and looked as though he was ready for trouble. We were denied entry, although we observed Arab children going in and out freely. He indicated that no photos were permitted. Nevertheless, I managed to snap this surreptitious semi-self-ie of me, the guard and the entry point.

Elliot Fixler

With the Rabbi and my buddies at Palm Beach Gardens
Chabad synagogue.

Four of my seven
grandchildren
(l-r) Scarlett, Jack,
Sasha, and Max.
c.2015.

Small memorial marker commemorating Bilke's Jewish Holocaust victims.

Detail from top of memorial marker depicting deportation of Jews in cattle cars.

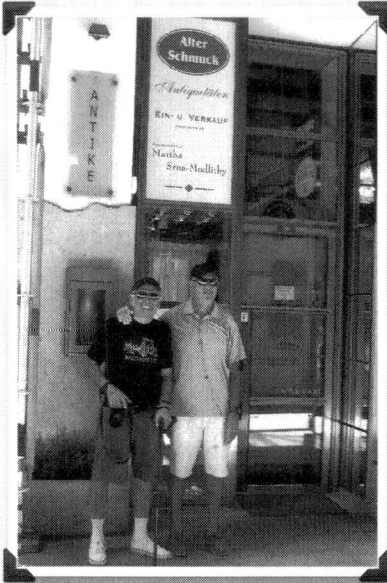

With Mickey Gottlieb. A couple of *Alter Schmucks* in Vienna. NOTE *Schmuck* means "Jewelry" in German.

Mickey exploring the bronze genitalia in the pocket of a statue of Leopold Von Sacher-Masoch, the namesake of masochism, in Lviv, Ukraine.

Raymond and the Dummy.
Raymond Kolkmann, looking for trouble on a European cruise we took together
The dummy is the one on the left (I think).

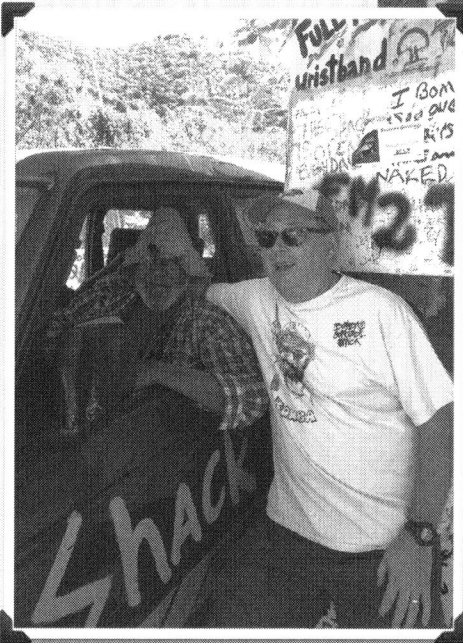

Ray Kolkmann on the island of Tortola in the British Virgin Islands, befriending the proprietor of a bar located across the street.
The proprietor parks there in his truck in order to keep an eye on the bar. The walls of the bar are covered with photos of bar patrons performing a variety of sexual acts while on the premises.

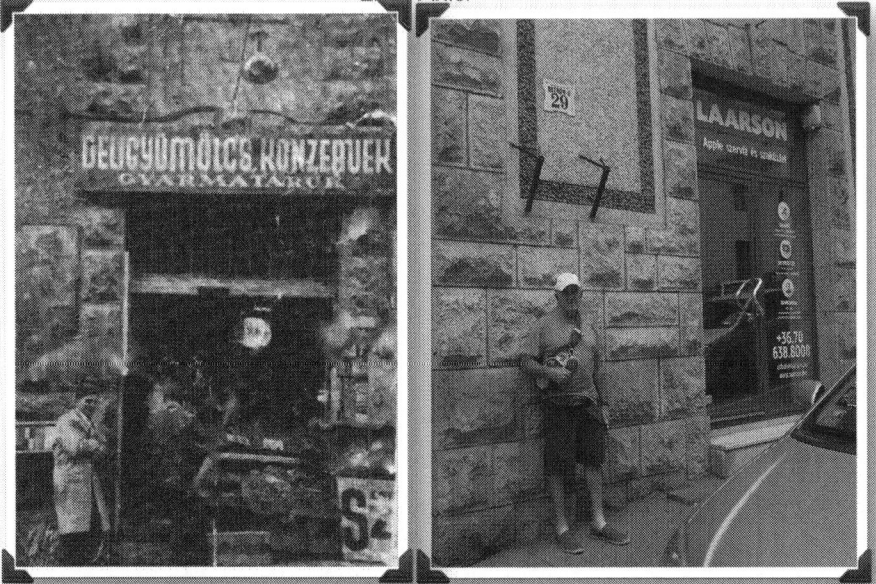

The building where I was probably born in 1944, located at Ostrum Utca 29 in Budapest, Hungary.

(left) As it looked in 1942, with my biological father, Marton Adlersheim standing in front of his grocery store

(right and below) As it looks these days, home to a computer repair shop

Coming full circle from apples to Apple Computers.

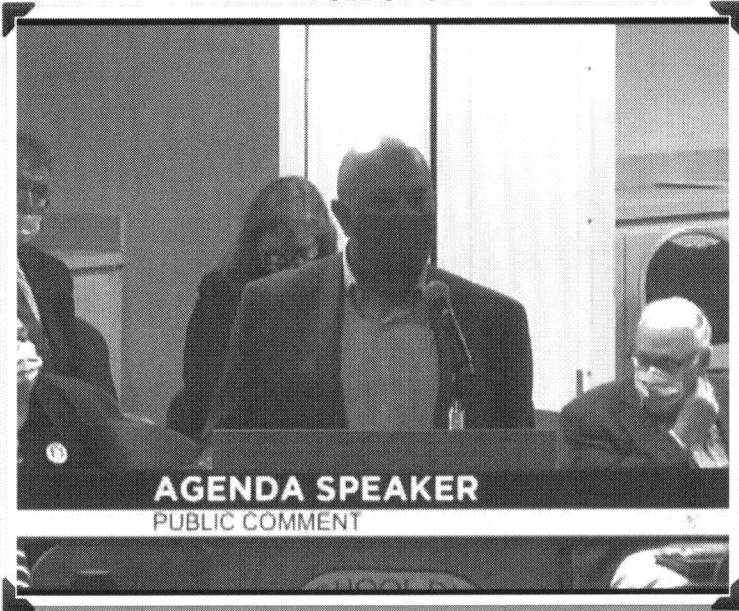

Testifying at the Palm Beach County School Board regarding a
Holocaust-denying high school principal. 2021.

With Tony Provenzano.

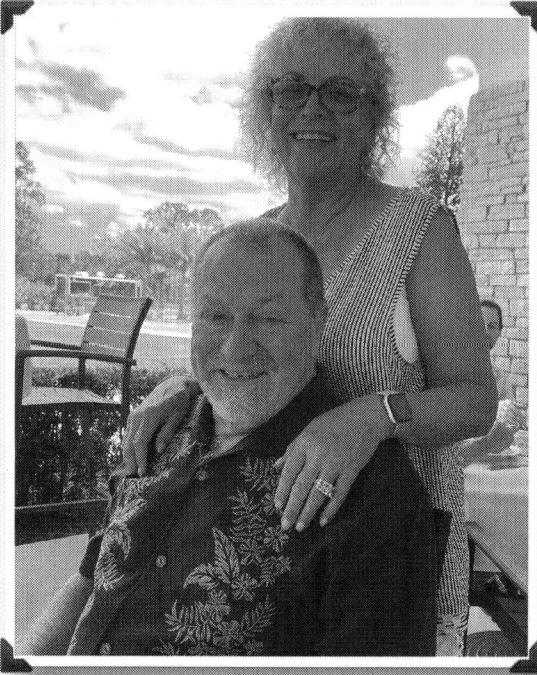

Terry *(seated)* and Christina Simone from Colorado visiting me in Palm Beach Gardens. 2021

Rob Burke *(standing)*, Michael Paolercio and me *(seated)* at the Burke home.

Patty and me stopping for lunch with the Simones during an annual ski trip to Colorado.

Lorraine *(r)* with caregiver, Patty Melcarek.

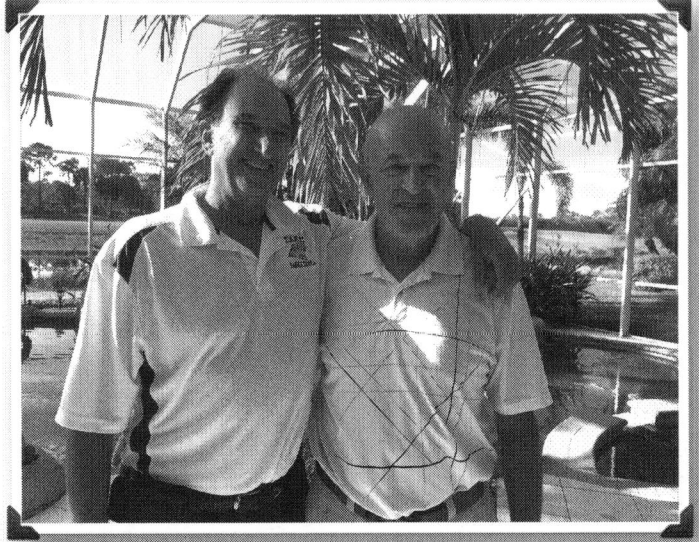

With my lifelong
friend, Dr. Richard
(Snip) Polisner at my
Ironhorse home.

With my buds in the Dominican Republic
*(l-r) M*e, Michael Paolercio, Irv Sparage, Rob Burke and Anthony
Paolercio from New York

510

(l-r) Mary Kolkmann, Jan Rudnicki, Pam Festa, Dave Festa, Lorraine, Anna Rudnicki, Raymond Kolkmann, and me.

With me dressed as the world's largest Leprechaun lawyer on St. Patrick's Day with Rod Huebers at Mar-A-Lago.

Tony and Marguerite
Provenzano at Mar-A-Lago

Jack and Sasha Fixler.
c.2019

When Jay was growing up in the 1970s, I had season tickets to
New York Yankees baseball games. He today shares season
tickets with his brother and a friend. Here Jay is taking Sasha,
Jack and me to a Yankees game.

Stacy and Jay with kids in our pool at our Ironhorse home.

(l-r) Sarah, Kyla, Eric, Levi and Luca Kuhn. c. 2019.

Kyla, Sarah, and Luca. 2022

Sarah and Kyla in stills from an exercise video aimed at pregnant women.
Video may be viewed at Sarah's website, Juna.co. The company provides prenatal and postpartum information and guidance.

Jason, Stacey Lager Fixler, Sasha, and Jack.

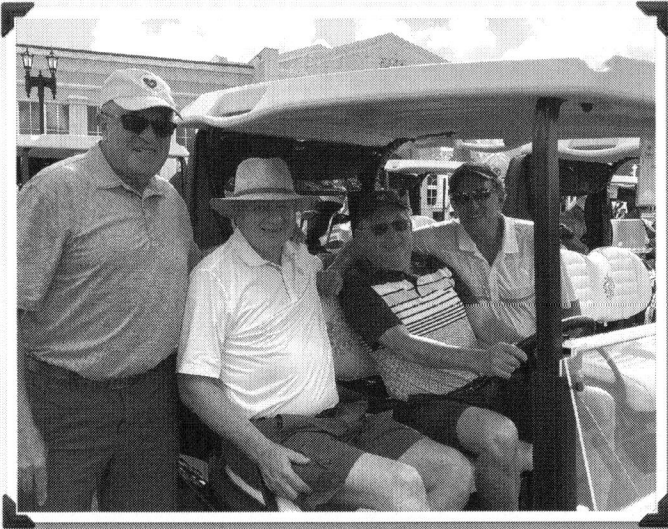

Chabad Golf Outing at Trump International. *(l-r)* me, Rod Huebers, Ray Kolkmann, and Richard Polisner.

Halloween party with *(l-r)* Cindy and Stuart Israelson, Marguerite and Tony Provenzano, me and Lorraine. 2019

Aliquam Vitae *(Collage of Life)*

Elliot Fixler

Appendix

Elliot Fixler

FULL CIRCLE

A 2010 letter written by my friend, Dr. Richard Polisner in response to my request for a letter of endorsement in my effort to obtain an appointment to an immigration judgeship. His humorous epistle was probably the reason I did not get the job. I love him anyway.

1/2/2010

Dear Ms. Layne, Dear Ms. Tolson,

I have probably been friends with Elliot Fixler longer than anyone. We met in 1952 and have been close since. I am proud to be able to call Elliot my friend.

Elliot has favorably touched people's lives wherever he has chosen to live or work. He has always been one of the most cunning, sneaky members of our entire cult group of friends. His legal career essentially began in 1960 when I would pick him up at the corner with his football gear while successfully arguing to his Dad that he was headed to the synagogue.

Imagine how ably he could argue when he left home only to encounter "my love of my life" who was German Catholic. He frequently was able to leave her in tears by destroying all of her arguments about religion. And she graduated UB Phi Betta Kappa. Mr. Fixler could certainly press his point. His hard work and integrity was most manifest in his passion for sports where he was dramatically mediocre (except in his own mind). His strongest attribute those days was his uncanny ability to know the rules and bend them frequently for his own gain on the court. However, when he didn't get his own way he begged for forgiveness and even was known to resort to tears when arguing didn't work out well. He also used this tactic in his personal life. I don't know how he was in court??????

Mr. Fixler has always been a family man, putting family first ahead of his own career and entertainment. (Just ask his first wife), The poor woman never had a chance. She's not been the same since the divorce. However, Elliot was able to make this trauma of divorce into a positive. i.e. spending more time with his then office manager and pouring himself into his office work and his devotion to helping others insurance companies against their insured's.

Law school was a passion of Elliot's. He always wanted to study the law and help people. This passion was aided by the fact that law school was a draft deferment from Viet Nam.

However, Elliot does have an incredible family, a beautiful wonderfull wife and successful delightful children. I would highly recommend him for a Judgeship. This job could be good for him to get out of the house, have something worthwhile to do and most importantly to get out of his wife (and Kid's) hair so they can have some peace.

Feel free to contact me at any time for further information. (or to embellish on any of Elliot's life, really!)

Dr. Richard I Polisner

An article from the March 1, 1982, issue of "Connecticut Today" magazine describing our island wedding

OTHER-WORLDLY WEDDINGS

By Jill Menkes Kushner

"Love and marriage go together like a horse and carriage," according to the refrain of a once-popular song. Well, the song may have slipped from the "Top 40" charts, but it seems that marriage is back in style. After falling from grace during the 1970's, weddings have once again become popular. In 1979, over 25,000 Connecticut residents tied the knot... so there must be something to it!

And, just as taking the vows has returned to vogue, so have the more traditional-style ceremonies. As one observer notes, "All of the recent weddings I've gone to have been traditional: church ceremonies with receptions afterward in a hall, or at home. It seems to reflect the (conservative) swing in morality; it's a reaction to the 1960's 'barefoot on the beach' type of wedding. People

are getting away from the extravagant and back to the norm."

Sounds dry, doesn't it? Indeed, most weddings seem pretty staid nowadays. Occasionally, says a

to change its rather barren appearance. As Mr. Fixler puts it, "The island was basically rock. We brought tons of soil out on a barge, and planted a number of trees and flowers." This effort transformed the rock into a romantic setting suitable for the occasion.

Once the island had been made more attractive, Mr. Fixler had a small logistics problem — getting the guests to the wedding! He hired the operator of the Thimble Islands ferryboat, and recruited his best man to bring people across the water. The wedding invitations even included the injunction: "Don't miss the boat; or you'll miss the wedding!"

Finally, the big day arrived. Aside from a few guests who suffered a touch of "mal de mer", and others who got a little soggy from the choppy waters, the wedding proceeded without any problems. The couple were married under a traditional

Jewish "chuppah" (canopy) (also transported for the event). And, afterwards, the over-one hundred guests enjoyed the festivities; in fact, the experience was described by some as

and they know about unusual creations: two of their products — a "Big Mac" that measured 42" in diameter and weighed 319 pounds, and an eight-foot cherry pie baked in honor of Washington's birthday — appeared in the Guinness Book of World Records.

In addition to constructing the multiple-tier cakes with lights, fountains, and sparklers, Benny DiMarco is especially proud of an innovation he introduced last summer — a cake without the table. Instructed by the betrothed couple to "do something different", he had a macrame holder made, which gracefully cradled the cake as it hung from the top of an outdoor tent. As Benny notes, "Luckily, there wasn't much of a breeze!"

Another outstanding DiMarco cake featured a specially-made cage to fit inside the structure of the cake's small pillars. The cage contained — you guessed it! A pair of

live doves, which were released into flight by a hidden switch. Definitely a little something to "liven" up the party.

Benny does add that most people

And, just as taking the vows has returned to vogue, so have the more traditional-style ceremonies. As one observer notes, "All of the recent weddings I've gone to have been traditional: church ceremonies with receptions afterward in a hall, or at home. It seems to reflect the (conservative) swing in morality; it's a reaction to the 1960's 'barefoot on the beach' type of wedding. People

to bring people across the water. The wedding invitations even included the injunction: "Don't miss the boat; or you'll miss the wedding!"

Finally, the big day arrived. Aside from a few guests who suffered a touch of "mal de mer", and others who got a little soggy from the choppy waters, the wedding proceeded without any problems. The couple were married under a traditional

betrothed couple to "do something different", he had a macrame holder made, which gracefully cradled the cake as it hung from the top of an outdoor tent. As Benny notes, "Luckily, there wasn't much of a breeze!"

Another outstanding DiMarco cake featured a specially-made cage to fit inside the structure of the cake's small pillars. The cage contained — you guessed it! A pair of

are getting away from the extravagant and back to the norm."

Sounds dry, doesn't it? Indeed, most weddings seem pretty staid nowadays. Occasionally, says a Stratford photographer, the betrothed couple will ride to their reception in a horse and buggy. But this seems to be as outrageous as people are willing to get.

Unless, of course, like Elliot Fixler, you happen to own an island. Elliot, a winter resident of Carmel, New York, purchased one of the Thimble Islands in Branford last year with a friend. The purpose? To provide him with a summer home, and a unique locale for the wedding of Elliot and his bride Lorraine.

The first problem with the property, which measures a quarter-acre at high tide and is appropriately named "Mother-In-Law Island," was

Jewish "chuppah" (canopy) (also transported for the event). And, afterwards, the over-one hundred guests enjoyed the festivities; in fact, the experience was described by some as "other-worldly". As Elliot Fixler notes, "I wanted this to be something special for my wife." Certainly, it was special. And unforgettable as well.

Many of us, of course, will not experience such a trip to Fantasy Island on our wedding day. Still, there can be some excitement in the ingredients for an otherwise traditional affair. Benny DiMarco of Luigi's Pastry Shop in Trumbull says that couples seem to be quite interested in spectacular cakes and desserts.

Benny and his brother John have been operating bakeries in Bridgeport and Trumbull for fifteen years,

live doves, which were released into flight by a hidden switch. Definitely a little something to "liven" up the party.

Benny does add that most people are getting away from big weddings with over 250 guests. Due to rising costs, they are paring down their guest lists. He also feels that people are having far more garden and home affairs, as well as having cocktail parties instead of more expensive sit-down dinners. As with everything else in our lives, the economy has affected even the most special events we treasure.

However, traditional or not, and unusual or not, people do seem once again to be interested in getting married. It remains to be seen whether all of this knot-tying will continue; and in what fashion the knots will be tied.

523

A 2001 article from an unidentified publication about my daughter,
Sarah's basketball career:

Mahopac senior named Courier Athlete of Month

Fixler has been the spark for Mahopac

By Skip Pearlman
Sports Editor

MAHOPAC – It wasn't the way Sarah Fixler wanted to end her career in a Mahopac High basketball uniform. But when the buzzer sounded to end last week's Class A semifinal at the Westchester County Center, it was clear that an era was over for the Mahopac girls.

Fixler has been running the Indians' offense for the last five years, and closed a terrific career with a solid showing in her third consecutive Class A semifinal.

The fact that Mahopac has lost all three of those semifinal appearances does not sit well with the 5-5 point guard, but there's no denying she's been terrific at what she does for the Indians.

Mahopac has lost only a handful of games in her five years, and ran off a streak of 50 consecutive regular-season in-section victories, a streak that

(Continued on Page B2)

Sarah Fixler

ended early this year.

Fixler averaged 15 points, 8.2 assists, 3.1 rebounds and three steals a game this season, and was named the Putnam Courier's January/February Athlete of the Month for her outstanding contributions.

Fixler was a team captain this season, and was a great playmaker and a deadly outside shooter. She earned her third consecutive All-Section nod recently, and was named All-League for the fourth time. Fixler was also named to the Section 1 All-Tournament team, and closed her stellar career with

1,243 points. She was the fourth Mahopac girl to eclipse the 1,000-point mark.

"In terms of this season, it was a season of transition and change," first-year coach Mike Hunt said, "and Sarah was a stabilizing factor from the beginning. The players are looking at a new coach and new players, but she was in the program for five years, and she led by example."

Fixler only missed one game this season, out sick, but returned with a vengeance, according to Hunt.

"In the game she missed, she was as sick as could be," he said. "Yet she came back the next day and got 20 against North Rockland. When the team saw that, they stepped it up. I can't say enough about her effort level. She's a true team leader, and that's what you want as a coach. She made my job easier, she was always willing to do what was asked of her, and always with passion and effort. Hers will be a name that's well-established, and remembered, because that's the type of basketball player and person she is."

524

Acknowledgements

I would like to express my deep appreciation to the following individuals without whose assistance this book could not have been produced:

Jason Fixler, my son

Mickey Gottlieb, my friend

Sarah Fixler Kuhn, my daughter

Dr. Richard I. Polisner, my friend

Patty, my partner

Peter Weisz,
my collaborator, editor, and publisher without
whose guidance and skill I could not have
produced this book.

About the Author

orn just days after the Nazis marched into Budapest in 1944, the Jewish child who would grow up to become attorney Elliot Fixler managed to miraculously survive the Holocaust. Traveling to Czechoslovakia, then Israel, and finally settling in Buffalo, Fixler grew up to become a successful trial lawyer, trying cases from Connecticut to California. His reputation for courtroom pyrotechnics placed him in the center of countless fascinating cases. An ardent sports fan, his success in the courtroom was matched by his children's many triumphs on the basketball court.

After relocating to Florida in 2004, Elliot settled in Palm Beach Gardens where he currently lives. He is an active member of the Chabad of Palm Beach Gardens.

Made in United States
Troutdale, OR
08/16/2023